A Diplomat in Environmentalist's Clothing

To Matthew and Martine,
my brother and sister in
Christ, with the prayer
that at least some of my
stories will prove entertaining,
informative or even inspiring.

Ray Robinson
May 3, 2017

Author's last official photo before leaving Ottawa, 1991.

A Diplomat in Environmentalist's Clothing

A MEMOIR

RAYMOND M. ROBINSON

Toronto and New York

Published in 2014 by
BPS Books
Toronto and New York
www.bpsbooks.com
A division of Bastian Publishing Services Ltd.

ISBN 978-1-927483-75-6 (paperback)
ISBN 978-1-927483-77-0 (ePUB)
ISBN 978-1-927483-76-3 (ePDF)

Cataloguing-in-Publication Data available from Library and Archives Canada.

Cover: Gnibel
Text design and typesetting: PressBooks

Printed by Lightning Source, Tennessee. Lightning Source paper, as used in this book, does not come from endangered old-growth forests or forests of exceptional conservation value. It is acid free, lignin free, and meets all ANSI standards for archival-quality paper. The print-on-demand process used to produce this book protects the environment by printing only the number of copies that are purchased.

To my remarkable wife, Ardith, who, despite a near-lifetime of destructive illness, constantly battled to be the wife and mother she wanted to be. Diana, James, and I will forever see you as our family hero.

CONTENTS

Part III. A Mission in New Zealand

Part IV. Becoming an Environmentalist

ACKNOWLEDGEMENTS

This book is full of references to people, some named, some not, who have supported Ardith and me at times of need during our life journey. In these preliminary paragraphs, I want to acknowledge those who played an important role in bringing this book into being. I think, for example, of my former colleagues Bob Connelly, John Herity, Carol Martin, and Bill Couch, whose contributions to protecting the environment are reflected in the text. They spent many hours reviewing my manuscript and making helpful suggestions. Another important collaborator was Stephen Hazell, formerly of the Sierra Club and the Canadian Wildlife Federation. Although I consulted him because of his key role in the enactment of environmental assessment legislation, he chose to read the entire manuscript, and I very much appreciated his comments. Many personal friends also read all or portions of the emerging book, and their supportive, encouraging reactions helped me overcome those times when I wondered if I was producing something useful. My children, Diana and James, were among those encouraging supporters, and James even shared the text with several of his friends.

I want, however, to say a particularly strong thank you to Rev. Dr. Ed Hird of St. Simon's Anglican Church in North Vancouver. He is a much published author, most recently releasing *Battle for the Soul of Canada,* who not only read every word of my manuscript, providing helpful comments throughout, but also, through his own editor, brought me to the attention of Don Bastian. Don diligently ferreted out bureaucratese wherever it raised its ugly head, reduced my paragraphs to manageable length, and provided chapter headings that were turn-ons instead of turn-offs. He made kind comments about my writing, but it is certainly the better for his involvement.

I want also to express my appreciation to Steve Terrell (www.steveterrell.ca), an accomplished photographer in the Vancouver area who worked hard to bring almost all of the photographs in this book to the level of quality needed for printing. The dramatic landscape photo on the cover is his. His website is well worth a visit.

Finally, I wish to give credit to my friend Gary Bounsall, whose design expertise and suggestions contributed greatly to this book's excellent cover design.

PREFACE

"I can only answer the question 'What am I to do?' if I can answer the prior question 'Of what story or stories do I find myself a part?'" So writes the Christian philosopher Alasdair MacIntyre. I take his words to mean that we can understand ourselves and our role in the world only if we understand the stories that have shaped who we are and thereby determined how we see and relate to that world. The stories in this account are designed to help me achieve at least a partial understanding of my purpose and place and to inspire my readers – especially my children – to explore their own stories with the same objective in mind.

PART I

MY ORIGINS

CHAPTER 1

ROMANTIC ADVENTURES AND CONFLICTED DNA

It was the spring of 1936. A young woman not long past her twenty-second birthday was standing at the dock in Southampton with her mother, stepfather, and younger sister, who were saying their goodbyes. She was pretty, blonde, athletic, outgoing, and very excited. She was about to leave England on a luxury liner for a multi-week voyage through the Suez Canal to a pearl-shaped island off the southern tip of British India. It was the adventure of a lifetime, but she had no idea how much that adventure was going to change her life. Indeed, given how wonderful her life had been to that moment, it is doubtful that she would have boarded that ship if she had known what lay ahead.

She lived in what her family would probably have called "comfortable circumstances." That was no small achievement during the Great Depression of the 1930s. Unemployment was at extraordinarily high levels all over the world, and Britain, like North America, was no exception. Those hard times were fostering great political and social change, nowhere more obviously than in Mussolini's Fascist Italy, Hitler's Nazi Germany, and Spain, whose terrible Civil War would result in yet another European Fascist state.

Betty, for that was my mother's name, would have been scarcely aware of the turmoil going on around her. She lived a sheltered life in a substantial home in an idyllic country setting near England's southern coast not far from Christchurch in Hampshire. Indeed, one of her greatest joys was riding her horse in the New Forest, so named by William the Conqueror when it was set aside as his royal hunting preserve in 1079, only thirteen years after he invaded England. Like other young people of her social class, she had attended a boarding school from an early age and, later, unlike most of her peers, a Scottish finishing school in Edinburgh. Captain of her school's field hockey team and outgoing by nature, she excelled in those things that make a young girl popular. Having inherited some musical genes from her mother, who was a skilled violinist, she also played the cello. Her best friend at school in Edinburgh lived with her parents in a castle on the Scottish coast. Betty often spent happy weeks there completely insulated (as she was in her own home) from what was going on in Britain let alone the rest of the world. Her sheltered circumstances probably contributed to her uninhibited approach to life, an approach that was to have life-changing consequences.

The voyage to distant exotic Ceylon (today's Sri Lanka) must have been a joy from start to finish, with anticipation mounting as Colombo drew closer. This city was not her destination. She was on her way high in the hills to a tea plantation owned by her aunt and uncle. Little in her previous life could have prepared her for the sights, sounds, and smells of Ceylon. About all that there was in common with her native England was the colour green. Steamy equatorial heat, masses of sweating people, and the sounds of a language not her own reminded her of how far she was from home. The journey from coastal Colombo was spectacular, with steep cliffs, narrow winding roads, hills and mountains covered with tropical foliage, and, here and there, the ordered green patches of the ubiquitous tea plantations. Now and then there were glimpses of exotic birds and animals, including the elephants so widely used by the Ceylonese for heavy work. Tea and rubber introduced by the British after coffee succumbed to leaf disease had made Ceylon one of the most profitable parts of the British Empire. The planters lived in a style that most of their fellow Britons living in cool, rainy, Depression-era England could only dream of. Betty was living the dream, and she thought it would never end.

A big part of that dream was the constant round of parties and visits. Betty's relatives' home was within a few hours' drive of Trincomalee, a magnificent natural harbour that was at the time one of Britain's most important naval bases in that part of the world. A steady stream of handsome young officers in their sparkling dress whites populated the planters' parties. Pretty Betty soon attracted a bevy of admirers, but she had eyes only for one. His name was George Symonds, and she spent many happy hours with him in the secluded places to which his MG frequently carried them. Unfortunately, this idyllic romance proved ill-fated. Betty discovered

My father, Lieutenant, later Commodore, George Symonds of Britain's Royal Navy (on left), with my mother, Betty, Ceylon, 1936.

that she was pregnant. Neither George nor Betty wanted to marry, and that meant that Betty's dream and care-free life had come to an abrupt end.

The voyage home to England was very different from the one to Ceylon. It seemed to last forever. The on-board parties did little to reduce Betty's sadness, and the movement of the ship did little to reduce her nausea. But a warm welcome awaited her at home. Her mother's response to her situation had been totally supportive and in no way condemning. That very much reflected the sort of person her mother was. Winnie was one of several children born to an Anglican vicar and his wife in a small southern English village. The vicar certainly came by his occupation honestly, coming as he did from a long line of "clerks in holy orders." His Bodington family tree had been traced back to a "yeoman," typically an agricultural worker, during the reign of Henry VIII. For one hundred and fifty years thereafter, this designation was applied to the men in the family; suddenly, in the early 1700s, it was changed to "gentleman." No one knows how that immense social jump occurred. During the 1800s, more specific designa-

My great-grandmother Knipe, née Sackville-West, UK, c. 1900.

tions replaced the generic one, for example, solicitor, doctor, army officer and, in greatest numbers, clerks in holy orders.

Winnie's life was more home-centred than Betty's. She married at a young age in 1913. Her husband, Edward Knipe, was the younger son of a well-to-do family with a long aristocratic lineage. Edward's mother, née Sackville-West, was descended from a Norman knight who accompanied William the Conqueror to England in 1066. His descendants amassed considerable wealth over the generations and several achieved high positions, including Thomas Sackville, Lord High Treasurer to Queen Elizabeth I and later James I. Sackville, who was created first Earl of Dorset by James I, was Queen Elizabeth's third cousin through Elizabeth's mother, the unfortunate beheaded Anne Boleyn. Anne's father's sister was Thomas's grandmother.

Thomas was also an astute businessman (dealing in iron foundries and land) who greatly increased his inherited wealth, but his most important contributions to English life were in the literary field, where he is ranked by some with Francis Bacon. A committed Protestant, he was jailed as a young man for airing his beliefs while visiting Rome. It took Elizabeth's intervention to free him. Much later, he represented the Queen in the Netherlands where the Protestant Dutch were battling a Catholic Spanish army seeking to reassert control over that part of Europe. He was very critical of Elizabeth's inadequate support for the beleaguered Dutch and ended up being recalled. Clearly he was not intimidated by his royal cousin; later, while serving as one of her senior advisors, he was banished from the Court for six months for his impertinence.

Later in his career, he was given the sad duty of informing Mary, Queen of Scots, that she was to be executed. He is said to have done this with as much kindness as possible. For his time, he was remarkably tolerant, strongly believing that every person should follow his or her conscience in matters of religion except when it resulted in actions dangerous to the State.

One of Thomas' descendants, Vita Sackville-West, an early- to mid-twentieth century writer and close friend of the more famous Virginia Woolf, lamented in a book she wrote about her ancestors that Thomas had wasted his literary talent by focusing on his political career. Most of her other ancestors she dismissed as rogues or worse. From my study of them, I would add the category of "incompetents." Consider, for example, the court-martialled Major General whose influence at Court secured for him the post of King George III's Secretary of State for America during the American Revolutionary War. He so mismanaged the logistics and interfered with his generals' decisions that he deserves a statue in Washington for his contribution to the Revolution. On the other side of the ledger is a gallant cavalier who served as the top adviser of Charles I during the Civil War that ultimately cost the King his head. That cavalier ancestor provoked the King's wrath by repeatedly urging compromise to meet Parliament's demands and end the war.

My cricket-playing friends no doubt would give top honours among these ancestors to the debonair third Duke of Dorset, who, in the late eighteenth century, used his considerable resources and great personal skill to promote that quintessentially English game in his own country. While in Paris as Britain's Ambassador to the King of France, he successfully promoted cricket among the French aristocracy. A tour of France by an English team was planned, but was cancelled at the storming of the Bastille. Depriving France (and its subsequent empire) of cricket is a little-known result of the French Revolution. Another ancestor was twice Lord Lieutenant

Knole, Sackville-West ancestral home, Kent.

(Viceroy) of Ireland; he was fired for incompetence the second time around, no small feat given his friends at Court. Thomas's descendants still occupy the family seat called Knole, a 365-room country house in Kent where my mother's paternal grandmother was allegedly born and which served as the setting for Virginia Woolf's fantasy novel *Orlando*. Like so many other ancestral homes, it now belongs to Britain's National Trust. Knole has what is arguably the finest seventeenth century interior in Britain. Most of the Great Houses frequented by visitors display eighteenth-century interiors.

Mom's paternal grandfather was descended from a relative newcomer to Britain named Knieper, a member of the court of William and Mary of Orange (in the Netherlands), who jointly assumed the British Crown in 1689 at the invitation of Parliament. William and Mary were replacing James II, who had been forced to flee to Ireland because of his secret plans to restore Roman Catholicism in Britain. The famous Battle of the Boyne in Ireland ended James II's hopes of regaining his throne. Our family name later became Anglicized to "Knipe."

I first learned of Mom's interesting ancestry when I went through her papers after her death. She never spoke of it. In an egalitarian country like

Henry VIII's solid silver furniture, King's bedroom, Knole.

Canada where acceptance of a title has resulted in the loss of citizenship, it is difficult to relate to the social importance still given in much of Europe, especially Britain, to titles. There are, of course, socio-economic classes in North America and notions of old and new money, but they seem more flexible. That said, income distribution in Britain today is actually more equitable than in the United States (though not in Canada). What fascinates me as a history buff is the thought that people whose DNA is linked with mine played a sometimes important part in events centuries ago that helped create the conditions under which so much of the English-speaking world lives today. It makes history come alive in a special way. There is not a lot of scope for pride in ancestry, however, given that so many of those ancestors demonstrated what happens when absolute privilege carries with it little or no accountability. My DNA must be very conflicted.

Two daughters, Betty and Barbara, quickly followed my grandmother Winnie's marriage, but tragedy was not far behind. Her husband, Edward, a lieutenant in the King's Own Scottish Borderers, was killed in the huge World War I battle of the Somme, in 1916. Distraught, Winnie, with her two

My grandfather Lieutenant Edward Knipe – killed at the Somme, 1916.

babies, returned to live with her parents in the lovely old vicarage. Edward's parents, who made sure they lacked for nothing, enabled the girls to attend very good schools. Winnie used her comfortable circumstances and widowed status to become one of the first women in England to own a car. Her taste for ever-faster vehicles grew over the years, and, even when she became the grandmother of adult children, she was still known for speed. A ride with her could be hair-raising. In addition to many photos, we have in our home some wonderful reminders of that time: the vicar's solid oak roll-top desk; a painting of the picturesque village for which he had spiritual charge, as seen from the window of his office in the rambling old vicarage; and a large photographic portrait of the beautiful, elegant Victorian lady born a Sackville-West who was Edward's mother and Mom's paternal grandmother.

When the girls were older teenagers, Winnie married again. Her new husband, William Hunt, always known as Bill, came from modest circumstances in a small village in Kent but had managed over the years to put together a stock market portfolio that enabled him to live at home full-time

My mother, Betty (seated), with her sister, Barbara, and mother, Winnie, Hampshire, 1918.

and pursue his hobbies of dog breeding (he had one hundred Sealyham terriers) and bees (fifty hives). Betty and Barbara vastly preferred the terriers.

Bill's life had been a colourful one. One of his first jobs of consequence was escorting the sons of Indian princes between England and India to enable them to study at English schools or universities. He received many a present from his wealthy charges, which in due course formed the basis of his investments. One memorable experience had to do with the oldest son of the King of Siam (now Thailand). That unfortunate young man had gotten into a knife fight at Oxford, and the British Government, which was wooing the King, was determined to avoid any scandal. It was Bill's job to escort the disgraced prince back to Bangkok. The Siamese King was so grateful for how this incident had been handled that he threw a two-week party in Bill's honour. Bill later said that it was an experience like none other in his life.

The King also gave him many presents, some of considerable value, including a magnificent set of twelve elephant figurines in ascending size

My mother, Betty, at age sixteen, Hampshire, 1930.

carved in black ebony with ivory tusks. Three of them still survive in our home today. Bill made the great mistake prior to World War I of investing much of his growing capital in czarist Russia; he lost it all, thanks to the Bolshevik revolution. However, he correctly anticipated the 1929 stock market crash, hedging his investments in such a way that, unlike so many others, the depression years were good to him. As a result, he was able to continue providing a comfortable home for Winnie and her daughters. Bill never lost his willingness to take a risk. Indeed, shortly after World War II, when it was forbidden to move capital out of Britain, he converted his assets to diamonds preparatory to leaving for Canada and mailed them in rolled-up newspapers, a few at a time, to my mother in Victoria, B.C. He never lost one.

My mother, Betty, her mother, Winnie, stepfather, Bill, and five of a hundred Sealyham terriers, Hampshire, 1931.

CHAPTER 2

NEAR DEATH AT BIRTH, AND WARTIME EXPERIENCES

Returning to Betty's story, the warmth with which she was welcomed by her parents and younger sister when she disembarked from the liner at Southampton made up for the unseasonably cool, drizzly weather. She spent the remainder of her pregnancy at the family home in Hampshire, but my actual birth, on March 19, 1937, took place at a small nursing home in Hendon in northwest London. It was a terrible ordeal for all concerned. Twin sons were born, but the first quickly died. I, the second, was very weak and nearly died as well. Although Betty recovered quickly, physically, the continued weakness of the surviving child, the loss of his twin, and the ordeal of the previous few months all took their toll. The family decided that a complete change of scene was needed. When I was six months old, they embarked on a tour of Canada and the U.S. West Coast. They had no idea that Betty would never see her homeland again.

The tour did much to lift their spirits. They enjoyed sightseeing as they travelled by train across Canada before turning south to spend some months in California. The sun, beaches, and spontaneous, outgoing behaviour of their American hosts brightened their mood, and Betty was soon her sparkling, extroverted self again. A highlight was visiting Hollywood, where they met British film star David Niven, who was very welcoming. They moved up the West Coast, and, crossing into Canada, found themselves in the sleepy little outpost of Empire at the southern tip of Vancouver Island, named, appropriately enough, Victoria. Clearly, Betty had an eye for uniforms, or at least the men in them, because she quickly became enamoured of a Canadian artilleryman, CE (Ted) Robinson. Betty and Ted married, and her parents and sister returned to England just as World War II

My stepfather Captain Ted Robinson before leaving England for the invasion of Sicily, 1943.

was beginning in Europe. My future was to be affected, if not determined, by all of these events.

For nearly a year following the birth of my half-brother Keith in March of 1940, the three of us followed the man I believed to be my dad over six thousand kilometres across the country from Vancouver Island to the Atlantic. We stayed in a succession of army bases. My very first memory of Dad is of him getting into the back of an army truck near Halifax in the spring of 1941 before embarking for Europe. Mom then drove my baby brother and me all the way back to Victoria in our dark red 1940 Dodge sedan. We travelled mainly through the United States because there was no Trans-Canada Highway in those days. Mom told me that, wherever we went, I announced to everyone that my dad had gone to war and we were treated like heroes, even though the U.S. itself had not yet entered the war. She also told me that the love and support she received from so many Americans during that long, lonely trip did much to ease her fear and pain at seeing her husband sail into harm's way.

We lived in a big old house in Victoria's quiet, leafy, waterfront suburb of Oak Bay along with my dad's parents and his younger sister, also named Betty. Both of Dad's brothers were in the armed forces. His oldest brother, Mark, was a Group Captain (Colonel) in Britain's Royal Air Force (RAF), and the youngest, Bill, was a Sergeant in Vancouver's Seaforth Highlanders, also deployed in Britain. In addition, later in the war, Dad's younger sister Betty married Lieut. Phil Frewer, the gunnery officer on Canada's most successful warship, HMCS *Haida,* which sank seventeen German vessels, a Canadian record. I carried the bride's train dressed in a green velvet Little Lord Fauntleroy suit with breeches and stockings that I detested, though walking under the archway of naval swords held by the groom's brother officers when exiting the church almost made it worthwhile. Fourteen years later, Christine, the eldest daughter of that couple was the flower girl at my own wedding. Christine later became a beautiful, vibrant wife and wonderful mother before she was taken from us far too young. One of my best memories is of seeing her riding off on the back of her husband's big motorcycle in 1980 looking like a teenager with her long black hair flowing behind her.

My mother helped the war effort by driving a truck collecting scrap metal, and my paternal step-grandmother organized social events for servicemen, many of whom visited our home. We were very much a household at war. Thankfully, all of our family's fighting men returned safely, but my mother's younger sister, Barbara, who was in the women's RAF, was killed by a German bomb. It was a terrible blow for both Mom and her parents. Poor Grandma Winnie. She lost both her first husband and her youngest daughter to German military action, twenty-seven years apart.

Living in my step-grandparents' house proved to be the source of a remarkable coincidence. About thirty years later, I moved from the Foreign Service to the newly created Department of Environment. My first boss, a very distinguished wildlife biologist, grew up, like me, in Victoria. I told him about my childhood home and particularly about the large cherry tree in the backyard that made it possible to climb out of the back balcony and down the tree without anyone knowing I had left the house. It turned out that his childhood home also had such a tree that he used for the same purpose. It was, of course, the same house. His parents had sold it to my step-grandparents shortly before the war began.

Dad had a tough front-line war. He was a Forward Observation Officer

(FOO) with the Canadian artillery. That meant he accompanied the advance infantry units, along with a radioman, to guide the artillery fire. He fought through Sicily, mainland Italy, France, Belgium, Holland, and into Germany – in other words, everywhere in Western Europe except the Normandy landing and the subsequent breakout. Two radiomen were killed beside him, but he was never even wounded. The only physical damage he sustained came from falling asleep in the southern Italian sun after swimming and burning his behind so badly that he was hospitalized for two weeks. To that indignity could be added, I suppose, the dog bite he received from our family pet as he marched up our path in late 1945, resplendent in his Major's "crowns" and campaign ribbons. We always excused the poor colour-blind dog because he could not differentiate between postman blue and army khaki.

This unfortunate incident proved prescient. Always on the frontline and at high risk for so long, Dad found it difficult to adjust to civilian life. Mom had no doubt changed as well during the four years that her husband was absent. During the time he and Mom had been apart, they had not only changed but had become virtual strangers. My parents' marriage became one of the casualties of war; sadly, I grew up without him or my younger brother Keith in my life. When I was ten, Dad moved from Victoria to Vancouver, and Keith returned to live with his paternal grandparents in the big old house where we had spent the war years. Sadly, despite being near each other, Keith and I had only occasional contact. Four years later, when Dad remarried, Keith moved to Vancouver to join him. I had infrequent contact with Dad and even less with Keith during my teenage years. Dad and I had very occasional contact during my teenage years at boarding school and, later, university in Vancouver, but he always treated me like his own son. When he and Keith left, Mom told me that my real dad was dead. The news that my hero dad was not my own added immensely to the pain of his departure. That pain is still with me sixty-six years later. Many years ago, I wanted to take Dad to one of the great reunions in the Netherlands where Canada is still celebrated as the primary liberator from the Nazis, but he died of cancer before I could do so.

Understanding history is, or ought to be, a big part of knowing who and what we are. In World War II, Canada had well over a million men and women in uniform, ninety percent of whom were volunteers, including all who served overseas, despite a population of only eleven million. Almost a

My hero dad returns, here seen with Mom, Keith, and me, Victoria, early 1946.

fifth of allied soldiers landing in the first wave on the Normandy beaches were Canadian – all on Juno beach – and our per capita fatal casualties during the war were about twenty percent higher than those of U.S. forces. (In World War I they were thirteen times higher.) At the end of World War II, Canada had the third-largest surface navy and the fourth-largest air force in the world. No one watching most U.S. and British war movies would be aware that Canada was even in the war much less realize the extent of its contribution. Unfortunately, such movies have been the public's primary source of information about World War II for generations. Not surprisingly, many Canadians, not to mention our American and British allies, have little or no appreciation of what Canada did during what was surely the most morally justifiable war in history (despite the vindictive Treaty of Versailles ending World War I, which, most historians contend, was the root of the conflict). I am a product of that era and this lack of appreciation saddens me. Gratitude for the sacrifices of earlier generations makes us all better than we would otherwise be. We must not forget.

Chapter 3

A PRIVILEGED EDUCATION, AT A STEEP PRICE

My birth father, George Symonds, was not dead. He survived the war and rose to the rank of Commodore (equivalent to an Army Brigadier General) in Britain's Royal Navy. Indeed, he was Commodore, Hong Kong, when Ardith and I were living in New Zealand in the late 1960s. He proved to be a gentleman as well as an officer in that he fully honoured the promise made in 1936 to provide funds for my education. As a result, Mom placed me in private school from the age of five (St. Michael's in Victoria up to grade nine and St. George's in Vancouver thereafter), initially as a day student and then as a boarder. I disliked those schools very much, especially the latter, not least because I was bookish, bright, and nonathletic, a combination certain to encourage bullying.

My school experience was the opposite of Mom's and she could not understand my constant pleas to leave the schools or at least become a day student. That lack of understanding, coupled with the long periods during which we were separated from one another, created a coolness that lasted until my retirement years when both she and I made a special effort to reconnect. I gradually came to understand that her determination with respect to my schooling was not just a reflection of her own upbringing, but a central element of what distinguished her social class in England. She saw it as her parental duty to raise me properly, an attitude shared by my birth father, who provided the necessary funds. There were times after her initial divorce and between her subsequent marriages when her circumstances were difficult; she worked at many low-paying jobs in sharp contrast to the wealthy families of the boys who were my schoolmates. Yet she never touched my education money.

Seated beside older teacher and my classmates, St. Michael's School, Victoria, 1951.

Given Mom's commitment to and sacrifice for my education, I have, on occasion, wondered whether the benefit of that education outweighed the cost. I clearly benefited on an academic level. I was given a good classical education with emphasis on Latin, English grammar, and literature, along with British and Canadian history, math, and general science. I learned to speak and write well in English and to read, though not speak, French. (A degree of fluency in French came much later.) That ability to speak and write undoubtedly served me well in the career that followed. On the downside, the bullying, which continued for years, and the lack of nurture by my mother undoubtedly caused me emotional harm.

Year after year, Alan Brown, the closest of my few friends at St. George's, was my academic rival for top marks. He was also reasonably athletic and was thus spared the poor treatment I routinely received. The school was a brutal place, with the senior boys empowered to inflict corporal discipline on the younger boys. Staff oversight of this authority was not impressive; I do not doubt that abuses occurred. When I became a prefect in my final year, I refused to use the cane. This, no doubt, only served to add

My mother, Betty, in Victoria, 1953.

to my wimpish image. Alan and I often talked about the changes that were needed.

I made my career elsewhere, but he stayed in Vancouver, determined to make a difference. In due course, he became the headmaster of St. George's and changed it beyond recognition. Today, it is a very different place than the one he and I condemned so long ago. Sadly, Alan died prematurely of Parkinson's, but we used to lunch from time to time when I visited Vancouver from Ottawa. He expressed his sorrow at how badly I had been treated more than once. That helped, because I sometimes wondered if I had exaggerated my experiences in my own mind. Clearly I had not.

Another friend I had at St. George's was quite a character. Most of the rest of us were in awe of him. Night after night, he would sneak out of the dormitory to visit one of his several girlfriends, who lived in the residential area that surrounded the school. To our innocent ears, the tales of his many conquests were spellbinding. He also had a taste for wine, which was accommodated by regularly sipping from the bottle kept in the kitchen for use in communion services in the Anglican school chapel. He would add water to maintain the level in the bottle. He was eventually caught in both of these activities and summarily expelled. I do not know which sin was viewed as the more heinous. Later he moved out of the province and became a successful retailer with his own airplane. I once made the big mistake of letting the fact that he had been expelled slip in the presence of his adult children. Was he ever annoyed! I hope that he has since forgiven me.

During most of my time boarding at St. George's in Vancouver, my mother and her second husband owned and operated the Dawson Hotel in tiny Dawson Creek, B.C., "mile zero" of the Alaska Highway. I sometimes visited them at Christmas and also spent the summer of 1954 with them. I recall it vividly because of my role in rebuilding the local radio station. My job was central to the success of that major project. For weeks I spent all day in the hot sun pulling nails out of what must have been thousands of boards saved from the demolition of the previous radio station for reuse in the new building. No doubt this inspirational introduction to recycling pointed me towards my future career in the field of the environment. Another inspiring job was helping a huge German immigrant knock down a cement water cistern in the basement of the Dawson Hotel. My job was to aim a stream of water at a point just above the drill bit of his jackhammer so that the water would gently trickle into the hole being made in the cistern wall and keep the dust down. My attention would inevitably wander and the water would hit the hole full blast, spraying all over my fellow worker, making it appear that he was suffering from a bad case of German measles. It was then my turn to be inundated with a torrent of German curses. I am grateful that my ignorance of that language maintained my innocence, especially since my attention often wandered.

My winter visits to Dawson Creek exposed me for the first time to the reality that cold can hurt. In the temperate maritime climate of the West Coast, even record lows could not achieve that effect. Snow-free winters at sea level were not unusual, and some years the mercury never dipped below freezing. The contrast with Dawson Creek could not have been greater. I will never forget the awful pain in my face that I experienced one Christmas Eve when walking from the Dawson Hotel to church.

Over the course of her life after her first husband left, my mother was married again twice, once very unsuccessfully to the man who was in the hotel business and once, for the final time, very happily. Her love affair with men in uniform clearly continued. Her third husband, Clyde Fraser, was a

Mountie who, at six feet four inches and built to match, cut a dashing figure with his red serge and walrus mustache. His last post was as head of the RCMP detachment in the Vancouver suburb of Richmond, but he and Mom retired to Victoria to be near to her parents. Mom was, not surprisingly, very close to her mother; she had been thrilled when Winnie and Bill had moved to Victoria from England after World War II. I spent many a summer living with my grandparents during my school years. Thankfully, there were no bee hives; sadly, there was only one dog. There was an abundance of English cooking, including gooseberry tarts with custard, a favourite of theirs but not mine – too sour.

When I was in grade 11, I experienced a life-changing encounter. Basil Robinson (no relation), the son of one of our "masters," as we called our teachers, returned from his diplomatic post in Paris to visit his family in Vancouver. He was encouraged by his father to meet with me to talk about a possible diplomatic career. We spoke for an hour; both his account of his work as a First Secretary at our embassy in Paris and his description of Canada's idealistic foreign policy inspired me. From that time on, I focused on doing whatever was necessary to become a Foreign Service Officer. Five years later as a newly sworn-in member of the Foreign Service, I walked into Basil's office in Ottawa and received a very warm welcome. At that time, he was Senior Foreign Affairs Advisor to Prime Minister John Diefenbaker, but he later rose to become Canada's top diplomat. To be honest, however, the process of my getting to Ottawa owed much more to good luck than good management. I will say more about that later, but first I should talk about something much more important – my love life.

Chapter 4

LOVE WITH A FUTURE, UNIVERSITY WITHOUT DEBT

While at St. George's, my contact with the opposite sex was limited to the organized school dances with the young ladies from two girls' private schools, York House and Crofton House, which were within easy driving distance. We wore our navy blue blazers, school ties, and grey slacks while they came looking like Christmas packages with crinolines, bows, and long white leather gloves. No wonder the innocents among us saw them as creatures from another planet, desirable, to be sure, but not at all like us. Ardith McMillan, my wife-to-be, was among them, but we did not meet at that time.

When I first started attending the University of British Columbia (UBC), I focused on my studies and had a very limited social life. That changed, thanks to a blind date arranged by my cousin, Morris Treasure, from Edmonton; Morris was temporarily in Vancouver to obtain work experience related to his father's business. He was eager to go out with a striking-looking girl he had just met, but she was willing only if her girlfriend could come along as well. I was needed to round out the party. The outing, at least for me, did not go well. I was so nervous that I drank too much and made a very poor impression. I thought that I would never see my date again, but Morris's aspirations made sure that I did. The next encounter went much better, and in due course my date and I were going out regularly.

My partner was, of course, Ardith, who was to become my wife a little over two years later. When I met her, she was living only a few blocks from my boarding house. Her parents then decided to build their dream home in the British Properties, an exclusive residential area in the upscale suburb of West Vancouver. Because it was located on the side of one of the mountains that overlook Vancouver's harbour, I faced a long drive up steep hills in my old, underpowered car. I used to say that it was powered by ardour for Ardith. I ended up eating at Ardith's new home so often that my landlady reduced my rent. Indeed, after a time, I wondered whether Ardith's mother Martha was courting me by serving all my favourite foods, especially green peas and mashed potatoes. (Neither was on the menu after our marriage; grounds for divorce?) I later learned that there was some truth in my suspicion. I was perceived as a much better suitor for her daughter than a particular alternative. Ardith's father, Jim, was also welcoming, but her older brother, Bruce, a fellow UBC student, initially made it pretty clear that he did not share his parents' enthusiasm. Happily, he has long since come around.

If there is one word that is dominating the public discourse these days, it would be "debt." While Canada's public debt per capita is much lower than that of almost every other industrial country, personal debt in this country is at record levels. It saddens me that, for many young people in particular, much of that debt reflects expenses incurred in securing a university education. Those like me who entered Canadian universities in the '50s were spared that terrible burden. I was able to pay my annual tuition fee of $240, pay my monthly room and board of $60, and operate a car from what I earned selling bus tickets in the summer and at Christmas for a long distance bus company. It helped that gas cost twenty-five cents an imperial gallon (4.5 litres) and that car insurance was also very cheap. With only eight thousand students, UBC then was less than a sixth of the size it is now. The huge campus had far fewer buildings and free parking abounded. I actually drove between some classes. For a student to live like that today would be completely impossible.

I worked in New Westminster, a distant suburb of Vancouver, at a brand new bus depot serving the Fraser Valley, which stretches inland about 150 kilometres and south to the U.S. border. Working as well for the Greyhound Bus Company, I also sold tickets for buses travelling all over North America. When I first started, I thought I would never be able to remember the different bus routes, the names of the stops, the prices, the departure times, and the bays from which they would depart, especially with a lineup of impatient customers reaching to the door. Somehow my brain adapted, and soon it was second nature.

More challenging was coping with the drunks, of whom there were many. The company policy was that I had to sell them tickets but the bus driver had the right to refuse entry if he judged them to be too drunk. Typically, a drunk customer would buy a ticket from me, be refused entry onto the bus, lose his ticket while waiting for the next bus, purchase another ticket, and be refused again. This could go on all evening with the customer, not surprisingly, getting ever angrier (and often drunker). When the last bus left sometime after midnight, a swing at me was the only logical recourse. More than once, I used the wheels on my chair to get out of the way just in time. Fortunately, however, the police station was next door and they soon got to know my voice. Sadder were the occasions when a street person would ask me to call the police for a place to spend the night. Many of the regulars were greeted by name in a friendly way by the responding police officers.

On one occasion a woman getting off a long distance bus was about to give birth; after calling for an ambulance, the other ticket clerk and I flipped a coin to see which of us would attend her in the restroom. Fortunately, he lost, but the birth, he told me, went well. Another time a short, elderly Chinese man smoking a pipe made a beeline for the restroom after arriving on one of the older buses without toilets. He ran into the glass wall which separated the bus bays from the waiting lounge. His pipe almost disappeared down his throat as he rapidly descended to a seated position. It was a strange sight, but also dangerous for him. Fortunately a quick-thinking passerby slapped him hard on the back, and out popped the pipe. Even more frightening and not in the least funny was the time a burly logger also made a beeline for the restroom. He went right through the glass, which came down from the ceiling like a guillotine, missing him by inches. He could easily have been killed. After these and other incidents, the bus company finally put striping on the glass.

The eighteen months in total that I spent in that bus depot were educational in a way that my time in school was not. I had lived a relatively insulated life, far from the harsh realities that dominate the lives of so many others. The bus depot provided a small window into that other world.

One of the perks of working for a bus company was getting reduced fares on long distance trips. I travelled in this way to Edmonton to visit relatives and once went to San Francisco to join Ardith and her family, who were attending a convention related to her father's work. Speaking at the convention was Governor Adlai Stevenson of Illinois, who was running for president against the incumbent, General Dwight Eisenhower, who was the Allied Supreme Commander in Europe during World War II. Ardith's father got us all into the hall for the speech.

It was my first exposure to a political speaker of this calibre; I was deeply impressed both by the delivery and the content. Stevenson was a very thoughtful man; many view him as one of the better presidents that the U.S. never had, intellectually superior to his opponent. That said, Eisenhower's diplomatic skills had been central to the success of the British/American alliance during the war. Eisenhower's opponents tended to discount his intellectual abilities and to portray him as an affable golfer, but his insightfulness was demonstrated in his final speech before handing over his office to the much younger Jack Kennedy. In that speech Eisenhower first used the phrase "military-industrial complex," warning of its growing power and expressing the view that it would change America for the worse in fundamental ways. He was absolutely right, but, given the role that the U.S. played in the post-war world, those changes were probably unavoidable.

Chapter 5

AN ABRUPT CLOSE TO MY UNIVERSITY YEARS

While attending UBC, I lived in the home of a delightful elderly lady, Catherine Reynolds, who had lost three sons, all pilots, in World War II. Her surviving son was the CEO of a copper mining company and she had no need of income from students. She did, however, have a need for the company of young people; I was, for four years, lucky enough to be one of them. Her meals were magnificent, as she was an excellent cook and not constrained by a budget. High-quality steak was common and the desserts were to die for. For herself, she particularly loved ice cream in its "purest" form: vanilla. Devoutly religious, she would give up ice cream for the forty days of Lent, a real sacrifice. It was really something to watch her go through a whole container of ice cream on Easter Sunday. Her great love was her talking parrot, a large green macaw. She delighted in giving us surprise treats on special occasions, such as apricot brandy in our breakfast juice glasses; tossing that back unawares sure woke you up. Both Ardith and I grew very fond of her, and we often visited her home in subsequent years. She was particularly thrilled to see our first child, Diana, as we passed through Vancouver en route to New Zealand. Unfortunately, she passed away while we were "down under."

One of my fellow boarders was of particular interest. He was a refugee because of the unsuccessful revolt in 1956 of the Hungarian people against their Soviet oppressors. He was one of two hundred forestry engineering students at Sopron University who escaped with their professors to the West as Soviet tanks crushed the revolution. Sopron's School of Forestry Engineering was incorporated into UBC and, for years after, Hungarian names could be found scattered through B.C.'s large forestry industry.

In 1956 I experienced a remarkable evening thanks to my new Hungarian friend. Sopron had a centuries-old tradition of celebrating the university's founding with a night of revelry and song. Perhaps because of the religious origin of the university, the communist regime had banned this celebration. Now, for the first time in many years, the celebration could take place without fear of arrest or worse. Needless to say, it was a wild affair. The students were dressed in their high-collared uniforms similar to those in the 1950s Mario Lanza film *Student Prince* set in nineteenth-century Heidelberg. They held their magnificent beer steins in the air as they sang traditional drinking songs, sometimes standing atop the tables. As the only non-Hungarian present, I could not understand a word, but occasionally my friend or another student would explain what was being said or sung. What I could understand was the joy that had been unleashed after so many years of oppression. Little did I know that, two years later, I would come face-to-face with one of the agents of that oppression.

During my years at university, from 1954 to 1958, I was active in the model Parliament to which the student body elected members affiliated with the national political parties. It was just a debating group, but was a lot of fun for those of us who were interested in the political process. On one occasion, we were invited to the University of Washington in Seattle to put on a performance showing off the Canadian parliamentary system or some reasonable facsimile thereof. We had one Tory (Progressive Conservative) member with a posh British accent who used to bring his rolled up umbrella to pound on his desk to underline his points. We knew our American hosts would get a kick out of him. Of more serious interest were our two Communist members, especially since U.S. Senator McCarthy's anti-Communist investigations during the mid-1950s had provoked near hysteria with respect to Communist infiltration of the United States. Because of our Communist members, the model Parliament was refused permission to cross the border. The U.S. Consulate General in Vancouver said that the rest of us would be welcome if we left the two Communist members behind. Naturally we rejected that proposal and it looked as though the visit would not take place. Eventually, the Consulate General relented, and the resulting publicity made sure that our model Parliament commanded a much bigger audience in Seattle than it would have done otherwise. The antics of our umbrella-equipped Tory and the fervency of the Communists' rhetoric delighted those who came to see us.

My university years were to come to an abrupt end in 1958, much sooner than I had anticipated. Dean Soward, the University's leading expert on foreign affairs, had taken a special interest in me. He recommended that I try the entry exams for the Foreign Service to gain experience for a more serious attempt in the future. Successful candidates were typically older than I and had graduate degrees and/or relevant work experience. Only twenty and an undergraduate, I had no expectation of success. At that time, the procedure for entry included four levels of testing. The first level was an elaborate multiple-choice test of general knowledge. The second was an interview with Public Service Commission officials to determine personal suitability. The third consisted of writing essays on three of twelve possible topics. The fourth and final level was an interview with a panel, which, for Vancouver applicants, consisted of two Canadian diplomats of ambassador rank, the executive vice president of Macmillan Bloedel, British Columbia's largest forestry firm at the time, and a dean from the UBC faculty.

I was able to get through the first three levels without much difficulty, but, when I entered the room for the final interview, my heart sank. To say that I felt intimidated is an immense understatement. I was scared stiff.

Everything changed when I heard the first question. "Please describe for us the prospects for an Islamic Republic divided territorially by a much larger hostile power." The question referred to Pakistan, which, at that time, still included East Pakistan, later to become the separate Republic of Bangladesh. Pakistan was the subject of my graduating paper and my confident, full, and knowledgeable answer reflected that fact. The dynamic of the meeting was completely transformed. My interrogators were visibly impressed; my answers to their remaining questions were undoubtedly less impressive, but they were delivered with confidence. That crucial first impression had done the trick.

PART II

BECOMING A DIPLOMAT: OTTAWA AND LATIN AMERICA

CHAPTER 6

NEW BEGINNINGS, BOTH FOREIGN AND MARITAL

Nonetheless, because of my youth, I was genuinely surprised when, a few days before my twenty-first birthday and weeks before I was granted my undergraduate degree, I received a telegram offering me the post of probationary Foreign Service Officer (FSO) at the princely salary of $350 a month (about the same as what I earned at the bus depot, but without overtime benefits). That unexpected offer and my acceptance changed everything, especially my relationship with Ardith. What were we to do?

Ardith and I were very fond of each other, but neither of us had given any thought to the possibility of marriage. I had been lonely, and the warm welcome of Ardith's family had made me feel very comfortable. She was pleased that her parents liked her boyfriend, but the prospect of leaving Vancouver and going to distant Ottawa was not a happy one. Her mother was clearly concerned that the relationship would be unlikely to survive if I left on my own. She was a very strong personality and did not hesitate to put a lot of pressure on her daughter to respond positively to me if I proposed. I did not want to lose the only girl ever in my life, nor did I want to walk away from Ardith's family, who had been so good to me. Her father was concerned that both of us were too young, but my excellent prospects made up for that.

Eventually, Ardith succumbed to her mother's pressure and a wedding date was set. I needed an engagement ring and approached my grandfather for help. He still had several diamonds left from those he had used to move his assets out of Britain. He was more than willing to help, and quickly brought out a black velvet box for my inspection. When he opened it, I was stunned. It looked like a tiny version of the Milky Way. He said that I could select one large one and two matching smaller ones, which I did. I had enough money to pay for the setting, which was very simple, but the resulting ring, especially on Ardith's small hand, was striking.

The manner of presenting it, however, was not. One late summer evening, I chose to take her to beautiful Queen Elizabeth Park, a former quarry that had been turned into a garden of considerable beauty. We stood at the edge of the quarry in the long grass and I repeated my proposal. Ardith held out her hand and I tried to put the ring on her finger. In my eagerness, I dropped it; the seeming eternity of worry that followed robbed the moment of any possible romance. What was I going to tell my grandfather if I could not find the ring? We did not dare move and the poor light meant that our fingers did the looking. Eventually one of us felt the ring, and both of us gave massive sighs of relief.

Ardith had gone to business college after graduating from York House school. She had obtained a decent job at BC Telephone (now renamed Telus); living at home, she had managed to save some money. After our engagement, she used that money to purchase a small, brand new, British-made convertible which was to carry us across the country to Ottawa. The weather was beautiful that summer; our frequent outings together with the top down are a happy memory for us both. I had no difficulty driving up the hill to Ardith's parents' home in that delightful, very peppy little car.

In late July of 1958, a couple of days before I left the bus depot for good, I was interviewed by the "Roving Reporter" from CKNW, the local radio station. A few years ago, I happened to come across the copy of the interview tape I was given. It is often said that wisdom comes with age; I have to say that my own experience has not generally supported that assertion. However, when I listened to that pompous know-it-all commenting on the issues of the day, I realized that I had learned one thing – how little I really knew. I guess that is the beginning of wisdom.

Our wedding day, August 2, 1958, was as beautiful as the rest of the summer. The church was located near the foot of the mountainside on which Ardith's parents' home was located. It was a very pretty church and had been delightfully decorated, but that did nothing to calm my nerves. It helped when I saw Ardith coming down the aisle; she was so beautiful. I remember little of the ceremony itself, but the reception in her parents' home is much clearer in my mind. Their view was spectacular: the whole harbour, the city, and the ocean beyond were below us. A regatta covered

I wed Ardith McMillan, West Vancouver, August 2, 1958.

English Bay with white sails, and we could clearly see the mountains of Vancouver Island and Washington State's Olympic Peninsula to the southwest as well as the striking, snow-topped volcano, Mount Baker, to the southeast. Finally, we were off to a hotel near English Bay for our last night in Vancouver. If Ardith were writing this, she would no doubt add the complaint that, because I was sick on my wedding night, she had to go out in the wee hours in her going-away finery to find a drugstore; not the most romantic beginning.

The next day was Ardith's turn to be upset as the full impact of leaving her home and family hit her and hit her hard. She must have cried almost all the way to Penticton, our first overnight stop. My terry cloth shirt was soaked, especially the right shoulder. After visiting many places in the United States and Canada as well as several relatives during the weeks that followed, we stopped our eastward journey in beautiful old Québec city because money was running low. We turned back to Ottawa, found a small, brand new, one-bedroom apartment in the city centre, and bought a sofa bed. That sofa bed, a couple of folding chairs, and a carpenter's table left over from the construction of the building served as our only furniture for several months. (Later, Ardith's parents sent us her bird's-eye maple bedroom set, which we still have.)

We were appalled to learn that a deposit was required before we could occupy the apartment, especially since it would be three weeks before any paycheque would appear. Short of funds, Ardith bought a huge turnip for ten cents to fill our stomachs, thereby provoking our first marital crisis: I hate turnip with a passion. The crisis was overcome when Ardith traded it for two cabbages from the resident caretaker.

Our food problems continued, though less severely, until Ardith added to our meagre income by using her experience at BC Telephone to get an even better job at Bell Canada. I particularly remember the saga of the disappearing leg of lamb, Ardith's favourite meat. Our plan had been for it to last a whole week. George Cowley, one of my fellow probationary Foreign Service Officers, who was much later to become our first child's godfather, came over with his housemate for dinner. Ardith and I watched with horror as the two of them ate the whole roast.

I should say something about Ardith's job, not just because it enabled us to eat regularly, but, more importantly, because it was the last one she was able to have outside the home. She was one of only two women in an office of Bell Canada out of which two hundred telephone repairmen worked. She was responsible for reviewing the job orders, for determining how many workers and how much time was required to do the tasks set out, for establishing a budget to cover expenses, and for reviewing the claims for those expenses once the work was completed. By 1950s standards, she was treated courteously, and the men agreed not to tell vulgar jokes in front of her. However, she had had to undergo pointed questioning about her pregnancy plans when applying for the job, and it was common for the men to comment on her appearance.

CHAPTER 7

MY DIPLOMATIC EDUCATION BEGINS

I reported for duty in the elegant East Block of the Parliament Buildings on September 15, 1958. My career had begun. My first day was not, however, without embarrassment. As another new appointee and I followed a more senior officer to the place we would be sworn in, I pulled my handkerchief out of my pocket only to scatter confetti all over the floor. I was in my one and only hand-me-down suit, which I had put on to leave the wedding reception. I had just become Canada's youngest diplomat, and it was showing.

One of the reasons I was attracted to a career in the Foreign Service was the nature of Canada's foreign policy. "Pearsonian" diplomacy, as it was sometimes styled, reflected Canada's capacity and willingness to serve the United Nations in a peacekeeping role. Lester Pearson was Canada's top professional diplomat before entering politics and becoming Foreign Minister. In the latter position, he played a central role in bringing about the United Nation's first peacekeeping intervention, for which he was awarded the Nobel Peace Prize. That peacekeeping force was established to supervise the cessation of hostilities and the withdrawal of British, French and Israeli forces following the Suez crisis in 1956. The crisis arose when Britain and France, on the pretext of protecting the canal from a prearranged Israeli incursion, occupied Egypt's Suez Canal, which Egyptian president Nasser had just nationalized. It had been operated by an Anglo-French company since its construction in the nineteenth century. Canada's longstanding focus on being willing and able to participate in U.N. peacekeeping and on pursuing policies that would make us acceptable as a peacekeeper began at that time.

In 1958, when I entered the Foreign Service, Pearson was leader of the

Liberal Opposition. Prime Minister John Diefenbaker's Progressive Conservatives formed the government, having just won a massive majority after decades of Liberal rule. Nonetheless, Diefenbaker, a populist prairie lawyer with a deep commitment to human rights, fully supported the foreign policy initiated by Pearson. While some critics ridiculed Canada's idealism as "boy scoutism," it was widely supported by the public and over the years came to be regarded by many as a characteristic of Canada's national identity.

While I found the Department to be generally welcoming, I did experience some negative feedback because of my youth. Particularly discouraging was my encounter with Norman Robertson, Lester Pearson's successor as Under-Secretary, as the top professional diplomat was known. It was traditional for the Under-Secretary to host a reception for incoming FSOs. When our host spoke to me, he inquired about my age, experience, and education. Clearly disturbed by my answers, he remarked, before moving to the next guest, that hiring me would appear to have been a mistake. Some of my colleagues seemed to hold the same opinion. It did not help that I looked even younger than my age. Having a seeming teenager in the group must have been galling. That mistake was never made again, which is no doubt why I still hold the record as Canada's youngest diplomat.

There were just over twenty of us new FSOs in 1958, including one woman. Today, the percentage of successful female candidates is many times higher; over a quarter of Canada's ambassadors are women. Sally, our one woman, was very impressive, but she later married Arthur Kroeger, another of our group, and had to resign. Moreover, as a diplomat's wife, she was not allowed to work when abroad. Today, the Department tries hard to find postings where both spouses can serve and Canada has also negotiated reciprocal agreements with many governments allowing the spouses, male or female, of serving diplomats to find paid employment in their host countries. Arthur was to rise to become one of Canada's most senior and most respected public servants, but poor Sally was to die far too young of a brain tumour. What a loss! It is good that we cannot see our future.

CHAPTER 8

THRUST INTO THE COLD WAR

Typically, new Foreign Service Officers were kept in Ottawa about eighteen months before going abroad on their first postings. That period was usually divided into three training assignments. I first worked in the Protocol Division where, as I learned to describe it, we were engaged in the care and feeding of foreign diplomats. We dealt with vital matters such as disposing of parking tickets, getting dogs out of quarantine, and monitoring the purchase of tax-free liquor. A few of those accredited to our country abused their privileges by reselling liquor. I caught one consul moving fifty cases of whisky a month. He was sent home. I guess I could say that one of the lessons I learnt during my months in Protocol was how not to behave while representing my country abroad.

A task of more consequence was telling Communist bloc diplomats whether they were permitted to travel outside Ottawa. That seemingly innocuous role led Ardith and me to an encounter with the feared KGB, the Soviet Union's notorious secret police, that changed our perceptions of the cold war forever. My task was simple enough. Each time a Soviet, Polish, or Czech diplomat applied to travel more than twenty-five miles from the centre of Ottawa, I would telephone the embassy concerned with the Department's response. That response depended upon whether or not the diplomat's country of origin had recently denied travel approval to a Canadian diplomat. When denying permission to travel, I would emphasize that Canada believed in freedom of travel for diplomatic personnel, but was obliged to respond when permission to travel was denied to our own personnel. The first time I did this, the Soviet official who received my call asked me to put it in writing. I checked with my superiors and declined. I was told that each new officer in my position was always asked the same question. I might add that Soviet Bloc diplomats staying in sleepy little Ottawa found it a real hardship to be denied the delights of Montréal.

Not long after I had begun my new job, Ardith and I received an invitation to the 1958 annual celebration of the Great October Revolution at the Soviet Embassy. Because of the difference between the Russian and Western calendars, the celebration took place in early November.

You can imagine how excited we were upon arrival at the intimidating-looking Soviet Chancery, as the primary building of an embassy is known. It was located in Ottawa's elegant old inner residential area of Sandy Hill. We parked our car, walked in the oversized front door, and passed through a foyer into a large, attractively decorated ballroom. The Soviet diplomats and their wives were lined up along one wall, but each couple moved quickly to greet whoever was entering and then, if our own experience was any indication, stayed with them all evening.

The couple who stayed with us were Rem Krassilnikov and his very attractive young wife, Irina. They spoke reasonably good English and we found them to be pleasant company. Irina was upset that evening because her children had reached the age where they had to be sent back to Moscow for their education. It was easy to empathize.

Rem greatly enjoyed dancing with my beautiful wife, but he seemed to enjoy his vodka even more. As the evening progressed, he became more and more inebriated and, perhaps to show off to Ardith, he began to talk about her family and neighbourhood. He knew what her father did for a living, that she had a brother at university, and that they lived on the side of a hill with a beautiful view. Ardith was stunned and not a little frightened. When she whispered in my ear what Rem had told her, I instantly shared her upset. We left not long after. Rem gave us a small carving as a gift. I had it checked for "bugs," but it was clean. We kept it as a reminder of the lesson learnt.

That experience was a serious wake-up call for me. Thirteen years earlier, Igor Gouzenko, a cipher clerk in the Soviet Embassy in Ottawa, upon learning that he and his family were being transferred back to Moscow, decided to defect, carrying with him cipher books and 109 files. These files revealed that Canada's wartime ally had a massive espionage network across this country and into the United States. The news became public and created a significant backlash against the Soviet Union, also spurring the creation of more sophisticated counterintelligence capabilities within

Canada. Britain's MI5 and the United States' FBI were involved in debriefing Gouzenko. They made use of the information obtained in pursuing such high-profile traitors as Klaus Fuchs in the U.K. and Julius and Ethel Rosenberg in the United States. Gouzenko's expertise and knowledge are also believed to have played a role in uncovering the "Cambridge Five," a group of highly-placed spies in Britain.

What Ardith and I experienced meant that, despite the counterintelligence efforts made by Canadian authorities in the immediate post-war years, the Soviets had rebuilt their network to the point that they had both the manpower and the inclination to look into the personal history of a very low level Canadian diplomat (and his wife) who had been in his position only a matter of weeks. If they had been looking at Ardith's background, how much more must they have been looking at mine. I wonder if they spoke to the Communist members of UBC's model Parliament who had initially been denied entry into the United States and with whom I had demonstrated solidarity.

When I reported the incident, the lack of surprise on the part of the Departmental Security Officer reinforced my concern. He implied that Krassilnikov was a KGB officer; I later saw his name in a published list of KGB members. Never again did I fall into the trap of discounting the Soviet threat, something which, in reaction to U.S. Senator McCarthy's excesses, I had earlier been inclined to do. I was to experience further evidence of the nature of our Soviet opponents in my next job – but more of that later.

We also had some very pleasant contacts with foreign diplomats, among them a young Indonesian, Sutikno, who was to meet his wife Umi in Ottawa. Sutikno, his embassy's most junior diplomat, lived in our apartment building, and Umi was the governess for the Indonesian Ambassador's children. We got to know them while they were getting to know each other and, not surprisingly, we were invited to their wedding. Covered by the TV networks, it was billed as the first Javanese Muslim wedding in Canada, taking place at the Ambassador's residence. It was a very elegant affair featuring a superb Indonesian banquet. What especially sticks in my mind was the conclusion of the short, simple ceremony. At that point, the Ambassador, standing in for the bride's father, invited the bride and groom to sit on each of his knees and then pronounced them to be of equal weight (i.e. in his affections). It was a touching gesture.

The night before, Ardith had been the only non-Indonesian at the bride's

Ardith helps with Umi's Indonesian wedding preparations, Ottawa, 1959.

party; I had been the only non-Indonesian at the groom's party. My party was uneventful, but Ardith helped decorate the large cloth "egg" which served as a fertility symbol. Indonesian tradition also called for a rooster under the marriage bed the first night, but placing this living fertility symbol in the basement had to suffice. Its effectiveness was, however, in no way diminished. Umi and Sutikno went on to produce thirteen children.

My next Protocol adventure had its origin in the Vatican and was very different in every respect. It started with the news that Pope Pius XII had died. The phone began ringing with callers from across the country asking whether to lower flags to half mast on Federal Government buildings. All my bosses were away, and I did not have a clue. I studied my manuals but could find references only to honouring the heads of state or government of allied or Commonwealth nations. I felt instinctively that Canada should respond in a positive fashion, and I sought guidance accordingly from an Assistant Under-Secretary (a very high rank despite the sound of it). He quickly dismissed me from his office. It was clear that he had no interest in getting involved in such a sensitive issue. It was sensitive because at that time, Canada did not have diplomatic relations with the Vatican, and Catholic-Protestant relations in Canada were less cordial than they are now.

I returned to my manuals with a vengeance, finally finding an obscure clause permitting, in special circumstances, the honouring of a friendly nation which was not an ally. I wrote a memo to the Minister arguing special circumstances and rushed it directly to the Under-Secretary's office for signature. My reward came an hour later when I saw the flag lowered on the Langevin building just across Confederation Square from the East Block of the Parliament buildings where my office was located. A heady sense of my own power grew as I imagined thousands of flags being lowered all over our huge country.

I was only twenty-one and three months on the job. It could only get better. It didn't! My new sense of self-importance quickly evaporated when I noticed a half hour later that the flag on the Langevin building had gone up again. It turned out that the Foreign Minister, who was from mostly Protestant Vancouver, was having second thoughts. Eventually, the decision to lower the flag was made, but with the ironic result that, because of our time zones, flags were down very briefly in the predominantly Catholic East and much longer in the predominantly Protestant West. I am happy to report that the manuals were quickly revised after this incident to provide explicit instructions to future probationary FSOs. My experience would not be repeated.

Many years later, fourteen years after my retirement, I was asked to headline a conference in Ottawa for young up-and-coming public servants on the theme of openness and accountability. I prepared a detailed paper on governance (appendix XIV) for distribution to attendees but also wrote a speech for oral delivery. In it, I included the story about the Pope's death and the flag and added the following, somewhat preachy, paragraph.

> The point of this story is that public servants, even at very junior levels, can influence events in our country much more than we realize. In this instance, the decision to lower the flag for the first time in Canada to recognize the death of a pope was a step forward for this country, however small, in our evolution towards the inclusive, tolerant, accepting society that we have become. It was also a prelude to establishing diplomatic relations with the Vatican a few years later. In other words, what public servants do, visibly or not, matters. That means that your attitudes, values, ethics and professional competence also matter. Moreover, these characteristics will undergo greater scrutiny as

> Canada's Public Service becomes more transparent and accountable. That is, or should be, what this conference is all about – helping you to realize what a high calling public service is and how important it is for you to develop the attitudes and skills needed to live up to that calling.

Despite the seemingly insubstantial nature of my work in the Protocol Division, I look back at those few months as truly instructive, an excellent beginning to my career. I saw up close the nature of our Cold War opponents, I experienced how much even very junior public servants could (should?) influence events and I learned how not to behave when representing one's country abroad. Not a bad base on which to build!

My next training assignment was in the Consular Division, the part of the Department that focuses on assisting Canadians abroad. I was given responsibility for managing our consular relations with Hungary, Bulgaria, and Romania. Canada had no embassies in these Communist countries, and our interests there were looked after by the British. Most of my time was focused on Hungary, where a particularly harsh regime had been established after the Soviet army put down the revolution of 1956. Several Canadians of Hungarian origin, sometimes accompanied by Canadian-born children and spouses, had made the mistake of visiting their homeland, often to see ailing relatives. The Hungarian authorities had refused to let them leave, declaring them to be Hungarian citizens, but at the same time treating them as foreigners and not allowing them to work. These people survived on money that the Canadian Government sent through the British Embassy.

From time to time, the Hungarian Affairs Attaché at the Polish Embassy in Ottawa would visit me to make the point that, if Canada were to establish an embassy in Budapest, these people would be allowed to leave. In other words, they were being held hostage in order to pressure Canada to take an action – establishing an embassy – that would enhance the respectability of the Soviet-imposed regime. To me, that Hungarian Attaché became the ugly face of Soviet imperialism.

Every time I met with her, I remembered the stories of Soviet oppression and brutality told to me by my Hungarian fellow boarder in Vancouver two years earlier. It was another important reminder early in my career of what the Cold War was about.

Chapter 9

INTO THE MUCK OF DIPLOMACY

I have described my first two assignments in the Protocol and Consular divisions. My third assignment was in what was then called the American Division, specifically the section of that division dealing with transboundary water and other environmental problems. (I, of course, had no idea that twelve years later I would be playing a major role in that section, much less that it would lead me into a totally new career.)

The work was very different from what I had experienced in the other two divisions. My first task was to write a memorandum proposing a strategy for dealing with a cross-boundary flow and water quality problem affecting an Alberta river. I had never written anything like that in my life; worse, I knew very little about the subject matter. I frantically read through the file, talked to some of my fellow officers, and attempted to put together an approach to the problem. I will never forget the response of the Divisional Director when he called me in to discuss the memo. "Nicely typed," he said, referring to the one element in the memo that had nothing to do with me. I was clearly on a steep learning curve.

Later, I negotiated dredging agreements with the United States. These were designed to ensure that the channels in the Great Lakes Seaway were kept clear for the huge number of lake and oceangoing vessels that travelled that immense inland waterway. You might call it the muck of diplomacy; the objective in each case was very simple: get the Americans to pay for the lion's (eagle's?) share of the cost and use as much Canadian labour and equipment as possible. Not a lot of idealism there! Nonetheless, the lessons learned were valuable and practical, complementing my immensely different experiences in the Protocol and Consular Divisions.

The most exciting moment in any diplomat's career is learning the location of his or her first posting. Mine was Bogota, the capital of Colombia, about which all I knew was that it was a great coffee producer. The first order of business was beginning Spanish lessons for both Ardith and me. My studies of Latin and knowledge of French made it much easier for me to learn another Romance language, especially one whose pronunciation came easily to the tongue. To my ear, Spanish is a beautiful language, and I love Latin music. We began to read as much as we could about Colombia and, of course, we had to make the usual practical preparations for departure.

Despite Ardith's job, we remained cash poor, and that meant taking out a substantial no-interest loan from the government to pay for our new car, formal clothing, furnishings, additional silverware, glassware, china, and other items befitting our new status. We thought it appropriate to take with us some Canadiana to display to our Colombian guests. We chose a French-Canadian carved wood mug and two Inuit (Eskimo) soapstone carvings. We had no idea how embarrassing that mug would prove to be.

We also needed to take our diplomatic passports with us, but mine proved very difficult to obtain. The effort to do so provided yet another useful career lesson – this time in bureaucratic inflexibility. It turned out that I was not a Canadian citizen despite having lived in this country almost my entire life! When I entered Canada at the age of six months in 1937 with my mother and her family, I did so as a visitor. The record of my arrival still existed; that unfortunate fact precluded a discretionary judgement assuming that I had entered as an immigrant. I was told by the Registrar of Citizenship himself that I had to become a landed immigrant and wait five years for my citizenship. In the office, my colleagues teased me by removing any "Canadian eyes only" documents, but the real dilemma was choosing the appropriate travel document. It looked as though I might have to travel to Colombia on a British passport, hardly the best identification for a diplomat representing Canada.

Fortunately, a further search of the records was made, which found that in 1949, two years after the Canadian Citizenship Act came into force, my mother had registered herself and me as landed immigrants at Victoria's Pat Bay airport immigration office. My landed immigrant status was counted from that date, easily meeting the five-year residency requirement. The Registrar of Citizenship himself presented me with my citizenship certificate and expressed his regret over what had occurred. I also received a form in the mail asking whether I had adjusted to life in Canada, had obtained a good job, and other questions of that nature. I did not fill it out, but I took away from this incident a real sympathy for those caught on the wrong side of inflexible bureaucratic rules.

The next decision was choosing the method of travel to Colombia. In this, we were influenced by a couple who lived on the top floor of our building. He had recently retired from an ambassadorship in the Foreign Service, and the two of them had taken a friendly interest in Ardith and myself. They suggested that we drive our new car to New York where it would be put on a ship destined to Colombia, and, in essence, do the same for ourselves. They made the suggestion more attractive by offering to meet us in New York and show us the "Big Apple." Accordingly, we made reservations on a passenger freighter that was leaving for Colombia at about the same time as the freighter carrying our car. It was late spring in 1960, the weather was beautiful, and the drive down the gorgeous Hudson valley on the parkway across the river from storied West Point was stunning. We broke our journey in Poughkeepsie, a delightful historical town with an equally delightful inn.

Our friends lived up to their promise by taking us to that great musical, *West Side Story*, which had recently opened on Broadway. The next day we dined at the famous Copacabana night club, which proved to be our last edible meal for several days. It turned out that the cook on our freighter had quit; unfortunately, a crewman had been drafted to replace him. It was a disaster, as all of the dozen passengers, or "prisoners," as we came to call ourselves, heartily agreed. Laundry facilities were not much better; Ardith found herself hanging her unmentionables in the engine room, often to a chorus of whistles. To add to the memorable character of the voyage, we ran into a big storm in the Caribbean. The crew told us to put our lifejackets under our mattresses to keep us from being thrown out of our beds. It worked, but only barely.

On the positive side, we made friends with a young Colombian couple who were returning to Bogota after his studies in dentistry in the United States. I also met a Colombian police lieutenant who had been attending an anti-guerrilla training course in the United States. If I had been a guerrilla I would have been very frightened of him. Much later, I was able to use him as a contact when I was writing about rural violence in Colombia.

Chapter 10

SEISMICALLY SHAKEN IN COLOMBIA

Our arrival in the Colombian Caribbean port of Barranquilla left us in no doubt that we were in the tropics. Both of us were dressed inappropriately: jacket and tie for me and crinolines, stockings, and the like for Ardith. Canada's honorary consul in Barranquilla met us at the dock and quickly had to apply cold water to Ardith's neck lest she faint. He whisked us to his home for a brief rest and then to the airport for the relatively short flight to Bogota.

Getting off the aircraft at that elevation was a very different experience. We were at 2625 metres (8612 feet) above sea level, and the air, what there was of it, was cool and refreshing (the average high in Bogota was only 19°C). We stayed at the Tequendama Hotel in the city centre while looking for a permanent residence. It was modern and comfortable and located only a few blocks from the embassy offices. Our hotel was also directly across from the bullring, a central feature in Colombian life.

We were greeted in both a standard and also an unusual fashion. The standard greeting was coming down with "Bogota Belly" – dysentery, painful and unpleasant, but not life-threatening. The more spectacular greeting came in the form of an earthquake, which was almost strong enough to throw us out of our sickbed. The hotel had been built to resist such tremors; it swayed magnificently, especially on the fourteenth floor, where we were staying. Leaving Bogota three years later, almost to the day, on the same floor of the same hotel, we had the same frightening experience. Our coming and our going were clearly marked.

Shortly after our seismic experience, our car arrived in Bogota and was delivered to the hotel garage. To my delight and surprise, it was completely unmarked. I got in and started the engine. I had totally forgotten that I had

Canada's diplomatic team in Bogota, dressed for work, 1960.

ordered a standard shift to avoid possible problems with repairs. The car lurched ahead into a concrete pillar. The two-tone paint job that resulted was an ongoing reminder of my stupidity.

We had made another car-related mistake. Colombia tightly restricted the import of cars, but it periodically allowed the replacement of taxis. Bogota had just received several dozen of them, all the same make and model as our car. I will never forget the constant cries of "taxi, taxi," wherever we went, despite our diplomatic licence plates. I took the desperate step of placing a Canadian flag in our windshield, but then encountered cries of "Ingleterra" (England) instead. We were still flying the Red Ensign in those days with its Union Jack in the corner and the Canadian coat of arms in the fly. The Colombian response did not do much for my sense of national pride, but it was better than "taxi." When the car first arrived in Bogota, it carried Ontario licence plates, which have at their centre a crown topped by a cross. Some Colombians apparently thought it was a papal crown and would cry out, "El Papa" (the Pope), and even make the sign of the cross. "Taxi" was quite a comedown.

One of the main hazards of driving in Bogota was that competing bus lines travelled the same routes. If drivers from different companies spotted passengers ahead, a race would ensue, and woe betide the wretched motorist caught in the middle.

Writing these words has brought to mind our one and only traffic accident during our three years in Colombia. I mentioned that one of my tasks in my first assignment in Ottawa in the Protocol Division was fixing parking tickets. Diplomats are immune from the enforcement of their host country's laws; while the more responsible among them voluntarily respect those laws, there are always those who ignore them, especially with respect to parking and speeding. In my day, the Ottawa Police routinely ticketed vehicles in violation despite their distinctive red diplomatic licence plates. The Foreign Affairs Department was left to return the tickets to the police unpaid with the standard explanation about immunity. With respect to accidents involving injury or loss of life, the embassy concerned could be asked to waive immunity to allow prosecution. Because almost no country responds positively to such a request, expulsion of the diplomat in question becomes the only real sanction.

Protection of diplomats from foreign harassment or persecution is the overarching objective of this immunity. Staging accidents in order to blackmail foreigners was, for example, standard KGB fare, and, the argument goes, routine waiving of immunity would undermine the principle of absolute protection. Canada was the only nation I know of that did not allow its diplomats to hide behind immunity over traffic violations in countries where we had no reason to believe that such laws were likely to be used in an inappropriate way to target our personnel. (I do not know if that is still true.) Thus, when a drunk driver slammed into our car at an intersection in Bogota, my fate was in the hands of the Colombian judicial system.

The incident itself was straightforward enough. One evening, Ardith and I were driving home on a wide, almost traffic-free street in one of Bogota's upscale residential neighborhoods. We reached a traffic light with a left-turn arrow and proceeded to execute a left turn once the arrow turned green. A jeep coming towards us failed to stop, and hit our front passenger door with a loud bang. Fortunately neither Ardith nor I was injured, but we were badly shaken. The two men in the jeep were clearly drunk. A woman who had been coming out of her house at the moment of impact rushed over to us and kindly offered to call the police. She also invited us, but not the two men, into her home to wait for a squad car. It was a very long wait, and we greatly appreciated the comfort of her living room.

Once the police arrived, the game began. Both men were, by this time, showing less evidence of drunkenness, and they vigorously contested my account of the affair, adding for good measure that I had insulted Colombia and Colombians. More importantly, I saw them give money to the traffic police, something I was not prepared to do. While the version of events that the police obtained from the woman who had witnessed the crash supported me, I was not surprised that the report submitted by the police to the magistrate was in favour of the jeep driver. Accordingly, accompanied by my witness, I was required to appear before the magistrate to answer the charges made in the report.

It is a mark of how upset I was at the time of the accident that I had not remembered what a beautiful woman my witness was. The magistrate was clearly enchanted by her appearance and charming manner. He not only questioned her at length but asked her back twice more. Things were looking up, and one of the court clerks told me that I would be pleased with the magistrate's decision.

Then, everything changed. The magistrate was among several who were being investigated for corruption. When charges were finally laid, the investigating judge reversed all the decisions that were on the point of being issued, and that included mine. I was found guilty and ordered to pay a substantial fine, which, as a good Canadian boy scout, I did. My insurer had to pay the cost of repairing the jeep as well as my own car. Sometimes the moral high ground is expensive.

CHAPTER 11

NOT FOR THE FAINT OF HEART

If I had to sum up Colombia in two words, they would be "extreme contrasts." In almost every measure I can think of Colombia lives up to that description. The country is legitimately known for violence, yet, with its many universities, libraries, writers, and poets and its place as arbiter of the Spanish language in the Americas, Bogota is also regarded as the Athens of South America. Similarly, despite the propensity for violence, including a three-year civil war between its two political parties at the end of the nineteenth century and an even longer one in the mid-twentieth century, Colombia was largely ruled by civilian governments throughout the nineteenth and twentieth centuries. While some of these governments before the latter half of the twentieth century were scarcely democratic by modern standards, at least they were neither extremely dictatorial nor militarist like so many other Latin American regimes.

Another area of contrast is between the rich and poor. Colombia, despite its considerable natural resources and growing economy, continues to rank among the most inequitable in the world with respect to income distribution. Finally there is the topography: the stunning high, cold Andes and the steamy equatorial jungle (including part of the Amazon basin), great plains and spectacular waterfalls, the sun-drenched, tourist-filled Caribbean coast, and the much darker, incredibly wet Pacific coastline. I could also cite the contrast between the modernity of urban centres like Bogota and Medellin or Cali and the beautiful colonial charm of an untouched town like Popayan.

Bogota was the Spanish regional capital for an area now encompassing Colombia, Ecuador, Venezuela, and Panama. After Simón Bolívar, the great liberator of northern South America, defeated the Spanish in the years following 1810, he also chose Bogota as his capital. Before the Europeans arrived, Bogota was the centre of the Chibcha nation, one of the Americas' most advanced indigenous societies. Their gold artifacts are a wonder to see. It was there that the legend of Eldorado was born. *Eldorado* means "the golden one"; the legend comes from the practice of sacrificing a human being by throwing him in a lake after covering him in oil and gold dust. Venezuela and Ecuador left Bolívar's republic in the 1830s, but Panama did not leave until the beginning of the twentieth century. Its departure was facilitated by the U.S. in order to ensure control of the soon-to-be completed Panama Canal. Colombians still resent that loss.

Because Bogota is the third-highest national capital in the world, the effects of altitude are of concern. These are experienced in various ways by different people. In theory, the human body is supposed to adjust to reduced oxygen and air pressure levels by increasing the number of red corpuscles in the blood. This typically takes about two weeks. Some people, however, do not adjust fully and can experience a number of continuing effects. In my case, the principal continuing effect was on my digestive system. It got so bad that I actually fainted in the office from what the doctor later described as malnutrition. Enzyme supplements were sufficient to overcome that problem, but breathing while playing tennis, for example, or climbing eight stories to our office during a power outage could be very challenging. Indeed, on days when our office building was without power, I would telephone the Ambassador and tell him not to come in. I recall in particular that, not long after our arrival, we were asked by the Ambassador to participate in a square dance demonstration at a reception held on Canada Day, July 1. I have never felt my heart pound like that.

Another effect that could be particularly devastating to visitors was the speed with which they would be affected by alcohol at that elevation. We always warned our visitors about this danger, but, not surprisingly, many forgot or simply chose to ignore us. I had to develop new skills to deal diplomatically with inebriated VIPs. Older people were also inclined to fall asleep more readily. I recall sitting beside a very elderly Canadian Cabinet Minister who was representing Canada at a conference. My job was to gently wake him up every time he nodded off. That also expanded my diplomatic skill set.

Not only human beings and animals were affected by the altitude. This was clearly demonstrated whenever we drove off Bogota's high plateau down towards the *tierra caliente* (hot country). The car engine would get stronger and stronger as we got closer to sea level, ultimately gaining about twenty percent in power. Of course, it would lose that power on the way back up when it was needed most.

As in Spain, bullfighting is a deeply ingrained part of Colombian culture. Given my own aversion to hunting for sport, I am not really sure what to say about *la corrida de toros* (running of the bulls), as bullfighting is described in Spanish. Ardith and I attended our first bullfight not long after our arrival in Bogota. The ring, located in downtown Bogota, looked like a brick Coliseum and was packed. There were three basic price divisions in ascending order: *sol* (sun), *sol y sombra* (sun and shade) and *sombra* (shade). We sat in the shade fairly high up. Those attending were frisked at the entrance to prevent them bringing in bottles or perhaps weapons, but it was customary to bring wineskins. These were held well above the mouth and a fine stream of wine would hopefully hit the right spot. Often, friends would toss their wineskins to one another, frequently forgetting to reattach the screw-on tops and thereby spraying everyone in between.

We went two or three times more with friends but never became *aficionados,* as fans are called. Bullfighting is an exercise in the control of a very dangerous animal by skilled and courageous participants. Aficionados see the movements as a kind of high-risk ballet. The parades, costumes, and rituals are colourful and interesting to see, but the outcome rarely differs. That said, the danger for the matador is real; many have been gored and some have died. I guess bullfighting is an acquired taste.

Flying over the Andes has its own special character, particularly when flying in relatively small aircraft and landing at small airstrips. I will never forget taking off in a World War II vintage DC 3 from Pasto in south-western Colombia. Pasto is a little lower than Bogota at 2500 metres above sea level, and the plateau on which it is located drops off sharply to a valley below. The airstrip is located on one of the few flat areas next to the edge of the plateau. You can imagine how I felt as the plane slowly lifted from the runway and promptly plunged down into the valley before gaining sufficient speed to rise, barely, above the peaks beyond. Not for the faint of heart!

CHAPTER 12

FINDING A HOME

When Ardith and I arrived in Colombia, we were determined to connect with Colombians and not simply live within either the diplomatic social round or the surprisingly active world of the sizable English-speaking community (Americans, Britons, and Canadians). That worthy objective proved ultimately unattainable for reasons about which I can only speculate. Colombia's social structure was probably a major factor. Our socio-economic counterparts lived in circumstances much more modest than our own and were not comfortable inviting us to their homes. Nor could they afford to entertain us in restaurants. We could invite them to our frequent receptions and dinners, but the relationship was of a one-way nature. The Colombian upper class had no interest in associating with diplomats below ambassadorial rank, and I was way below. Thus we were obliged to find our friends among the expatriate community.

Finding a place to live was our first priority. Initially, we rented a large apartment in a low-rise building located in an upscale neighbourhood. It proved unsuitable, but we were lucky enough to find an attractive two-bedroom bungalow surrounded by larger homes somewhat further from the city centre. A British diplomat and his wife lived across the street. The house was centred around a tiled atrium featuring magnificent tropical plants reaching almost to the large skylight above. Beyond the atrium, at the back of the house, was a good-sized dining room opening onto a walled garden. The two bedrooms were to the left, also at the back of the house. To the right of the dining room were the kitchen, laundry room, and maid's quarters. To the left of the entrance hall and atrium at the front of the house was a large living room, which led through sliding doors into a smaller den. By leaving those sliding doors open, we could create an excellent space for large receptions reaching from the den through the living room and the atrium into the dining room.

The layout of the house was ideal for entertaining. Typically we gave buffet dinners for a maximum of thirty-four guests because our set of Rosenthal china was for 36 (as were our silverware and crystal). Ardith would make the meals with the help of our live-in maid and we would hire two people to serve. Most of Ardith's meals were very well received, but we had one disaster. She made the Greek dish moussaka, which, for some reason, did not go over well. We ate that moussaka for many days thereafter and to this day we cannot abide it.

I mentioned earlier the three pieces of Canadiana that we had purchased in Ottawa to display in our home in Bogota. One – the French-Canadian carved wooden mug – was on display for only one party before being hidden deep in a drawer. Its disappearance was my quick response to a question posed by one of our guests: "Why do you display a carving depicting the face of your ambassador?" The resemblance was uncanny and its further display in Bogota was out of the question.

It did, however, later serve as a remembrance of a man both of us came to like very much. Jean Morin was not a career diplomat but had been given the ambassadorship in Bogota as a reward for his important role in securing the 1958 landslide election victory of Prime Minister Diefenbaker. To be more specific, Mr. Morin had been the Progressive Conservative party's principal bagman in Québec, at that time a traditional Liberal stronghold. Diefenbaker won the most seats in Québec of any Conservative in Canadian history up to that time. Generally speaking, there are very few political appointees among Canadian ambassadors, but our missions in Washington, London, and Paris constitute the exception. These are often headed by politically prominent Canadians.

The Ambassador was not, however, content with his appointment in Bogota; he spent much of his time lobbying friends in Ottawa for a transfer to Europe. He was ultimately successful. I remember his delight as we saw him and his wife off on their way to beautiful Portugal. He came from a very wealthy seigneurial family and, although trained in law, he had never practiced his profession. While he was as much a novice as I at the diplomatic business, he and his very artistic wife related easily to members of Colombia's upper classes and were excellent hosts. Despite their consistent courtesy, I think they did see the likes of us as semi-servants. During receptions or dinner parties, Ardith was often ordered to their kitchen to oversee their intimidating three hundred-pound female cook, Maruja, whose strange behaviour, including howling at the full moon, had unnerved her employers. I will never forget having to force Maruja, with the help of the chauffeur, to leave the residence preparatory to the Ambassador's departure for Portugal. There was nothing in the diplomatic manual to prepare me for that.

One of my first "calls" after getting settled in my new office was at the Royal Bank of Canada's Bogota branch where I met the Canadian staff, including the man who would later steal (marry) my secretary. I was astonished to recognize one of his colleagues who had lived only four houses from me in Victoria when we were both eleven. His last words to me as I exited the bank were, "You never gave me back my Lone Ranger book." He was right. Be sure your sins will find you out!

We attended many a party with Royal Bank personnel and became particularly close to an accountant from New Brunswick named Alan Caldwell. In due course a young member of the Swiss Embassy named Anne, who was about Ardith's age, joined our group. She was a great addition, full of fun, energy, and curiosity and bright as a button. Alan was a bit older, but his behaviour at parties masked that fact. Several months later, Anne was told that she was to be transferred to the Swiss Embassy in Havana. The United States had broken relations with the newly established Castro regime in Cuba somewhat earlier, and the Swiss Embassy there, having accepted responsibility for representing American interests, needed more staff. Anne was faced with a big decision, which became the trigger for deciding to tie the knot with Alan and to leave the Swiss Foreign Service. Their wedding and the happy celebration that accompanied it took place in our home.

The following week Alan's colleague Dick Fuller married Eileen, my secretary from Vancouver who, I can now say, was the best-educated secretary I was ever to have. Because of the short-sighted and sexist personnel policies of the day, she ultimately had to resign just because she got married. Fortunately, a replacement was not immediately available and I benefited from her continued presence in the office for about a year. Their marriage took place in Bogota's elegant Country Club, but Ardith earlier hosted a surprise bridal shower for Eileen in our home.

Although Dick and Eileen remained in Bogota, Anne and Alan moved immediately after their wedding to the much lower and therefore much warmer city of Cali, one of Colombia's regional capitals, where the Royal Bank also had a branch. We have happy memories of periodically visiting them there. As diplomats we were seeing the world through a cocktail glass. Their lives were grittier; I still recall the visit to a large meat market in Cali full of unspeakable sights and smells where Anne bargained like a native and was fazed by nothing.

We vowed to keep in touch when we left Colombia, but had no idea how much our lives would later be intertwined. The link was to be the younger of their two daughters. Anne and Alan spent the rest of his career in various South American and Caribbean countries, and, by the time they retired to Puerto Plata in the Dominican Republic, he headed the Royal Bank of Canada's extensive operations in that part of the world. Bored in Puerto Plata, they began building and selling condos to the many Canadians who holiday there. Both of their daughters earned degrees at Queen's University in Kingston, Ontario, where Anne and Alan bought a second home for their children to use. They also used it themselves when visiting Canada.

Fast forward to the mid-to-late eighties, when I was heading the office in Ottawa that became the Canadian Environmental Assessment Agency. I was surprised one day to see a familiar face from the past. It was Paula, Alan and Anne's younger daughter, who had just earned a degree in Environmental Science. She looked a lot like her mother and had her vivacity and intelligence. She was looking for a job, and we had a temporary contract position open. I left it with my staff to decide whether to hire her, and she easily qualified.

Paula proved to be a first-class worker and rose over the years to become a director in the Department of Environment and, later, in other parts of government, including its powerful centre, the Privy Council Office. Then, in a surprise move that was a reversal of my career pattern, she entered our diplomatic service, initially as the Senior Trade Commissioner in Sao Paulo, Brazil, later as number two in our very important embassy in Mexico, and now, at the time of writing, as our Consul General in Dallas. She sought my advice when she was also offered the alternative of an ambassadorship to a small country. "Choose substance over title" was my response, and she obviously agreed. As Canada's Consul General in Dallas, Paula is responsible for managing our relations with five states, which, collectively, have more trade with Canada than Germany and France combined.

Anne and Alan used to visit their daughter regularly when she was still working in Ottawa, and we would see them each time until we moved to Vancouver. They occasionally visited us on the West Coast, and sometimes we saw them in Ottawa when we were visiting our son, James, and his family. Far too young, dear Anne, whom we miss greatly, died of cancer in Kingston in late 2009, but we have continued to receive visits and phone calls from Alan, who travels extensively. One highlight was Alan's 2012 visit to Vancouver accompanying Paula, who was serving as the only Canadian resource person at a recurring conference of presidents of American State Senates that was held in Vancouver that year. Thirty states were represented. All four of us also had a reunion with Dick and Eileen, who, unknown to us, had retired near Vancouver. A week later, I was the only person present at their fiftieth wedding anniversary celebration, other than Eileen's sister, who had also been at their wedding in Bogota. To close the circle further, I met Eileen and Dick's daughter, a senior Foreign Service Officer, who is currently serving as our ambassador to Chile, an important Canadian trading partner. It was a joy talking to her and seeing her parents again.

Chapter 13

COLOMBIA'S POLITICAL SCIENCE EXPERIMENT

In 1960, Canada's embassy in Bogota was very small, with an ambassador, a political/consular officer (me), one senior trade commissioner, and one junior trade commissioner supported by two Canadian secretaries and a Canadian file/cipher clerk. There were also two Colombian receptionists/typists, a Colombian commercial assistant, a film librarian, and two drivers. The office occupied the eighth floor of a downtown office building. Today there are twenty Canadians and fifty-six Colombians on staff located in a stand-alone building in a distant suburb (close to where Ardith and I lived during most of our posting there). That growth reflects not only Colombia's place as South America's third most populous country and its growing trade with Canada, but also the recent signing of a Canada/Colombia Free Trade Agreement. Bogota's own growth has been remarkable. Its population was a little over a million when we lived there in the early '60s. Fifty years later it is close to ten million.

My work at the Embassy was essentially divided into two parts. The first was dealing as needed with the Colombian government and writing reports for Ottawa about political conditions in Colombia. The second was looking after all Canadians living in or visiting Colombia except for those who were being assisted by the Trade Commissioners. The need to meet with Colombian officials arose only rarely and usually involved such matters as seeking Colombian support for a Canadian initiative at the United Nations or making arrangements for official visitors from Canada to Bogota. Much more of my time was spent in writing reports for Ottawa about Colombia's complicated political situation and the continuing rural violence.

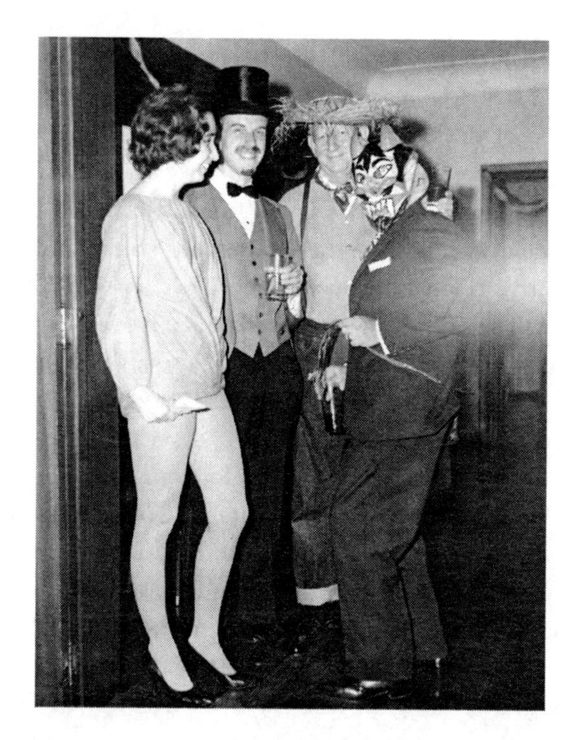

Ardith and I show that diplomacy is not all work, Bogota, 1961.

A word about Colombia's difficult history is needed. Both the political situation and the continuing violence had their origin in a multi-year civil war between the two principal political parties with the familiar names of Liberals and Conservatives. These parties came into being not long after Simón Bolívar established the republic. They fought a three-year war from 1899 to 1902 but did not again resort to violence on a large scale until 1948. That second war, known as "La Violencia," lasted even longer and cost about three hundred thousand lives. It was brought to an end through a military coup, and the leaders of both parties were exiled. Most Conservatives went to Franco's Spain and most Liberals to Mexico.

The new military dictator, General Rojas, was initially well received by the people of Colombia, but, over time, harsh measures, corrupt behaviour, and a refusal to restore democracy turned the people against him. In a near-bloodless revolution during which the banks shut down, Rojas was forced to flee the country, and the Liberal and Conservative leaders were invited back. Neither trusted the other, and the challenge for them both was to prevent a repetition of history. They came up with an ingenious system of government under which they would effectively share power for twenty-four years.

On the face of it, this would seem to make elections irrelevant, but they came to play a role much like the primary elections that choose party candidates in the United States. The elections determined the ideological bent of individual members of the House and Senate, and co-operation between similarly oriented members of both parties would enable legislation to proceed. The presidency was determined by popular vote, but cabinet membership and other important appointive positions were always divided equally between the parties, as were members of Congress. The system came to an end in 1978.

The civil war ended at least six years before our arrival in Bogota. It had been fought almost entirely in rural Colombia. The substantial loss of life and the disruption to the Colombian way of life had, however, left an ugly residue – what could best be described as a depraved taste for violence, at least on the part of some. Through contacts made through the police lieutenant whom I had met on the boat coming to Colombia, I was given some graphic briefings describing the challenges faced by Colombian authorities in dealing with this residual taste for violence.

What was happening was that seemingly peaceful *campesinos* (peasants) would come together from time to time for a night out. That night out might well consist of stopping a bus and massacring everyone on board, often in a slow and cruel fashion. Putting a halt to these terrible atrocities was extremely difficult because those perpetrating them had no base camp and there was no way of knowing when or where the attacks would occur. My police informants explained that their only effective tool was infiltration of the groups of *campesinos*. Finding suitable people brave enough to serve as infiltrators was a major challenge. Such people could most commonly be found among the relatives of those massacred, presumably motivated by revenge. Moreover, the infiltrators had to be prepared to participate in such massacres since they would not be given advance notice of the next outing until they had proven themselves. Only with advance notice would the police have any hope of catching the perpetrators in the act.

From time to time, the Ambassador would make an official visit to one of Colombia's regional capitals. When he made his official trip to Cali, the regional capital where our friends Anne and Alan were living, I was asked to accompany the embassy car and chauffeur while he travelled by plane.

We were escorted by eight soldiers in two jeeps equipped with machine guns. In the predawn darkness, our car became stuck in the mud. Half of the soldiers helped push us out while the other half scanned the jungle-covered hills on either side of us, holding their automatic weapons at the ready. We eventually got moving again, but it did not ease my mind to think about the horrific details I had learned during the police briefings. I could still see the graphic photos of mutilated bodies piled around a bullet-ridden bus. I later learned that a bus was attacked earlier the same night only fifty kilometres from where we were stuck.

Frankly, the account of the violence given to me by my police contacts made my mind boggle. It also made it a little easier to understand the decades of better-organized violence that followed our departure from Colombia. A mix of drug lords, left-wing revolutionaries, and right-wing paramilitaries have, at various times over the years, dominated parts of rural Colombia and used this propensity for violence for their own ends. The Colombian government has eliminated the worst of the violence through a mix of negotiation, successful military action, and limited amnesty. Nonetheless, there are still parts of Colombia that are decidedly unsafe, and the threat of kidnapping remains high.

My overly-long, detailed analyses of Colombia's giant political science experiment that I regularly sent to Ottawa proved to be exercises in my own entertainment. When I returned to Ottawa, I made the mistake of visiting the Latin American division and looking at what disposition had been made of my many reports. File without distribution was the norm. As a political appointee, my Ambassador boss in Bogota was unable to provide the guidance that I would have received from an experienced diplomat. I did, however, receive a great deal of inspiration from Viron P. "Pete" Vaky, the senior political officer at the U.S. Embassy in Colombia. Pete had spent his career in various Latin American countries and spoke Spanish as though it were his mother tongue with only a slight Argentinean accent. Of Greek descent, his colouring was dark and he could easily pass as a Latin American in any crowd. I remember standing with him near a large anti-American demonstration that was going on in front of the Congress. He was about to start mingling with the protesters when he stopped and looked at me. He explained that he could not safely enter the crowd accompanied by such an obvious gringo. His hesitation was truly ironic, given

"Diplomacy is easy on the brain and hell on the feet" – Ardith and I with Luann Vaky (centre) at a reception in Bogota, 1962.

Canada's decision to maintain relations with the Castro government in Cuba had made us popular with left-wing movements in Latin America.

Pete, who had a good understanding of what was going on in Colombia, often shared his insights with me. Ardith and I became very fond of him and his beautiful blonde wife, Luann, whose intelligence was matched by her considerable talents as a singer and dancer. I will never forget her singing "I'm Gonna Wash That Man Right Out of My Hair" from the musical *South Pacific* put on by the English-speaking community. Pete was later to return as U.S. Ambassador to Colombia, and he ultimately became U.S. Assistant Secretary of State for Latin America. It was a privilege to know him and his talented wife. We reconnected once in Washington, D.C., many years later, along with the British diplomat and his wife who had lived across the street from us in Bogota.

Chapter 14

BECOMING A CONSULAR ANGEL

A fair amount of my time in Colombia was spent helping Canadian residents and visitors in my role as vice consul and, later, consul. Several anecdotes will illustrate best what that work entailed.

I will begin with Harry, who operated a gold-dredging barge on the substantial Magdalena River that bisects Colombia. It is about the size of Canada's Fraser River (which reaches the Pacific just south of Vancouver). He worked for a Vancouver-based gold mining company that operated several dredges. As a result of a dispute with his employer, he left his dredge barge on the Magdalena and moved with his wife and two young children to Cali.

I had seen Harry and his family once at the Embassy offices, but I did not encounter him socially until July 1, Canada Day. At our diplomatic posts abroad, July 1 is very busy. Bogota was no exception. At midday, the Ambassador and the rest of the diplomatic staff would receive the local VIPs: Cabinet members, Congressmen, prominent businessmen, and other ambassadors accredited to Colombia. In the evening, the Ambassador's residence would be filled with a very different crowd: Canadian expatriates, many of whom were determined to drink back what they had paid out in taxes. Mixing the two crowds would have set back relations with Colombia several years, and having the Canadian party first would have left the official residence in no fit condition for the VIPs.

You can imagine how surprised I was when Harry showed up at the VIP party along with a woman who was not his wife. She was equipped for the occasion with a huge handbag, fashionable at that time, which was put to immediate use. Harry walked straight to the bar, seized an unopened forty-ounce bottle of Seagram's VO, and placed it in his companion's handbag.

I protested, and he pointed out in a crude fashion that there was very little I could do about it with all the VIPs present. He had a point. He and his friend proceeded to drink almost as much as they had stolen before leaving just before the last few VIPs. In Cali, he had opened an unsavoury night spot named the Canada Key Club; reportedly he included in his advertising the assurance that customers could rely on the quality of the liquor served in his establishment because it came straight from the Canadian Embassy.

That account is simply to establish Harry's character. The real story is more dramatic. I was seated in my office when our receptionist, Rosita, called me to say that some police officers wanted to see me. Three men in plain clothes came through my door, but I soon discovered that only two were from the police. The other was a *contrabandista,* a smuggler, who, it turned out, had been supplying smuggled liquor to the Canada Key Club. The smuggler had complained to the authorities about receiving bad checks from Harry.

My Spanish was pretty good, but I had them repeat the story because I could scarcely believe what I was hearing. Harry had disappeared, and the police wanted to know if I knew where he was. I did not and was so informing them when my intercom loudspeaker interrupted us with the sound of Rosita telling me in Spanish that Harry had arrived in the reception room and wanted to see me.

The three men jumped to their feet and proceeded at speed down the hall towards a thoroughly alarmed Harry. I moved as quickly as I could behind them; as the policemen grabbed Harry, I announced that this was *territorio Canadiense* and that they could not arrest him. It took some time to get the point across, but in due course the three men withdrew to the elevator lobby on the other side of the glass wall that separated it from our reception area.

I now had to turn my attention to Harry, who was looking much relieved. His mood changed dramatically when I informed him that we could not give him asylum and that he would have to leave. He responded in words not suitable for this account; I made it clear that, if necessary, the trade commissioners and I would push him out the door. Our rules are very clear on this point. Canadian embassies must not be used to provide safe haven from the due process of local law unless there is clear evidence of abuse and discrimination.

Eventually, Harry agreed to leave, and moved towards the door. The three men on the other side of the glass moved closer as well. Harry hesitated and moved back, and this process was repeated two or three times. It was straight out of a Laurel and Hardy movie. Finally, Harry left and disappeared into the elevator with the two policemen flanking him.

A few moments later, the elevator operator (we still had them then) came rushing into our reception area shouting for "Señor Cónsul." She explained that the policemen had roughed Harry up, and he had called for help. Now it was appropriate for me to provide him with consular assistance. Isn't it wonderful how the bureaucratic mind works!

I immediately called a senior police officer to whom I periodically sent gifts of Canadian whiskey. I explained the situation; after he had stopped laughing, he agreed to radio the policemen involved and order them to bring Harry to his office. He asked me to be there to help work out a solution. I ended up arriving before Harry and his escort.

When Harry saw me, he just about fell on my neck with joy. Prison in Colombia is no picnic, and Harry was very scared. It turned out that the Canadian gold mining company owed Harry a separation payment required under Colombian law; it was enough to cover the bad checks he had given to the smuggler. Against our regulations, I agreed to pay the smuggler the money owed out of my personal account if Harry signed his separation payment over to me. The police agreed to drop all charges, which allowed Harry and his family, who were my primary concern, to leave the country.

I telephoned the gold mining company and persuaded them to pay for flying Harry and his family home to Vancouver. To me, that is what Canadians should be able to expect from their consuls. It saddens me greatly when I hear of instances that fall so far short of my service to Harry and his family. As for breaking the rules, I knew only too well from my difficulties in obtaining a Canadian diplomatic passport what it is like to be on the wrong side of bureaucratic inflexibility. Harry was not going to jail or his family into poverty because I was scared of breaking a rule. The closure of the Canada Key Club in Cali was a bonus.

A question to the reader: What does it take to turn an archaeologist into a diplomat? Answer: A shipwreck. One morning I received a telephone call from Cartagena on the Colombian Caribbean coast. The agitated young man with whom I spoke was an archaeology student from McGill University in Montreal who had been working as a crew member on a yacht. The yacht had capsized in a storm near the coast, and he had barely made it to shore. He had no identification and no money. I sent him enough money to get him to Bogota. He stayed with Ardith and me until we could confirm his identity, issue him a passport, and see him on his way back to Canada with an airline ticket purchased by his family. We really enjoyed his company, but the impression that we made on him apparently changed his life. He replaced his archaeological courses with others better suited to a diplomatic career and, a few years later, joined me as a Canadian Foreign Service Officer. He was to have a very successful career.

On another occasion, Ardith and I were instrumental in saving a Canadian journalist's life. The journalist in question, Ian Sclanders, was visiting Colombia on behalf of *Maclean's*, Canada's English-language counterpart to *Time* or *Newsweek*. I do not remember what story he was pursuing; probably something to do with the rural violence. We had him to dinner at our home on a couple of occasions, and I had arranged to meet with him to act as translator in some interviews we had organized. When he did not show up, I made the necessary apologies, but assumed that something else had caught his attention. When I got home that night and told Ardith what had happened, she became very worried and insisted that we go to his hotel. We found him in his room lying on his bed looking near death; I called Augusto Biagi, a good friend whose wife, Peggy, was Canadian. Augusto served as the Embassy's unofficial doctor. He rushed over, called an ambulance, and moved the visiting journalist to a private clinic. Our visitor was bleeding from a stomach ulcer and had, Augusto later said, perhaps five hours to live.

Ian stayed in our home for his two-week convalescence before returning to Canada, and from time to time thereafter we would hear from him. Years later, we visited Washington, D.C., where he was working. He invited Ardith and me to a remarkable picnic in the beautiful Virginia hills. James M. Minifie, the CBC's celebrated Washington correspondent, was the fourth member of the party. We had three wines, two caviars, exquisite meats and poultry, and elegant salads, all served on china with silver and crystal. All we lacked were the servants and the Rolls-Royce. This was our friend's "thank you," and it was clearly heartfelt.

Another visiting correspondent, Gerald Clark from the now defunct *Montreal Star*, who was writing a book on Latin America, provided me with an interesting insight into a little-known part of Colombia's history. He had read of the short-lived Communist Republic of Tequendama located in the coffee hills below the high plateau on which Bogota is located. I had never heard of it, but, with a little research, I discovered that back in the 1920s the peasant farmers working in the large coffee estates near the little town of Tequendama had risen up against the land owners, killed some, and forced the rest to flee. At that time, there were no roads connecting Bogota with that area and, because of the steep mountains, travel was very difficult. Nonetheless, the Colombian government sent soldiers to put down the revolt and restore the land to its legal owners. The soldiers were defeated by the peasant farmers, and Bogota chose to leave them alone. The leader of the peasants declared the founding of the Communist Republic of Tequendama. It continued to exist in its "independent" state until the mid-1950s when the military dictator General Rojas negotiated its re-integration into Colombia in return for the construction of a road that would facilitate the export of coffee and bananas. He also promised official recognition of the status quo with respect to land ownership. The *Montreal Star* correspondent asked me to drive him there, which I was happy to do.

The journey was hair-raising. The road was narrow, winding in the extreme, and flanked by cliffs falling away on one side and rising steeply above us on the other. There were three real dangers: erratic drivers, the absence of signs and barriers at hairpin turns, and the risk of rockfalls or road washouts. White crosses marked those places where vehicles had gone over the edge, and sometimes they almost formed a fence. Periodic roadside shrines were often surrounded by what seemed to me strange offerings: piles of sealed beam units (headlights).

Eventually we entered the territory of the former republic, which was clearly marked with signs. Imagine, if you can, steep hillsides covered with a mix of broad-leafed banana trees and coffee plants, the latter growing in the shade of the former. We passed a woman working among the coffee plants and stopped to talk with her. With me as translator, my visitor asked questions about Tequendama's history. Did she and her husband own their own land and did they know about the land ownership transfer generations earlier? They did own their land, but she had heard only vague rumours about a land transfer. Did she know the current Communist mayor of Tequendama? She had heard of him but, in response to further questioning, clearly had no idea what Communism meant. We asked if she had ever visited his farm, which we knew to be prosperous and located further up the same road on which she lived. She replied that over the course of her life (perhaps fifty years) she had never been that direction on the road, only the other way leading to the village.

We were not able to speak to the mayor, but we did have an interesting conversation with the village priest. Although at that time the Roman Catholic Church was generally regarded as being anti-progressive in Latin America, many individual priests held very different views and often acted upon them. Such was the priest in Tequendama. He understood the history of the former republic well, and he explained how he and his predecessors had developed excellent relations with the "Communists," most of whom regularly attended mass. He supported the land reform, and believed it should be applied more generally in Colombia.

I suspect that, in that latter belief, he would not have found automatic support from many of his parishioners. The reason would not arise from opposition to the idea, but rather from a total lack of awareness of the rest of the country. At the peasant level, Colombia's rugged topography isolated communities to such a degree that they would not understand that what happened in one community would have significance for another. Said more simply, there was little class consciousness on a national level among the peasantry, whereas the upper and middle classes knew exactly what policies served their interests. Various events since, including the communications revolution, have changed that situation.

One of my more unusual consular responsibilities was the protection of about thirty Canadian evangelical Protestant missionaries, many from Alberta's Prairie Bible Institute, who were living in Colombia. Despite my Anglican boarding school upbringing, I was essentially an agnostic and regarded these missionaries as an embarrassment to Canada in Catholic Colombia. The Ambassador, on the other hand, a Roman Catholic, was even more embarrassed at the poor treatment sometimes meted out by his fellow believers to these missionaries. He ordered me to be zealous in their protection.

At that time, Colombian law still banned all non-Catholic religious worship but that law was not enforced in urban areas. In small rural communities, it was a very different matter. The missionaries would be harassed by having their electricity and water turned off; some were even jailed. My job was to get the power and water restored or to get the incarcerated missionary released. In the process, I developed a totally undeserved reputation as a consular angel. One of the missionaries whom I had assisted lived with his wife and family not far from Bogota. On more than one occasion he and his wife invited Ardith and myself to dinner in their very modest home. We always got our own special sermon along with a very warm welcome. While I did not change my religious beliefs, I did develop respect for these people, who, out of a clearly genuine concern for Colombians, were prepared to live in circumstances so much worse than they would have experienced back home in Canada. Years later, on the other side of the world, I came to better understand what motivated them.

CHAPTER 15

RECEIVING VISITORS

Early in our Colombian posting, we received news that my younger brother Keith was getting married. He had also just earned an engineering degree from the University of British Colombia and won a scholarship to attend the prestigious engineering school at the University of Illinois at Champaign-Urbana. He went on to obtain a master's degree in soils engineering, a specialty of that school. (Many years later, I attended a conference at that university and lectured there.) Although he travelled widely later in his career, he was in no position as a student to visit us in Bogota. He worked and lived in Seattle, San Francisco; Perth, Australia; and Johannesburg, South Africa before finally settling in Vancouver.

Keith headed his own company for many years but eventually sold it to become a senior vice president in a very large engineering firm. In that position, he was responsible for overseeing the underground work for the construction of the subway system that links Vancouver's airport to the city centre completed just in time for the Winter Olympics in 2010. More recently, he has played a similar role with respect to the new urban rail link under construction in Calgary.

It has been a source of sadness to me that our separate upbringing has meant that Keith and I do not have the shared memories and experiences that would be part of a normal sibling relationship. I am pleased, however, that, at this late stage in our lives, we are able to see each other from time to time. Keith and his first wife had two children, a boy and a girl who were a little younger than our own.

One visitor to Colombia gave rise to a lifelong friendly association. He was Herb Gray, at that time a young, newly elected Member of Parliament from Windsor, Ontario. I cannot remember what brought him to

Colombia, but I do remember our first meal together. Ardith and I invited him home for dinner. Because he was the first MP we had ever met, let alone invited into our home, we were anxious to make a good impression. Colombian meat varied considerably in quality, perhaps because it was not hung for long. Usually we ate *lomito* (tenderloin), but even it could sometimes be tough. That night we made the huge mistake of choosing prime rib, and it was just like rubber. Ardith had cooked it in a wine sauce that turned a bright pink, in sharp contrast with the yellow stuffed eggs sprinkled with paprika surrounding the roast. What a disaster. To make things worse, my effort to open the wine destroyed the cork, which disintegrated before I could remove it. Herb was the soul of understanding, but it is perhaps not surprising that the next night he invited us out to dinner. Later he mailed us a thank-you gift: an automated corkscrew.

In subsequent years, as Herb and I climbed our respective career ladders, I would encounter him from time to time, most often in the dry cleaning establishment that we both frequented. Always the greeting was warm, and often we chuckled over our shared memories when we were both starting out. He was elected in thirteen general elections, making him the longest continuously-serving Member of Parliament in Canadian history. Later Herb became Deputy Prime Minister and, for a brief period, acting leader of the Liberal party during the party leadership race that Jean Chrétien won. On a couple of occasions, I was asked to brief him on environmental issues, and each time the warmth that began in Bogota was rekindled.

My happiest memory of him, however, was at the annual Parliamentary Press Gallery formal dinner many years later, in 1990. I had been invited to attend by a Canadian Press correspondent. At such dinners the Governor General, the Prime Minister, and other party leaders were expected to deliver amusing speeches. Ed Schreyer, the former premier of Manitoba, was at that time the Queen's representative in Canada, and, despite his somewhat stiff demeanour, proceeded to deliver an absolutely hilarious speech. He constantly referred to us all as "my subjects," and he frequently instructed his red-coated aide to note the name of anyone who responded inappropriately to his remarks. All that was lacking was the cry, "Off with their heads." Prime Minister Mulroney gave a professionally crafted, amusing speech, but he was not nearly as funny as Schreyer. The New Democratic party leader, Alexa McDonough, who was a real lady, was given a down-to-earth speech to deliver, which, while containing some funny lines, did not do justice to her gracious personality.

Herb Gray, who spoke third in his role as acting Liberal party leader, surprised us all. He was the opposite of charismatic, and most commentators considered his name reflective of his image. Referring to his party's leadership contest, he spoke of the growing movement across the country, which he characterized as Graymania, to draft him for the leadership. He described the rapturous reception he received from elderly ladies, who fainted wherever he went. As he continued, we in the audience periodically stood waving our white serviettes above our heads and shouting, "Herb, Herb, Herb." It was hilarious. There is little so attractive as self-deprecating humour. Herb Gray was a decent, hard-working politician with a minimal ego, and I was privileged to know him, however distantly.

The only visitor of international note whom we met while in Colombia was His Royal Highness Prince Philip. Along with the British diplomats and their wives, we Canadians were invited to the joint reception given by the British and Canadian ambassadors in Prince Philip's honour and to the corresponding reception in the presidential palace, hosted by Colombia's president, Alberto Lleras Camargo. At the palace, Roger Bull, the Embassy's junior Trade Commissioner, and I were talking when the Prince came over to ask about our impressions of Colombia. I became nervous and tongue-tied, but Roger saved the national honour by replying calmly and coherently. Many years later, I did somewhat better when meeting another Royal, Her Majesty Queen Beatrix of the Netherlands, but that encounter fits better in another part of this narrative.

We were not only visited by strangers. Friends and family came as well. We particularly enjoyed spending two weeks travelling around Colombia with Ardith's parents and brother. One of the places we visited was Colombia's second-largest city, Medellin. At about 1500 metres above sea level, it enjoys a truly delightful year-round climate. Courtesy of an acquaintance of mine who was a Colombian Congressman, we were able to stay at the city's elegant country club. I will never forget the luxurious surroundings, artificial waterfalls, superb food and service, and glorious tropical flowers. We spent an evening at the Congressman's magnificent home, where we met his beautiful wife and children. Their lifestyle approached that of the minor aristocracy in an earlier Europe. The contrast with the conditions under which the vast majority of Colombians lived could not have been starker. It was hard not to feel conflicted as we enjoyed the beauty and graciousness of our surroundings and hosts.

Another place we visited with my in-laws was the storied city of Cartagena on Colombia's Caribbean coast. Cartagena and Canada's Québec city are the only two cities in the Americas whose original walls are still intact. (San Juan, Puerto Rico, almost qualifies.) Cartagena is the port where the Spanish gathered their galleons together in convoy before proceeding across the Atlantic with their treasures of silver and gold. Convoys were essential to protect against constant attacks from British, Dutch, and French privateers and pirates. Cartagena itself was once attacked by the British, and I remember visiting the high point above the city where a group of nuns threw themselves to their deaths rather than face the ravages of the attackers. The romantic view often held in the English-speaking world of the pirates of the Caribbean is certainly not shared in Latin America.

One of my favourite cities in Colombia was Popayan, in the south near Ecuador. My visit there would have been like travelling back two centuries if one could but remove the cars and electric lights. The Spanish colonial architecture was beautiful, and several homes were furnished in the period and open to visitors.

My oldest friend, John Craddock, whom I had known since age seven when we both lived in Victoria, also came for a visit. I can still see the alarm in his face as he knocked on our bedroom door after his first night with us and asked what was meant by the sounds of machine guns and mortar shells that could be heard in the distance. Influenced by Latin American stereotypes, he fully expected an armed revolution. It happened that the neighbourhood where we lived was not far from an army firing range, which may have helped keep the rent within the range of my modest rank.

In truth, at that time, Colombia was politically stable and in no danger of armed insurrection. However, that did not rule out street protests sometimes requiring the use of water cannons. I particularly recall the imaginative way in which university students protested a proposed hike in fees. In Colombia, as in some other Latin American countries, university campuses were generally immune from police intervention. This practice was designed to protect intellectual freedom. I cannot imagine that this immunity would apply to investigations of murders or other serious criminal activities, but it certainly applied to political protests. Taking advantage of this immunity, the students started capturing buses on their routes through

Ardith and I enjoy a German Christmas in the Claessens' home, Bogota, 1961.

the campus. If memory serves, the number was approaching fifty when the continued refusal of the authorities to cancel the fee hike led to a change of tactic. The students started to burn the buses, one each day, and, after about the tenth, the fee hike was cancelled. While the Colombian government's restraint may impress some, I do not believe that the lesson learnt by the students was particularly healthy.

Bogota had a substantial German community, including the descendants of many who had arrived long before World War II. Ardith and I became friends with Nena and Karlfried Claessens, who, between them, represented the pre- and post-war German immigrants. Nena's family had arrived decades earlier, but Karlfried had immigrated to Colombia from the chaos of post-war Germany with scarcely a penny in his pocket. He had worked at all sorts of menial jobs before establishing himself as the sole distributor of a line of German machine tools. By the time we met him, he had married Nena, had had two adorable children who looked like Hummel figures, and had built up a substantial business.

Drafted as a teenager into the German army, Karlfried served in North

Africa in Rommel's Africa Corps as a driver. Retreating from the British after the pivotal battle of El Alamein, he became separated from his unit and was captured by a British patrol. Much to the delight of the British soldiers, Karlfried's open half-track was full of wine and champagne. Karlfried, who spoke English, was included in the party which followed and became very friendly with the officer commanding the patrol. Subsequently, Karlfried was sent to a POW camp in Canada where he spent the balance of the war. He fell in love with our country and vowed to return. Unfortunately, in the immediate post-war period, we were not accepting German immigrants, and Colombia was his alternative.

He had not, however, abandoned his dream of coming to Canada, and, with my encouragement, he visited some Canadian cities to decide which one would be best for establishing a business. He chose Toronto, and I had no hesitation recommending that he and his family be given visas. His entrepreneurial spirit is precisely what our economy needs. His machine tool business prospered in Canada and is now headed by his son (who no longer resembles a Hummel figure). We have kept in touch over the years with phone calls, letters, and occasional visits. I remember in particular a visit he made to Ottawa when I was heading the Environmental Protection Service. He arrived in my office accompanied by a retired British Major General, the young officer who had captured him in the desert so many years earlier. It was a fascinating conversation, and the story was picked up by the newspapers.

One of our favourite outings from Bogota was to visit Palanquero, a Colombian air force base down in the Magdalena Valley. We had become friends with a Canadair engineer and his wife who lived at the base. His job was to oversee the servicing of the CF-86 Sabre jets that his Montreal-based company had sold to the Colombian government after Canada downsized our air force following the Korean War. Sabre jets had tangled with Soviet-made MIGs throughout that war. The base was surrounded by thick jungle full of creatures both interesting and, sometimes, dangerous.

I have a vivid memory of sitting in the darkness on the veranda of the officers' mess overlooking the brightly-lit swimming pool. Out of the jungle came a three-toed sloth moving at the pace unique to that creature. Its slowness was hard to believe. It eventually arrived at the water's edge, hesitated as though contemplating a swim, and then slowly turned back towards the jungle. After what seemed an eternity, it reached a power pole and started a tortuous climb. Up and up it went, but ever so slowly. We started to become alarmed when we realized that at the top of the pole were live wires. Tension on the veranda mounted as the sloth grew ever closer to them. Just when it seemed that the creature was about to breathe its last, it stretched its long arm to a nearby tree branch and swung off the pole. We all gave a loud cheer.

CHAPTER 16

PARQUE EL CANADA

Our most precious souvenir of Colombia is a tiny silver engraved plaque conveying the gratitude of the "Junta Pro-Parque El Canada del Barrio Santa Ines" (Canada Park Council of the Saint Ines District). Behind that plaque lies a very touching story.

Not long before we arrived in Bogota, the city's mayor came up with a clever scheme to involve embassies accredited to Colombia in the care of the city's parks. He named several of these parks after particular countries and invited the embassies so honoured to take an interest in them. Parque El Canada was located in one of the city's poorest districts on the side of a hill far from the elegant residential areas where the likes of us made our homes. I was given the job of organizing some kind of response to the mayor's invitation.

My first visit to the park is not easy to forget. It consisted of an empty city block of dirt and unkempt grass around which, on often steep hills, were clustered thousands of the tiny brick homes, mostly in poor condition, which made up this district of twenty thousand people. Few homes had electricity or running water. The city had put up two flagpoles and the old Canadian Red Ensign flew beside Colombia's yellow, blue, and red flag. Our flag was upside down, but I did not have the heart to say anything about it. In any case, it reflected the distress I felt upon looking around me.

In the middle of the park was a small brick kiosk, and, on the day I visited, about eighty children were crammed inside getting a lesson on how to read and write from Agente (Constable) Leopoldo Tiria. He was a member of the Policia Infantil (Children's Police), who were assigned to city parks and playgrounds. Tiria was barely able to read and write himself, but he was doing his best in difficult circumstances. When I learned that this was the

On one of my periodic visits to the St. Ines District, Bogota, c. 1960.

only "school" in the district, it became obvious that a proper teaching facility was needed. Building one in that park became our objective. Canada had no aid program in Colombia, and we recognized that raising the necessary funds would be the first order of business. As an immediate gesture, some of us bought and installed children's play equipment: swings, slides, teeter-totters, and the like.

Over the next few months, we were able to secure the help of personnel in the Royal Bank of Canada and others in the Canadian community as we put together a series of fundraising events. Visiting Canadian groups and even some individuals were taken to the park and asked to contribute. I remember in particular a large delegation from the Toronto Board of Trade, including a member of the Eaton family, which was bused to the park and welcomed by the children, who had been taught to sing "O Canada." There was scarcely a dry eye among our visitors, and the contributions were generous. (That time I made sure the flag was right side up.)

We also held benefit evenings, sometimes with gambling tables. I never expected our own home to become a gambling den even for one evening. I

Constable Leopoldo Tiria shows great patience.

also never expected the Royal Bank's accountants to be so skilled at operating the tables. I guess it is a part of their training that is not well publicized.

We also found an architect who was prepared to donate his services and a contractor who was willing to direct volunteer labour from the district. We made deals for the necessary materials, and soon the construction of the new school was underway.

Once the building was completed and supplied with both electricity and running water, it became clear that it could be used for several purposes that would bring real improvements in the lives of both adults and children throughout the Santa Ines district. We had built so much more than a school. It became a part-time medical clinic, a place where nurses taught proper hygiene to mothers, a setting for adults to learn to read and write, a library, and even, on Saturday nights, courtesy of the Canadian Embassy, a film theatre. (For most attendees it was their first experience of a film.)

As I got to know the people of Santa Ines better, I also learned more about their problems. A recurrent theme was the high price they had to pay for basic foodstuffs at their one and only retail outlet. It happened that a Canadian organization called "Cooperatives Everywhere" sent a representative to Bogota to help decide whether or not Colombia would be the next

With Ambassador Ted Newton, Constable Leopoldo Tiria, and Parque El Canada schoolchildren, Bogota, 1963.

country they focused on. (They later picked one of the Caribbean islands.) I talked to the representative about Santa Ines, and he suggested setting up a consumer co-op, offering to put me in touch with the right people in the Colombian co-operative movement.

My Santa Ines contacts were excited by the idea and began talking it up with the residents. They immediately ran into a major opponent: their first newly appointed permanent parish priest. (It is a mark of their poverty that a district that large had not previously been able to support a permanent priest.) I had come to know the priest, who was an elderly man from Spain in, I suspect, not the best of health. He was clearly bothered by the altitude. He was nonetheless a decent, loving person, and I had no doubt that his opposition to the idea of a co-operative was founded in a fear of anything sounding remotely like communism. He had spoken against the co-operative at Mass, and it was clear that, if we were to make any headway, I would have to change his mind.

Cooperatives Everywhere was an extension of the co-operative move-

First completed classroom and original kiosk of Parque El Canada, Bogota, 1963.

ment founded by St. Francis Xavier University in Antigonish, Nova Scotia. That movement grew out of the fishermen's co-operatives promoted by Father Francis Coady and his fellow priests who taught at the university. Later, Father Coady founded the Coady Institute dedicated to educating people about co-operatives. Canada's National Film Board had made a documentary called *The Rising Tide*, showing Father Coady's work with the fishermen. The Spanish version, which was in our embassy film library, was just what I needed to reach the reluctant priest. I organized a film evening in the new school building featuring *The Rising Tide*, a speaker from Colombia's own co-operative movement, and a film I borrowed from the American Embassy showing the U.S. Peace Corps doing similar work in rural Greece. It was important to put the speaker in between the two films so that no one would leave.

The weather was not the least co-operative – it was very cold and wet. Worse, the priest had a cold and refused to attend. I went to his tiny house behind the church and begged him to join us. I offered to drive him in the embassy car and told him about the great films we had to show. He finally agreed to come, but he was not in his most receptive mood. All that changed when he saw his fellow priests vigorously working with the fishermen to organize the co-operative that was to change their lives. Next Sunday he was equally vigorous in promoting the co-operative project. All that remained was to secure credit and organizational help from the Colombian co-operative movement. The new co-op store was soon up and running, and it greatly reduced the cost of food for those very poor people. The private store remained in business, but it lowered its prices to match those at the co-op.

On special occasions, our friends in Santa Ines almost always invited the Embassy to send a representative. One such occasion was the appointment of the first permanent priest whom I have already described. I attended along with our receptionist, Rosita Duarte, but I was to pay a considerable price for having done so. The plan was to attend a Mass and a celebratory lunch. I had asked Rosita to accompany me because I was unfamiliar with Roman Catholic liturgy and I wanted to copy every move she made.

The interior of the church was so stark that it would almost have satisfied John Knox, the austere founder of the Scottish Presbyterian Church. There were no pews, but two chairs had been brought in for Rosita and me. They were placed near the front of the church, facing the humble altar. Everyone else was standing and, as the priest proceeded with the liturgy, all eyes appeared to be on us. That changed when a dog entered the church and began sniffing around the base of the altar. I feared the worst, and both Rosita and I had difficulty suppressing smiles. Suddenly Rosita's chair collapsed. Everything stopped. Our hosts were much embarrassed and insisted upon replacing both of our chairs so that they would match. Fortunately, only Rosita's dignity was harmed, and the Mass resumed once our new chairs were in place. Afterwards, we went to the lunch, where Rosita and I sat at the head table. Rosita ate nothing and told me to do the same. I did not see how I could possibly do that without offending our hosts. I was rewarded for my efforts with three days of painful dysentery. What we do for Queen and country!

I want to say something about Rosita. She not only was a delightful person and a great dancer (you should have seen her doing a rhumba with a full glass on her head), but was also a real asset to our embassy team. She came from an upper-class Colombian family and was teased about work-

Ardith next to Ambassador (centre), Mrs. Newton and Rosita (left) in front, and U.S. Embassy's Pete Vaky (wearing glasses), Bogota, 1963.

ing for an embassy in order to obtain a diplomat husband. Whether or not that was true, she did succeed. Sometime after we left Colombia, she married a British diplomat who later became an ambassador. Upon retirement he was knighted, and Rosita now carries the title "Lady." It could not have happened to a nicer person.

It was one thing to erect a school building; it was quite another to secure the teachers to work in it. Our method for so doing, I have to admit, was devious in the extreme. The Ambassador hosted a gala gambling night in the official residence, to which we invited Colombia's Minister of Education. He said he would drop in for a few minutes, but we were able to keep him there all evening. My job was to keep his glass full, not a difficult task, but the challenge for our friends from the Royal Bank was rather greater. As operators of the gaming tables, they were to ensure so far as possible that he won. They largely succeeded, another tribute to their secret training. Just before the Minister left, flushed with his gambling successes and my bar-tending, the Ambassador asked him for two teachers. He cheerfully agreed, and the next day a formal diplomatic note was sent to thank him. We needed to raise money to cover all other costs, including supplies, but the teachers' salaries were paid by Colombia's Department of Education.

Chapter 17

LEAVING COLOMBIA

Our Swiss friend Anne's decision to marry our Canadian friend and banker Alan rather than accept a transfer to Cuba had a parallel in our lives. Not long after the Soviets responded to the threat of U.S. military action by withdrawing their missiles from Cuba and bringing to an end the crisis that had could have lead to World War III, I was told that we were to be transferred from Bogota to Havana. I avoided that move in a much less drastic way than Anne. I came down with both amoebic dysentery and amoebic hepatitis, turned a delightful shade of yellow, grew my first beard, endured the joys of arsenic treatment, and lay in bed for three months.

The post in Havana was occupied instead by George Cowley, our best friend in the Foreign Service despite having once eaten our week's supply of meat at one sitting. He later told us what we had missed. The cover job was to make consular visits to various Canadian religious communities, mostly nuns from Québec, who were scattered around Cuba; the real job was to look for evidence of Soviet military activity. Our friend, an adventurous character, was tall and fair-haired. He noticed that the Russian advisors almost always wore blue blazers and grey pants. So attired, he wandered all over the place and was never challenged. I have to admit that I sometimes wondered if my friend was embellishing his account a bit. However, a few years ago, a secret agreement between the U.S. Kennedy administration and Canada's Diefenbaker government was made public under which, according to press accounts, Canada agreed to foster relations with Cuba and share information obtained thereby with the United States. I guess George (and nearly myself) had been a part of that undertaking.

I have to say something more about George if only to underline that, even within bureaucracies, risk-taking innovators can be found. His first post had been Tokyo where he was responsible, among other things, for managing Canada's university scholarship program for qualified Japanese students. That entailed publicizing the program, screening applicants, and sending the names of recommended candidates to Ottawa for consideration by a panel of academics. However, the decision was made in Ottawa to end the program on the seemingly reasonable grounds that Japan was too rich a country to merit such aid.

George, in his passionate way, was outraged, arguing that it was in Canada's interest to have Canadian-educated Japanese in potentially responsible positions in such an important Canadian trading partner. It is a sound argument, but it proved ineffective. Stubbornly, George ignored Ottawa and continued the search for scholarship students. He advertised for and screened candidates as before, but sent the names of the best to those individual universities across Canada where appropriate courses and potential scholarship funding existed. He placed them all, continuing his private program each year until his tour in Tokyo ended. Clearly, he was the right choice to be "our man" in Havana.

Before ending the account of our time in Colombia, I should say something about our one out-of-country trip (except for a holiday in Canada) during our Bogota posting. It was to the much smaller neighbouring country of Ecuador, whose capital Quito is even higher than Bogota. The purpose of the trip was to prepare the way for a Canadian embassy in that city. The decision had been made to locate one Canadian diplomat in Ecuador with the title "Chargé d'Affaires" (acting ambassador). Our Ambassador in Bogota would be dually accredited to the president of Ecuador and would make periodic visits.

Quito is a much smaller city than Bogota, but what we noticed most as we flew into Ecuador's capital was the profusion of red tiled roofs. In Bogota the tiles were a brownish grey. In some ways the brightness of those roofs expressed the character of the city, which we found to have an upbeat, relaxed atmosphere. There were far fewer modern buildings than in Bogota, which gave Quito a very colonial feel. Indeed, Quito's colonial centre is a World Heritage Site. The setting is truly spectacular. The hotel in which we stayed was right at the edge of the plateau on which the city is located. Below us was a valley flanked by high mountains that seemed to go on forever. Our visit lasted only two weeks and centred on discussions with the Ecuadorian Foreign Ministry and a search for a suitable office.

There are no funny anecdotes to relate, but I do want to pay tribute to Colombia's beautiful neighbour. Environmentally it is a remarkable place, one of the most diverse in the world and home to the unique Galapagos Islands. I have been told that Ecuador is the only country in the world that has the "Rights of Nature" written into its constitution. In the many years since our visit, Ecuador has become a major oil exporter and a magnet for foreign investment. Canadian firms have invested over $2 billion in the country, primarily in oil and gas, and there are over two thousand Canadians now resident there.

There was a particularly touching moment at Bogota's airport when the time came for us to return to Canada. We were talking with some of our friends when Ardith noticed that a small group of people from the Santa Ines District were standing not far off, apparently too shy to approach us. Constable Tiria of the Children's Police readily caught the eye in his brown uniform. We went over to them and there were many *abrazos* (hugs) and tears before Tiria gave us the little engraved silver plaque that I mentioned at the outset of the story about Parque El Canada. It was an encounter and a gesture that we will never forget.

Forty-eight years later, in a suburb south of Vancouver, I told this story as part of my congratulatory speech at Dick and Eileen Fuller's fiftieth wedding anniversary party. (The reader will recall that Dick worked at the Royal Bank of Canada in Bogota and married Eileen, my secretary at the Embassy. If memory serves, he very skillfully operated the roulette table at the Ambassador's residence at the Parque El Canada fundraisers.) Afterwards, Dick, who had returned to Bogota later in his career to manage the Royal Bank, described how the Canadian community continued to raise funds and to help the people of Santa Ines District long after Ardith and I had left Colombia. That warmed my heart and brought back many memories.

I should add that I had a lot of fun giving that congratulatory speech. I made a particular point of praising Eileen. She had a degree in English from the University of British Columbia and was a walking, talking thesaurus. My reports to Ottawa on conditions in Colombia were greatly improved by her contributions. Her son and her daughter, who, as I mentioned earlier, is currently Canada's Ambassador in Chile, apparently knew little of their mother's accomplishments in this area; it was a treat to watch their faces.

Near the end of my remarks, I added that Ardith, who was unable to attend the celebration, had told me to say something nice about Dick. I had earlier explained how long it had taken me to forgive him for taking away such a good secretary. For a long time I said nothing and everyone started to laugh, except Dick. Then I said, "He's a banker." Everyone groaned. "He's not a Wall Street banker," I added. One or two clapped. "He's that great gift from Canada to the world – a Canadian banker." There was a roar of approval. Canada's conservative, well-regulated banking system is among the best in the world; partly for that reason this country was largely spared the credit squeeze and economic downturn caused by the sub-prime mortgage crisis in the United States and elsewhere. Bankers are never popular, but they are currently more appreciated in Canada than in most places.

Chapter 18

ETERNAL PROBLEMS: FROM ELECTRONIC SPYING TO THE MIDDLE EAST

Home leave in Vancouver followed our departure from Colombia, but real life did not hit us until our return to Ottawa. There is a phenomenon known as allowance withdrawal symptoms, one feature of which is fainting in liquor stores after seeing the prices. Tax-free they are not. We found an attractive modern two-bedroom apartment on the Rideau River, which bisects the city, about a ten-minute drive south of the city centre. I was delighted to learn that my new assignment would be in the Middle Eastern Division, where I was to be responsible for managing our relations with Israel. One effect of this assignment surprised me and gave me an insight into the major crisis of that era which had nothing to do with the Middle East.

Because my new position involved routine use of clandestinely obtained information, I needed an upgraded security clearance, i.e., beyond Top Secret. Part of that clearance process entailed a tour of the Communications Security Establishment of Canada (CSEC), Canada's national cryptologic agency, whose very existence was secret at that time. (It was "outed" by the CBC some years later.) During the Cold War, the CSEC was primarily responsible for providing signals intelligence (SIGINT) data to the Department of National Defence regarding the military operations of the Soviet Union. As I toured the establishment and learned with growing amazement about the remarkable extent of its capabilities, I came to understand the degree to which we in the West were able to follow what was happening in the Soviet Union through sophisticated monitoring and analysis of communications in that country. (This is well before satellites orbiting the earth revolutionized the spy business.)

What also became clear to me during my indoctrination tour is that we were able to determine through SIGINT that the Soviet Union was not mobilizing for war during the frightening confrontation in 1962 between the Soviet Union and the United States over the Soviets' insertion into Cuba of nuclear missiles aimed at American cities. The Soviets had comparable SIGINT capabilities, and they would readily have been able to determine that the United States, in contrast, was preparing for military action against Cuba. That places the confrontation between Soviet Premier Khrushchev and U.S. President Kennedy in a somewhat different light. Using the analogy of a poker game, Kennedy knew that Khrushchev was very likely bluffing, whereas Khrushchev knew that Kennedy very likely was not. The stakes were too high for either to be sure, and Khrushchev, having intimidated the young president when they had first met in Vienna, may well have thought Kennedy incapable of pulling the trigger.

Moreover, there was also the risk of a fatal error. The U.S. Navy discovered three of four Soviet nuclear-armed diesel-electric submarines hiding in the Sargasso Sea presumably preparing to help break through, if so ordered, the U.S. naval "quarantine" of Cuba that was preventing Soviet freighters from carrying military equipment to the world's newest Communist nation. The Soviet Navy Captain commanding the four submarines must have been sorely tempted to fire his nuclear torpedoes in response to the U.S. pressure tactics that ultimately forced three of his submarines to surface. Clearly, we all owe a lot to his restraint. That said, I think it is still fair to conclude that the world was not as close to the nuclear precipice in 1962 as has been generally supposed. There is nothing like good intelligence to reduce the risk of mistakes.

Alert readers will no doubt recognize CSEC as the organization at the centre of the controversy surrounding Canada's alleged electronic espionage activities aimed at foreign political, commercial, and industrial activities. In an angry statement of condemnation, the president of Brazil has accused Canada of spying on her country's energy and mining sectors. The Prime Minister's reaction was to express concern but avoid substantive comment.

Subsequently, it was alleged that Canada through CSEC had cooperated with the United States in electronic surveillance of world leaders at the 2010 G8 and G20 summits in Toronto. "No comment" was the effective response. Later allegations emerged accusing Canada of ongoing cooperation with the United States in electronic spying aimed at heads of state and other key individuals and institutions in a broad range of friendly and not-so-friendly countries. Given the long history of cooperation in intelligence matters between Canada and the United States, these accusations should come as no surprise. More disturbing for many are the most recent allegations of spying on Canadians, which CSEC is legally enjoined from doing. CSEC contends that the incident cited involved collecting only "metadata," i.e., information generated as technology is used such as the time and place a cell phone is operated. I understand that the objective was to develop a database for typical movement patterns from an airport. There was no invasion of individuals' actual communications and, therefore, in CSEC's opinion, no violation of Canadian law. According to Ministers' statements in the House, the Canadian Government agrees, but many critics nonetheless regard the tracking made possible by metadata collection to be unacceptably intrusive.

During World War II, the United States, Britain, Canada, Australia, and New Zealand maintained a very close relationship in sharing covertly obtained intelligence. That partnership, today called the Five Eyes Alliance, developed further during the NATO/Soviet Cold War, as did the electronic technology that fed it. Canada did not put in place a network of overseas human spies, but our electronic surveillance capability ranked with the world's best. I do not doubt that our capability in this respect has continued to strengthen in the years after the Cold War. Indeed, Professor David Skillicorn from Queen's University School of Computing calls Canada the world leader in the collection of electromagnetic intelligence. With a CSEC staff of nearly two thousand and an annual budget approaching $400 million, the Canadian Government seems determined to maintain this level of excellence.

Over the course of the coming year, CSEC is scheduled to move into what has been called the most expensive government building ever constructed in this country. No doubt it will be superbly equipped. The standard justification given for CSEC's work is defensive, identifying and providing protection from foreign electronic attacks on Canadian data systems and seeking out potential terrorist threats. However, even a person as technically challenged as I understands that CSEC's remarkable capabilities can be just as easily applied to offensive activities aimed at foreign competitors. According to Brazil's president, that is exactly what is happening. On the face of it, stealing other people's secrets seems a very un-Canadian thing to do. Yet I can also understand that tying one or both very accomplished electronic hands behind our national back, so to speak, in an increasingly competitive global environment where our own secrets are routinely targeted, may be seen by some as carrying "boy scoutism" too far. Moreover, for the Government of Canada to engage in a candid public debate in this country in front of a world audience about the wisdom of or need for spying on foreign competitors would require admissions about our activities which could, to put it mildly, be a bit awkward. Our partners in the Five Eyes Alliance would not be overly thrilled, either, and Canada clearly has no interest in damaging its longstanding and important relationships with these partners.

A cynic might conclude that we just need to get better at the spying to avoid being caught. That would be an unfair conclusion. The revelations about Brazil and the G8 and G20 summits flow from material made public by U.S. National Security Agency whistleblower Edward Snowden, granted asylum in Russia. Canadian academic experts commenting on the Brazilian complaint say they are convinced that Canada had no special interest in the alleged Brazilian targets and, if involved, was undoubtedly doing so as part of its routine co-operation with its Five Eyes Alliance partners. That said, a CBC news crew visiting Brazil pointed out that Canadian firms had successfully bid on concessions in Brazil's energy sector. CSEC chief John Foster confined his reaction to observing that Canada has an independent commissioner who has "full access to every record, every system and every staff member to ensure that we follow Canadian laws and respect Canadians' privacy." Obviously that reassurance will not satisfy Brazil, which has ordered an inquiry into the matter and sought Russia's co-operation in interviewing Snowden. I will leave the last word to a Brazilian congressman who told a CBC reporter that the people of Canada will have to decide whether such spying activities are in keeping with Canadian democratic values. He then conceded that Brazil probably spies as well.

Obviously the revelations produced by Snowden have domestic as well as international implications. Concerns are being strongly expresssed in Canada and the United States about the seemingly unlimited ability of our governments to monitor private communications. Instinctively I identify with these concerns, but, as a former professional diplomat, I recognize that we are living in a world that is much more unpredictable than the one in which I worked. Despite our more limited technical capabilities in my day, it was in many ways both easier to identify our enemies and to predict their likely actions then than it is now. Identifying threats and predicting events are at the heart of security. It may well be that the price we have to pay for the level of security we all desire is acceptance of the intrusions that today's technology makes possible.

To return to my work in the Middle Eastern Division, several of my fellow FSOs were experienced Arabists; some had studied at the American University in Beirut. However, there were no Jewish FSOs in the Division or anyone else with a particular understanding of Israel and its history. I therefore decided to immerse myself in Jewish and Israeli history and to learn something of Judaism.

Israel in the 1960s was an interesting mix of peoples in a state of transition. So different were many of them from each other that a cynic might argue that the hostility of the surrounding Arab states was needed to maintain Israeli unity. The founding philosophy of the Israeli state came primarily from the European Jews, the Yiddish-speaking Ashkenazi, and it included not only a strong sense of community best exemplified by the kibbutz but also a recognition of the importance of maintaining strong ties with foreign supporters, especially the United States.

The Middle Eastern Jews, the Sephardim, tended to be less educated and less connected to the West. "Sabra," a kind of cactus known in English as Prickly Pear, was the nickname given to Israeli-born Jews who were allegedly prickly on the outside and sweet on the inside. Their distinctive characteristic was a sense of self-reliance and independence. In the 2010 Israeli census, Sabras made up seventy percent of the Jewish population. Some of them, no doubt, regarded the European Jews as products of their persecuted past, too inclined to look to others for help. One of those Sabras was a friend of ours, Tova, a former Israeli army sergeant who was the beautiful wife of a fellow Canadian Foreign Service Officer. I always had trouble imagining her cradling an Uzi submachine gun.

A major factor in unifying the Israeli people has been universal military service for both men and women. In the Armed Forces all the Israelis of different cultures and ethnicities were stirred together, so to speak; that mixing process has had a considerable impact on Israeli society.

My eighteen months in the Middle Eastern Division and my studies of Jewish history and religion left me with a lifelong interest in that region and even affected my religious views. I moved from being an agnostic to becoming a vague theist because I could not believe that the Jewish people, after going through so much for so many millennia, could have survived and returned to their "promised land" without some kind of divine intervention in history. There is no other human saga like it. Ironically, most Israelis, who tend to be much less religious than most Americans, would probably not agree.

The issues which arise from and contribute to the long-standing Israeli–Palestinian impasse are at the heart of the most important and most dangerous divisions affecting the world today. Those divisions have affected all of us in greater or lesser degree over the past decade; however they play out in the years ahead, they will continue to have a major impact. For that reason, I have put together in appendix I a few descriptive and analytical thoughts for interested readers on that very troubled part of the world. I believe them to be well worth reading.

CHAPTER 19

A NEW CHILD AND A NEW FLAG

To return to my own story, my youth and an appearance that made me seem even younger continued to bother me even after having served my first posting abroad. I recall one weekend in 1964 when I was serving as duty officer. That meant reviewing all communications received by the Department over the weekend to see whether any matter required urgent attention. News came that the prime minister of Cambodia was threatening to resign. His departure could have resulted in political chaos. Canada was one of three nations serving on each of the three Truce Commissions (Cambodia, Laos and Vietnam) established after France's withdrawal from what had been French Indochina. I contacted those responsible for managing our relations with that part of the world and they prepared an urgent message for our Foreign Minister to send to the Cambodian prime minister asking him not to resign. My job was to take it to the Minister for signature.

Canada's Foreign Minister at that time was Paul Martin, Sr., whose son was to become Prime Minister many years later. Martin Sr., in an earlier portfolio as Health Minister, had introduced the Canada Health Act establishing universal access to healthcare in our country, an accomplishment of which his son is very proud. He did not, however, have a background that seemed to fit him for the role of Foreign Minister, and some Foreign Service Officers were uncomfortable with him in that position. Martin was probably aware of their condescending attitude; he took some satisfaction in bypassing the departmental hierarchy from time to time by telephoning mid-ranking officers directly to seek their views on issues of the day. I had never met him but considered him to be a man of principle. Despite representing Windsor, which, like its neighbour Detroit, is an automotive city, Martin had refused to allow the sale of tens of millions of dollars worth of trucks to the South African Police during apartheid. British Leyland did not hesitate for a moment to fill the gap created by Canada's commitment to principle.

Mr. and Mrs. Martin lived in an upper-floor apartment in an attractive building next to Ottawa's most elegant residential neighbourhood. I rang the enter-phone and was asked by Mrs. Martin to check with the concierge and bring up any newspapers. I did so and entered the elevator. On the way up I was nervous about meeting the Minister and was trying to look as old as possible. (I am not quite sure how you do that.) I knocked on the Martins' door, and Mrs. Martin opened it. As soon as she saw me, she exclaimed, "Why, you're just a baby!" She might as well have kicked me in the stomach. Into the room came the Minister in his undershirt, not a prepossessing sight, and, already profoundly embarrassed, I did not know which way to look. I walked into the living room in a daze, managed to utter a few words, and handed him the telegram. He read it and remarked with mock severity, "Does this not constitute interference in Cambodian domestic affairs?" I knew little of Southeast Asia but blurted out the first thing that came to mind: "The Cambodians must want us to interfere if we are on the Truce Commission." "Good answer," he replied, and signed the telegram. I left very quickly.

Our eighteen-month stay in Ottawa was marked by two important events, one for our family and the other for the country.

Our family event was the birth of our first child, Diana, in 1964. The birth was mildly unusual in that I was one of the first fathers in the Ottawa area permitted to attend the great event. We had one of the very few obstetricians who favoured the practice, and he worked out of the only hospital that permitted it. I was able to use the breathing exercises we learned at the pre-birth classes to help Ardith through the final stages. I blew in her ear and she followed the pattern. The birth was so quick that the doctor had scarcely arrived when Diana made her entry. (Like her father, Diana tends to be impatient.) The worst part for Ardith had been earlier in the day when she had come to the hospital with false labour. They had insisted on her remaining in the boiling, humid heat on a rubber sheet. It is a wonder she did not melt. Our biggest concern at the time had been whether our child would be born on June 30 or on our national day. As it happened, she popped out at nine o'clock at night, three hours before Canada's birthday. July 1 is a particularly busy day for Canadian diplomats abroad and we did not want it to be Diana's birthday as well. As with most new parents, our lives were changed forever, much for the better. Diana was a beautiful baby who has long since become a beautiful adult. We are very fortunate.

The event of importance to the country was the unveiling of our new maple leaf flag on February 15, 1965, a truly unforgettable day. It was a very cold morning when I joined thousands of others in the snow on Parliament Hill to watch our new flag unfold for the first time. There was a quiet cheer as it reached the top of the flagpole. It hung limply for a moment before the wind came up and we saw the red and white as it was meant to be seen. A roar came up from that staid, mostly Public Service crowd and went on and on. Never have I shouted so loud or for so long. I had no idea that I would feel that way. It was as though my patriotism had been dammed and was suddenly broken.

The fact that two months later we were in New Zealand, our next posting, where the flag had been raised officially for the first time anywhere in the world because of the International Date Line, was icing on the cake. I will never forget the pride that I felt when, as Acting High Commissioner, I was driven in the official car with that flag flying from the fender. It was a far cry from flying the old Red Ensign at our previous post in Bogota to shouts of "Ingleterra."

The Red Ensign was an excellent flag when it was adopted. Britain's Union Jack in the corner reflected Canada's membership in the Commonwealth, and the emblems of France, England, Scotland, and Ireland in our coat of arms represented the countries that together formed by far the largest part of our European heritage. However, in the decades after World War II, Canada became a very different place, politically and culturally. Moreover, it was on a course that would lead to even greater change. A flag was needed that looked to that multicultural future in which the main links that bind us will be our magnificent geography and, hopefully, a tolerance for differences, not our ethnic history. Prime Minister Lester Pearson, who had replaced John Diefenbaker while we were living in Colombia, was determined to find such a flag.

Hundreds of designs were submitted, some very bizarre, but the heraldic experts who advised the committee reviewing each proposal insisted that the design be as simple as possible and that Canada's official colours of red and white be predominant. The flag chosen not only meets those criteria; it features the most recognizable of all Canadian symbols: the maple leaf. Moreover, it contains no features with which only Canadians of a particular ancestry can identify. In short, it is a flag for the future, not the past. Some opponents continued to dismiss it as "Pearson's Pennant," but the design that was picked was not the Prime Minister's first choice. He preferred a flag with three red maple leaves on a single stem on a white background with narrow blue borders representing the Pacific and Atlantic Oceans. Personally, I am very glad that the heraldic experts' criteria won out.

PART III

A MISSION IN NEW ZEALAND

CHAPTER 20

A BEAUTIFUL HOME DOWN UNDER

Ardith had found it difficult to adjust to life in Bogota and was not keen to go abroad again. I thought it might help if we were sent to a more benign setting that was closer to our own country culturally. We were allowed to express our preferences with respect to postings but considered ourselves very lucky if those preferences were respected. After reviewing several post reports that described living conditions, I requested a posting to Wellington, New Zealand. I was delighted when, a couple of months later, I received news that this was where we were to go.

Despite the political and social stability of that beautiful country and its cultural similarity to the English-speaking part of Canada, Ardith did not share my enthusiasm. She agreed that New Zealand sounded lovely, but she did not relish returning to the diplomatic round, entertaining guests and attending receptions and dinners. We received help in overcoming her reluctance from a very unexpected quarter.

We had come to know the older single gentleman who lived in the apartment next door to ours. He often gave me a lift to work, as his office building was near mine. I can still remember the great surprise I felt when he parked his car in a space assigned to the Deputy Minister of Agriculture. He had given no indication of his high rank during our visits. He was separated from his wife and estranged from his children, and he became for us a kind of adopted uncle. We told him about our posting to New Zealand and about Ardith's concerns about returning to the world of diplomacy. It so happened that he was about to make an official visit to New Zealand, and he promised to give us a full report. He was as good as his word, and the country he described on his return to Ottawa sounded like it was flowing with milk and honey. Moreover, when he called upon the Canadian

High Commissioner, Ken Burbridge, who would soon become my boss, he made a point of going to sit in the office I was to occupy in order to report back to "my good friend, Ray Robinson," on the accommodation. The High Commissioner, very much outranked by his important visitor, was suitably impressed, no bad thing.

Unfortunately, Ardith's fears persisted even as we made our preparations to leave Ottawa. There was a real risk that she might decide to stay in Vancouver with Diana at the home of her parents, whom we were visiting en route to New Zealand. The day before we were to move out of our apartment, she had an emotional crisis and I telephoned the Deputy Minister for help. He left a meeting in his office to come to our apartment immediately. He spent the rest of the afternoon talking with Ardith and reassuring her about the beauty and welcoming friendliness of New Zealand. It helped; when we boarded the train for Vancouver, Ardith's mood was much better. We will never forget our neighbour's kindness and generosity.

The trip across Canada did even more to improve her mood and mine as well. It was a wonderful experience. We had what was grandly described as a "drawing-room," which was the best kind of private compartment. Such accommodation was warranted because of our baby. The porter checked on Diana while we ate elegant meals served in the beautifully appointed dining car, but we carried her with us when we sat in the glass-roofed observation car. The views through the Rockies and further west towards the Pacific coast were spectacular, and we arrived in high spirits to a warm welcome in Vancouver from Ardith's parents and, later, from my family in Victoria. The flight to New Zealand was broken with an overnight stop in Hawaii, a delightful benefit. In those days, babies were able to sleep in small baskets attached to the storage containers above the passengers' heads, a practice that later was deemed unsafe.

Our excitement at our first view of Aotearoa, the Maori word for New Zealand, knew no bounds. Aotearoa means "the land of the long white cloud," and the country was living up to that description. We landed on April 15, 1965, at Auckland, New Zealand's largest city, with no idea of how transforming our stay in that beautiful country would prove to be. Because of the length of the journey from Hawaii and our baby, we were authorized to spend the night there.

Auckland is located in a beautiful volcanic setting around a splendid harbour, and it made a great first impression. We had to be alert when going for a stroll because we had never before experienced cars driven on the other side of the road. It was vital to look in the right direction when crossing the street. We were also quickly reminded of the importance of the dairy component of what was then New Zealand's most important industry, agriculture. An enormous bowl of very thick whipped cream accompanied the meal delivered to our hotel room, a fact that sticks in my mind because, after placing it on the bed, I accidentally sat in it. I guess you could say it was the first impression I made in the country that was to be our home for nearly six years.

What we could never have imagined was the immense impact those years would have on the rest of our lives. Indeed, the challenge I am facing as I write these words is to see New Zealand once again as we first saw it rather than through the prism of the love we now feel for that precious country.

As I said earlier, our former neighbour in Ottawa described the country to us as a land of milk and honey. He certainly got the milk right, but at that time you would have had to substitute wool for honey. There were sixty million sheep in the country, about twenty for every human being. I well remember looking down from the aircraft as we flew from Auckland to Wellington at the countless little white dots on beautiful, rolling green hills. I could also see at least two volcanoes, as well as lakes and a section of desert before Wellington, situated at the southern tip of the North Island, finally came into view. The large, beautiful, almost round harbour, reminiscent of San Francisco, was backed by brown hills, and the houses, stacked up on steep hillsides, were also reminiscent of Wellington's bigger Californian counterpart.

The airport was located on a fairly narrow isthmus, almost the only flat land available. New Zealand's capital is notorious for its near constant and often strong winds. The airport was particularly exposed to wind, and the welcoming Canadians from the High Commission first saw us with our hair standing on end. We were in good company. Almost all the deplaning VIPs in subsequent years who warranted photos in the newspaper displayed a similar shocked look.

The first order of business had to be finding a suitable place in which to live. In some diplomatic posts abroad, the Canadian government, in addition to owning a large, fully furnished, prestigious residence for the Ambassador or High Commissioner, also owns several lesser residences that are occupied by foreign service personnel. Canada owned only one such residence in New Zealand, and it was occupied by the Senior Trade Commissioner. A handsome house with an attractive garden, it was located in the Hutt River Valley on the far side of Wellington's large harbour. That valley was home to three suburban cities: Petone on the coast, with its mix of modest homes and industrial areas such as car assembly plants; Lower Hutt, which was almost entirely residential and contained some upmarket housing; and Upper Hutt, quite a lot smaller and farther up the valley. We liked the Trade Commissioner's home and neighbourhood in Lower Hutt and decided to concentrate our search in that area.

Fortunately for us, a Danish businessman and his New Zealand wife had decided to return to Copenhagen and were happy to give us a long-term lease on their attractive and very suitable house. It was located in a small enclave of upmarket houses surrounded by an attractive golf course. Set on a substantial, beautifully landscaped corner lot, it made a good first impression with its two storeys, red brick and white stucco exterior, and handsome covered front porch with a rounded arch entryway.

Inside, it was perfect for both our family and entertaining needs. A sizable separate dining room that could have easily handled a table for fourteen was directly accessible from the entrance hall. The L-shaped living room was significantly larger. It had a wall of built-in bookcases surrounding an attractive marble wood-burning fireplace. The room could be accessed from the entrance hall through either end of the "L," ensuring good circulation at dinner parties, especially when heading for the buffet table in the dining room. Both living and dining rooms had beautiful hardwood floors, by far the best surface for occasionally messy entertaining. There was a small sitting room opening onto the enclosed back garden off the large eat-in kitchen as well as a laundry room and a half bathroom. The curving staircase rising from the entrance hall led to a spacious landing onto which opened a sizable master bedroom, a good-sized second bedroom with its own small sunroom, and a smaller bedroom where Diana and later her brother James slept. There was only one bathroom on that level, but it was very big and had a separate shower in addition to the large tub.

A particularly nice feature of the master bedroom was a wall of closets made of very attractive New Zealand Rimu wood with built-in drawers. Light reddish-brown in colour, the wood blended well with our bird's-eye maple bedroom furniture. Windowsills, frames, and doors throughout the house were made of the same attractive wood. From the many windows in the master bedroom, we had a lovely view of the beautifully treed and landscaped neighbourhood. Right outside one of the master bedroom windows in our own fully enclosed backyard was a glorious Pohutukawa tree, often called New Zealand's Christmas tree because its red blooms come out in December.

While central heating is common in New Zealand today, that was not the case in the 1960s. Our new home had no insulation in the walls or ceilings, and you could feel the wind whistling through the electrical outlets. Wellington has a temperate maritime climate, which means that it gets almost as cold as my hometown Victoria in the winter and is about the same as Victoria in the summer, with occasional hot days but mostly cool and breezy. Because of the very strong winds, especially in winter, Wellington can feel much colder than the thermometer indicates. Ardith nearly wore out a pair of fleece-lined boots keeping her feet warm inside the house during the winter months.

Initially, we tried to heat the house to Canadian standards, using the large portable electric heaters provided by the High Commission, but the cost proved prohibitive. In the colder months, we ended up living in the large kitchen and adjacent small sitting room as well as the upstairs. We closed off the oversized dining and living rooms and heated them only when entertaining. Surprise visitors necessarily received a chilly reception. We eventually installed insulation in the attic, which greatly improved wintertime temperatures upstairs.

CHAPTER 21

SINGING IN A FARAWAY LAND

Our entertainment allowance was sufficient for us to invite about sixty people a month to dinner, a level we were expected to maintain. Unlike in Colombia, we did not have a live-in servant but relied on a weekly cleaning woman and part-time gardener. As a result, we fell into the pattern of holding two good-sized buffet dinners a month. I supplemented that, as appropriate, with periodic business lunches. Sometimes we took a group of my contacts and their spouses to an evening meal at a dinner theatre.

Wellington today is a highly sophisticated city with many cultural attractions well out of proportion to its size and a host of excellent restaurants. That was not the case when we lived down under, but there was one very good French restaurant that we patronized from time to time. They made a lobster thermidor that I can still taste. The caterers we used for our buffet dinners were not overly impressive and were used by all our diplomatic colleagues. In egalitarian New Zealand, the catering staff would often greet our guests by name, and I sometimes got the impression that they knew them better than we did. I knew that the French restaurant always closed on Mondays and asked the manager if he would be interested in catering my diplomatic parties if I always held them on that day. He responded positively, and that became a staple of our entertainment. The quality of our food on such occasions improved tremendously, and the restaurant staff who served our guests did so with an elegance to match. Moreover, the restaurant provided all the plates, glassware, and cutlery. Amazingly, the per-guest cost hardly increased at all. Our parties were still remembered when we visited New Zealand years after our departure.

In all fairness, that was not just because of the food and service. We had

Ardith and I are ready for our first vice-regal dinner hosted by the NZ Governor General, Wellington, 1965.

a dear friend, Don Toms, about whom I will say more later, who was a truly gifted musician and singer. Although trained as a classical guitarist, his hobby was seeking out and singing unusual folksongs, especially those that told entertaining stories. Most were from Britain, his native land, but he also sang some particularly amusing ones drawn from New Zealand's pioneer past that were always well received. "Taumarunui on the Main Trunk Line" sticks in my mind. He could also be persuaded, especially in a party setting, to choose better-known melodies for others to sing along to. A fixture at our parties, he positioned himself at the corner of our large L-shaped living room where all could see him. He was exceedingly popular, as were a young Canadian couple, Gary and Everill Muir, working respectively as an exchange teacher and a social worker, who from time to time also sang folk songs in English and French, mainly drawn from Canadian folklore. The evocative melody "Un Canadien errant" from Québec and the rollicking "I'se the B'y" from Newfoundland were particular favourites. One of our prized possessions is a record the Muirs put out in New Zealand. Sadly, Everill's vocal chords were later damaged in a car accident. Otherwise, she and Gary might well have had a successful musical career. They had been scheduled to sing at a Shirley Bassey concert.

The two right-hand drive cars we had ordered from their respective factories before leaving Canada arrived shortly before we moved into our new home. That was very fortunate, since it was a good twenty-five minute run to my office in Wellington during rush hour. I was a car enthusiast and took particular pleasure in my brand new, dark blue Mercedes-Benz 280SE with grey leather upholstery. In those days the top-of-the-line "S" class had a strong six-cylinder engine just like its BMW competitor. Only the limousines had larger engines. We had also purchased a silver-blue Chevrolet Impala station wagon, an inappropriately large vehicle for New Zealand but one which was to lead to a massive transformation in our lives. Both cars were well-housed, the Mercedes in a separate garage leading to one street and the station wagon in a covered carport backing on the garage and leading to the other street.

My daily drive was actually quite enjoyable since it took me along the banks of the Hutt River to its mouth and then onto a motorway that skirted the edge of the picturesque harbour all the way to Wellington. On really stormy days, the waves actually reached the road, but usually I just enjoyed the scenery: lovely hills on one side and water on the other. From the Hutt Valley end of the motorway I could even see snow-capped mountains on New Zealand's rugged South Island across Cook Strait. Indeed, the mountain view was very reminiscent of that enjoyed from Victoria, B.C.'s waterfront drive looking across the Strait of Juan de Fuca at Washington State's snow-capped Olympic mountains.

We were able to spend the whole of our five-and-a-half-year extended posting in that lovely house and neighbourhood. Our general practitioner lived in the same enclave, about two blocks away, and that fact may well have saved our daughter's life. One weekend, when Diana was perhaps eighteen months old, she developed an exceedingly high fever, turned an alarming blue colour, and began to have convulsions. I called the doctor, who, at an earlier stage of his life, had driven race cars in South Africa. I heard him coming in his Jaguar all the way down the street. As soon as he arrived, he removed Diana's overly warm clothing and cooled her body with ice. Only then did he take her temperature, which, if memory serves, was about 105°F; goodness knows what it was before the ice was applied. We were never able to discover what caused this fever, but it passed quickly with no apparent consequences. There easily could have been brain damage.

Among our good friends in New Zealand were two families who lived, successively, in the house next door. Berwyn Gibbons, the matriarch of the first family, was an accomplished teacher of elocution. She made a significant contribution to New Zealand's dramatic arts, even founding a theatre school. The hall where it was located was later named after her and a memorial scholarship established in her name. Following the death of her husband, Ronald, she visited us several times in Canada. When she passed away some years ago, I sent a heartfelt tribute, which was read out at the memorial service. I know she is missed by many beyond her own family.

We also got to know her two daughters, Denise and Rosemary, both of whom have repeatedly visited us. Denise was accompanied on both visits by her husband, Buster, a highly successful dairy farmer who, sadly, is now deceased, and once by her younger daughter, Kirstie, currently recovering from a potentially fatal illness. Rosemary, a keen yachtswoman, moved to an idyllic island near Auckland after retiring from a career as a hi-tech banking systems consultant that took her to Europe and Australia. She accompanied her mother to Vancouver. Rosemary's elder son, Kingsley, an academic expert on China who is now lecturing in England, also visited us here in Vancouver while presenting a paper at the University of British Columbia. Berwyn's son, Derek, became a doctor and provided us with medical care during one of our several visits to New Zealand many years later.

The second family to occupy the neighbouring house was named McKeefry. John was an architect whose lovely wife, Bernadette, had her hands full with six preteens, one of whom became an Olympic rower. New Zealand's Cardinal McKeefry was John's uncle. When the fence between us was blown down in a storm, we became very close, and our children played together regularly. Bernadette rationed the number of children allowed to visit our house at one time so that Ardith would not be overwhelmed. Both families were extraordinarily kind to us during the several health crises we experienced during our New Zealand stay.

Chapter 22

WELLINGTON, WIND, AND THE WAHINE

With respect to Wellington's notoriously windy weather, I should recount one remarkable event in 1968 commonly known as the *Wahine* disaster, though some called it a miracle. The *Wahine* (Maori for "woman") had a capacity of over one thousand passengers, nearly two hundred crew, and hundreds of cars. It was one of the largest passenger ferries in the world at the time. Only two years old, it sailed regularly between Wellington and Christchurch in the South Island, often travelling overnight. On this occasion it arrived at the narrow, rocky entrance to Wellington's harbour at 5:50 a.m. just as a tropical cyclone that had caused great damage further north collided with a powerful Southerly coming up from Antarctica. Because the winds were reaching gusts of "only" 150 km/hr, the captain made the fateful decision to bring the ferry into the harbour. Within twenty minutes, the winds were surpassing 250 km/hr, and the ship was blown into the rocks despite the Captain's frantic efforts to turn it back into the open sea. A gash opened in the hull underwater and the propellers were damaged, leaving the ship completely at the mercy of the elements.

As I ate breakfast, I was completely unaware of this drama being played out in the harbour. I could see that the driving rain was moving horizontally somewhat faster than usual, but, given the nature of Wellington's winter weather, I gave it little thought.

I paid more attention when the wind blew down the fence on the driveway behind my car as I tried unsuccessfully to back out. I went back into the house, telephoned an American diplomat who lived a block away, and obtained a lift to work. From the car radio, we learned what was going on, and, as we travelled the motorway skirting the harbour, we looked in vain for any sign of the *Wahine,* hidden as it was by sheets of rain. Waves were crashing over the motorway to a level I had never seen before, and the car, a reasonably heavy one, was bouncing around. We reached Wellington without any damage, and my American friend dropped me off across the street from my building. Every time I tried to cross the street, I started to lose my footing because of the power of the wind and had to retreat into the shelter of a store entrance. I could see that the sidewalk in front of our building was covered with broken glass, and I began to wonder how I was going to get to work that morning. Then a man in yellow oilskins appeared, tied to the building with a long rope. He came towards me and I moved towards him and, just as I was again losing my footing, he grabbed me. I was very grateful to be safely inside the entrance lobby.

At about one o'clock in the afternoon, the *Wahine* turned in such a way as to provide some sheltered water on the side of the ship that had been punctured and there was some cessation of wind. Because the ship was listing badly and he feared that it would soon capsize, the Captain ordered the 610 passengers and 116 crew members to abandon ship. Altogether, 53 people died, including 6 crew members, a tragic loss, but the miracle, given the conditions, was that so many survived. Most were saved by a fleet of boats, largely privately owned, that set out towards the ferry as soon as the "abandon ship" order was given. It was like a mini-Dunkirk. When the wind dropped, the excess water that had been pushed into the harbour by the storm began to flow out to sea, drawing about two hundred people back towards the rocky harbour entrance. That is where most of the fatalities occurred. Hundreds of people were waiting on the beaches with hot tea and blankets for the survivors, a powerful display of New Zealanders' community spirit.

A subsequent Board of Enquiry found the captain at fault. In my totally non-professional and uninformed opinion, the underlying culprit was Wellington's notorious windy weather. The poor captain had had to bring his ferry through Wellington Harbour's narrow entrance in a gale so often that he did not appreciate that the one on that terrible day was about to become three times stronger than usual. The B.C. ferry service routinely cancels service on Canada's West Coast at wind speeds well below normal Wellington gales.

CHAPTER 23

THE "WOMB TO TOMB" ECONOMY

New Zealanders' sense of community was also reflected in the way they managed their economy. The country was, at that time, one of the world's most advanced welfare states in which the "womb to tomb" social support system provided a remarkable degree of protection from the normal ups and downs of economic cycles. In 1965, unemployment was almost non-existent, and incomes at the top and bottom of the socio-economic totem pole were extraordinarily close. I remember how astonished I was about two years after I arrived to watch a march on Parliament to protest the fact that unemployment had surpassed one percent. That figure represents, as any economist will tell you, a serious labour shortage. An incredible labour turnover rate of 300 to 400 percent at, for example, the car assembly plants, was a clear result.

This situation was the result of a mix of highly protectionist import policies, domestic support programs, and generous social programs. While some poverty no doubt existed at the time, it was not at all apparent on the streets of the country's cities. With such generous social programs and a labour shortage, New Zealanders seemed to be living in a welfare state utopia insulated from what was going on in the rest of the world. Prices were very low by Canadian standards for food and housing, but luxuries, including cars, could be very costly. The economic and healthcare security enjoyed at that time by the people of New Zealand appeared to be significantly greater than that enjoyed in Canada (where unemployment of five to six percent was common). On the other hand, the standard of living for most New Zealanders, as measured by the size of homes, number of possessions, and disposable income, was lower than that enjoyed by their employed Canadian cousins.

Maintaining such a generous welfare state with very full employment depended in large part upon the prosperity created by the sizable, secure British market for a range of New Zealand agricultural products such as wool, meat, and cheese and upon the high price of wool, at that time the most important of New Zealand's exports. When the wool price dropped by thirty percent in 1967, and the security of the British market was threatened by Britain's planned entry into the European Common Market, unemployment rose from one to five percent within the year, and inflation began to rise. Continuing low export commodity prices and the energy crisis of the 1970s aggravated the situation, and by the mid-1980s the country was facing serious balance-of-payments problems. Its protectionist and economic support policies were abandoned or profoundly altered with the help of advice from a team of economists from the University of Chicago's very conservative School of Economics. The New Zealand in which we had lived was changed beyond recognition.

During our periodic visits to the country during the late 80s and early 90s, we watched this change happening with disbelieving eyes. The social tension was palpable. A reasonable degree of economic growth and a better trade balance were achieved in the more open, diverse, and competitive environment that was created, but that achievement came at a considerable social cost. Unemployment remained high, the gap in incomes increased immensely, social programs were less generous, and the protectionist barrier around New Zealand was almost completely dismantled, even to the point of allowing non-New Zealand airlines to carry domestic traffic, a very uncommon practice.

Chapter 24

THE REMARKABLE MAORI

The indigenous Maori people (about fifteen percent of the population today) and the immigrant Polynesian "islanders" from the South Pacific, especially from Western Samoa and the Cook Islands (both of which were at one time administered by New Zealand), were generally at the bottom of the socio-economic totem pole. It is therefore not surprising that they paid the highest price for the creation of a harsher, more competitive economy. Such indicators as seriously disproportionate rates of unemployment and incarceration make that all too clear. As a result, there has been a rise in racial tension (although much less than in many other parts of the world).

On the other hand, over the years, efforts by successive governments to give the Maori people a pride of place in New Zealand governance and culture have been impressive, and we in North America could learn some lessons in this respect from our friends down under. For example, the Maoris have their own court system, and four out of eighty-four Members of Parliament must be Maori. In effect, Maoris are doubly enfranchised in that they also possess the right to vote for candidates not so allocated as registered voters in the regular parliamentary constituencies where they live. As a result, there are many more MPs with Maori blood than the allocated four. In addition, their language not only has official legal status but its use is actively encouraged. Intermarriage has been so extensive over the generations that there must be few, if any, "pure" Maoris left in New Zealand.

A word about Maori origin and history is needed. The Maori people are thought to have migrated to New Zealand from tropical Polynesia (possibly from the unknown legendary homeland of Hawaiki) in large ocean-going canoes around the ninth to thirteenth century. Those arriving in Aotearoa (New Zealand) found a land very different from tropical Polynesia. New Zealand not only was colder, but also was much bigger in area than the islands from which they would have come. (Indeed, New Zealand is larger than the total land mass of the rest of Polynesia.)

In addition, they encountered unusual fauna, including the largest bird in the world, the four-metre-tall flightless Giant Moa, and the world's greatest aerial predator, the giant Haast's Eagle. Both are now extinct. New Zealand is also the only place in Polynesia with snow-topped mountains and even glaciers. The South Island's stunning Southern Alps cover more area than the Alps in Europe. The North Island also has one main chain of mountains and several volcanoes.

Before the coming of the Pakeha (white man) to New Zealand and the creation of a Maori written language, all literature, including many legends and *waiata* (songs), was passed on orally between generations. The most widely recognized expression of Maori culture is the "Haka," a war dance or challenge. The Haka was performed before the onset of war by the Maori as late as the nineteenth century. It has since been immortalized by New Zealand's world-class national rugby team, the All Blacks, who perform this dance before every game. Genealogy is very important in the Maori culture; orators often begin traditional presentations by listing their ancestors. The different tribes trace their roots back to specific canoes that brought their ancestors from legendary Hawaiki.

Maori culture is also expressed through striking facial tattoos. Full-face tattoos, or *moko*, among the Maori tribes were predominantly a male activity. Female forms of *moko* were restricted to the chin area, the upper lip, and the nostrils. Today the *moko* still lives on as an increasing number of Maori are opting to display them to preserve and connect with their culture and identity. Intricate wood carvings of motifs similar to the tattoos, often of mythological figures, continue to be widely produced.

Dutch navigator Abel Tasman was the first European to encounter the Maori, in 1642. In 1769, British explorer James Cook established friendly relations with some Maori tribes. By 1800, visits by European ships were relatively frequent. British–Maori relations were initially reasonably amicable, and, in 1840, representatives of Britain and Maori chiefs signed the Treaty of Waitangi. This treaty established British rule, granted the Maori British citizenship, and recognized Maori land rights. However, rising ten-sions over disputed land sales led to conflict in the 1860s. The resulting Maori–British wars took their toll on the Maori, but the real killer was European disease. Eventually their population dropped to about 100,000 but today has risen to about 650,000 (with another 120,000 living as immigrants in Australia).

Maoris live in all parts of New Zealand, but predominantly in the North Island where the climate is warmer. Many hold high positions in New Zealand society and have made important contributions to the country over the years. Some of the Waitangi Treaty's provisions regarding land rights have not been respected. and a judicial process is in place for compensating Maori for land that was illegally confiscated or otherwise alienated.

Chapter 25

ADVENTURES IN PUBLIC RELATIONS

The Canadian High Commission in Wellington at that time was almost exactly the same size as our embassy in Bogota – four Canadian diplomats (the High Commissioner, myself, and two Trade Commissioners), three other Canadians, and about half a dozen New Zealand employees. It is called a high commission rather than an embassy because it is located in a Commonwealth country (a country formerly part of the British Empire). The original Commonwealth countries all had the same head of state, the British monarch, which meant that the monarch could not accredit an ambassador to him- or herself. Instead the prime ministers of each Commonwealth country would accredit High Commissioners to each other. Later, when republics became common within the Commonwealth and the Queen could accredit ambassadors to them, it was decided to retain the name "High Commissioner" to underline the special historic relationship. Otherwise, in terms of international law and diplomatic status and privileges, embassies and high commissions are equivalent.

Canada's High Commission occupied the whole of an upper floor of a modern office building that served as the New Zealand headquarters for Imperial Chemical Industries. The location was ideal – on the other side of St. Paul's Anglican Cathedral from the Parliament Building. New Zealand Foreign Affairs and other government offices were nearby, and I could easily walk to most of my appointments.

My New Zealand work experience was very different from that in Colombia largely because the culture and lifestyle of New Zealand were so similar to Canada's. There were no Canadians in distress to help, no missionaries to protect from persecution, and very few visitors from Canada requiring help from the likes of me. We certainly did not save anyone's life.

Also, the Canadian community, which was fairly large, blended into local society and we had hardly any contact with them. As for making friends among the locals, so difficult in Colombia, that was a joy. We remain close to many of those friends even today, more than forty years after we left that hospitable land. We have also flown down under six times over the years and have welcomed many "kiwis" to both our Ottawa and Vancouver homes.

My work in New Zealand fell easily into two areas: public relations and diplomatic reporting. The former consisted mainly of giving speeches to service clubs like Rotary, church groups, business luncheons, academic institutions, and the like. While the content and presentation were tailored to the individual audiences, a common theme was the need for all the white countries of the Commonwealth to demonstrate solidarity with nonwhites by adopting common policies and practices in opposition to South African apartheid.

Just as ice hockey predominates in Canada, the dominant secular "religion" of New Zealand is rugby. As a result, many New Zealanders had mixed feelings about contacts with South Africa and its pro-apartheid regime because they wanted the New Zealand All Blacks to play against South Africa's Springboks as often as possible. Typically, Maoris are disproportionately represented on New Zealand's national rugby teams but, in 1960, New Zealand sent an all-white team to tour South Africa in deference to apartheid. That action provoked widespread protests in New Zealand and, when the next opportunity came to send a national team to South Africa, the New Zealanders decided not to do so. However, in 1970, the South Africans said they would accept Maori players as "honorary whites" and a mixed-race New Zealand team was sent. That action was not in keeping with the boycott that Canada was urging. (The Australians and British were also maintaining "rugby relations" with South Africa.) I used to argue in my speeches that the division of the world that would follow the end of the Cold War would likely be North/South rather than East/West and that we white nations needed to begin now to build bridges across the international racial divide. Obviously, one way of so doing was to vigorously oppose the apartheid regime.

I remember in particular a strongly argued debate that was held at Wellington's Victoria University. I was speaking in support of Judith Todd, the beautiful, articulate daughter of Garfield Todd, a New Zealander who became Prime Minister of Southern Rhodesia when it was still a British colony. He tried to create a multiracial political system but was replaced by Ian Smyth, who held the opposite view, carrying it so far as to declare independence from Britain and wage a civil war against black insurgents. Judith travelled the world speaking against Smyth's regime and, by extension, against South Africa's apartheid. Opposing us in the debate was a South African diplomat who argued that South Africa and, by extension, white Rhodesia were much-needed bulwarks against communism in Africa. In the short term and in a narrow military sense, he had a point, especially given the role of the Cuban military in former Portuguese Africa. Judith focused on the inequities and abuses that result from a racially based regime. I emphasized the long-term harm to Western interests that would result from support for apartheid both during the Cold War and in the kind of world that would likely emerge following its end. I remember really putting my heart and soul into the debate that day. I was probably trying to show off in front of Judith.

Another interesting audience was the national governing body of New Zealand's Presbyterian Church. I made essentially the same points but added a spiritual dimension. I pointed out that in a situation where there are oppressors and oppressed, it is most often the oppressors who develop hard hearts and become thereby resistant to the teachings of the Christian faith. It follows that the church should discourage their congregants from identifying with hard-hearted oppressors.

Some audiences were particularly daunting. I remember on one occasion attempting to make a serious presentation on Canadian foreign policy to a Mothers' Union meeting at which almost all the participants were knitting. The click of the knitting needles continued throughout my talk and was remarkably distracting. I had real trouble maintaining the thread of my presentation.

Another speaking event proved positively painful. I guess you could say that it is seared into my mind (and elsewhere). The Canadian High Commissioner, my boss, had been invited to open New Zealand's National Highland Games, to be held in a beautiful seaside town called Tauranga halfway up the east coast of New Zealand's North Island. He was going to be away and I was offered as a substitute in my capacity as Acting High Commissioner.

The great day arrived, and Ardith and I drove to the main entrance of the large race track where the event was to be held. I was fully kitted out in a tam o' shanter, lacy shirt, kilt, sporran, and tartan knee socks – a brae, bonny sight! I was, however, completely eclipsed by my beautiful wife, who looked very glamorous in a short flowered silk dress. The chief of the games, Andrew Fleming, and a lone piper met us at the entrance and we were "piped" to a raised platform that had been set up in front of the main stadium. There was a row of metal chairs on the platform for the VIPs, such as the mayor, city councillors, and the local member of parliament. After introductions, Ardith was seated, and I stood in the centre of the platform behind a microphone. In the grassy oval within the track were assembled the massed pipe bands of New Zealand, a truly impressive sight. They proceeded to march around the racetrack past the VIP platform as I took the salute. I like bagpipes and drums, and it was a very stirring experience.

Once they had reassembled, I was expected to say "a few words." As my friends know well, that is constitutionally impossible for me. Instead, I took a few moments to tell the tale of a community in Nova Scotia founded by Scots in the early nineteenth century that chose to sail, in its entirety, to the North Island of New Zealand in the late 1800s. The community they founded still exists in New Zealand today. I said a few more words about great Scotsmen who had played major roles in Canadian history and concluded by declaring the games open. There was polite, impatient applause as I went to my assigned seat.

At this point I should add that the month was January, the southern hemisphere's equivalent of July, and it was very sunny and hot. I had already discovered how warm a heavy kilt could be, but I had not mastered the art of smoothing a skirt-like garment under me as I sat down. As a result, my upper thighs landed on a red-hot metal chair. I let out a yell, leapt to my feet, and endured the howl of laughter that poured out of the packed stadium behind me. It did not seem very funny at the time, but, as I look back, the largely unsuccessful efforts not to laugh by the VIPs seated around me were truly hilarious. Only Ardith looked concerned, bless her. New Zealanders are very egalitarian people and seeing a stuffed shirt get his must have been truly delicious. At least it was an entertaining start to the games.

Sometimes the public relations activities were of a more tangible nature. On the occasion of the bicentenary of Captain Cook's circumnavigation of New Zealand, our Information Officer, who was a New Zealander, and I came up with the idea that Canada mark the occasion by presenting a West Coast totem pole to the people of New Zealand. Ottawa agreed, and a prominent British Columbian carver was commissioned to fashion a pole that would tell the story of Captain Cook's visit to Canada's West Coast. Because it was very tall, it had to be divided into three pieces and carried to New Zealand by three Canadian destroyers. I was Acting High Commissioner at the time of its arrival, and I had the dubious pleasure of helping New Zealand Prime Minister Keith Holyoake unveil the pole in a howling wet "Southerly" that was already doing a better job of unveiling Canada's gift than we were. At least the great man always recognized who I was after that. Indeed, many years later as leader of a Canadian environmental delegation visiting New Zealand, I was presented to Sir Keith in his new role representing the Queen as Governor General. He remembered our shared ordeal, which provoked much laughter. The totem pole was installed in Gisborne, where Cook first landed.

The next day, in much better weather, I stood stiffly at attention beside a Royal Canadian Navy Captain at a very different ceremony. The commanders of his squadron's three ships were behind us and about a hundred "Jack Tars" armed with rifles were behind them. The location was a Maori Marae (tribal community and spiritual centre), and the occasion was a formal welcome by the Maori tribe whose traditional lands encompassed that area. A lone facially tattooed Maori warrior clad only in a short feathered kilt approached us with a sharp wooden spear in his hands. He did a fierce dance with grotesque grimaces and much sticking out of his tongue (which appeared extraordinarily long). The most dramatic moment was when he thrust the spear inches from my nose and I had to repress any urge to flinch. He then laid a large feather on the ground. By picking it up, the Navy Captain and I signified that we came in peace. In response, the sailors behind us lifted their rifles to the sky and fired a *feu de joie*. That meant that each sailor fired his rifle immediately after the man next to him. Had it been dark, the muzzle flashes running across the line of riflemen would have been striking to watch.

Afterwards, the Maoris put on a wonderful display of singing and dancing including the famous and fierce "Haka" challenge that precedes every game played by New Zealand's always impressive "All Blacks" rugby team. All that was missing to complete this Victorian-era event was a white pith helmet for me.

A much more personal ceremony took place when the three Canadian

Our son James' baptism onboard HMCS Yukon, Wellington Harbour, 1967.

destroyers made their official visit to Wellington. Our son, James, born eleven months earlier, was christened by the naval chaplain in the ward room of HMCS *Yukon* using the inverted ship's bell resting on a Canadian flag as the font. Later, James' name was engraved on the bell, which today sits in the Halifax Maritime Museum. The local newspaper featured a photograph of the event along with a story, and both were sent by wire service to Canada and picked up by many newspapers across the country. I took great delight in sharing a large, glossy photo of the christening with the guests at James' wedding in Ottawa many years later.

Fortunately, no photo was taken of James' hapless father trying, in accordance with naval custom, to pour the unused water in the font into the harbour. The bell was very heavy and I was warned that if I dropped it, I would follow it. I held on well enough but stupidly poured it into the ever-present wind, thereby becoming thoroughly christened myself.

CHAPTER 26

SUCCESSES AND FAILURES

My diplomatic reporting responsibilities mainly focused on three areas: Britain's negotiations aimed at joining the European Common Market, the Vietnam War, and developments in Malaysia. New Zealand was given special access to Britain's negotiations with Europe because of the immense effect that the Common Market's exclusionary agricultural policy would have on New Zealand's vital export trade to Britain. It would mean the end of "Commonwealth Preferences." Canada and Australia would, of course, be affected as well, but the impact on both countries would be proportionately much less significant.

Simply put, we wanted to know what was going on, and, since the British were often reluctant to brief us to the extent that we wanted, we approached the New Zealanders as well. My contacts in the New Zealand Foreign Ministry were more than helpful. If they were busy, they would hand me the files for me to make notes and would always make time to answer my questions. As a result, our reporting on this subject was much praised by Ottawa. What my bosses in Ottawa did not know was that I understood very little of what I was sending them. Much of it was highly technical, and I was simply parroting what the New Zealanders told or showed me.

As for the Vietnam War, Canada was a member of the International Truce Commission set up after France's withdrawal from Indochina and not a participant in the war. New Zealand, on the other hand, was a belligerent, like Australia, and had access to information which we did not. The Australians were more reticent in sharing what was going on, but the New Zealanders adopted the same approach with me as they had done for the Common Market negotiations. From 1965 to 1970, the years Ardith and I were in New Zealand, U.S. involvement in Vietnam escalated immensely, and New Zealand's inside knowledge of the development and pattern of that escalation was of real interest in Ottawa. Once again, we were praised for our reporting.

With respect to Malaysia, New Zealand had been involved in that part of the world for a long time and had sources we did not. As a result, we were the first of Canada's diplomatic posts to report to Ottawa that Singapore had decided to leave Malaysia.

I also served as Canada's liaison with New Zealand's Security Service. One of the Service's top officials, Tim Bennett, and his wife, April, were among our closest friends; they exchanged visits with us long after we left New Zealand. Sadly, Tim passed away some time ago, but April has visited us twice since, and we maintain a warm friendship. (Diana stayed with her when visiting New Zealand a few years ago.) The liaison work was normally pretty routine, but we had one crisis. A young New Zealand diplomat serving in Ottawa was, along with others, compromised by the Soviets. I argued that he should be allowed to return home quietly rather than be potentially exposed as part of a Canadian undercover operation aimed at the Soviet diplomats involved. Ottawa agreed, and the New Zealanders were very appreciative.

On two occasions, I participated in the negotiation of what are called "air bilaterals," agreements governing the frequency of commercial air flights between countries. I was so successful at this activity that Canadian Pacific Airlines went from weekly service to every other week after the first round, and lost the right to fly to New Zealand entirely after the second round. I still have the Canadian Pacific Airlines cufflinks given to me to mark the occasion. The problem was that Air New Zealand could link up with Air Canada in Los Angeles and tap the Canadian market without having to land in Canada and give anything in return. Air New Zealand was under strong pressure at the time from its British and Australian partners to reduce Canadian Pacific Airlines' presence in the South Pacific.

I mentioned earlier our dear friend, Don Toms, who used to sing folk songs at our parties. He was New Zealand's Director of Civil Aviation. During the second round of negotiations, he sang a specially composed song at a party we gave to welcome our new High Commissioner Ronald Macdonell. (Coincidentally, Macdonell was a former Secretary General of the UN's International Civil Aviation Organization, which was headquartered in Montreal.) Don's song told the story of a Canadian Pacific Airlines Captain sadly saying his final goodbyes in an Auckland pub. I sent the words verbatim to Ottawa as an all-too-accurate predictor of the results of the negotiations.

Sometimes we had fun carrying out the instructions we received from our masters in Canada. When Canada's Navy decided to get rid of the aircraft carrier Bonaventure, we were among the many diplomatic missions told to try to sell it to our host country, a truly ridiculous instruction given that its crew requirement would have consumed almost the whole New Zealand Navy. Nonetheless, the Trade Commissioner and I formally called upon the Minister of Defence with this exciting offer. There was much laughter on all sides, and we toasted the navies of both countries.

Not surprisingly, we made several friends among the New Zealand diplomats who were frequent guests at our social gatherings. One, Ken Piddington, went on to become New Zealand's Environment Commissioner; I had the great pleasure of collaborating with him in mutually beneficial visits and personnel/information exchanges years later when I held a comparably senior environmental position in the Canadian government. In the mid-1980s, Ken arranged for me to be the only non-New Zealander at a national conference, chaired by New Zealand Prime Minister Lange, aimed at developing new legislation and institutions for protection and conservation of the environment. It was a very exciting and productive experience. I recommended that the assessment and review process be kept at arm's length from the managerial systems of government so that it could provide unbiased advice to the government and unbiased reporting to the public, a view that Ken also held. The model ultimately adopted largely reflected this view.

Sadly, I long ago lost contact with Ken, but Ardith and I have been fortunate to maintain a relationship to this day with one dear couple formerly with New Zealand's Foreign Service, Hugh and Natasha Templeton. Early in his diplomatic career, Hugh had played an important role in negotiating New Zealand's withdrawal from administering Western Samoa under a League of Nations/UN Trusteeship in place since the end of World War I. In 2012 he accompanied New Zealand's prime minister on a trip to Samoa to celebrate the fiftieth anniversary of that event.

Hugh eventually left the Foreign Service to enter politics, and I had the great joy on one of my visits to Wellington of meeting with him in his office while he was serving as a senior Cabinet Minister. Like me, he has long since retired, but, unlike me, his views are still sought on issues of the day, and he is occasionally asked to look into one issue or another on behalf of his government. We maintain a lively e-mail correspondence, and, when he visited Vancouver in 2009, we spent a lot of time together. The years simply melted away.

CHAPTER 27

THE TWO SIDES OF PIERRE TRUDEAU

I said earlier that normally there was no need for me to help Canadian visitors to New Zealand. There was one very important exception. Canada's new prime minister, Pierre Trudeau, chose New Zealand for his first official overseas trip, and I was responsible for helping organize it. What that meant in practice was that I kept Ottawa informed of what was being arranged by the New Zealanders and passed on to my New Zealand counterparts Canada's comments and suggestions.

The visit was successful, but I have to say that my perhaps unrealistically positive view of our new prime minister (no doubt the result of the Trudeaumania phenomenon then sweeping Canada) took something of a beating. Up close, he seemed cold and distant. His interaction with an audience clearly depended upon his view of that audience. For example, he must have been bored by an audience of high school students, and it showed very clearly. He was not much better when meeting with the New Zealand Cabinet.

On the other hand, when stimulated, he was really impressive. I had arranged a TV interview with New Zealand's premier interviewer, a man just as good as Britain's much more famous David Frost. Just before the interview, Romeo LeBlanc, Trudeau's press secretary, who later became Canada's Fisheries Minister and then Governor General, scolded the Prime Minister in rapid French for his poor performance at the high school and said that he needed to do a lot better with this interview. (The interviewer told me later that he had understood this exchange and had taken heart.) The questioning was superb, Trudeau was clearly impressed, and he responded accordingly. It was one of the high points of the trip.

Later, the Prime Minister received a formal welcome at the local Maori

Marae. The Maoris have a great oral tradition and many are superb orators. The local chief was clearly one of the best, and his presentation was both colourful and stirring. He called Trudeau the "Great White Heron from Across the Seas," a very high compliment. The Prime Minister's response, given off-the-cuff, was passionate and moving, one of the best speeches of its kind I have ever heard. Even some of the hard-bitten reporters sitting around me were wiping the occasional tear from their eyes. His theme was the mutual enrichment that comes from the mixing of and respectful interaction between differing cultures. I guess you could say that Trudeau was something of a selective, very able chameleon. He took on the colour of his surroundings and, if they stimulated him, proceeded to outshine all others.

The New Zealanders did a wonderful job of organizing his visit – nothing went wrong – and a lot of the credit for that rubbed off on me. As a result, when I returned to Canada, I was asked to manage his planned tour of Southeast Asia. Fortunately, knowing as I did that it was really the New Zealanders who achieved the earlier success, I turned down the offer. Things were bound to go wrong on a tour of that kind, and I did not want to be anywhere near it.

Chapter 28

THE GREAT DIANA DIAPER CAPER

I do not want this account to turn into a travelogue, but it would be remiss of me not to say something about the beauty of New Zealand. We made a number of motor trips to different parts of that lovely country during the years that we lived there, but we actually saw even more of it during six visits after our departure.

What strikes me most is the remarkable variety that can be found in a relatively small area. Canada is a vast country, and the huge variety in our terrain is to be expected. New Zealand has just as much variety in much shorter distances. I remember well the beautiful beaches and green hills of the semitropical north as well as the giant Kauri gum trees. Canada has nothing like that; yet New Zealand, in its rugged South Island, has mountain ranges every bit as magnificent, if not more so, than the Rockies. Its nineteen thousand kilometres of coastline range from idyllic, sandy beaches devoid of any human presence to fjords that equal or surpass those of Norway. The people of New Zealand add to the attraction of their country through their down-to-earth, forthright behaviour and welcoming attitude as well as their exuberant enjoyment of their own outdoors. Extreme sport is very much a part of that enjoyment; it does not surprise me that bungee jumping originated in New Zealand. So did jet boats that move at speed through whitewater and, for those who want something very different, rolling down hills inside giant transparent plastic balls. Each to his own! I will tell only one travel story because what happened during it was later to have such an important impact on our lives.

I call our first motor holiday in New Zealand the "Great Diana Diaper Caper" for reasons that will become obvious. James was not yet born and Diana was still in diapers when we set out from Wellington up the west coast of the North Island. The largely deserted sandy beaches were beautiful, contrasting pleasantly with the green hills inland. Later we moved away from the coast onto what is called the Desert Road running through a very dry, but not sandy, rolling plain and past two extinct but dramatic volcanoes. New Zealand's volcanic origins are often very evident. As was so sadly demonstrated by the earthquakes in Christchurch, New Zealand, like Canada's West Coast, is part of the Pacific Ocean's seismically sensitive "Ring of Fire." Beautiful Lake Taupo, a trout fisherman's heaven, soon appeared, and we quickly found a waterside motel.

Today's New Zealand has some of the best tourist infrastructure in the world, but the situation was very different in the 1960s. Motels tended to be pretty primitive, and laundry facilities were often lacking. Diapers, more specifically the washing thereof, became a dominant concern. Everywhere we went, we washed Diana's diapers in the bathroom sink and hung them all over the room to dry. The problem became so overwhelming that at one point I thought of tying a diaper to the radio aerial both as an appropriate sign of our passage and as a symbol of surrender. Finally, we encountered a motel that advertised laundry service. We wasted no time in making use of that service, but the result, to put it mildly, was unexpected. The diapers were returned stacked and starched – stiff as boards! Poor little Diana! Clearly, our diapers were not recognized as such, despite the obvious evidence of the use to which they had been put. New Zealand diapers, called "nappies," were made of heavy, flannel-like material and were generally square in shape. The North American diapers we were using were made of a gauze-like material and were rectangular in shape.

Undaunted, we continued our journey, encountering further evidence of New Zealand's volcanic origins in the geothermal region surrounding Rotorua – bubbling mud, highflying geysers, and everywhere the pervasive smell of sulphur. There was also a wonderful place where we could watch Maori carvers at work, and we have two truly beautiful examples of their creations in our living room today. Years later, we returned to Rotorua to watch the national dog trials in which the country's best sheepdogs, mostly border collies, competed for top honours. We were immensely impressed by their skill and intelligence. We had, of course, no idea that, many years thereafter, we would have a border collie of our own. It is a truly unique breed.

Our final Diaper Caper destination before turning back towards

Wellington was the well-equipped, very comfortable Waitomo Hotel situated next to the famous caves of the same name. (This hotel washed the diapers and did not starch them.) The caves are accessed through an underground river, and they are famous because their roofs and stalactites are covered with glow-worms. Visitors sitting in small boats are told to keep completely silent so that the glow-worms do not turn off their lights. The sight is truly awesome, like a miniature version of the Milky Way in 3-D; one of nature's jewels.

Unknown to us, a young couple from Auckland were honeymooning at the hotel. We did not meet them or even notice them, but they certainly noticed us. Nearly three years later and in circumstances best described elsewhere in this narrative, they and we met at a seaside camp. We were to learn with amazement the role they had played during the intervening years in bringing about truly transforming changes in our lives.

Our journey home to Wellington took us through the delightful West Coast town of New Plymouth, dominated by Mount Taranaki (then called Egmont), a superb Fuji-like snow-topped volcano. I remember so well picnicking among the green, rolling hills dotted with fluffy white sheep near the base of that beautiful mountain. We were able to purchase a large wool tapestry depicting that scene, and whenever we look at it, we are carried back to that idyllic afternoon so long ago, so far away.

Recalling the Diaper Caper brings to mind a somewhat more painful incident from Diana's early years. When she first learned to climb out of her crib, she came happily into our bedroom to wake me up. I would not have minded except for the very early hour. After the third morning, I pretended to stay asleep in the hope that she would tire of this practice and stay in her room. The little voice saying "dada" got louder, and suddenly I felt this terrible pain in the middle of my face. Diana had picked up my hard-soled slipper and whacked me firmly on the nose. We have often joked since that that incident established our relationship. I have always been an obedient father.

CHAPTER 29

THE END OF A DREAM

The reader might be forgiven for thinking that we were living a truly charmed life with interesting work, plenty of friends, lovely surroundings, very comfortable economic circumstances, good prospects, and, above all, a beautiful, healthy daughter. The reality, as is so often the case, was very different. Perhaps because of the insecurities of my early years and the reaction to my youth within the Foreign Service, I was driven by an ambition to become Canada's youngest ambassador. Not long after my thirtieth birthday, I was promoted to counsellor, a fairly senior diplomatic designation. That only intensified my ambition. I was only one promotion away from being eligible to head one of the many small diplomatic missions that Canada has scattered around the world. (Larger missions require ambassadors of more senior rank.)

The problem was that Ardith not only did not share my ambition but positively feared it. She cried when she heard I had become a counsellor. Ardith is a very sweet, gentle person who never put on airs and thought it unbecoming to draw attention to herself. She was not at all comfortable in the diplomatic world. She never said so because she did not speak disparagingly of others, but I am sure she found some of those with whom we interacted intimidating and self-important. There were many others who proved to be very supportive friends, including our neighbours, but the round of diplomatic parties weighed heavily on her. The resulting tension between us grew steadily but, when she became pregnant with our second child, our attendance at maternity classes together did create something of a compensating bond.

James' birth on November 23, 1966, could not have been in circumstances more different from those when Diana entered our world. Instead of in a large city hospital, the birth took place in a small house not far from where we lived. It had been converted into a four-bed maternity home, run by two dear old midwives who were at the point of retirement. Also, instead of nearly melting with the heat, Ardith was really cold in the unheated delivery room. James was a lot larger than Diana had been and the birth was correspondingly slower and more difficult. Nonetheless, the breathing exercises Ardith and I had learned together did help, and there were no complications. The maternity home operated on a principle that was precisely the opposite of the assembly-line hospital care that predominates today. Ardith stayed there for the minimum requirement of two weeks after the birth, living like a queen. She was fed beautiful meals with vegetables fresh from the garden, and James was cared for like a prince. Not surprisingly, she did not want to come home.

James was both a very happy baby, rarely crying, and a very big one. His head was larger than that of his two-and-a-half-year-old sister and his body soon matched it. In photos of diminutive Diana holding up her baby brother, she almost disappears behind him. Despite James' good humour and Diana's cheerful acceptance of him, Ardith's reluctance to return home from the maternity home proved prescient.

She fell into what was thought to be classic postpartum depression, but it went on and on. After five months, she had to be hospitalized, initially in Wellington. She was soon transferred to a long-term care facility in Hamner, located in the foothills of the South Island's magnificent Southern Alps. She was to remain there for several months before returning home. I visited her on a number of occasions and took her for drives in the beautiful countryside. She was usually fairly calm, but she had lost so much weight that she appeared almost skeletal. The doctors said it was "nerves."

While Ardith's prolonged absence brought home to me how much I missed her, it also underlined how difficult our situation was becoming. Diana had for some time already been attending a preschool. This preschool was run by a wonderful woman, Glen Charlton, who became central to our ability to cope. That dear woman was willing not only to keep Diana all day and overnight through the week but also to do the same for five-month-old James. The children were home with me on the weekends, and I have to admit that Monday mornings never looked better.

To be honest, from this distance in time, the months and even years that followed are often blurred in my memory. Sometimes the children were with us, sometimes they were not. Sometimes Ardith could cope, but much of the time she could not. There were worse symptoms and further hospitalizations, ultimately resulting in a diagnosis of schizophrenia.

I was increasingly coming to the realization that my dreams of an ambassadorship were just that – dreams. How could Ardith be an ambassador's wife with that kind of illness? I would like to say that I accepted the loss of my dream, but the truth is that I was very angry. So near and yet so far! Not surprisingly, Ardith found my bouts of anger hard to deal with, even though I tried not to direct them at her. She began to talk about returning to live with her parents in Vancouver, together with the children, which added to my despair. Indeed I think it is fair to say that, for a time, it was only her inability to travel, because of her illness, that kept us together.

Chapter 30

A CAR SALE THAT OPENED A DOOR

Ardith's inability to travel also meant that we would not be able to return to Canada at the end of our normal three-and-a-half-year posting. We were, as a result, given a two-year extension. I decided to replace our oversized station wagon with a smaller vehicle that would be easier for Ardith to drive, and I put the wagon up for sale. That sale was to open up a whole new world.

Gordon Pellow, the buyer, was a charming man, a little older than I. He owned the principal funeral business in Hamilton, New Zealand's fourth-largest city, 525 km north of Wellington. Hamilton is bisected by the meandering Waikato river, located in dairy country and surrounded by beautiful, rolling green hills. Our station wagon was to become New Zealand's first silver-blue hearse. (It looked really great with the little fringed curtains made by Gordon's wife.) That was not a use I had anticipated, but a buyer is a buyer and I was pleased that it sold so quickly.

Some weeks later, Gordon called me with an invitation both to speak to his Rotary Club and to stay at his home. My acceptance meant that I got to meet his delightful wife, Margaret, a New Zealander who had been a ballerina in London and now taught her skills to others as well as caring for her two teenagers. I will never forget Margaret standing at the sink with one leg resting on top of the kitchen counter. Flexibility personified!

I think it is fair to say that people in the funeral business tend to be the objects of unkind comments and generalized characterizations, if not caricatures. Gordon and Margaret were the opposite of the caricatures: witty, travelled, cultured, full of fun, and very much enamoured of one another. I really enjoyed this couple's company, and we began to exchange visits. Ardith liked them as much as I did. Gradually, over several months, we shared some of our health and marital problems with them, and they responded by respectfully and sensitively talking about their faith and its central importance in their relationship with each other. I respected them, but remained unconvinced. Ardith was more receptive.

Our Hamilton friends were Presbyterians, but they maintained close relationships with like-minded people in other denominations. Among them was a remarkable couple, about six years older than us, who lived in Tauranga on the North Island's east coast, not that far from Hamilton. Ian Crawford, a New Zealander, was teaching high school English when we met him. He had attended university in Canada where he met his Canadian wife, Millie. She became a very successful real estate agent in southern Ontario while he taught.

Both have a great love for children, and they saw it as their Christian ministry to adopt children whom no one else would adopt: those who were too old, were racially mixed, had health problems, or were otherwise disadvantaged. After adopting several and having one of their own in Canada, they made the very costly decision to move to New Zealand because they thought that the country's "womb to tomb" welfare state would be a kinder place for their "disadvantaged" children. (They had no way of foreseeing the immense impact of New Zealand's later balance-of-payments problems and the tough remedies proposed by the Chicago School of Economics on New Zealand's society.)

Ian and Millie continued adopting children, reaching a total of thirteen (plus two of their own), including two with life-threatening illnesses who eventually died. We had, by that time, come to know them and their family, including the two children who died, and we knew how deeply they felt that loss. At the same time, they also rejoiced in the certainty that those two dear ones would be with Jesus for eternity. I am moved to tears as I write these words. I will never forget their home, where we saw so many different-looking children (Maoris, Africans, Native Americans, Orientals, and their own Caucasian children) interacting with one another and their parents so warmly. Think of the UN and add God's love. Ian and Millie are Pentecostals; Ian later became a pastor in New Zealand's Assembly of God (AOG) Church. A couple of years ago, they sent us photos of Ian's eightieth birthday celebration, a large and very colourful costume ball. Most of their progeny were present, including some who now live in England and Canada.

Both of us were awed by Ian and Millie's example of Christian love and inspired by Gordon and Margaret's relationship, but I was still resistant to the idea that I could have a personal relationship with God. It took Ardith making concrete arrangements to leave with the children to bring me to the point where my need overcame my reluctance. We deliberately did not tell our Hamilton friends of Ardith's plans because we knew they would be upset. Our efforts at secrecy were, however, blown in a way we could never have anticipated. It was Gordon and Margaret's custom to pray for us each day in their home in Hamilton. As they did so, they became convinced that something bad was happening right at that moment in our lives. They prayed about what to do, and Gordon felt inspired to call his friend, Frank Garrett, a Presbyterian elder and prominent businessman in Wellington, to ask him to go to our home urgently.

Next morning, a Saturday, Frank called me to say that the Pellows wanted him to visit us. Both Ardith and I were very upset over her impending departure, which was only three days off. I tried to discourage him, but he would not take no for an answer. He arrived and there ensued a lengthy exchange in which I put forward every reason I could think of for not accepting his invitation "to invite Jesus into my heart." Frank's response to each argument was to read me a relevant scripture verse. Indeed, he was constantly flipping through his Bible as I spoke. He told me much later that scripture references were coming into his mind even before I said anything. No wonder I lost the argument. Finally, Ardith, who had said little, and I knelt to pray a prayer of repentance, seeking forgiveness and asking Jesus into our hearts. To be honest, I was still not convinced, but I felt I had nothing to lose and potentially a lot to gain. To be even more honest, I also figured that our visitor would leave if I prayed the prayer.

CHAPTER 31

RUMOURS OF ANGELS

I felt nothing after the prayer beyond relief that our visitor was leaving. But by next morning, I knew that something extraordinary had happened to me. For Ardith, this experience was really a reaffirmation of her childhood beliefs and the changes in her that resulted were modest. They did not need to be dramatic. For me, it was very different. My priorities changed remarkably and nearly instantly, with concerns about my career greatly diminishing and concerns about Ardith's health and wellbeing correspondingly rising. Ardith saw those changes and cancelled her travel plans. Perhaps the change in her was to be more forgiving because I was still no bargain as a husband. The Holy Spirit had a lot of work to do in me – still does after over forty-five years. To my mind, that was a miracle every bit as remarkable as Ardith's dramatic healing nearly two years later (and of even greater consequence).

There was more. A few weeks later, a friend gave me a book written by David Wilkerson entitled *The Cross and the Switchblade*. Wilkerson was a rural American pastor who had been appalled by the drug culture and gangs of inner-city New York. He established a remarkable ministry to those caught up in that seemingly hopeless world. His success rate, through using what he called the counter-addiction of the Holy Spirit, was extraordinary, far better than conventional detox programs. The book was an inspiring account of the establishment and growth of his ministry, but it also contained teaching on what Wilkerson called the "Baptism of the Holy Spirit." He concluded by inviting the reader to seek this blessing. I had never been exposed to this teaching, but I found the biblical references to be compelling. I also remember thinking, as I looked at myself in a large mirror on the wall, that what had already happened to me was a much bigger miracle than what I was now being asked to believe. Accordingly, I asked Jesus to baptize me in the Spirit with the same evidence as that experienced by the Apostles on the day of Pentecost, and He did. That blessing and associated gift has remained with me ever since, and it has often been a source of great comfort.

A couple of years later, Don Wilkerson, David's younger brother, came to Wellington to speak in a number of churches from various denominations. I accepted the responsibility of organizing part of this speaking tour and of driving him to some of his appointments. Don was a fascinating man with much broader interests and knowledge than critics often associate with rural American pastors. However, what I remember most, apart from the fervour and insight in his preaching, was his observation that preaching in different denominations had given him a much better understanding of the varied ways in which God deals with His people. In a reference to his Pentecostal background and my membership in the Anglican church, he said, "You will understand that it was just as hard initially for me to see God in the order as it probably was for you to see him in the apparent chaos." He was absolutely right. What is essential among Christians is that we are agreed on the divinity of Jesus and the fact that He gave Himself on the cross to enable all of us to receive God's forgiveness for our sins. How we celebrate those truths can vary immensely. Sadly, David died recently, but Don is still active in ministry.

My return to the Anglican church of my childhood did not follow automatically from our conversion because I felt it had let me down. It was the High Commission's film library that provided the vehicle for that reconciliation. We loaned our National Film Board documentaries to individuals, schools, churches, and other groups all over New Zealand. In 1969 we reached the extraordinary figure in that little country (then three and a half million) of several hundreds of thousands of film viewings a year, that is to say, individuals times films seen. For example, if a group of three hundred people saw four documentaries, that would count as twelve hundred viewings. What we did not know was that our locally engaged film librarian, Hector Robbie, a New Zealander, was a former missionary who often accompanied films sent to churches with notes suggesting how the film in question could be used to illustrate spiritual points.

One of Hector's regular customers was the Vicar of St. Augustine's, Petone (the Anglican pastor in the suburban city next to where we lived).

Hector had recognized at once what had happened to me (a marked reduction in arrogance was probably the key giveaway), and he told me about his secret ministry. Meeting Ian Tweddell, the Vicar, followed in due course. Ian and I bonded almost immediately. The rest, as they say, is history. Ardith was confirmed as an Anglican in Ian's church since she wanted to declare her commitment publicly. Subsequently we also participated in a ceremony reaffirming our wedding vows before a God in whom we now believed. While Petone's Anglican church remained our spiritual home, we often attended evening services at Petone's AOG (Pentecostal) Church, whose passion and exuberance we admired and where we also saw some miraculous occurrences.

One such occurrence sticks in my mind. We were seated, as usual, near the back of the packed church, which was worshipping God in its accustomed joyful and somewhat noisy fashion. Half a dozen leather-jacketed "bikers" came in and stood at the back. Clearly there to make fun of the holy rollers, they periodically shouted rude remarks. Such an approach is a lot less effective in a boisterous Pentecostal church than it would be in an Anglican one, and they were easily drowned out. We were close enough to hear them, and I noticed that they became a lot quieter as the service proceeded. After finishing his hard-hitting sermon, the pastor called upon those who did not yet know Christ to come forward to "ask Him into their hearts." To my astonishment, three of the bikers did so, and the other three said absolutely nothing.

Over time, I saw several healings and other evidence of the supernatural power of God at that church. I came to understand better than I had that real Christianity is not simply a code of behaviour or a theology explaining the otherwise unexplainable. It is an ongoing encounter with a real and powerful God who wants to interact regularly with His children. At the same time, He is profoundly respectful of man's free will. Initially, I had great difficulty understanding that concept, but I have come to recognize that man's free will is at the heart of the Christian experience.

Let me put it this way. Each of us has been given the right to say yes or no to God. If you believe, as I came to, that God created all that exists, then the notion of saying no to Him is truly awesome, indeed frightening. Why, one might ask, would an omnipotent and omniscient God permit such independence? I believe the answer is extraordinarily simple. God created us in order to love Him and we cannot do so unless we are free not to love Him. Upon this reality hang all the horrors and all the God-honouring moments of history. Man is free to choose and act upon evil, and he has done so countless times over the millennia. Man is also free to respond to God, and he has done so countless times over the millennia. When people ask why God did not stop this or that atrocity, it is because He has chosen to respect man's free will even when it leads to terrible evil.

That said, it is clear from biblical accounts that God has intervened in history to achieve certain specific purposes, very often in response to prayer from those who believe fervently in Him. For those of us who have come to believe in God, expectant prayer is both our means of communicating with Him and of opening ourselves to His guidance and intervention in our lives or in the lives of others. In the remainder of this account, I hope from time to time to draw from my own erratic spiritual journey over the years to illustrate this important reality.

Chapter 32

FROM EUPHORIA TO DESPAIR

Sometime after our conversion, we were given a striking reminder that God is reaching out to us far more than the other way around. We accompanied Gordon and Margaret to a Christian young people's seaside summer camp. We sat down for tea with the counsellors, among whom was a young couple who kept looking at us in an almost stunned way. It transpired that they had been on their honeymoon a couple of years earlier at the Waitomo Hotel. The reader will remember my earlier description of the millions of glow worms in the nearby Waitomo caves. The young couple had seen us there and "the Holy Spirit," in their words, "had laid it upon their hearts" to pray for us ever since. Needless to say, the faith of all present was given a great boost by this "chance" encounter. All of us were also given an object lesson in the power of obedient, persistent prayer, and Ardith and I were reminded that God was seeking us long before we became conscious of Him.

I have mentioned two couples who played important roles in the lead-up to our Christian conversion. Now I want to talk about a couple, Eric and Julie Sherburd, who played an important mentoring role in our lives after we had become Christians. Eric had been the pastor of a sizable Baptist church in Tauranga. After having the same experience with the baptism of the Holy Spirit as I had had after reading Wilkerson's book, Eric and Julie decided to move to Wellington to pursue their spiritual calling in a secular setting. In other words, Eric would work in the business world but actively involve himself in Christian activities on evenings and weekends. In time he developed and pastored, in co-operation with others, a large fellowship drawn from a number of denominations. We met him and Julie through that work and developed a warm friendship that has persisted to this day. Whenever we had problems, and we certainly did, he and sometimes they would be there for us, guiding, supporting, and praying for us. Their circumstances were tough – four children to support and a new profession to learn – but that did not keep them from coming to our aid whenever Ardith's illness threatened to overwhelm us and undermine our faith. Christians talk about God's provision. There is no question that Eric and Julie were very timely provisions from God in a very needy period of our life.

Let me illustrate. Ardith's second hospitalization was the most frightening that she experienced in New Zealand. She was much sicker than she had been the first time. Her body was so wracked by psychotically induced fear that she was in great physical pain. The only relief came from medications that produced a vegetable-like state. Electroconvulsive therapy (ECT), commonly known as shock treatment, was repeatedly applied without anaesthetic and without informing me. Ardith had nightmares about that procedure for years, believing that she had been gang-raped. I cannot help thinking that those awful memories created a kind of post-traumatic stress that made her underlying symptoms even worse. The ECT also wiped out memories of important family events.

Because she was in the Wellington Hospital rather than on the South Island as before, I was able to visit her regularly, but it was difficult to remain optimistic in these circumstances. I guess I thought, with the naïveté of the new Christian, that some kind of divine bubble should have enveloped us and protected us from the vicissitudes of this life. Ardith and I were being disabused of that notion in a pretty direct way, and sometimes it was all too easy to doubt the reality of the changes that had affected us so powerfully. That is where our friends, especially Eric, came in – comforting, encouraging, exhorting.

One incident stands out. I was invited to give two talks in Christchurch, the South Island's largest city, one at noon to a Chamber of Commerce luncheon and the other at seven at night to the New Zealand Institute of International Affairs at Canterbury University in the form of a lecture on Canadian foreign policy. I arrived in Christchurch the night before, utterly exhausted, and quickly collapsed on my bed at the airport hotel. I was normally able to handle speaking assignments fairly easily, but, in my stressed state, the events of the next day were worrying. Moreover, I had not had the time or energy to prepare my material as well as I should have. I had difficulty falling asleep, and, well into the night and in a half-awake state, I simply asked God to help me. I began utilizing the prayer gift given to me at the time I was baptized in the Spirit but in a totally new way. Gradually, my tiredness lifted, and I found myself almost exhilarated and increasingly full of energy.

I finally fell asleep, and, when I awoke in the morning, I could not believe how well I felt and how clear my mind was. The luncheon speech I gave was full of humour and was very well received by a crowd that clearly wanted entertainment more than information. The more serious evening presentation was supposed to last forty minutes with about thirty minutes for questions afterwards. So enthusiastic was the response and so prolonged was the questioning that I was on my feet for three hours.

Clearly something remarkable had happened, and I returned to Wellington the following day in a state of near euphoria, convinced that I would find Ardith completely healed. I bought a bouquet of flowers at the airport and rushed to the hospital. When I found Ardith's bed empty, my spirits soared further. I asked the nurse where I could find her and she pointed to a door with a small window. I looked in the window and saw Ardith on the floor of a padded cell in a state of considerable distress. I threw the flowers down and ran from the hospital. Somehow I got back to the office and telephoned Eric. It took a while, but with his help, I was eventually able once again to develop a measure of positive expectation.

Looking back at that difficult time, I can see a parallel between myself and the Israelites as they were being led by Moses out of four hundred years of slavery in Egypt. I had experienced my personal parting of the Red Sea in our conversions, as well as a great deal of other evidence of God's love for both of us and of His willingness to intervene in our lives and in the lives of others. Yet, when I encountered another challenge or setback, I forgot, like the Israelites in the desert, what had been done for us, and fell into despair. Eric served as my Moses, getting me back on track.

In time, Ardith slowly improved and was able to come home again. She was, however, both fragile and dependent. With the help of our friends and Glen, that wonderful woman who cared for our children, we were able to cope, but only barely. We had less than one year left to stay in New Zealand, and I wondered what the future would hold.

Chapter 33

A REMINDER OF COLOMBIA

About this time, we had a welcome distraction, a festival of tall ships in Wellington's magnificent harbour. Among them was a sizable three-masted white schooner that served as a training vessel for Colombia's Navy. Because of our earlier posting in Bogota, Ardith and I were invited to a reception on board. Not many of the naval cadets could speak English, and few, if any, of the New Zealand guests could speak Spanish. I soon found myself acting as an interpreter, surrounded by guests and cadets. Accompanying the cadets was a Colombian army officer, a priest who was serving as the ship's chaplain. Perhaps because of the chaplain's presence, we began talking about religion, and I explained that I attended an Anglican church called St. Augustine's. I also explained that because it was St. Augustine's day this coming Sunday, our Bishop would be speaking at a special service to mark the occasion. The Colombian chaplain asked if he and some of the cadets could attend. I said that they would be most welcome, and we made arrangements to pick them up on Sunday.

The Colombian navy had based itself on Britain's Royal Navy, and their uniforms were virtually identical with Britain's and therefore almost the same as those worn by New Zealand sailors. The Colombian army had patterned itself after the German army, and the chaplain appeared to be wearing a German uniform. Thus, when this seemingly German officer and these seemingly New Zealand naval cadets, none of whom otherwise looked the part, arrived at St. Augustine's, the parishioners were filled with surprise and curiosity. I did my best to explain the ceremony to the chaplain and the half-dozen cadets with him, but my Spanish vocabulary predated my recently acquired Christian faith. Nonetheless, our guests tried to follow along as best they could.

When it came time for the Bishop's presentation, I tried to translate it, thereby earning many angry looks from parishioners wondering why I was talking during the sermon. St. Augustine was a remarkable fellow who lived an exciting life both before and after his conversion. A talk about him could have been very stimulating, but the Bishop opted for a more academic approach. Whether it was the quality of my translation, the content of the Bishop's address, too much of the night before, or all of the above, the chaplain fell asleep, as did a couple of cadets. Later, they awoke with a start and, clearly well trained, fell to their knees. Unfortunately for them, we were standing singing a hymn.

During coffee afterwards, all was explained. I did my interpreter bit for the Bishop, Vicar, and others and ensured that our guests made it safely back to their tall ship. I think I was forgiven for talking during the sermon.

CHAPTER 34

ARDITH'S DRAMATIC HEALING

At the beginning of April in 1970, three years after her first extended hospitalization and two years after we became Christians, Ardith suffered a further series of severe psychotic episodes and entered the hospital for the third time. After a few weeks, she was sent home in what was described as a catatonic state because, as the doctor put it, "we can do no more for her." She lay in her bed for three days in a state of complete withdrawal, her face pale and her eyes dull – what a layman might call a kind of conscious coma – neither eating nor drinking.

Then on May 8, at nine o'clock at night, she got up, face full of colour, eyes sparkling, fully coherent, and remarkably energetic. She went downstairs, prepared food, and ate a large meal, all the while declaring that she had been healed.

I thought she was delirious, but this kind of super health continued, and the next day I phoned Ian Tweddell, the Vicar of St. Augustine's, to tell him what had happened. (Ardith had been a volunteer secretary for the Vicar and was often at the vicarage. The Vicar and his family had been very supportive during our ordeal.) He responded with an extraordinary story. On the evening of May 8, he, his wife, Leona, and their children had attended a healing service at an Anglican church fifty kilometres away in Upper Hutt conducted by John Harris, an Anglican clergyman visiting from Australia. He was one of the leaders of a well-attended weekly healing service in St. Andrew's Cathedral, Sydney, led by a remarkable man whom I later came to know, Canon Jim Glennon. At about nine o'clock, Reverend Harris concluded his talk on "The Power of Jesus Christ to Heal Today" and invited those present to come forward for the laying on of hands. The Vicar's eleven-year-old son, Marcus, rushed to the front of the church with his mother in hot pursuit, fearing embarrassment. Marcus asked for prayers for "my mother's friend who is sick," meaning Ardith. Marcus' mother did the same, naming Ardith, and the result, many kilometres away in our home, must have been instantaneous.

We had not even known about the healing service, much less what Marcus was going to do. I will never forget the look on the psychiatrist's face when Ardith came bouncing in to his office at the hospital two days later. Nor will I forget what he said as we were leaving: "You will understand how difficult it is for me to accept the explanation you have offered, but I cannot deny the result nor would I wish to." That healing from catatonia made it possible for us to return to Canada in September of 1970 at the end of our two-year extension beyond the normal posting period.

Other symptoms of Ardith's illness resurfaced after we were back in Ottawa, and many struggles followed. But the catatonia did not return, and she was never as bad as before that remarkable proxy healing. Moreover, the memory of God's dramatic intervention did much to bolster our faith during times of stress. About thirty-five years after we left New Zealand, Diana spent several weeks there and, at our request, went to Tauranga where the Vicar's widow, children, and their spouses and children now live. She brought our love and thanked Marcus, now a father with two grown children of his own, for his faithfulness so very long ago. Marcus's sister, Margaret, and her husband, Tony, hosted Diana and have visited us twice in Vancouver. We exchange e-mails regularly. Margaret is a writer and is encouraging me in my efforts.

Before leaving New Zealand, I was from time to time invited to speak to a church audience about our journey into faith. After Ardith's remarkable miracle, such invitations increased in number, and the Anglican Bishop of Wellington decided to give me a letter stating that I "could be trusted with a message." This letter turned me into a kind of lay preacher, and I found that I spent many a Sunday in or away from Wellington speaking in Anglican and other pulpits. As I saw it, the miracles of salvation and healing did not belong to us but rather to the whole church, and it was my responsibility to share them as widely as possible. I had no idea that by so doing I was placing my government career in jeopardy.

The time finally came for us to leave beautiful New Zealand and the many friends who had come to mean so much to us. There were a lot of tears, and not just on the part of ourselves and our friends. That wonder-

Our children, Diana and James, just before we leave New Zealand, 1970.

ful woman, Glen Charlton, who had looked after Diana and James for so long, had developed a deep attachment to our children, especially James, who had come to her as a baby. She was childless, which no doubt added to her pain. We were so pleased to learn sometime later that she and her husband, David, had had a daughter of their own, Elizabeth, with whom we are still in touch.

What we did not appreciate as much as we should have was that James was losing one of his "mothers" with whom he had bonded after spending so much time with her since the age of five months. He had been the mascot of the day care and the apple of Glen's eye for over three years. No wonder he was so happy and bubbly all the time. Understandably, his moods became much more changeable after his arrival in strange new surroundings in far-off Ottawa. In other words, he began to experience ups and downs like the rest of us. The depth of his connection to the woman he had called "Mummy One" became clear twenty-five years later when we learnt from Elizabeth of her mother's premature death. James was very moved, and he told me that he had hoped to visit her one day in New Zealand.

The flight home to Vancouver, except for an enjoyable overnight break in Hawaii, was highly forgettable, as might be expected when travelling with a six-year-old and a very active four-year-old. James prepared me for the ordeal by spitting up his cookies on my suit jacket as we drove to the Auckland airport. He recovered remarkably quickly. Indeed, once on the plane, he became so rambunctious that the cabin crew moved us into the empty first-class compartment to protect the rest of the passengers. That was an unexpected benefit. Diana and James even got to visit the pilots on the flight deck, something that would be impossible in today's security-conscious world.

Ardith's parents met us at the Vancouver airport and whisked us to their lovely mountainside home with its spectacular views. They had made extended visits to us in New Zealand on two occasions, once with Ardith's brother, Bruce, so they were not strangers to our children. What was strange was our reaction to our own country. We experienced the phenomenon known as "culture shock," beginning with amazement at how large the cars were. I remember visiting a huge supermarket and being stunned by both its size and the variety of products on offer. We had become used to shopping at the local butcher's and greengrocer's. On one occasion I actually drove on the wrong side of the road, narrowly avoiding a collision, something I never did during all our years in New Zealand. We had been away from Canada for nearly six years, and it showed. Our children spoke with New Zealand accents, which caused some amusement and even some incomprehension on the part of relatives. Later in Ottawa, other children teased them about the way they spoke, and it was not long before they had adopted Canadian speaking styles. However, I can still hear a trace of the kiwi in some of the words Diana uses. We spent most of our time in Vancouver while on home leave, but we also visited Victoria to see my mother, her retired Mountie husband, and my grandmother. My step-grandfather, Bill, had passed away while we were in New Zealand, an event that had caused me deep sadness. He had been my substitute father, and I missed him very much.

I remember those initial weeks back in Canada with a mixture of understanding and embarrassment. Not surprisingly, Ardith and I were full of the wonders we had experienced in New Zealand, and I was eager to talk about them to anyone who would listen. Given the dramatic changes that had occurred in our lives, such enthusiasm was, perhaps, understandable.

However, looking back, I can see what a pain I was. Not surprisingly, given my glibness and insensitivity, no one fell to his or her knees after hearing our story. That said, it is a fact that a few of those with whom I shared our life-changing experiences, including my mother, Ardith's brother, and my first stepfather's second wife, were to have similar conversion experiences in their own lives years later.

PART IV

BECOMING AN ENVIRONMENTALIST

Chapter 35

"PERSECUTION" IN OTTAWA; "IMMERSION" IN THE GREAT LAKES

We arrived in Ottawa in the fall of 1970 after home leave in Vancouver, and I reported to work to receive my new assignment. There was a telephone message waiting for me from an officer in the Privy Council Office (PCO). PCO is the nerve centre of the Canadian government, serving as a kind of Prime Minister's Department as well as the Cabinet Secretariat. Its nearest American counterpart would be the White House, except that the staff are drawn almost entirely from career public servants. The political staff are concentrated in the much smaller Prime Minister's Office (PMO). I was suitably impressed and returned the call quickly.

I was asked whether I would be prepared to be temporarily seconded to PCO to organize Prime Minister Trudeau's planned trip to Southeast Asia and to accompany him as he made his visits. I declined, knowing that the invitation was based on the success of the Prime Minister's visit to New Zealand. The New Zealanders, not I, had done the work on that visit, and they would not be helping me organize this one. As a "reward" for my lack of co-operation, my own department gave me a dead-end job of minimal interest. I was naturally disappointed, but not as distressed as I would have been before my newfound faith had brought my extreme ambition into balance. The next blow was much more challenging.

I received a memorandum from the Director of Personnel informing me that I had been removed from the promotion list and would no longer be considered for any foreign posting on the grounds that I "had lent my position to the propagation of a particular creed" (a beautiful example of bureaucratese). The memo concluded by characterizing this activity as an act of poor judgement and inviting me to consider resignation. I should explain that, under Canada's Public Service Act, I could not be summarily dismissed except for acts of "moral turpitude." Clearly there was none of these, and my performance reports up to that time had been very good. Ending any prospect of career advancement or overseas posting and leaving me in a dead-end job was the extent of the sanctions available.

Obviously, the grounds cited as the basis for this disciplinary action reflected the many occasions when I had described our Christian conversion and Ardith's healing in various New Zealand churches. It was scarcely a subversive activity, and it was done on my own time and at my own expense. Canada's new High Commissioner in Wellington, who had arrived about a month before I left, had written a scathing attack on my "inappropriate" activities.

My boss' boss, Klaus Goldschlag, a very senior officer who was Jewish, concluded upon learning about this memo that I was being persecuted for my religion. He took up my cause with a vengeance. He eventually won the departmental battle that ensued and immediately appointed me to a senior position in the part of the Department that dealt with Canada–U.S. trans-boundary environmental matters. That appointment enabled me to play a central role in negotiating with the United States an agreement to clean up the polluted Great Lakes. The success of those negotiations led in turn to a new career in the recently created Department of the Environment (also known as Environment Canada). Ardith was able to remain in Ottawa, relieved of her responsibilities as a diplomatic hostess, and I was able to speak freely about my faith. Moreover, the new career took me to bureaucratic heights beyond my imagining and allowed me to exercise my belief in Christian stewardship – our obligation before God to care for His creation. I see this series of events as a wonderful example of God bringing good out of bad.

The Trans-boundary Environmental Affairs Section where I found myself from 1971 to 1973 was part of the United States Division. A lawyer by profession, my new boss came across initially as a crusty, arrogant, abrupt man. His wife, I later learnt, was seriously ill. With some trepidation I told him that my prayer group was praying for her. He was overcome, and it was not long before he and his wife prayed the same prayer of conversion that Ardith and I had. They also began regularly attending our weekly multi-denominational charismatic prayer meetings. (Most of our two hundred and fifty regular attendees were Roman Catholic because that is by far the largest religious denomination in Ottawa, but the leadership was drawn from several denominations.)

Later, my boss was diagnosed with a heart ailment requiring surgery. Several of us laid hands on him and prayed with dramatic results. Having experienced a great warmth rush through his body, he declared himself healed. His doctor was skeptical but could find no evidence of his heart condition, and surgery was cancelled. Eager to share his newfound faith, my boss organized a large family gathering at his lakeside cottage in the beautiful lake-filled resort and vacation area north of Toronto known as Muskoka. (He was a wealthy man, and the "cottage" was actually a fifteen-room mansion with several outbuildings. He also had a classic 1920s mahogany speedboat.) He took me along for support.

Once the clan were assembled, my boss explained to their horrified ears that he had come to Christ, strongly emphasizing my own role. This drew many unfriendly glances in my direction, which grew even more unfriendly when my boss proceeded to describe the healing of his heart and promptly dove into the icy lake water – it was October – to demonstrate how well he was. I was no more prepared for this act than was his family, and I have to say it tested my faith. He not only survived this experience but lived for many years thereafter, regularly playing tennis and skiing. A surgeon's knife never went near his chest. We lost touch some time after I left Ottawa to retire to Vancouver, but a few years ago I received a cheque in the mail from a lawyer representing my former boss' estate. He had died peacefully in his sleep and had left me a small bequest. It was a touching if unusual gesture.

There are two images that come to mind when I think about my first and biggest challenge in my new job managing Canada–U.S. environmental relations. One is of a paratrooper hitting the ground running and the other, perhaps more apt given my lack of training, is of being thrown into a pool in order to learn to swim. I was asked to play an ever-increasing and ever more central role in the negotiation of the world's first major international environmental agreement. It can be legitimately characterized as a global environmental milestone. I am talking about the Canada–United States Great Lakes Water Quality Agreement signed by President Nixon and Prime Minister Trudeau in 1972.

A fuller explanation of the need for the Agreement and a characterization of its content are set out in appendix III. It is sufficient here to say that shallow Lake Erie in particular had such low levels of dissolved oxygen that it could no longer sustain fish life. Algae, fertilized primarily by phosphorus produced by various human activities, was decomposing on the bottom and absorbing the oxygen. Canadian scientists discovered that we were nearing the point where this process would become irreversible. That discovery provided the impetus for the negotiation of an agreement that would require massive and rapid reductions in phosphorus inputs. We also needed to set the stage for dealing with the many other contaminants that future technology would be able to identify and address.

My own role in the lengthy negotiation process began modestly: organizing planning meetings, ensuring the right people were present, taking minutes, assigning tasks to various experts in the several disciplines involved, and writing or editing reports. Initially, it was almost like working in a new language because I had little understanding of the subject matter and no familiarity with the scientific terms that were used routinely. My brain had to adapt and fast, much as it had done many years earlier when I began selling tickets at the bus depot to earn my way through university. I guess I am a quick study because I soon found both my ability and my role evolving. Our team was headed by a very senior diplomat who had many other demanding responsibilities. As a result, he tended to preside rather than lead. As his number two, I found myself increasingly acting as de facto team leader, pulling together contributions from the environmental and other experts and frequently serving as the principal spokesperson at the actual negotiating sessions. When specific technical issues were debated, the lead would be taken by the appropriate expert, but I would find myself summing up the positions taken and discussing ways in which we could reflect our conclusions in the proposed agreement.

The initial draft agreement provided by the United States was, in our judgement, far too vague, and our counter draft was much more detailed and demanding. I sent it by diplomatic courier to our embassy in Washington for urgent delivery to the U.S. State Department. The urgency reflected the fact that we were shortly to meet in Washington with our U.S. counterparts. It was important that our draft be on the table along with the American one to improve our chances of achieving our objectives. I was, therefore, appalled to receive a telephone call from the Canadian Embassy's Counsellor responsible for environmental issues telling me that the mail clerk had reported that the draft agreement had been sent to our Consulate

General in New York by mistake. I started to pray that this error would somehow be corrected and, before too long, my contact called me back to say that he had found the draft in his in-basket when he had returned to his office from the Embassy mailroom. Neither he nor the mail clerk was able to explain how the draft got there, but the bottom line is that he delivered it to the U.S. State Department in time.

There were some amusing moments during the months of negotiations which followed. For example, one of our team members was a blunt engineer representing the Province of Ontario named Bill Steggles. Halfway through the negotiations, one of the U.S. team members, a salty old U.S. Coast Guard Captain responsible for regulations controlling discharges from ships, remarked that he had finally figured out how Robinson and Steggles worked together. Robinson reached out and appeared to be patting the Americans on the back but he was really feeling around for the best place for Steggles to stick the knife in. I must admit we did have the "good cop, bad cop" routine down pretty well. It was an excellent early lesson for me on the value of federal–provincial co-operation.

Another key player on the team was Charles Bourne, an English-born-and-educated law professor from the University of British Columbia who was spending a year in Ottawa on loan to the Department of External Affairs (as our foreign ministry was called at that time). He had a mind like a steel trap, a great asset, but I remember him best for initiating the great "which" hunt. Unlike his U.S. counterpart (who became a great friend of mine, even visiting us here in Vancouver after my retirement), Charles strongly preferred the relative pronoun "that" to "which." As we moved to finalize the agreement, Charles went through it, changing virtually every "which" to "that," thereby becoming forever known to us all as "Charles, the which hunter."

One other anecdote is worth relating as a matter of historical interest, but it is not in the least amusing. H. R. Haldeman, President Nixon's Chief of Staff, headed the U.S. team that came to Ottawa to prepare for the president's visit. He is the most senior of the White House officials who later were jailed because of their role in covering up the infamous Watergate burglary that led to President Nixon's resignation. That was all yet to come, and I had no idea how powerful this man seated across from us was. What I can say is that he was extraordinarily arrogant as he peremptorily demanded this and that arrangement. Finally, the senior Canadian diplomat at the table felt it necessary to point out that we were in Canada and that our views had to be taken into account. The word "livid" is associated with anger, and it literally means "turning white from the loss of blood to the head." That was Haldeman's reaction, but, to his credit, he bit his tongue.

The Great Lakes Water Quality Agreement was not just the first of its kind in the world; it has been extraordinarily successful. Both the initial problems identified in the Lakes and the nature of the Agreement's remarkable success are described in appendix III. I would, however, be very remiss if I did not pay tribute to two individuals who played crucial roles in bringing such an effective agreement into being: Frank Stone and Jim Bruce. Jim, as Director of the Canada Centre for Inland Waters in Burlington near Toronto, led the team that discovered that the phosphorus release from the bottom sediments was becoming irreversible. That discovery brought home how little time we had to reverse the eutrophication process in Lake Erie. Moreover, he was able to persuade his American scientific counterparts of the validity of the Centre's conclusions, thereby providing much of the impetus needed for the negotiations to begin. Jim also played a key role during the actual negotiations. The respect in which he was held by his American colleagues was very evident. He went on to occupy top positions in Canada's Department of Environment and he became, after his "retirement," the number two official of the World Meteorological Organization in Geneva. Jim was one of Canada's gifts to the international community.

Frank was an ambassador-level Foreign Service Officer on loan to the Department of Environment, occupying the same position as I assumed on a permanent basis two years later in 1973. He looked and talked like a cross between an untidy academic and an Ottawa Valley farmer. However, he had one of the best conceptualizing minds I have encountered. It was he who conceived of and articulated the institutional elements of the Agreement that transformed it from a simple short-term gross pollution control arrangement into the dynamic instrument that brought about ever-better protection of the Great Lakes as our detection technology improved in subsequent years. Frank went on to become Canada's High Commissioner to Pakistan and later received other ambassadorial appointments, but he died much sooner than he should have. I wish I had told him how much I admired him and how much he was owed by our country.

These two men personify the happy marriage between science and diplomacy that produced this groundbreaking Agreement. The far-sighted structure we created not only has stood the test of time but has, for four decades, brought real benefits to the largest navigable inland water system in the world and to the tens of millions of people who live around it. To be part of this process was for me both a real privilege and a remarkable learning experience. It kindled in me a deep concern for protecting both our environment and the people who are or could be adversely affected by harmful changes in that environment.

That heightened and informed concern is very much in keeping with the concept of Christian stewardship – of our obligation before God to care for His creation. Stewardship is an integral part of my Christian faith. With hindsight, I can also see that the lessons I learnt through my "immersion" in the Great Lakes played a huge part in the measure of success I was later to achieve in my subsequent nearly twenty-year career in the environmental part of government. More broadly and more importantly, the effectiveness of the cleanup process itself is proof that success can be achieved in addressing the environmental challenges that science identifies, provided there is the political will to put in place what is needed.

CHAPTER 36

CANADA UNDER ATTACK

Soon after our arrival in Ottawa, we bought our first home: a lovely, long, stone and brick five-bedroom "high ranch" bungalow on a sizable, beautifully treed, and well-landscaped lot. It was located in an attractive neighbourhood among larger homes ten minutes' drive from the city centre and very close to two major hospitals and other medical buildings. Not surprisingly, there were many doctors among our neighbours, so many that some people called the area "Pill Hill." For those readers who know Ottawa, we were on Roger Road near the Smyth Road medical complex in Alta Vista. We later grew to love our home and even renovated and expanded it, but initially we wondered if we had made a big mistake. The reason will perhaps seem very strange.

In the twelve years of our marriage and of my working life, we had never owned a home. Nearly nine of those years had been spent abroad in low-cost environments where we also benefited from housing and other allowances and diplomatic tax-free purchasing power. Simply put, we had no idea how low the purchasing power of my basic salary was back in Ottawa. Nor did we have any idea of the cost of maintaining a house, especially a sizable one in an upscale area. Because our savings from those low-cost years abroad were substantial, the purchase price of the house presented no problem. Buying more or better furniture or even curtains for the very large living room, however, proved beyond us, at least initially, largely because we needed to install new central air conditioning, a new furnace, and new double paned windows. Unintentionally, we had become slaves to our home: house rich and cash poor. That said, the purchase proved in time to be inspired. It was a wonderful neighbourhood for the children, it was within easy walking distance to good schools, it had minimal traffic, and we had several neighbours with whom James, who still lives in Ottawa, remains friends to this day. It also proved to be a good investment.

When we returned to Ottawa in the fall of 1970, Canada was experiencing a major security crisis caused by bombings, kidnappings, and later murder carried out by terrorists in the name of Québec separatism. A Québec Provincial Cabinet Minister and a British Consul in Montreal were kidnapped. The Cabinet Minister was murdered, but the Consul was later released in a negotiation that resulted in the terrorists being permitted to leave for Cuba. Prime Minister Trudeau had activated provisions for special powers under the War Measures Act to combat this threat. Many Quebeckers were arrested without normal due process in an effort to head off further violence, an action which proved controversial, especially in Québec.

We were, of course, aware of these developments, but the full impact of what was going on did not really hit us until we took Diana and James out trick-or-treating on Halloween. A fellow Foreign Service Officer and his wife had invited us to join them and their children in the annual canvass for goodies. They lived in Rockcliffe, Ottawa's most prestigious neighbourhood, where the Governor General, the Prime Minister, and the Leader of the Opposition maintain their official residences. Most of the ambassadors and high commissioners accredited to Canada do the same. (One of the exceptions was the Malaysian High Commissioner, whose official residence was across the street from ours, two houses down.) Rockcliffe is a beautiful area situated beside the wide Ottawa River that separates the provinces of Ontario and Québec. There are many old trees and stately homes surrounded by substantial, attractively landscaped properties. It did not, however, look so beautiful on that occasion because of the large number of military vehicles and heavily armed soldiers patrolling the streets. Indeed, as our children set out excitedly on their door-to-door quest, trailing us behind them, we were escorted by two soldiers with their automatic weapons at the ready. I never thought I would ever see such a sight in Canada. After all, we are deservedly known as the peaceable kingdom. Happily, there has never been a repeat of that sad experience.

To return to more mundane matters, the winter of 1970–71 produced a record snowfall of fourteen feet (more than four meters) and provided us with a surprising benefit. The snowbanks were so high that they afforded us the privacy that our absent curtains should have. Neither of our children had ever experienced snow, but they took to it very quickly and even more enthusiastically. James and Diana, clad from head to toe in warm snowsuits and fleece-lined boots, quickly learned to make snowmen, snow forts, and snow angels, which are created by lying down in the snow and sweeping the white powder with the arms to create the appearance of wings. Throwing snowballs was, of course, a major part of the fun, but an even more enjoyable game soon developed accidentally.

Because of the substantial overhang of our roof, an ever deepening crevasse was created between our exterior walls and the mounting snow. Inevitably, James fell into the crevasse, and his sister soon followed. Fortunately it happened directly in front of our floor-to-ceiling living room picture window. Neither child could climb out, and they soon began banging on the glass. Just like the St. Bernard rescue dogs of Switzerland, I ventured forth to save them. Sadly, this turned into a game, and I was constantly putting my winter clothes on and off as I continued my rescue missions. There was not much tail-wagging on my part.

The most fun was had when we took them to the toboggan hills – racing down, trudging back, falling off, and screaming throughout. People living in places without real winters do not know what they are missing. As the children grew older, more sophisticated winter sports like skiing and skating became part of their lives as did ice hockey for James. I will never forget the ice-cold hockey arenas at six in the morning, heated only by the passion of over-partisan parents.

Of course Ottawa-style winter is not all fun. Living as we do now in comfortable retirement on Canada's mild coast, I remember well and do not miss in the least out-of-control cars skidding on ice or stuck in snow banks, driving in blizzards, the nightmare of freezing rain or ice storms, and the joys of keeping a long two-car driveway clear. That first winter in our new home taught me all about driveways. The record snowfall was made even worse because that particular season had few if any thaws. Normally Ottawa experiences several, which have the effect of reducing snow buildup. We could not afford a snow blower, and, as the snow banks mounted, I found myself unable to throw the snow high enough to keep it from coming back down. That once-wide driveway got narrower and narrower as the winter proceeded. Sadly, it did not get any shorter. James reminds me that he used to take great delight in being on the top of the snow pushing back what I was throwing up. Particularly disheartening was the city snowplows' habit of coming along our street just after I had finished clearing my driveway. The resulting wall at the end of the driveway usually contained packed-down, icy snow, very tough to shovel.

In subsequent years, we bought a snow blower for ourselves, and James was able to use it to earn money clearing neighbours' driveways. The challenge was ensuring that he did ours first. The reader will not be surprised to learn that, when James bought his own house many years later, our main housewarming gift was a very large and powerful snow blower.

CHAPTER 37

"COUNSEL FOR CANADA"

Because Canada and the United States share such a long boundary, air and water quality issues affecting both countries arise frequently. In addition, sometimes one country wishes to undertake an activity such as constructing a dam or diversion that could affect water flow or levels on the other side of the boundary. The Boundary Waters Treaty of 1909 sets out the obligations of each country to the other in such matters. The Treaty also enabled the creation in 1912 of the six-member International Joint Commission (IJC). The IJC exercises its responsibility in two different ways: by making binding decisions and by submitting, at the request of one or both governments, advisory reports on matters of concern. The decision-making authority is limited to matters involving increases in water levels caused by activity on the other side of the boundary. Such increases are prohibited except when approved by the IJC or explicitly covered by the written consent of the government of the affected upstream country. The normal route is to apply for an IJC Order of Approval. For example, the extensive flooding that accompanied the construction of the St. Lawrence Seaway, which enables oceangoing vessels to travel four thousand kilometres inland, is covered by several of these Orders of Approval.

My job at External Affairs included serving as "Counsel for Canada" (i.e., spokesman for the Government of Canada) at IJC proceedings. IJC hearings are typically held near the site of the subject of the hearings, and my role meant that I was able to visit several places in our huge country that I might not otherwise have seen. Sometimes I travelled to represent the Government outside of IJC proceedings. One such occasion stands out in my memory.

Some history is needed. Boeing, the giant aircraft maker located near

Seattle, greatly increased its production during the Second World War and needed more electric power. In 1942, the United States successfully applied for an IJC Order of Approval to raise the height of power-producing Ross Dam on the Skagit River, which flows south from British Columbia into Washington State. In the event, the height of the dam was not at that time increased, but the Order of Approval remained in force. In the early '70s, Washington State's Bonneville Power Commission indicated its intent to raise substantially the height of the Ross Dam using the authority of the old wartime Order of Approval.

Environmentalists in both British Columbia and Washington State were outraged at the prospect of the Skagit Valley becoming an artificial lake because the Valley contains a mix of coastal and inland flora, including masses of rhododendrons, that is considered by experts to be unique. Acting on behalf of many of these environmentalists, a Vancouver lawyer, John Fraser, who to this day is a strong advocate for environmental causes, was considering challenging the IJC Order of Approval in court on the grounds that it had not been acted upon for so long and that the concerns which the IJC would have to address in the 1970s were not given any consideration at all in the wartime atmosphere of 1942. The group that John Fraser represented was called the ROSS Committee, always spelt with capital letters because it was an acronym for "Run Out Skagit Spoilers," a clear indication of the general mood. My task was to make the opposing case at a large, angry meeting in Vancouver convened by Fraser, not a fun prospect.

The Canadian government's position was straightforward enough. The IJC Orders of Approval provide an essential legal underpinning for numerous water level–changing projects along the international boundary across the country. The most important is the St. Lawrence Seaway. A challenge in court questioning the validity of such an Order could open the way for challenges elsewhere that are not in the Canadian interest. Needless to say, this view was not very popular, and I found myself engaging in a fairly sharp exchange with Mr. Fraser. I had no idea that I would one day be working for him.

In 1973, as mentioned earlier, Frank Stone returned to the diplomatic service from his temporary position as Director of International Relations in Environment Canada. The vacancy seemed tailor-made for me, and I hesitated not at all when I was invited to apply for it on a permanent basis. I saw the opportunity as heaven-sent. Becoming a diplomat in environmentalist's clothing not only corresponded to the new interests I had acquired through my work with the Great Lakes cleanup, but, more importantly for our family, it would enable me to provide a permanent home for Ardith without the stress of going abroad. It would also remove any constraints with respect to sharing my beliefs. I had, however, no idea what this move might mean in terms of career progression. Environment Canada was a very large department full of scientists and engineers, and I thought it rather unlikely that, with my limited qualifications, I would advance much beyond the position that was being offered to me.

My duties were similar to those in my last position but with one very big difference: perspective. Working for Environment Canada meant that I would always be trying to maximize protection for Canada's environment rather than managing a particular part of the larger relationship with the United States. Thus, I would use my knowledge of international affairs to encourage and equip my former diplomatic colleagues to find creative ways to encourage our American friends to respond meaningfully to our environmental concern of the moment. My staff and I would prepare detailed advice and briefing papers that explained what was at stake and outlined the best case that could be made. It might sound like duplication, but what it provided was depth and knowledge for diplomats whose own knowledge of and background in environmental issues were typically limited. I also dealt directly with officials of the U.S. Environmental Protection Agency. We often shared a similar perspective, and it sometimes proved possible for us to resolve potential problems in both directions before diplomatic intervention was required.

Environment Canada was divided into "Services," each headed by an Assistant Deputy Minister (ADM) who reported to the Deputy Minister, the permanent head of the Department. He or she in turn reported to the Minister of the Environment, who was both a member of the Cabinet and a Member of Parliament. I was located in the relatively small policy and planning service, but the main work of the Department was in the much larger services dealing with such matters as national parks (which was added later), atmospheric environment (weather), fisheries and oceans (later made a separate department), forests, wildlife, land and water management, and environmental protection (i.e., pollution control).

During my nearly four years heading International Affairs, I dealt with almost all of these services from time to time and came to respect enormously the quality and dedication of the people who worked in them. In short, they understood and loved what they were doing, and that made for a very good and productive working atmosphere. Many were highly respected in their chosen fields well beyond government and often well beyond Canada. An example was my boss, a distinguished wildlife biologist. His international reputation and contacts were very helpful in the role he played in bringing about the first Stockholm Environment Conference and the subsequent creation of the United Nations Environment Program (UNEP), headquartered in Nairobi.

Blair Seaborn, the Environment Department's Deputy Minister in the 1970s, was, like me, a former Foreign Service Officer who, at a much earlier point in his career, had served as Canada's Commissioner on the tripartite (India/Canada/Poland) Truce Commission in Vietnam set up after France's withdrawal from Indochina. On one memorable occasion I accompanied him to a meeting with visiting U.S. Secretary of State Henry Kissinger because there were, as usual, some environmental issues on the agenda. As soon as Secretary Kissinger entered the meeting room, he made a beeline for Blair and gave him a big hug. I had to wait until we were driving back to the office to find out that Dr. Kissinger's enthusiasm upon seeing Blair had to do with Vietnam. Blair was reluctant to give details, but he told me that, while he was serving on the Truce Commission, he had been helpful in conveying messages between Hanoi and Washington. For Kissinger to react like that, Blair must have been very helpful indeed.

I might add that I have a great deal of respect for Blair, who played a crucial role in the development of Environment Canada in its early years. It was created from parts of various departments, and he sometimes had to deal with rivalries and jealousies among the heads of those various parts. His diplomatic skill was much needed. I saw him as both a mentor and a role model. He had so much integrity and was not easily intimidated. I remember one occasion when a Minister wanted to use a government aircraft to take some friends to visit the Arctic. Blair flatly refused to sign off on this obvious misuse of government funds. I should add that, in my experience, such abuse was rare. After his retirement, Blair very successfully chaired more than one environmental assessment panel managed out of the office that I headed at that time.

One result of the role I played was that I became known to many in the Department, especially at the senior levels. Thus, when the Assistant

Deputy Minister heading the Environmental Protection Service (EPS) decided to strengthen the policy and negotiating skills within EPS, he thought of me. I was invited to apply for the recently vacated position of Director General of Air Pollution Control despite my very limited knowledge of that area of work. The invitation notwithstanding, I was genuinely surprised to receive the appointment, given that the others under consideration were so much more knowledgeable. Fortunately, the directors reporting to me were first-class, and, despite their undoubted disappointment at losing out to an uninformed outsider, gave me excellent support. My learning curve continued and got a little steeper.

My new job allowed me to reconnect with the International Joint Commission. Although the Commission was set up to deal with boundary waters, both governments asked it to play a role with respect to trans-boundary air pollution issues as well. To that end, the Commission established an International Air Quality Advisory Board with three Canadians and three Americans. I was soon appointed Canadian Chair of the Board and, together with my five colleagues, began investigating complaints about trans-boundary air pollution.

One investigation was particularly memorable for a reason that will no doubt amuse the reader. The issue was pretty straightforward. Reynolds Aluminum in upstate New York was emitting fluoride, a by-product of aluminum processing. Much of this fluoride was crossing the St. Lawrence River and landing on a First Nations reserve near Cornwall, Ontario. The effect was to contaminate the grass being eaten by the cattle on the reserve with the result that the cattle were losing their teeth. I visited the reserve on behalf of the Board. To demonstrate the seriousness of our purpose, I agreed to put my head inside a cow's mouth. Talk about air pollution! That was gross! I do not recommend including that procedure in future investigations, but I am pleased to report that we were able to persuade the New York authorities to impose tighter controls on Reynolds.

The Air Pollution Control Directorate was responsible for testing automobile emissions in a lab located in the Ottawa area. When I visited it for the first time, the manager suggested that we use my car to demonstrate how the process worked. To my embarrassment, it worked all too well. My car failed, but a few adjustments to the carburetor later it smelled like roses, so to speak.

The main challenge in my new area of responsibility was to negotiate agreed air quality objectives with all of Canada's provinces. The whole point of federalism is to allow different parts of the country to make their own decisions within a defined range of responsibilities. That said, there are real advantages in having common standards in many fields, including environmental protection. The Canadian government has authority to legislate in the area of health protection, which includes airborne contaminants, but some air pollution is not considered a threat to health and was traditionally regulated by the provinces. We established a federal–provincial task force and began to examine a long list of contaminants. Over time we were able to agree upon a set of objectives for both federal and provincial air-quality programs.

The agreement came just before the Deputy Minister asked me, as the newest of the EPS Directors General, to become acting Assistant Deputy Minister (ADM) in place of my boss, who was moving to another job. I had been Director General of Air Pollution Control for less than a year, and I fully expected to be returning once a new ADM had been found. To my amazement, I was confirmed a few months later as Assistant Deputy Minister heading the Environmental Protection Service. A new and very exciting chapter in my life had begun.

Chapter 38

"EMPIRICAL CHRISTIANITY"

For several pages, I have been focusing on my career and saying nothing about our home life. It was much more tumultuous than my relatively ordered office existence, and I may have instinctively been avoiding the subject. One of the consequences of writing a memoir, of course, is that it forces the writer to think about periods in his life that he might prefer to forget, especially periods when he felt that he performed poorly. We have on our refrigerator door, along with many family photos and paintings by our talented granddaughter, a cartoon given to us by a friend. It depicts a very harried-looking young father standing beside his equally harried-looking wife, who is seated on a couch. Facing them are their two children, a girl perhaps eight years old and her shorter brother perhaps two to three years younger: a perfect description of our family in the early '70s. The caption reads, "Your mother and I are feeling overwhelmed. You are going to have to bring yourselves up."

It is easy to understand why our friend gave us the cartoon. Ardith's health challenges and my struggles to cope with her dependence and with the long hours entailed by the increasing responsibilities of my work made us perfect candidates to be the couple it depicted. We never said those words to our children, but our actions – our performance – would have very often spoken for us. However, I am much comforted by the biblical teaching that God looks upon the heart and regards the motivation that He finds there as more important than the performance. Fortunately, at least from this distance in time, our children share this perspective and greatly admire their mother for her brave battle to play the role she wanted to play despite the challenges she faced. They knew that, despite her sickness and my absences, Ardith and I wanted to be good parents. Most of the time our motives were right, especially Ardith's, even if our performance might have been lacking.

The move from New Zealand to Ottawa, the purchase and refurbishment of our new home, and the adjustments in our lifestyle for both the children and us all presented challenges and therefore stress. Psychotic episodes can be triggered in sufferers from schizophrenia by external stress and Ardith began again to exhibit symptoms of the illness that had so beset her in New Zealand. Hospitalization was needed not long after we had settled in. Sadly, a second hospitalization in Ottawa proved necessary some years later, but the catatonia from which she had been healed through prayer in New Zealand never returned, and the psychotic episodes were less severe and often shorter than they had been down under. Indeed, there were periods of relative wellness. During such periods, the side effects of the inadequate medication available at the time could unfortunately be almost as debilitating as the illness.

I wrote earlier about what Christians call "God's provision," especially helpful, supportive people coming into our lives just when they are most needed. That happened again and again, sometimes in a church-related context, sometimes in a medical context. For many years, a wonderful, loving, holistic doctor, Libuse Gilka, cared for us in Ottawa. Her close associate, Saul Pilar, who shared her approach to medicine, moved to Vancouver not long before we did; he became our primary medical caregiver after our arrival on the West Coast. Over several years, we received support from members of the interdenominational charismatic prayer group about which I wrote earlier; some of these became close friends. I warmly remember a dear woman who was a teacher and a Grey Nun. The love she radiated and the inner peace she reflected were delightfully contagious; it was always such a joy just to be near her.

We attended an Anglican church in Ottawa's West End, a fairly long freeway drive from our home, because we had heard such good things about the rector (minister). For fifteen years he had directed a leprosarium in India. He became another very supportive figure for us, and we have warm memories of our attendance at that church. Much later, he left his role as pastor of a church to become a full-time counsellor ministering to people with emotional problems. We were much involved in helping establish that ministry, for which, when she was able, Ardith served as a volunteer secretary and receptionist.

There were also some fellow public servants who shared our faith and who became friends and prayer partners. I think in particular of an English couple whom I first met in 1971 when he was working for the Government as a senior economist specializing in energy matters. He had previously been with Royal Dutch Shell in the Netherlands. He later became Canada's top energy regulator, and we occasionally worked together on behalf of our respective agencies. In the more than forty years since we met, he and his wife have become our dearest friends despite the fact that, for most of that time, we lived in different cities. Their example, their practical support, their encouragement and, above all, their prayers have been so important to our well-being and to the maintenance of our faith, especially when Ardith's illness periodically resurfaced over the years. Now in their retirement, they work with the poor through the Salvation Army in Ottawa.

I titled this chapter "Empirical Christianity." Let me explain what I mean by "empirical." I wrote earlier at some length about the miracles of salvation and healing that were central to our early Christian experience in New Zealand. One of the better-known passages of Scripture has to do with "doubting Thomas." In John's account, Thomas, one of John's fellow apostles, cannot believe that Jesus has risen from the dead until he actually touches His wounds. In a gentle rebuke, Jesus responds: "Because you have seen me, you have believed; blessed are those who have not seen and yet have believed." I have some sympathy with Thomas because I would almost certainly not have believed in God, much less in the claims of Christ, if I had not experienced the transformation in my own life that I described earlier. The other miracles I saw later strongly reinforced that belief. In that sense you could say that, like Thomas, I saw (experienced) before I believed. As a consequence, I hold in awe those who believe so deeply despite not having had experiences as dramatic as mine.

I do recognize that faith, as the Bible puts it, is a gift from God so that no one can boast about having it. Yet, when my faith is tested, I am able to look back at these miracles and be encouraged. I cannot deny what I have seen and experienced. In that sense, I am an empirical Christian. Although the research scientists I later directed would have questioned the methodology, my initial prayer, however reluctant, was for me an experiment, and I was amazed that the results completely supported the hypothesis put forward by believers in Christ. I was not predisposed to believe, but their experiences and mine coincided, the essential element in proving a hypothesis.

Said another way, having successfully tested what I could – that Jesus is able to supernaturally transform and heal those who come to Him – it became reasonable to accept as valid His other claims as recorded in the Bible, such as the promise of eternal life. "Seek and you will find" is the Bible's challenge to us all, believers and skeptics alike.

CHAPTER 39

CONFRONTING ACID RAIN: FACT VS. FICTION

Becoming the Assistant Deputy Minister (ADM) at the head of the Environmental Protection Service (EPS) after such a short apprenticeship made my immersion in the Great Lakes seem like a swim in our apartment's pool. The broad range of challenges that the new position brought with it made my learning curve even steeper. In chapter 44 and appendix IV, I describe several of these challenges and the changes I made as well as the structure and activities of EPS. The single issue that dominated my years heading the Service was acid rain. Before getting into the specifics of that particular problem, I would like to say something about the origin and structure of EPS.

In the late 1960s, growing evidence of pollution and its damaging effects as well as calls for action such as Rachel Carson's seminal book, *Silent Spring,* were inspiring widespread environmental concern. The United States Congress responded by developing what became the National Environmental Policy Act (NEPA). NEPA was to have a far-reaching impact within and beyond the United States, which I will discuss later. One of the issues to be decided by Congress at that time was the form of the agency that should be created to carry out the environmental objectives of government.

There were two models under consideration: a separate, stand-alone agency or a service within an existing large department. Examples of the latter are the Fish and Wildlife Service and the National Parks Service in the U.S. Department of the Interior. Congress chose the agency model, and the U.S. Environmental Protection Agency (EPA), which was to be headed by an Administrator, was born. In Canada, we opted for the service model, and our counterpart to EPA was named the Environmental Protection Service (EPS), to be headed by an ADM within the newly created Department of the Environment. A Canadian ADM equates with a U.S. Assistant Secretary. The range of EPS responsibilities in Canada was very similar to that of EPA in the United States. I was the third person to serve as ADM of EPS, and I did so from 1978 to 1982.

Appendix V focuses on acid rain. It recounts the initial success we had in working with the U.S. Carter Administration through the joint working group structure set up to develop a control agreement and how that work came to an end with the election of a new U.S. president. What followed was a multi-year public campaign to encourage U.S. co-operation in ending the acid emissions. These emissions were threatening tens of thousands of Canadian lakes as well as forests, limestone buildings like those on Parliament Hill, and even human health. While Ontario's giant nickel smelters produced a great deal of the sulphur that was the primary cause of the acid rain, eighty percent of the acid deposition in Canada was coming from coal-fired electrical power plants in the United States, especially in the Ohio Valley. Appendix V adds further details about the nature of the problem and explains the remarkable lengths to which we went to persuade a reluctant U.S. administration to curtail sulphur emissions from power plants. It proved necessary for Canada to appeal directly to both the American public and the U.S. Congress over a period of ten years before the needed Canada–U.S. acid rain control agreement was achieved in 1991.

The Canadian campaign in the United States was begun under my watch. Our most effective work was spreading information, especially through magazines catering to outdoor enthusiasts, working with U.S. environmental and other organizations, such as the powerful National Rifle Association with its many duck hunters, and lobbying Congress. On a personal level, I sought out or accepted speaking engagements in American cities where I could preach the anti-acid rain gospel. Initially I sometimes appeared on panels that included a spokesman or two for the electrical utilities or others opposed to acid rain control. After a while, I learned not to participate in such panels for a very simple reason. My opponents could say anything they wanted, however outrageous, but I could not. I had to adhere strictly to what was scientifically established and use language like "the preponderance of evidence" or "the research to date strongly suggests." My presence and the measured language that I used merely tended to legitimize my opponents' fact-free assertions. I had, however, no shortage of opportunities to speak on my own. I have no idea how many American audiences I addressed but it would have numbered in the dozens over a two-year period. Once I was even invited to address the annual meeting of the New England electrical utilities association held in Boston. I received a very polite reception with minimal questioning; I found myself wondering why I had been invited. In a disarming display of American candour, one of my hosts made the reason very clear. "We wanted to see what our enemy looked like."

My most memorable speaking experience took place in Cleveland, Ohio. I was invited to address the city's premier business luncheon club. I was also told that the speech would be carried on a large number of cable TV outlets. Upon arriving at the hotel ballroom where the club met, I was stunned to see, posted at the entrance and around the walls, blue-uniformed men wearing flak jackets and carrying automatic weapons. Sensing my astonishment, my host assured me that this was solely for my protection in response to threats allegedly uttered by the coal miners' union. I have to say that I was not much reassured. I should explain that the principal sources of the coal burned by the power plants of the Ohio Valley were the mines of southern Ohio. That coal was very high in sulphur and the Ohio miners were afraid that strict acid rain controls would force the electrical utilities to buy low sulphur coal from the western United States instead.

I was, of course, aware of this situation, and my speech was tailored to an Ohio audience. After setting out the case for control, I addressed the coalminers' concerns head-on. I pointed out that, sooner or later, sulphur emissions would have to be seriously curtailed. There would be two options for so doing: bringing in low sulphur coal from the West or installing "scrubbers" in the power plants' smokestacks to remove the sulphur before it is released into the atmosphere. If the coalminers of southern Ohio wanted to protect their future, I argued, they should be putting pressure on the electrical utilities to install those scrubbers. It took some time, but eventually the coalminers' union accepted that message and became reluctant allies.

Despite our failure after President Carter's departure from office to make any progress through the joint working groups towards securing a Canada–U.S. acid rain control agreement, we did not completely abandon our efforts to make our case directly to the new administration. I remember in particular accompanying my boss, Mme Jeanne Sauvé, Minister of the Environment, to Washington. (She was later to become, as Canada's Governor General, a very gracious representative of Her Majesty the Queen.) The first person upon whom we called was James Watt, President Reagan's first Secretary of the Interior. His cavernous office made an immense impact with its huge floor-to-ceiling stone fireplace and the heads of virtually every North American animal worth hunting covering the walls. I immediately thought of Teddy Roosevelt, perhaps because of his association with parks and hunting. Secretary Watt received us in a very courteous and friendly way. However, to every point we made about the need to control acid rain, he replied, in effect, that we should leave "market forces" to address the problem. We pointed out that there was no economic link between the sources of the problem and the places where the impact was most serious and that there was an international border involved as well.

It soon became clear that we were making no impression, and we prepared to take our leave. As we departed, Secretary Watt made a comment that only I among the Canadians present understood. It was a reference to biblical "end times" and his point was that, since these would soon be upon us, there was little point in concerning ourselves about matters like acid rain. Frankly, I was so taken aback by the remark that I chose not to explain the meaning of his words to the Minister and her accompanying staff. For me, Christian faith entailed stewardship, a responsibility before God to care for His creation. I had never before heard Scripture used to make the opposite argument. The last place I expected to hear it was in a discussion of a major trans-boundary environmental issue between members of the Canadian and United States Cabinets.

The Minister and I later called upon a senior official at the U.S. State Department. He initially received us very courteously, but, as we pressed our case, that courtesy wore thin, and I felt that he was not being as polite as he should have been to a member of the Canadian Cabinet who was also a very gracious lady. It was entirely legitimate and appropriate for him forcefully to present his government's view, but not in a discourteous way. I said as much, and we left. It was not one of my better moments, and I am not proud of losing my cool. I guess it reflected the frustration we were all feeling. Afterwards, the Minister gave me a big hug and called me her "knight in shining armour." That raised my spirits.

The reader may better understand the level of frustration we were experiencing by reading this excerpt from a speech I gave to the National Academy of Sciences in Washington, D.C., in 1982. The full text is in Appendix VI.

> A major casualty of this manipulation of expertise has been an earlier agreement among Work Group I scientists on an environmental loading objective. There was general acceptance during the work group process that a loading of twenty kg of wet sulphate per hectare per year would offer a reasonable level of protection for most aquatic systems. Now, at the eleventh hour, the United States side of the work group completely refuses to accept this figure as a loading target. What makes this situation particularly disturbing, even absurd, is that at a twenty-three-nation conference in Stockholm on acid rain last summer, the United States representative endorsed a total sulphur-loading target approved by the conference that is nearly twice as demanding as the one produced in the Canada–U.S. work group. The Stockholm target is expressed in terms of total sulphur deposition, which complicates the comparison, but if you calculate the emission reductions required to achieve that target, it is almost twice as stringent as the target earlier accepted within the work group.

Chapter 40

CANADA-U.S. CO-OPERATION: AN ACID TEST

In October of 1982, a few months after I left my job heading EPS, I was asked to perform one last task in the acid rain campaign. It was to write and deliver, to the most prestigious American scientific audience we could find, the National Academy of Sciences in Washington, D.C., the speech from which I quoted in the previous chapter. Because of the blunt message it contained, the speech was approved at ministerial level and by our Ambassador in Washington. It was titled "The Rule of Law Between Nations – An Acid Test." Rather than presenting yet again a comprehensive summary of the scientific evidence supporting the need for acid rain control, its main theme was that Canada–United States trans-boundary environmental problems had been successfully addressed over the past several decades because the two countries were prepared to be guided by the results of joint or co-ordinated production of scientific data. I pointed out that, by manipulating these data for non-scientific reasons rather than allowing the scientists of both nations to work together freely within the acid rain joint Canadian–American task force structure set up for this purpose, the U.S. administration was not only refusing to face the reality of acid rain but was causing great damage to the institutions and principles that had governed Canadian–American environmental relations for the greater part of the twentieth century.

The speech was unlike any other given up to that time by a Canadian spokesman on this subject in that it directly contradicted a claim being made by the Administration to the U.S. Congress and public. That claim was that the work in the Canada–U.S. task forces set up to address acid rain was proceeding satisfactorily and that there was, therefore, no need for specific additional Congressional action. Copies of the speech were sent to every Senator and Representative. It is reproduced in appendix VI. I commend it to those interested in reading a succinct history of Canada–U.S. environmental relations.

Sadly, as noted earlier, it took until 1991 for a Canada–U.S. acid rain control agreement to be signed. Happily, the agreement has proven reasonably effective. A virtually identical agreement could have been signed as early as 1982 based on the understandings achieved by U.S. and Canadian scientists in the working groups. Instead, both countries needlessly endured nearly a decade of avoidable acidic damage. How blind are we who choose not to see.

One memory from my years at EPS has little to do with the environment but a lot to do with a major problem facing the world today. I was asked to brief a visiting group of "White House Fellows," highflying career civil servants from Washington, D.C., who had been selected for a year of special studies and travel. In the evening I attended a dinner given by the U.S. Ambassador in honour of these visitors. I sat beside a very intelligent and thoughtful man who was the CIA's Director of Satellite Programs.

We spoke about many issues, but what sticks in my mind is the comment he made about Congressional attitudes towards orbiting hardware as opposed to analysts. He said that he never had any difficulty getting funds from Congress to put yet another spy satellite into the sky, but he could not persuade the politicians to pay for enough analysts to understand the information that was being produced by the growing number of satellites. The result was information overload, an early indicator of a problem that today threatens to undo the advances in efficiency achieved by the Internet. If memory serves, no less a player than Microsoft has spent about $40 million trying unsuccessfully to create software to help computer users make a quick and easy differentiation between useful and useless information. One of my son's friends is a brilliant consultant in Toronto who has developed a method, tailored to specific activities, of training personnel to make this much-needed differentiation more efficiently. He is able to cite significant increases in productivity that flow from the application of this training. My conversation with the CIA's Director of Satellite Programs took place over thirty years ago, and we are still grappling with the fact that more information does not necessarily equate with better understanding, much less contribute to higher efficiency.

Chapter 41

AN EXPERIMENT IN COMMUNAL LIVING

The stories that make up our lives and help create who we are are not always flattering. What follows is a perfect example. When Diana was about eleven and her brother James eight, Ardith and I came to the conclusion that our daughter would benefit from a Christian boarding school experience. As part of our search for a suitable school, we visited one located in Brockville, a small town on the banks of the St. Lawrence River an hour's drive south of Ottawa. The school had been founded by an evangelical Christian community that had pooled its resources and purchased a very handsome, grey stone, former Roman Catholic seminary perched on a hill overlooking the river. All the staff and their dependents lived on the site, some in the main building and some in mobile homes. The former seminary included a fair amount of land, which the community had developed into a farm with both crops and animals. Among the animals were horses, and riding was one of the main outdoor activities for the students. Our daughter, who had learned to ride, was delighted, and I suspect that all other considerations melted away in her mind when she saw her favourite animals.

We were very impressed by the calibre of the staff we met, by their obvious commitment to their students, and by the attractive setting. It was midsummer, and the headmaster suggested that I take a holiday from my office and that our whole family be their guests at the school for a couple of weeks. We all did so, even our two young miniature apricot poodles. Ardith and I were given a tiny room – it seemed like a monastic cell – and our two children were "adopted" by two of the resident families. Ardith worked in the kitchen, and I was assigned some pretty basic agricultural tasks, best forgotten.

The community was highly disciplined, we discovered, and very hierarchical. Their central credo was "joy through repentance," a concept reflecting biblical teaching with respect to seeking forgiveness and receiving God's grace. James did not like the firm discipline he received from his seasoned temporary "parents" and resented not being with us. However, Diana blossomed. She bonded with the childless couple who cared for her indulgently and delighted in riding and helping look after the horses. Initially Ardith enjoyed the companionship with the other women working in the kitchen, but that was to change later. For me, the overwhelming feeling was relief. Others were not just helping me care for my wife and children; they had essentially taken over the job.

Consequently, I hesitated not at all when we were invited to continue the arrangement after the two weeks were up. It was suggested that I commute to my work. James was upset, Ardith was uneasy, and Diana was delighted. The arrangement continued well beyond the beginning of the school year. Sometimes I stayed overnight at our home in Ottawa, but most of the time I slept in Brockville. Inspired by the biblical accounts of the early Christians living communally, I was increasingly thinking about selling our home, giving the money to the Brockville community, and making our permanent residence there. Ardith was very opposed to this plan and grew increasingly upset over her experience of living in this highly structured extended family. She felt controlled and invaded, not least because of the emphasis on repentance and confession of personal failings. For me, that practice was less invasive and more helpful. All of us struggle with our better and worse instincts, and having someone else take on part of that very personal burden added further to my sense of relief. Eventually, Ardith's concerns won out. We left Diana there to complete the school year because she was so happy, but the rest of us returned to life in Ottawa.

I have since given a fair amount of thought to what attracted me to the Brockville community. I think it comes down to this. My three greatest burdens were largely taken from me: caring for my wife, whose illness created a greater than usual dependence, caring for my children, who presented the usual range of parental challenges, and struggling with my own shortcomings. If I am truly honest, I also felt that my willingness to give everything I had to that community demonstrated what a good Christian

I was. In truth, it demonstrated the precise opposite. I was running away from the responsibilities that God had given me.

The stay in Brockville taught me something about myself, but it also gave me an insight into the attraction that many cults have for those who join them: the complete removal of personal burdens. If we are to grow morally and spiritually – the essence of the Christian journey – then we have to face our burdens, not run from them. (I am not saying that the Brockville community was a cult, merely that its attractions and some practices mirrored one.)

I recently talked to our daughter about her happy experience in Brockville. She said that it had done her a great deal of good. Not only had it strengthened her beliefs and values, it also, because of the small size of the student body and of the individual classes, had enabled her to develop close relationships with girls much older than she. When she later entered the junior high school near our home and encountered the usual backbiting and bullying, the confidence she gained in Brockville enabled her to brush it all off. I was delighted to learn that my "mistake" had had one very good result. For James the stay in Brockville remains, as it does for Ardith, a highly forgettable experience.

CHAPTER 42

OUR POLITICAL MASTERS

Canada had been ruled by the Liberal party since before my return to Ottawa from Colombia in 1963. It is essentially a centrist party with leanings to the left. Since 1968, the party had been led by the charismatic Pierre Trudeau, but his popularity had fallen as the country endured large budget deficits, high inflation, and high unemployment. He was opposed in the 1979 election by the Progressive Conservative's thirty-nine-year-old leader from Alberta, Joe Clark. Clark's youth, inexperience, and somewhat hesitant public manner worked against him. Nonetheless, as was apparent to those watching the House of Commons' newly televised proceedings, Clark was also capable of incisive wit. One of his most famous quips was, "A recession is when your neighbour loses his job. A depression is when you lose your job. Recovery is when Pierre Trudeau loses his job."

Clark won the May 1979 election and was sworn in on June 4, the day before his fortieth birthday, as Canada's youngest prime minister. Having won only two seats in populous, Liberal-dominated Québec, however, his party fell five seats short of a majority in the House. That meant that he would need the support of another party to enact legislation and stay in power. The six members of the Québec-based Social Credit party (commonly called Créditistes) would have met that need, and Clark was able to induce one of them to join the Progressive Conservatives. To secure the support of the others, Clark could have offered them official party status, which normally required at least twelve seats. Such status would provide money for research and staff as well as more opportunities to address the House. He also could have offered special co-operative working arrangements or even a coalition, but, in a decision that was to prove fateful, he chose not to do so. Instead, he decided to govern as though he did not continuously face the possibility of defeat in the House and another election.

The new Progressive Conservative Minister of the Environment was none other than the John Fraser with whom, readers may recall, I had crossed swords eight years earlier at a meeting in Vancouver organized by environmentalists who opposed increasing the height of an American dam that would flood British Columbia's unique Skagit Valley. Our exchange had been sharp but not disrespectful. I wondered if my new boss would remember the encounter. It was not long before I found out.

Almost immediately after his appointment, Fraser found himself at the 1979 annual meeting with provincial ministers of the environment. It was being held in the beautiful resort town of Kelowna, British Columbia, beside scenic Lake Okanagan in British Columbia's wine country. As head of EPS, I was a regular attendee at such meetings, and I arrived shortly after the Minister. I entered the hotel ballroom where a pre-meeting reception was being held and saw him talking to some of his provincial counterparts. He turned, saw me walking towards him, and came quickly forward with his hand outstretched. "Ray, great to see you again," were his first words, quickly dispelling any apprehensions I might have had. He went on to apologize for giving me such a hard time in Vancouver so long ago. It was the beginning of a relationship that grew into a friendship that I still prize.

A change in government provides an excellent opportunity to describe the relationship in Canada at the federal level between senior career public servants and their political masters. In the United States, when a new president is elected, it is customary for him to make thousands of "Schedule C" appointments to government departments and agencies. These appointments can reach three or four levels below cabinet members or agency heads. While such a large number of appointments can mean that many experienced and capable people are replaced by those without that experience, it also means that the new president's priorities and policies are more likely to be strongly reflected within the bureaucratic structure.

The practice in Canada is very different. Under the Public Service Act, all Public Service positions up to and including those immediately below deputy ministers and agency heads are protected from political interference. Appointments to positions covered by the Act are made through a competitive process supervised by the Public Service Commission and, hopefully, are made in accordance with merit. Deputy ministers and agency heads are what are called "Order-in-Council" (Cabinet decision) appointments and serve at the pleasure of the Government. Nonetheless, the vast majority of these appointments over the years have been drawn from the career Public Service, and very few are political. The prime minister makes the final decision on the selection, usually on the recommendation of the head of the Public Service, who is called the Clerk of the Privy Council. The "clerk," as he or she is generally known, is also the Secretary to the Cabinet and effectively serves the prime minister in much the same way that a deputy minister serves a minister. The clerk also heads the Privy Council Office, staffed entirely by career public servants, that acts as a nerve centre of government controlling, for example, access to the Cabinet and Cabinet Committees whose decisions are so important for the operation of government. As noted earlier, the much smaller Prime Minister's Office (PMO) staffed by political appointees focuses on the politics of governing.

The Progressive Conservative party, like the Liberal party, was also a centrist party but with leanings to the right. The centrists among them were often called "Red Tories," and Fraser was of that persuasion. Clark himself was usually described as a fiscal conservative but was progressive enough on many social issues to be sometimes characterized as a Red Tory. The moderate socialist New Democratic party, which held twenty-six seats in the House at the time, dismissed both parties as essentially the same: "Tweedledum and Tweedledee." During my career, I worked in direct contact with fourteen Cabinet Ministers, both Liberals and Progressive Conservatives. I was never able to perceive a clear pattern of ideological difference between them. The differences were of a personal nature: energy, relationships with colleagues, interest in the portfolio, personality, intelligence, and competence. On that score I was generally favourably impressed, and I found at least two of them, one from each party, positively brilliant.

In my experience, politicians are often viewed unfairly. The pressures on them can be immense, both personally and professionally. A Canadian Cabinet Minister, for example, has to stay in touch with his home constituency, representing as best he can its interests, while also serving in Cabinet and on Cabinet committees where he is required to help make collective decisions on many subjects beyond his own portfolio or personal experience. In addition, he has to run a department of government, guiding its policies and approving its decisions, and do battle with his colleagues on behalf of his department and its area of responsibility. Further, he is required to speak on behalf of the government with respect to his portfolio in the House of Commons, at House committees, elsewhere in the country, and possibly abroad. This is a heavy load, especially in the more demanding, high-profile portfolios. Canadian Cabinet Ministers are always selected in part with an eye to the province and region they come from. Doing battle with their colleagues on behalf of their province, city, and region is another component of the job description. So is the fact that the issues many of them have to deal with can be very challenging, not offering easy solutions. One of the characteristics of newly appointed ministers is that they soon develop red-rimmed eyes from studying the briefing notes prepared by their officials late into the night. Their jobs are not easy. I would never have wanted a political career.

One of the differences between the Liberals and the Progressive Conservatives in 1979 had to do with federal–provincial relations. Generally speaking, the Liberals were interventionists, inclined to assert federal authority and even expand it through the use of funding. Clark was elected on the basis of a platform that included rolling back some of these "federal intrusions." A particular target of his new government was federal–provincial "duplication."

One of my responsibilities was to appear periodically before Cabinet Committees on issues involving environmental protection. On one occasion I was accidentally invited into the Cabinet room for the agenda item preceding mine. The person I found making a presentation was none other than Gordon Robertson, Secretary to the Cabinet for Federal–Provincial Relations, a very senior and experienced public servant nearing retirement who had previously served as Clerk of the Privy Council (i.e., as head of the Public Service) before being replaced by Prime Minister Trudeau's political appointee, Michael Pitfield. Chairing the Committee was the Deputy Prime Minister, the second-ranking member of the Cabinet, who, like Clark, was an Albertan. After Québec, Alberta tends to be the province most opposed to federal intrusions. Others present included the new government's most senior ministers.

Robertson, a much respected figure who passed away at the beginning of 2013, approached his subject in a very interesting way. He went through a detailed comparison of the powers of a Canadian province and those of the sovereign nations that had signed the Treaty of Rome, thereby joining what was to become the European Union. On issue after issue Robertson showed that the ability of a Canadian province to inflict economic harm upon other provinces was significantly greater than that of those European nations that had inflicted war upon one other within easy living memory. He cited such issues as labour mobility, professional credentials, discrimination against out-of-province contractors, provincial government discriminatory purchasing practices and even the limited availability of out-of-province Canadian wine in provincial government liquor stores. The cumulative effect, he pointed out, was to balkanize Canadian markets and reduce our competitiveness with foreign producers, no small matter in a nation so heavily dependent upon exports. In these circumstances, he concluded, the last thing needed was any weakening of the Canadian union. The ministers' faces as they listened and the questions put to Robertson were very telling, as were their comments to one another when the presentation was over. It was clear that Robertson's argument had made a considerable impact.

The Clark government was in power for such a short time that I cannot be sure what effect this eye-opening exposé of Canadian economic disunity had on government policy, but it certainly impressed me. As it happened, it was not long before I myself was engaged in a related discussion. It had to do with the possible application of federal–provincial duplication avoidance policies to environmental regulation. I was invited to meet with Dalton Camp, whose name will be well known to Canadians of that era. Camp was the legendary éminence grise, the thinker behind the throne of the Progressive Conservative party, a role he had played for decades.

I had no idea what to expect, but I was determined to do my best to demonstrate the value of a continued federal role in environmental protection. Mr. Camp was courtesy itself, and we soon were deeply into the subject. I put forward two arguments, one related to health and one to economics. Under the constitutional division of federal–provincial powers, the protection of public health is a shared jurisdiction. The contaminants that are typically controlled by environmental regulation are often related directly or indirectly to public health. Given the importance of health protection, I asked, is it not wise to apply what I called "the double protection of federalism"? With respect to economics, I drew from Gordon Robertson's picture of economic disunity to argue that, if common standards of environmental protection are not applied across the country, provinces could use less stringent regulations as a means of attracting investment or providing a competitive edge to their own industries, thereby further balkanizing the country. Moreover, the effect of using lax regulations as a competitive tool could be to pull down standards to the lowest common denominator. Mr. Camp responded very positively to these points, but, as with the broader question of economic disunity, the Clark Government's term in office was too short to indicate whether my arguments had any effect.

I remember vividly a cold winter evening in 1979 sitting in John Fraser's parliamentary office where a group of us were celebrating his birthday. Several present were very much enjoying the conviviality of the moment, a fact that no doubt fuelled the very candid conversation about what lay ahead the next day. The Minister was in no doubt that his party was about to be defeated in a confidence vote in the House. Prime Minister Clark had won office on a platform that included a promise of tax cuts. His first budget included a proposed tax of eighteen cents a gallon on gasoline aimed at slowing the economy and curbing inflation. It was presented as "short-term pain for long-term gain." His erstwhile ally and fellow Progressive Conservative, Premier Bill Davis of Canada's most populous province Ontario, denounced the tax, which polls showed to be widely unpopular. Emboldened by the swing against Clark in popular opinion, the main opposition parties declared their intent to vote against the tax proposal, thereby defeating the government and bringing on another election. The five remaining Social Credit party members from Québec, who held the balance of power and were annoyed at Clark's earlier refusal to work with them, said they would support the Prime Minister only if the revenue from the proposed tax was allocated solely to Québec, a clearly unacceptable demand.

As the evening wore on, our host put on a display of his extraordinary talent as a mimic, copying the voices and mannerisms of fellow members of the House on both sides of the aisle. The subject matter had mostly to do with the impending defeat, but the mood was strangely upbeat; the challenge faced by the guests was to identify the individuals who were being mimicked. It was remarkably easy to do so, a clear tribute to Fraser's ability. Towards the end of the evening, he told us that one of his greatest fears as a minister was answering a question in the House of Commons in the voice of the questioner. He seemed completely resigned to the possibility that he would not have that problem much longer.

Clark's Progressive Conservatives did lose the confidence vote next day in the House and were defeated in the resulting February 1980 election by Pierre Trudeau's Liberals. The Liberals won with a comfortable majority, mainly because so many voters in Ontario switched their support from Clark to Trudeau. After 1982, as the economy faltered, Trudeau's popularity steadily waned. Facing almost certain defeat at the polls, he retired from politics in 1984. His Liberal party was crushed in the election held later that year by incoming prime minister Brian Mulroney's Progressive Conservatives. Indeed, Mulroney won the largest majority in Canadian history, including the vast majority of MPs from his home province of Québec, a traditional Liberal stronghold. One of them elected later in a by-election was to become one of the two most impressive politicians for whom I worked in my career. He later went on almost to succeed in breaking our country apart before becoming premier of Québec.

Chapter 43

PUBLIC, AND CHRISTIAN, SERVANTS

In 1971, shortly after our return from New Zealand, I became a regular attendee of a lunchtime Bible study group held at the National Energy Board, Canada's primary energy regulator. It was one of several such groups scattered throughout the federal Public Service, but I was not aware of one operating at that time in my own department, Foreign Affairs. A few years later, well after I had moved to Environment Canada, which had two Bible study groups, a few of us from different departments met in our home to consider creating some way of linking the different departmental groups.

The prime mover of this initiative was Don Page, a senior historian at Foreign Affairs, which, by that time, had its own study group. From this meeting the Public Service Christian Fellowship (PSCF) was born, to be co-chaired by Don, the real leader, and me. I was the decorative icing because of my high rank. Don was later to be appointed Vice President Academic of Trinity Western Christian University near Vancouver. He is currently Trinity's Professor Emeritus, Graduate Studies.

The plan was to arrange periodic weekend conferences with invited inspirational speakers and for Don, me, and possibly others to visit and encourage individual Bible study groups. We also hoped to increase the number of departmental groups. Don already had contacts with a comparable organization in Washington, D.C., and we hoped to arrange exchanges with our American friends. In the event, our prayers and efforts were well-rewarded. The PSCF grew to about fifty Bible study groups across the government, including one on Parliament Hill. We held several successful conferences, and contacts between the groups soon took on a life of their own. One Cabinet Minister and two other Members of Parliament were among those who addressed us. We also had a few American speakers over the years, and some of us visited Washington.

On one such occasion, I stayed in a magnificent old mansion that had assumed the title "the Christian Embassy." It was primarily a place of outreach to Washington's sizable diplomatic community, but it also served as a kind of elegant bed and breakfast for visiting Christian speakers. I was delighted to discover that one of the other guests was Dr. James Houston, the Oxford don who founded Regent College at my old alma mater, the University of British Columbia. The College was originally created to provide graduate theological education to lay people, but in 1979 it added a program to train students to become clergy. It was truly exciting to meet a man of such depth, scholarly achievement, and Christian commitment. I also missed by one night meeting Chuck Colson, one of President Nixon's former senior advisers who had been imprisoned for his part in the Watergate affair. After his release and personal conversion, he had founded a highly successful prison ministry. Sadly, he passed away recently.

My role as a founding PSCF Co-Chairman did provide me with some opportunities to meet some very interesting people and to be in some unusual situations. One such situation was particularly upsetting to our family football fan, James. I was asked to lead the Montreal Alouettes' prayer time before their game against our son's idols, the Ottawa Roughriders. I have to admit that I was really intimidated by the size of these huge men as they crowded around me to listen to my words of exhortation and to join in my prayers. I must have been truly inspired and inspiring because Montreal went on to crush Ottawa in the game. I do not know if James has yet forgiven me.

On another occasion, I was asked to lead a three-day mission sponsored by the Chinese Baptist Church for Vietnamese "boat people," refugees who had fled Vietnam, often in small boats, following the North Vietnamese victory in their home country. This was a very challenging invitation on several levels. There was so little in common between my audience and me, and I would have to speak through an interpreter. The Bible tells us that God's strength is made perfect in our weakness. I can tell you that I felt very weak indeed as I prayed about what to say and contemplated the circumstances under which I would have to deliver my remarks. In the event, God must have intervened because the words came readily; even having to stop after every sentence or two for the translation did not break the flow as I feared it would. I was later told by the church leaders that the response had been very positive. It is, of course, entirely possible that the interpreter, one of the pastors, merely gave his own excellent series of sermons over the weekend. Afterwards, I was presented with a beautiful painted wall hanging with an Old Testament inscription in Chinese that read, "My kindness shall never depart from thee." It was a perfect match in colour with the upholstery of the sofas in our living room, where it still hangs.

The most intimidating Christian audience I ever addressed was the annual dinner of the Ottawa Evangelical Ministerium, a gathering of evangelical pastors in the Ottawa area. What could I, a layman and decorative PSCF Co-Chairman, possibly have to say to these professionals? Fortunately I had the "boat people" experience behind me, and I truly believed that God would give me the necessary words, especially since there would be no interpreter to fill in the gaps. He must have responded to my prayer because I was invited back in a subsequent year. The theme I pursued that evening was the importance of congregations protecting and supporting their pastors and their families in regular, focused prayer. I urged the pastors to recognize that need and to set up prayer groups dedicated to that purpose.

Not long ago, I was asked to put together some advice for a young Christian public servant who wanted to know how best to reflect his faith in the workplace. I thought back to the many times I had spoken to gatherings of fellow public servants about that very subject. I was never much of a teacher or preacher but was an exhorter, a spiritual cheerleader. I used to use the word "servant" a lot because it is so much a part of Jesus' teaching and, of course, coincides with the formal name of the Canadian bureaucracy: the Public Service of Canada. I am repeating below the advice I wrote for that young public servant as a way of conveying what the Public Service Christian Fellowship (PSCF) was trying to do. I ask readers, especially those who do not share my faith, to consider what is written here and ask themselves what they would think of private sector employees or public servants who acted upon this advice. The scriptural quotations that I have used are taken from the popular paraphrase The Message.

> 1 Corinthians 9:19-22 – "Even though I (the apostle Paul) am free of the demands and expectations of everyone, I have voluntarily become a servant to any and all in order to reach a wide range of people: religious, nonreligious, meticulous moralists, loose-living immoralists, the defeated, the demoralized

– whoever. I didn't take on their way of life. I kept my bearings in Christ – but I entered their world and tried to experience things from their point of view. I've become just about every sort of servant there is in my attempts to lead those I meet into a God-saved life. I did all this because of the Message. I didn't just want to talk about it; I wanted to be in on it!"

This passage makes it clear – you have to meet people on their own ground. Ardith and I received a remarkable lesson in that truth even before we became Christians. [The reader will recall the story.] I sold a large American station wagon to a funeral director in a city 500 k north of Wellington, New Zealand, where we were living. It became the first silver blue hearse in that country decked out with little curtains sewn by the funeral director's wife. The funeral director, Gordon, invited me to speak at his Rotary club and to stay in their home. He and his former ballerina wife Margaret were a delightful couple, very much in love with one another in sharp contrast to the collapsing marriage in our own home. I invited them to visit us and we spent a lot of hours in each other's company. Over several months, they attended raunchy plays with us and otherwise entered into our lifestyle without hesitation or criticism, all the while displaying this remarkable love for each other which they gradually revealed was centred on the third person in their marriage, Jesus Christ. Clearly they were following Paul's example laid out in the Scripture verses quoted. For me that means that the first rule of the Christian in the workplace must be the acceptance of those around him without condemnation of their behaviour patterns.

The second lesson that I learned from Gordon and Margaret was that those who wish to witness to others need to earn that right. Their lives must be the witness before their words can be. In the workplace that means earning the respect of one's fellow workers in terms of attitude towards the work, of personal competence and of treatment of fellow workers.

Philippians 4:6 – "Don't fret or worry. Instead of worrying, pray. Let petitions and praises shape your worries into prayers, letting God know your concerns."

As in every other aspect of life, a Christian in the workplace is called to pray about his daily tasks and for those with whom and for whom he works. I admit that I tended to follow that instruction in times of stress and not as a regular pattern. I would undoubtedly have experienced much less stress if I had been more obedient to that scriptural admonition.

Clearly, these comments apply to any workplace but those which follow are tailored more to the specific circumstances under which public servants work.

Mark 12:17 – "Jesus said, 'Give Caesar what is his, and give God what is his.' "

A public servant needs to understand what he owes to "Caesar" and what he owes to God. Clearly it is the public servant's duty to serve the Government. That means not simply to work hard at the task at hand but to apply his imagination and creativity to helping the Government function as effectively and efficiently as possible. If he is in a position of preparing advice to Government, then that advice should be well researched and reflect sincere judgement. His obligation to God in this process is to ensure so far as possible that that advice is in accord with his Christ-informed conscience. As a practical matter, that means that he tells the truth whether or not that truth is welcome. I am not, I hope, being unduly naïve. Expressing advice in a manner most likely to be acceptable is normal practice but keeping the advice honest rather than self-serving or obsequious can still be feasible within those limitations.

The obligation to "Caesar" reasserts itself once the Government has made a decision on the matter which was the subject of advice. Whether or not the public servant agrees with what Ministers have decided, it is his clear responsibility to execute as vigorously as possible the will of those elected by the people. That responsibility goes beyond responding to the government of the day. He must also carry out the letter of the legislation under which he is functioning. The potential exists, of course, for a conflict to develop between a Minister's instruction and a particular legal requirement. It is the public servant's obligation to point out that legal requirement and even seek, in serious circumstances, the advice of the Justice Department. If the Minister persists and the Deputy Minister concurs, then I believe the obligation to Caesar requires that the public servant obey. If in the event that doing so would offend his Christ-informed conscience, then a request for reassignment or resignation would have to follow. If the issue is unclear, James 1:5 has the answer. "If you don't know what to do, pray to the Father. He will help."

Mark 10: 42-45 – "Jesus got them (his disciples) together to settle things down. 'You've observed how godless rulers throw their weight around,' he said, 'and when people get a little power how quickly it goes to their heads. It's not going to be that way with you. Whoever wants to be great must become a servant. Whoever wants to be first among you must be your slave. That is what the Son of Man has done: He came to serve, not to be served – and then to give away his life in exchange for many who are held hostage.'"

I repeatedly used the word "servants" in public addresses to underline the need for public servants to reflect Jesus' teaching as recorded in this well-known piece of Scripture. The Public Service is a hierarchy marked clearly by "rug-ranking," e.g. such perks as reserved parking spaces, large corner offices, comfortable couches and private washrooms. More importantly, there is a chain of command that reaches through the Deputy Minister to the political level. Obviously that chain of command must be respected and that was the theme of my earlier remarks. Yet Jesus' teaching appears to turn that chain of command on its head. What we must understand, however, is that what Jesus is talking about is attitude not authority. A Christian public servant must treat those around him, especially his subordinates, with courtesy, respect and compassion. To do so not only displays the attitude of a servant but also earns the right to share his faith. Keeping an open door and caring about one's fellow workers' problems are central components of this attitude. Taking seriously, for example, performance evaluations and trying to help those who are having difficulty are marks of a caring superior who understands what a Christian servant is called to be.

The idea of being a servant goes well beyond the immediate workplace. This is where the word public comes in. Bureaucrats, to use that unattractive word, are supposed to be servants of the public but so often their behaviour suggests the opposite. For the Christian, such behaviour is completely unacceptable. Caring about those for whom one's programs are designed is an integral part of carrying out Christ's admonition to be a servant. That applies both to those who have direct interaction with the public and those who design or manage public services.

Hebrews 10:24 – "Let's see how inventive we can be in encouraging love and helping out, not avoiding worshiping together as some do but spurring each other on ..."

The Public Service of Canada is very large and impersonal. Moreover, many of the jobs that exist within it are not very fulfilling and some are depressingly boring. Even with jobs that are intrinsically interesting, individuals can become discouraged by the apparent lack of opportunities for promotion or new challenges, especially in a contracting Public Service. Also their morale can become seriously impaired if their work is repeatedly devalued or their advice frequently ignored. With impending budget cuts, there is also fear about future employment. The Christian public servant, when faced with these conditions, has the reassurance of knowing that he is not only working for God but is loved by Him. His non-Christian workmate has no such reassurance. Reaching out in love and providing encouragement is as important in relationships with peers as it is with subordinates.

Matthew 18:20 – "And when two or three of you are together because of me, you can be sure that I'll be there."

It is also important to reach out to fellow Christians, encouraging them to come together for prayer and Bible study ideally on a regular basis. If a Christian public servant has a private office or ready access to a meeting room, it is appropriate to make use of that facility for group prayer but not on government time. Such gatherings should take place before work begins or after it ends or during the regularly scheduled lunch break.

Clearly the primary motivation of the PSCF was sharing Christ's message of redemption and salvation. A major part of that effort was to encourage its membership to be as "Christ-like" as possible in the workplace. As a former senior executive in government, I have no hesitation in saying that our country would benefit enormously if there were many more similarly motivated public servants running what is unquestionably the largest "enterprise" in Canada.

Chapter 44

STEPPING DOWN FROM EPS

Another major issue that I faced while heading the Environmental Protection Service was the impact on human health of lead in gasoline. I remember vividly a presentation made in Ottawa by scientists from the University of British Columbia on the effect of low levels of lead in the blood on the motor development of children. I had invited my opposite number in the Health Department to join us for this presentation, and he had brought several of his experts with him. Together we watched with mounting concern as the data demonstrated with increasing certainty that remarkably low levels of lead in blood have a significant impact on growing children.

At the end of the presentation, my colleague from the Health Department and I agreed that we had a moral duty to act. From that point on, while I remained at the helm of EPS, I pushed hard to put the necessary regulations in place. A major issue was finding an acceptable additive to gasoline as an alternative to lead. That issue was resolved, but it nonetheless took five years and a lot of vigorous exchanges at meetings with other departments and affected industry before the ban on lead in gasoline was imposed. Would it have happened anyway if I had not pushed so hard? Undoubtedly, but it might have taken a couple of years longer. Who knows how many more children would have suffered as a result? Later research showed that the scientists, in fact, had understated the problem. The effects were worse than supposed and occurred at even lower levels of lead in the blood than had been thought. A moral duty indeed!

I am one of those who saw emission-free hydrogen gas as the fuel of the future, initially supplementing and perhaps eventually replacing fossil fuels. Production of hydrogen gas is itself energy-intensive, and the most practical way at present of producing it in significant quantities without adding to climate-changing carbon dioxide emissions is with nuclear energy. In the 1970s, EPS entered into an experiment in partnership with Ontario Hydro, Canada's largest producer of electricity, to produce hydrogen gas through electrolysis at nuclear plants during periods of low demand for electricity. (Electrolysis separates hydrogen from oxygen by running electricity through water.)

We were motivated at the time by the need to reduce Ontario's dependence upon coal- or oil-fired power plants as a way of combating acid rain. Greenhouse gases and climate change were not yet central to our environmental concerns. The idea was to store the hydrogen gas produced in this manner at nuclear plants and burn it during times of peak demand to increase the generating capacity of those plants and reduce the need for power from plants dependent upon fossil fuels. It was also a way of maximizing the use of nuclear plants, which, unlike conventional power plants, are never shut down (except for maintenance) but continue to generate the same amount of heat during high and low peak demand cycles. In the event, Ontario Hydro chose not to continue the experiment primarily for financial reasons. I have always seen that decision as extraordinarily short-sighted. Unfortunately, EPS had neither the budget nor the facilities to pursue the experiment on its own.

I made it a regular practice to visit EPS regional offices across the country. They were on the front lines, so to speak, and necessarily had different perspectives on many of the issues that we dealt with. Those perspectives were very valuable to me, as were the exchanges I had with my provincial counterparts. While some provinces more than others resented the "Feds," I greatly respected the challenges which many provincial officials faced and always urged my staff to be as supportive and co-operative as possible. What happened on the ground was what mattered, and it was important that we in Ottawa not find ourselves in an ivory tower. The bigger provinces tended to take the lead in enforcing both their own and federal environmental regulations, while smaller ones looked to us for more assistance and intervention. Our job was to adapt accordingly.

Given my roots on the West Coast, I especially appreciated meeting with provincial officials in Victoria, where I could also visit my mother and grandmother. I also enjoyed meeting with my own staff at our substantial regional office in Vancouver. At that time, the Vancouver EPS regional office was located in the upmarket suburb of West Vancouver, not far from where Ardith's parents lived. I always stayed with them on those trips, a blessing for me and a saving for the government. On one such occasion, I attended over the course of three evenings a series of lectures at UBC's Regent Theological College given by London's celebrated Christian author and speaker, John Stott. I do not at this distance in time remember the topics he addressed in each lecture, but I do remember very well what happened to me during one of them. It was to change my life.

Some readers may respect my commitment to my work as head of EPS, and others will approve of my efforts with respect to the PSCF. But the truth is that I had become consumed by the challenges of both, and the long-suffering members of my family were paying the price. I had forgotten the lessons learned in New Zealand, and my priorities were not what they should have been. Ardith, in her desperate effort to fight her illness and the side effects of medication and still be a wife and mother to her husband and children, needed much more support and much more of my time and energy. My children had the right to have their father come home at a reasonable hour, not to be exhausted much of the time and not to be absent entirely on so many trips. I justified what I was doing because of the importance of my work both with EPS and the PSCF, but I also knew that both ministered to my ego much more than did the responsibilities of home. I had fallen into the same trap that I had with the Christian school community in Brockville: running away from my primary responsibilities.

I should not, therefore, have been so surprised at the answer I got when, during one of Dr. Stott's lectures, I silently asked God, "Why did you give me such a hard job?" "So that you could give it up," was the unmistakable answer that immediately flooded my brain. I had never had such a dramatic response to a questioning prayer before, nor have I since. I had and have absolutely no doubt that it was an answer to my question, but I spent months trying to persuade myself that all it meant was that I should pray more in my work.

I finally came to understand that the answer was aimed directly at my ego and my ambition. I was well regarded by both my political masters and my Public Service peers, and I was in the midst of the action. I did not want to walk away from that ego-massaging environment, but I had to. I informed both the Deputy Minister and the Minister that, because of my wife's situation, I considered it necessary to step down and seek a less demanding position. My decision was not without risk. There was no obvious alternative on offer, and I could not afford simply to stop working.

Both the Deputy and the Minister were very supportive and understanding, but their thoughts, no doubt, immediately turned to finding a suitable replacement. My thoughts were focused on what I was going to be doing next. I had only four days of uncertainty. I guess that is all that my faith could stand. The head of the small office that ran the government's environmental assessment process decided to leave, thereby creating an ideal vacancy. Because no promotion was involved, no competition was needed. Early in 1982, I found myself with the new, grand-sounding title of Executive Chairman, Federal Environmental Assessment Review Office (FEARO). Another new chapter in my life had begun.

CHAPTER 45

ENVIRONMENTAL ASSESSMENT LEGISLATION BLOCKED AGAIN

Because of my success at EPS, the staff at FEARO, I was later told, were delighted to learn of my appointment. They were fully aware of the challenges faced by the office, and they not unreasonably hoped that my arrival at the helm was an indication that the powers that be not only recognized those challenges but also saw the need for additional help. What a disappointment they were about to have! Instead of a hotshot as their new boss, they had inherited a sad sack.

Looking back, I can see that I was experiencing the classic symptoms of burnout. I felt like a failure, I had little interest in my new work, and my addiction to adrenaline, so magnificently fuelled by the atmosphere of combat that permeated my previous job, was now being experienced in the form of withdrawal. I would like to say that I got over this condition in a few weeks, but it was more like months. Fortunately, my immediate subordinates, Bob Connelly and John Herity, were first class and had no trouble managing the environmental assessment process despite my initial minimal input. Indeed, they were pillars of strength throughout my nearly ten years at FEARO. With their help, I came to understand the importance of the environmental assessment process to the effective management of government. I also learned the hard way about the considerable challenges that FEARO faced both in developing and managing that process as well as securing the authority needed to ensure that it was followed. That growing understanding fuelled my recovery, and I was soon throwing myself into the new tasks at hand.

While dependent administratively on Environment Canada, FEARO operated at arm's length from the Department, and, for policy purposes, I had a direct reporting relationship to the Minister. Along with the other Assistant Deputy Ministers, I, as head of EPS, had been a member of Environment Canada's Management Committee, which was chaired by the Deputy Minister. As head of FEARO, I continued to sit on the Committee, but as a courtesy. Although I was expected to keep the Committee abreast of important developments in the field of environmental assessment, it did not play a role in managing FEARO as it did with respect to the Department's individual Services such as EPS. As a consequence, I had very little contact with the Deputy Minister and met only very occasionally with the Minister. It was a strange new world, not at all at the centre of the action. That situation would change dramatically in the years to come, but I had no way of knowing that.

I will spare the reader a detailed description of the history and practice of environmental assessment at the federal level in Canada. I do, however, need to give enough history to provide a reasonable understanding of the situation in which I found myself and of the challenges that lay ahead.

Legislated environmental assessment began on this continent with the enactment by the U.S. Congress in 1969 of the National Environmental Policy Act, always known as NEPA. The circumstances of its passage are outlined at the beginning of chapter 39. That Act set out in some detail the obligation of U.S. federal departments and agencies to carry out the assessment of the environmental impacts of projects undertaken, funded, or regulated by those departments and agencies. The President's Council on Environmental Quality was established to provide detailed guidance and regulations and a measure of oversight for the environmental assessment process. It was not long before the need to apply NEPA's provisions to various projects across the United States became the subject of court case after court case. Critics say that the bureaucracy resisted this incursion into their decision-making processes, while those of a more charitable nature might say that the bureaucrats were operating in new territory and were simply making mistakes. Either way, projects were held up, and, in the eyes of NEPA's opponents, chaos reigned. (I should add that the situation gradually improved as U.S. civil servants learned to apply the rules in ways that would satisfy the courts.)

In 1973, newly created Environment Canada appointed a small group to recommend the best means of establishing a federal environmental assessment process in this country. The apparent chaos created initially by

NEPA in the United States was very much in the minds of Canadian decision makers, and, not surprisingly, there was reluctance to create a legal process that might result in a similar situation on this side of the border. Instead, a Cabinet Directive was formulated that called upon Canadian government departments to undertake the environmental assessment of projects initiated, funded, or regulated by them.

However, the Directive contained few details as to how this was to be done. A body called the Environmental Assessment Panel was established to oversee the process and possibly carry out public consultation as appropriate. Respect for the Directive varied among departments and it would be fair to say that its application was, to put it mildly, uneven. In due course, the Panel was renamed the Federal Environmental Assessment Review Office (FEARO) to distinguish it from the individual project assessment panels, but its powers were no greater. Indeed, power is too strong a word, as its tools were confined to persuasion and education.

Notwithstanding these limitations, FEARO's creative and committed personnel had, by the time I arrived, persuaded several departments to apply reasonable environmental assessment procedures to their projects and had undertaken a few public reviews of larger, more controversial proposals. In short, a process had begun to evolve, but it still needed to be codified and placed on a more authoritative footing.

The opportunity to move in this direction was created by the Liberal electoral victory in 1980 when Pierre Trudeau replaced the Progressive Conservatives' Joe Clark as Prime Minister. (I understand that Clark's environment minister, John Fraser, had told FEARO that he wanted the environmental assessment process placed on a legislative basis, but his government was defeated before any action could be taken.) The Liberal election platform contained a commitment to enact environmental assessment legislation, and FEARO naturally hoped to build on this commitment to secure government approval to submit an environmental assessment bill to the House. Indeed, shortly before I joined FEARO at the beginning of 1982, the new Liberal environment minister, John Roberts, had tried unsuccessfully to bring a proposal for environmental assessment legislation before the Cabinet. Despite the commitment in the new Liberal party's election platform, it had proved impossible to get the item on the Cabinet agenda. The reasons included a lack of consensus among affected departments in support of this initiative and concerns within the Privy Council Office itself over the appropriateness of one part of government fettering the decision-making power of another part.

Breaking through the wall of opposition within the Public Service had proven impossible at that time. The essence of the problem lies in the fact that, by its very nature, environmental assessment legislation must be aimed primarily at government itself, not just at the private sector, as is the case with most governmental regulatory intervention.

Further, the government's internal decision-making processes offer maximum opportunity for opponents within the Public Service to prevent any proposal they do not like from reaching Cabinet level. I described earlier the central role played by the powerful Privy Council Office. PCO is responsible for preparing – effectively controlling – the agendas of the various Cabinet Committees. Typically, a proposal affecting more than one department would be expected to reflect interdepartmental consensus or near consensus before being placed on the relevant agenda. The stated objective is to reduce demands on ministers' time. The effect of this practice is that senior officials in the affected departments are often left to make the value judgements and trade-offs that are a normal part of significant decisions. This is of concern because the public might reasonably expect such trade-offs to be made by publicly accountable elected politicians, the ministers. Continued failure to reach a consensus among affected departments can doom a proposal even though a minister or two may support it. A strong minister can usually get his proposal onto the relevant Cabinet Committee's agenda without such consensus but often at the cost of having all or most of his colleagues briefed to oppose him. A common result is a decision to send the proposal back to officials to seek consensus once again.

In my opinion, such consensus was not forthcoming with respect to environmental assessment legislation because senior officials opposed to this proposal correctly saw the legislation as a threat to their control over the flow of information and advice to ministers. That control is tightly held because the continued influence – read power – of those officials depends upon it. However, we were able, almost two years later, to achieve a compromise – the development of an Order-in-Council (Cabinet Directive) setting out the environmental assessment process in some detail.

To the surprise of many, Prime Minister Trudeau, conscious of his unpopularity as demonstrated in the polls, announced his decision to retire from politics. The Environment Minister at the time, Charles Caccia, a deeply committed and effective environmentalist, told me that the only opportunity to get the proposed Order-in-Council approved by the Cabinet would be at Trudeau's last Cabinet meeting, which would be coming up shortly. Suddenly we had a deadline, and the FEARO staff negotiating wording with the Justice Department had to pull out all the stops to get an acceptable draft ready in time. Some arguments with Justice over language remained unresolved, but, because the Order was supposed to be a "guideline" rather than a legally binding document, we reluctantly signed off on language we regarded as less than ideal. In that less than perfect way, the 1984 Environmental Assessment and Review Process Guidelines Order (EARPGO) was born. We had no idea how important that Order was going to become.

The EARPGO acronym sounds like a cheerleader's slogan, and that was certainly one of FEARO's functions, encouraging other parts of government to apply the Guidelines Order. However, we also acted as a coach, providing increasingly detailed advice on process and methodologies to the various departments. The Environmental Assessment and Review Process (EARP) was based on the premise that the primary responsibility for undertaking an environmental assessment should lie with the department or agency responsible for the project. Placing that responsibility on those departments was designed to encourage a culture of decision-making in which environmental effects would be automatically included along with financial, technical, and engineering considerations. For what we called initial evaluations, aimed at determining whether a more thorough environmental assessment was warranted, that work was typically done within the responsible department or agency. For larger, more sensitive, or more controversial projects, the work was often carried out by the actual proponent, which could well be a private sector corporation. If a more detailed assessment showed that there was potential for significant adverse environmental effects or that public concern warranted a public review, then, in accordance with the Guidelines Order, the Minister responsible for approving the project was expected to refer the proposal under consideration to the Minister of Environment for public review by an independent panel.

At that point, it became FEARO's responsibility to organize and provide support for the public review. Review panels were appointed by the Environment Minister on the advice of our office. Appointees normally included non-governmental experts in relevant disciplines who had no connection with the proponents or opponents. If, as was often the case, the project in question affected aboriginal communities, whether First Nation, Inuit, or Métis, we would also recommend the appointment of a native person to the panel, ideally with relevant technical or scientific expertise, but not from the affected band. One of FEARO's senior officers, occasionally me, would usually act as panel chairperson in order to promote procedural consistency. We were often able to make a small sum of money available to those intervenors whose applications for funding contained proposals for research or preparation of presentations clearly relevant to the issues before the panel. In addition, technical experts hired to advise the panel could provide a limited amount of advice to intervenors.

Critics of the process were always concerned about "levelling the playing field," and the modest attempts to assist intervenors were limited steps in that direction. Similarly, the hearing procedures themselves were designed to be "user-friendly" rather than court-like, that is to say, less intimidating. We wanted to hear from affected people, not just hired professionals. The high level of expertise on our panels, which often contained people very well-regarded in their fields, made them more than capable of telling the difference between informed and emotionally driven comments, but it was important that those affected have a full and fair opportunity to express their concerns. Surely being heard is at the centre of a democratic, open society.

In appendix VII, I have put together for the interested reader a number of anecdotes drawn from different parts of our vast country that both illustrate the points I have been making and tell us something about the people who live in this very large slice of the world's real estate. FEARO's panels and supporting teams operated in widely diverse places all over this land – from the High Arctic to Toronto, from Labrador to Vancouver Island. We became strongly aware of the ecological diversity and richness of Canada and also very sensitive to the fragility of some of our stressed ecosystems. What impressed me most, however, was our most important resource: our people. I am confident that those who choose to read appendix VII will be similarly impressed.

In every public review we managed we saw our fellow citizens working hard to influence decisions that could affect them, usually in circumstances that were controversial and sometimes deeply stressful. Everywhere we also found a deep concern for the natural environment, a sense that, collectively, we are and must be faithful stewards of this great land. The settings have been dramatically different: a tiny Inuit church on Baffin Island, an elegant ballroom in downtown Vancouver, a community hall in rural Prince Edward Island, a native meeting house near Shefferville, Québec, a resident's home in Etobicoke near Toronto's Pearson airport, a farmer's field next to Moose Mountain Creek in Saskatchewan, and an open-air First Nations' potlatch on the Pacific coast. Yet, in each of these, we found people willing to engage in respectful dialogue aimed at producing well-informed, sensitive decisions.

CHAPTER 46

A NEAR HUG FROM A QUEEN

Throughout the 1980s, FEARO continued to make advances in the methodology and application of environmental assessment. Following the issuance of the Guideline Order setting out the environmental assessment process, we created and funded the Canadian Environmental Assessment Research Council (CEARC), but not without opposition from some other departments. The Council was made up of leading academic and government scientists as well as environmental assessment practitioners. Some of the Council members undertook research projects with the limited funds that we had available. FEARO staff were active in the International Association for Impact Assessment (IAIA), and we developed good working relationships with universities in Canada and in other countries. Among these was the University of Aberdeen in Scotland, which had extensive experience with North Sea oil drilling and production. We also had a number of bilateral contacts with agencies similar to our own in other countries. I will focus on three: the Netherlands, New Zealand, and Australia.

At that time, the Netherlands was arguably the leading European country in the environmental assessment field. We developed a pattern of annual conferences, alternating between Ottawa and The Hague. So useful did these exchanges prove to be that the two governments decided to sign a formal agreement governing them. I will not soon forget the signature ceremony. It was timed to coincide with the visit to Ottawa of Queen Beatrix of the Netherlands. She did not, of course, sign the document herself, but instead presided over the signature ceremony. It took place outdoors on a beautiful sunny day beside the historic Rideau Canal locks that link the Canal and the Rideau River to the much larger and lower Ottawa River.

When I was presented to Her Majesty, I naturally told her that I was the son of a Canadian Army officer who had participated in the liberation of Holland from the Nazis. I regularly told my Netherlands colleagues about this connection with their country, and they always responded very emotionally and with a big hug. The Queen made a slight movement forward and then stopped. I like to think that I was almost hugged by a queen. Queen Beatrix, who at age 74 recently abdicated in favour of her son Willem-Alexander, spent the war years with her family in Ottawa where her younger sister was born. The maternity ward of the Ottawa Civic Hospital was declared Netherlands territory for the occasion.

I always attended the conferences with our Dutch colleagues held in or near Ottawa, but I went only once to The Hague. I was consistently impressed by the calibre of the presentations by both my own staff and the Dutch, and these occasions deepened my understanding of the technical and scientific side of our work. But I have to say that my warmest memory of my visit to the Netherlands was enjoying a rijsttafel (rice table), a magnificent Indonesian meal of superb proportions, hosted by our Dutch colleagues. Never have I seen such a variety of dishes.

Another warm memory arising from these exchanges was of a presentation made to me by the leader of the Netherlands delegation at the conclusion of one of the Ottawa conferences. He and one of his colleagues struggled onto the stage carrying a huge box covered with wrapping paper and an enormous bow. They put it down in front of me and he explained that it was a superb piece of European engineering brought across the Atlantic to assist us in our challenging work. Intrigued, I began to open it and discovered another box within. About four or five ever-smaller boxes later, I finally came to the gift itself. Before revealing what it was, it is important to underline that the business of environmental assessment is predicting the future – what effects are likely to result from the project under review. I pulled the final wrappings off and out came a beautiful crystal ball, a superb piece of European engineering indeed! It still graces the mantelpiece in our living room and carries me back to those interesting days so long ago.

I earlier mentioned when describing my move to Environment Canada that it was populated with people of remarkable accomplishment and commitment, many of them well known nationally and internationally. That was equally true on a much smaller scale with the staff in FEARO. I saw this most clearly during international conferences where it was obvious how much respect there was for the work we were doing in Canada in this new, expanding field. We were among the leaders in the world, and it is instructive to note that the European Union's Directive on Environmental Assessment, which drew heavily from the Netherlands experience, contains concepts that have their origin in Canada. How ironic and sad it is that Canada is currently moving away from these advances even as they continue to be applied in the ever-expanding European Union.

We also developed exchanges with New Zealand and Australia, although they were much less frequent because of the distance and cost. Both countries, of course, are much more like our own than is the densely populated Netherlands. Moreover, they have large indigenous populations who, like our First Nations and Inuit, are often affected by major development projects. For that reason, we always included First Nations personnel familiar with environmental assessments in our delegations. The New Zealanders did the same with respect to the Maoris. While some of the technical exchanges were similar to those with our Dutch colleagues, we also gave particular attention to issues affecting our respective indigenous peoples.

One of those issues was the weight that should be given to what is called "traditional knowledge." Such knowledge was often of particular importance in providing us with a picture of the environment as it existed in earlier times. It was made up in large measure of the collective memories of the tribe that had lived in the affected area over the millennia. Mainly as a result of the long-standing efforts to develop land claims agreements in this country, a fair expertise has developed among consultants in pulling together the memories of tribal elders, traditional stories of the past, and archaeological evidence to help calculate the extent of the traditional territory occupied in earlier times by a particular tribe or band. That kind of expertise can also be applied to acquiring a picture of the state of the environment in the past. Exchanges with the New Zealanders in particular helped us hone this process so that it could be used more effectively in specific environmental assessments.

One exchange in particular with our friends from "down under" stands out in my memory. It took place in a rural setting north of Montreal, and we had a number of First Nations participants, including the chief and some elders from the tribe in whose traditional territory we were meeting. There were Indian dances in which we all participated and some traditional foods that we all enjoyed, but the highlight was a presentation put on to sensitize all of us to the collective trauma experienced by our native peoples as a result of forced attendance at residential schools. We watched a very moving documentary on the subject and then listened to native speakers talk about their own agonizing experiences. I have to say I wept and felt a great deal of shame, as did many of my colleagues. (Both the Canadian and Australian Prime Ministers apologized years later to their respective aboriginal peoples for the pain inflicted on so many by the residential school systems employed in their respective countries.)

The best part of working in FEARO was the spirit that animated those who were my colleagues. Perhaps there was something of the David and Goliath mentality because of all the opposition we encountered. One result was the good working relationship that existed between virtually all of us and which even led to some intra-office marriages. I have never met a group of people who cared so much about what they did for a living. Indeed for most I think it was probably more a calling than a living. It was their caring that appealed to me, but it was their competence that fuelled our success. That commitment and that competence were going to be tested in the late 1980s, only a few short years later, in a way none of us could possibly have imagined.

The panel reviews were the most visible components of FEARO's work, but some of the greatest achievements were in advancing environmental assessment methodologies and procedures. These achievements were recognized by professionals in many countries. Appendix VIII characterizes some of the contributions made by Canadians in and outside FEARO and its successor, the Canadian Environmental Assessment Agency.

Before jumping ahead in the narrative to 1990 to conclude this tribute to the men and women with whom I worked, I want to make particular mention of Ghislaine Kerry, my excellent special assistant over so many years. She added immensely to my own efficiency. Fortunately for her, I needed a lot of managing. After practicing on me Ghislaine became a very successful manager elsewhere in government.

One of my happiest memories is of the warmth and fellowship of the last Christmas party I attended in the Ottawa office. Perhaps it was because everyone knew I was leaving, and all the ladies wanted to dance with the departing boss. We had also experienced our most successful year ever.

The environmental assessment legislation on which we had worked so hard and for so long had been submitted to the House of Commons six months before and was certain to be approved. Some of those attending had written a stirring ballad with multiple verses about our struggles and triumphs sung to the tune of Gilbert and Sullivan's "Ruler of the Queen's Navee." (The lyrics sounded better than they read, so the reader will be spared them.) Euphoria reigned, at least for one night, and it felt really good.

PART V

PUBLIC AND PRIVATE CHALLENGES

Chapter 47

LIVING WITH SCHIZOPHRENIA

In October of 2012, I was asked to speak to 150 third-year psychology students at the University of British Columbia about living with schizophrenia. I gave a lot of thought to what I should say to those young people. I was very aware that many, maybe most, of them almost certainly would have some contact, professional or personal, with the awful disease that had had such an impact over so long a period on my wife, my children, and me.

As an aid to organizing my thoughts, I put together three lists describing in point form the effects on Ardith, the effects on me, and the effects on each of our two children. It was exceedingly depressing, very different from writing this memoir in which I have avoided such detail except where essential to our story. The professor who invited me explained that she wanted to encourage among her students feelings of empathy towards the individuals and families who suffer from the effects of schizophrenia. That was my challenge: appearing likeable and needy at the same time. I guess the Spanish word *simpatico* sums it up.

I had never done anything quite like this before: to speak in depth about such personally stressful events before so many total, possibly critical, strangers. I am an experienced public speaker, but this was different. I admit to getting somewhat teary-eyed as I recounted some of the particularly painful memories, but I knew that if I was less than candid the exercise would have little point. My prepared speech lasted twenty minutes and the question-and-answer period another thirty-five. It was clear from the number and nature of the questions as well as the many tear-filled eyes looking back at me that it had been "mission accomplished." There was a great deal of empathy in that room. Many students came up to thank me afterwards, some with stories of schizophrenia in their own families.

I was asked to do it again and also to meet with smaller groups of medical students (which I have since done). More importantly, in the context of this book, the preparations for my talk to the students inspired me to write a chapter specifically on schizophrenia, even though some of the content necessarily repeats what I have written elsewhere.

I have been concerned for decades about public attitudes towards mental illness generally and schizophrenia in particular, but the mix of the demands of my career and later full-time care for my wife left me with little time or energy to do anything about it. In some ways, the opportunity the professor gave me was a bit like releasing water from an overfull reservoir. I had to control the flow, always a challenge for me. Some time ago, a caregiving friend in Melbourne asked me to write out in detail what I did each day for Ardith. It took me a while and was a real downer, but, when I showed it to another friend, it opened his eyes as to what caregiving is all about. In this instance it was the truth, not the devil, that was in the details.

For that reason, the interested reader will find in appendix II the lists of the effects of schizophrenia on Ardith and me. I have omitted, however, the list of the effects on our children. I want to protect their privacy, but they were far from unscathed. In large measure they had to bring themselves up in an environment that was often very stressful and whose effects were sometimes experienced well beyond our home. For example, our son was sometimes taunted about his "crazy" mother. My daughter tells me that her mother's periodic threats to kill herself were particularly upsetting to her and her brother. Curiously, Ardith rarely uttered these threats in front of me, and, mercifully, she never tried to carry them out.

On a more positive note, neither of our children inherited any symptoms of their mother's disease, and both have been very successful in their chosen professions. I was talking with my daughter the other day about this very issue and she credits her own sense of independence and self-confidence in part to having brought herself up. That said, she also believes that she and probably her brother have suffered over the years from a form of post-traumatic stress disorder. I have described elsewhere how well she and her brother have done in their respective careers while acknowledging the greater challenges they have faced in their personal lives. Both of our children greatly admire their mother, notwithstanding the problems experienced in their youth, because she tried so hard despite suffering so much. She is our family hero.

With Ardith, James, and Diana, looking better than we were, Ottawa, 1967.

Ardith's emotional difficulties began in her early teens, at which time her parents decided to move her to a private school because of her "nerves." The stress of the diplomatic life at our first foreign assignment in Bogota necessitated psychiatric consultation, but she recovered reasonably well when we returned to Ottawa. Severe postpartum depression followed the birth of our first child in June of 1964, and was prolonged, perhaps, by fear of going overseas again, this time to New Zealand. She managed reasonably well initially when we arrived in Wellington in April of 1965. However, postpartum depression following the birth of our second child eighteen months later, probably aggravated by the pressures of the diplomatic life, went on and on, culminating in five months of hospitalization. Upon return home, she found it difficult to care for the children, and her resentment and fear of the social burdens flowing from my promotion mounted. That led, as I described earlier, to a marriage breakdown and her decision to leave with the children. While the faith we found in response to that breakdown transformed us and massively improved our relationship, it did not stop the schizophrenia.

One weekend in mid-1968, Ardith began to manifest what I came to recognize as classic psychotic symptoms: voices, delusions, and great fear. After twenty-four hours of mounting terror and in the middle of the night she ran out of the house in her nightdress with me in pursuit. There was a hospital only two blocks from us, and she got there just as I caught up with her. She was hysterical and incoherent, and the hospital staff concluded that she was running from an abusive husband. I was restrained and had to do a lot of fast talking to make the staff understand what was going on.

That was the beginning of my wife's second prolonged hospitalization and the start of our real nightmare. What had happened up to that point was just kindergarten. It was during this second hospitalization that she experienced the repeated bouts of electroconvulsive therapy resulting in some permanent memory loss, frequent nightmares, and the memories of being assaulted that I described much earlier in this narrative. Sometimes her terror was so great that the muscles of her body convulsed and she was wracked with pain. The medication she was given was so sedating she felt like she was swimming through molasses. She eventually came home, but, because of that strong medication, she seemed almost like a zombie. Nonetheless, with the help of Glen, that wonderful woman who looked after both our children, we coped – just.

The normal period for a Canadian diplomatic posting to New Zealand is three and a half years. By this time we had been there nearly four and a half, about the halfway point of the two-year extension we had been given because of my wife's health. When Ardith's psychotic symptoms returned yet again in 1970, I was worried that we would have to seek a further extension. The reader with a good memory will recall that this time her illness took a different form: catatonia. Indeed, she was still in a catatonic state when the hospital eventually sent her home, saying they could do little more for her. I have recounted earlier the extraordinary miracle she received in response to the request for prayer from our minister's young son. She was completely healed from her catatonia, and that healing allowed us to return home to Canada five months later. The catatonia never returned, but the psychotic episodes, though less severe, did. She endured extended hospitalization twice more during the twenty-one years that followed in Ottawa, and there was a lot of pain and stress in between. There were also times of relative normalcy, but they were tempered by the often oppressive side effects of the many medications Ardith had to take.

As I recall these events and think about some friends who have experienced schizophrenia in their families, I recognize how fortunate we have been to avoid two all-too-common effects of schizophrenia: marriage breakdown and attempted or successful suicide. We came very close to ending our marriage, but our newfound faith so transformed us that we have been able to remain together for nearly half a century since. With respect to suicide, I can only thank God that Ardith's repeated threats were never translated into reality.

Schizophrenia is a physiological illness that, unlike many socially more acceptable diseases, is generally unrelated to lifestyle choices (with the possible exception of harmful narcotic use). A healthy diet, good exercise, and plenty of sleep have their place in reducing the risk of heart attacks, strokes, diabetes, and even certain types of cancer. The risk of succumbing to schizophrenia, however, cannot be diminished through a healthy lifestyle or even by the kinds of brain exercises that are thought to ward off or slow Alzheimer's and other forms of dementia. Yet, as a society, we often seem to see those suffering from this cruel brain disease as lesser beings, somehow responsible for their unhappy circumstances. Sadly, many of those suffering from schizophrenia also hold the same view, which feeds their sense of guilt and worthlessness. That self-condemning attitude is reinforced by the reaction of others, a reaction that in large measure stems from fear of what schizophrenics might do. That fear is in turn often fed by insensitive news stories, television and movie dramas, and popular print fiction.

When we first faced the full horror of schizophrenia about forty-five years ago, attitudes towards all kinds of mental illness were pretty bad and making fun of people who were "off their rockers," to use a relatively polite term, was the norm in general conversation. Over the years since, a measure of political correctness has crept in, and at least some people are less inclined than they might have been earlier to use pejorative language when speaking of the mentally ill.

That said, I have to add that public attitudes during the intervening decades have improved much less than I hoped they would. The stigma remains for virtually all kinds of mental illness, but it is generally worst for schizophrenia or anything called psychotic. The attention given in recent years to post-traumatic stress disorder (PTSD), especially that associated with war veterans, has helped somewhat, presumably because it is relatively easy for the lay public to understand the relationship between the cause and the effect. Other forms of mental illness, especially psychotic illnesses like schizophrenia, are much harder to explain. Without understanding, it is difficult to generate empathy. When that lack of understanding develops into fear, the result is often contempt and hostility. Clearly, better public education is needed, but it is a difficult cycle to break. Sadly, these attitudes further imprison the individual whose mind is already imprisoned inside terrors and delusions that most of us can scarcely imagine.

I have seen that terror up close on countless occasions over many years. It is no less real than that felt by a person charged by a lion or attacked by a rapist. I noted earlier that the fear was sometimes so powerful that Ardith's muscles tightened all over her body, creating intense pain. Yet I am still unable to imagine what it must be like to lose control of one's mind to the point that virtually anything, however bizarre, might be believed or acted upon. To use a relatively benign example, many years ago a Toronto-based economist, who looked a lot like a younger version of me, co-hosted a regular business news program on TV. Ardith became convinced that it was me and believed that I was living a double life, a delusion that lasted a very long time. The fact that I was living and working in Ottawa made no difference. No amount of reasoning or reassurance or comforting makes any difference when a person's sense of reality has been altered by a psychotic delusion. How terrible that must be. Is that not a reason for pity, a motive for compassion? Does it not warrant a real effort to understand rather than condemn?

We were very fortunate both in Ottawa and Vancouver to find holistic general practitioners who cared for us over many years with imagination and compassion. In Vancouver, we also benefited from the help of caring and dedicated psychiatrists. However, that happy experience with the healthcare system was not universal. In my naïveté, I expected that attitudes among healthcare practitioners might be more enlightened than among the general public, but we have encountered over the years several examples of ignorance and popular prejudice among health professionals. These ranged from insensitive general practitioners who refused to listen to my advice about how to keep from frightening my wife to a dentist who refused to avoid adrenaline-based anesthetics despite my warnings, inducing three days of intense delusions and terror. The side effects of having to increase her medication to control these induced symptoms lasted much longer. More broadly, I often found her covered with bruises from the rough treatment she had received and from the restraints applied during her several hospitalizations in Wellington and Ottawa.

Most traumatic for my daughter and me was the process of forced hospitalization that took place in Vancouver about six years after our return to British Columbia from Ottawa. Together, we managed to convince Ardith to accompany us to visit a psychiatrist in an office near our home, and, after he had made the legally required determination that she was in need of treatment, we were able to get her to ride in the ambulance with us to the hospital without too much difficulty. The ambulance crew was kindness itself, and even the accompanying police officers were sympathetic.

The problem began when we arrived in the emergency ward at the hospital. The sergeant-major of a nurse who was in charge was brutal in speech and behaviour, sparking terror in my wife. She summoned two huge male attendants who promptly placed Ardith in restraints, provoking even greater fear on her part. When my daughter and I, who were already weeping, sought to protest, the nurse said she would have us forcibly removed from the hospital if we said another word. I turned for help to a young intern who was clearly upset at what was going on, but he said that he could do nothing. The nurse was in charge. I began to wonder if we had made a terrible mistake, but I am happy to say that, once she was transferred to the psychiatric ward, attitudes and treatment improved immensely. The result of a couple of months of hospitalization and experimentation with different brands of anti-psychotic medication called neuroleptics was very positive.

Ardith also encountered a brilliant and very compassionate young psychiatrist who continued to care for her as an outpatient over many years thereafter. Eventually, he moved to focus his attentions on those suffering from substance abuse and other horrors in Vancouver's notorious Downtown Eastside. Ardith is now cared for by a female psychiatrist who specializes in older patients. She has been a great help to us.

British Columbia's Mental Health Act made it possible to oblige my psychotically oppressed wife to receive the treatment that enabled her to live a life with much less fear and pain. In Ontario, corresponding legislation was changed decades ago to make it much more difficult to force seriously mentally ill people into care. This change was represented as an advance in human rights. I have to wonder how much needless suffering and even deaths through suicide have been caused by this change. It may have warmed the hearts of human rights activists, but not of those who love people who are seriously mentally ill. People caught in psychotic delusions cannot make rational decisions about their own care, and that is a simple medical truth. They need their loved ones and concerned medical practitioners to make those decisions for them. To me, leaving such afflicted people without the protection of the law is comparable to the decision made years ago to massively cut the number of psychiatric beds available. Can anyone doubt that many of the street people we see, a high percentage of whom are mentally ill, are in their present situations precisely because of these acts of societal indifference?

With the newer medications called neuroleptics, Ardith's psychotic episodes involving voices, delusions, and paranoia became less frequent and less intense. Provided I protected her from external stress, our home life became much calmer, though very constrained. From time to time crises flared, necessitating an increase in medication along with its unfortunate side effects, especially weight gain and now irreversible tardive dyskenesia (facial tics and other involuntary noises or movements). She takes additional medication to combat these side effects, but it is not fully effective. However, the alternative was worse, and we adjusted ourselves to living in a self-imposed cocoon with limited external contacts.

The onset about six years ago of Alzheimer's, initially masked by the overlapping symptoms of schizophrenia, especially confusion, created a whole new challenge. Travel, already limited to visiting our son, James, and family in Ottawa once a year, became impossible, and Ardith's dependence upon me for help with almost all basic human functions has grown steadily. It is sadly ironic that, as we finally settled into a life of carefully managed equilibrium, Alzheimer's made its ugly entrance and turned our lives upside down again. Lately, it has been concluded that Ardith also has symptoms of vascular dementia.

Recent studies have shown that mental illness in the aggregate places a greater burden on society in terms both of human suffering and of economics than do infectious diseases and cancer combined. Yet, far fewer resources are devoted by society to addressing mental afflictions than to better-known illnesses. Furthermore, far less money is being spent by the pharmaceutical industry on research into replacing the often ineffective psychiatric medications available today than is being devoted to research on new medications for a variety of other, less widespread illnesses. The reason for this situation, the experts say, is that brain functions are generally more challenging to research, despite advances in technology that enable us to "see" those functions more clearly, and therefore offer a slower and less certain return on investment. As a result, researchers in this field often find themselves at the bottom of a limited funding ladder. Our aging population and the growing incidence of dementia, especially Alzheimer's, will make this problem even worse if the increasing need and public concern do not bring about changes in funding priorities.

I talk briefly about Ardith's own experience with Alzheimer's much later in the book, but I wanted to say something here for the benefit of those readers who, like me, are full-time caregivers for dementia patients or other very needy family members. Caregiving is a very stressful occupation, especially when the one for whom you are caring is a loved member of the family. To the extensive demands of physical care are often added social isolation and the stress of seeing the loved one suffering or becoming estranged. There is also a great deal of frustration involved when the simplest tasks cannot be undertaken or re-taught. All this is to say that caregivers must look after themselves. I have been late, but hopefully not too late, in recognizing this truth. In May of 2013, at the instigation of my doctor, I enrolled in a professionally supervised exercise clinic called, appropriately enough, "Live Well." I was not exactly sedentary, but, except for walking our border collie, I had been exercise-adverse. My motivation came from the recognition that I needed to remain strong and, ideally, get stronger to care for Ardith's physical needs as her Alzheimer's and mobility both worsened. The results have been beyond my wildest expectations. I have become much stronger, and my endurance levels have increased immensely. While my progress was carefully measured after six months, I did not need the charts to tell me how much my body had improved. Part of this success undoubtedly reflected the considerable effort I put into the exercise routines, but I cannot claim a lot of credit even for that. I discovered that the attractive young female kinesiologist who oversees the program is a competitive weightlifter despite her very feminine appearance. Once I realized that she could lift me over her head and throw me across the room, my motivation increased enormously.

I realize that in today's world people of my age – mid seventies – are no longer viewed as old in the sense that they were during my youth. But I still remain amazed that a body as old as mine would respond so quickly and so well. Clearly I should have begun a program of this kind long ago, especially given the stress of both my family and work life. That is a message that is widely disseminated today but so often ignored, hence, among other things, the growing incidence of lifestyle-related illness. I recently came across an innovative effort to get that message across. A new member of the Live Well team told me that her father, a general practitioner working in White Rock, a distant suburb of Vancouver near the U.S. border, had recently written a book that approached this need based on an intriguing premise: that readers might relate better to health advice by identifying with the challenges faced by a fictional character in a novel. I contacted her father, Dr. Werner Spangehl, and asked him to characterize his book in a paragraph to be included in mine. This is his slightly edited response.

> *One Minute Medicine* is a fictional account of a forty-two-year-old lawyer who suffers a heart attack; the book follows his journey of recovery. The point of the book is that incremental life-style changes (that are within our control) can result in tremendous improvements in health outcomes. There are several things that make this book unique – first that it is written as a novel – so that the reader can identify with the characters and learn vicariously through their experiences. Second, that a relatively healthy young man can have a life-threatening heart attack (most men in their early forties feel they are invincible)! Third, the "book within a book" concept that gives specific but succinct information on "12 Habits of Healthy People." Many people know that "you are what you eat" and "exercise is the most powerful medicine," but many find it surprising to learn that social isolation, job dissatisfaction and marital discord are more toxic than smoking, high blood pressure, cholesterol and family history when it comes to determinants of health – and are also risk factors for heart disease! Hence, there is a lot of emphasis on social connection, spiritual reality, purpose, meaning and balance – and when all of these habits resonate in harmony, then true health or a full and vibrant life can be achieved.

One Minute Medicine is published by Peace Arch Publications in White Rock and, at this stage, is distributed locally. However, because the reaction to the book has been so positive, Dr Spangehl is looking into broader distribution through a national publisher. I will be obtaining copies for my children, both of whom are in their forties. I want them around to look after me when I really get old.

Inspired by my own experience and encouraged by our daughter, I have also hired Ryan Booth, a personal trainer, to help Ardith combat loss of mobility and strength. Ardith has responded surprisingly well to Ryan's gentle but persistent encouragement. Already she can go up and down stairs twice as fast as when she began. She has also started using the treadmill for short periods.

I recognize that this discussion of schizophrenia could be depressing, both for the reader and for me. There is, however, a silver lining. Ardith and I made our marital vows twice, once before a God in whom we did not believe and once before One who, in response to the effects of Ardith's mental illness, opened our eyes to His existence. The first set of vows failed, but the second held fast. On both occasions, the vows contained the same words, "in sickness and in health." It is in the valleys of life that we grow spiritually, and few valleys are deeper than those created by serious illness. Similarly, nothing tests love like crisis. It deepens or collapses. Ours deepened and is now being tested even more as Ardith's symptoms of Alzheimer's worsen. Writing this memoir and especially this chapter on schizophrenia has brought home to me just how different – how much worse – our lives would have been if we had not experienced that first encounter with God in New Zealand that so transformed our priorities. That life-changing experience gives me hope, and hope is the essential ingredient in continuing to be to Ardith what she now so desperately needs.

In 1984, seven years before we left Ottawa, our children gave us vanity licence plates for our new car. They read *RMR * AMR*, my initials and Ardith's on either side of a crown topped by a cross. The crown reflects Canada's status as a monarchy and appears on all Ontario licence plates. However, for us the crown represented Jesus, the linchpin in our marriage. We were reminded of that truth every time we got in or out of the car.

CHAPTER 48

ENTER, LUCIEN BOUCHARD

To say that the government changed is a massive understatement. As noted earlier, on September 4, 1984, after twenty years of briefly interrupted Liberal rule, Brian Mulroney's Progressive Conservatives (PC) won the largest majority in Canadian history, 211 seats compared with the Liberals' 40 and the New Democrats' 30.

For FEARO, there were two important implications: the Progressive Conservative party's platform contained a clear commitment to enacting environmental assessment legislation, and the possibility now existed that John Fraser might once again become my boss. It was he who had pressed for that commitment in the platform, and I knew he would work hard to ensure that it was met. Moreover, he was a committed environmentalist for whom I had a great deal of respect. However, Fraser was appointed as Fisheries Minister, and Suzanne Blais-Grénier, a former federal public servant from Québec with limited political experience, assumed the Environment portfolio. Some of her public comments drew criticism, especially from environmental groups, and she was replaced within a year by Tom McMillan from Prince Edward Island.

McMillan was keen and easy to work with, and he clearly was able to attract competent people to his personal staff. One of these was Elizabeth May, today a Member of Parliament and leader of the Green party but at that time an environmental activist from Nova Scotia. In the years I worked with her I developed a considerable respect for her integrity, knowledge, and commitment. Getting elected to the House was a significant achievement, but, as one of only two Green party MPs, she has less influence than her party's nation-wide popular vote might imply. Nonetheless, her voice can still be heard.

Despite the commitment in the election platforms of both the defeated Liberals and the victorious Progressive Conservatives to enact environmental assessment legislation, we knew from past disappointments that such commitments do not automatically translate into Cabinet approval for the submission of the promised legislation to Parliament. Indeed, when the Liberals were in power, we could not even get our proposal onto the relevant Cabinet Committee agenda because of opposition within the career Public Service. Consequently we gave a lot of thought as to what we might do differently this time around. We decided to do what we did best: engage in a public consultative process on the need for and the nature of environmental assessment legislation.

To that end, we developed a discussion paper setting out what such an act might look like. The final version had to be very vaguely worded because Minister McMillan, needed the support of his colleagues to make the government's tentative thinking public. That meant interdepartmental consultation, resulting in a paper with minimal content. Bob Connelly and I think it was Elizabeth May who said that the best thing in the paper was the Minister's photo. (He was a handsome fellow.) Nonetheless, we distributed it to all the provinces, territories, and other principal stakeholders, such as affected industry, environmental organizations, and aboriginal peoples. Over several months, we held meetings with each stakeholder in addition to informal public information hearings across the country. Based upon these meetings and hearings, we put together a report and developed a package of proposals.

I asked Stephen Hazell, whose important role in advancing the cause of environmental assessment legislation is described later, to act as one of several reviewers of an earlier draft of this book. In the 1980s, Stephen was legal counsel for the Canadian Wildlife Federation, and he later directed the Sierra Club. He currently heads an environmental law firm and serves on the faculty of the University of Ottawa's Law School. He commented that FEARO's consultative process on possible legislation was "hugely important" in that it enabled environmentalists to understand that FEARO officials were "more or less on the same wavelength" as the environmental community.

In April of 1988, I was asked to brief a newly appointed Minister heading another department on the subject of environmental assessment. He was Lucien Bouchard, best known today as the man who nearly took

Québec out of Canada. Bob Connelly accompanied me, both because his French was better than mine and because he knew a lot about the newly legislated Québec environmental assessment process that had triggered Bouchard's interest. In many ways it paralleled the federal process, especially in the use of an independent body to conduct public hearings on major projects.

Although he was new to politics, Bouchard was seen as a star in the Progressive Conservative party. The Liberals had become unpopular among many French-speaking Quebeckers following Trudeau's success in securing the adoption of Canada's new constitution over Québec's opposition. This disaffection had enabled Progressive Conservative leader Brian Mulroney to attract a sizable number of "soft" Québec nationalists to his party and thereby help win his huge majority in the House. Bouchard, a former classmate of Mulroney's at law school, was one of these "soft" nationalists, but his route into the House of Commons and the Federal Cabinet was more circuitous than most. It would take him to Paris, first, where the incoming prime minister sent his old friend to serve as Canada's Ambassador in 1985. By all accounts he performed very well in that post, and, upon his return to Canada, he was elected in a by-election to a seat in the House and immediately thereafter appointed to a minor Cabinet post.

The meeting with Bouchard went very well. Bob and I were both impressed by his knowledge and enthusiasm. I do not remember it, but Bob tells me that I remarked, upon leaving Bouchard's office, that it would not be long before this man became the new Environment Minister. I was right. Environment Minister Tom McMillan lost his seat in the November 1988 general election, but his Progressive Conservative party was re-elected with a substantially reduced majority. In the cabinet shuffle that followed, Bouchard became our new boss. Needless to say, my colleagues and I in both FEARO and Environment Canada were delighted. With his close ties to the Prime Minister, Bouchard was clearly the most politically influential Environment Minister Canada had ever had.

I remember only vaguely the Environment Canada Management Committee's first encounter with the new Minister, but I remember very well the first major task I was asked to perform for him. Prime Minister Mulroney had instituted a practice of asking each newly appointed Cabinet Minister to write him a letter setting out what that Minister hoped to achieve. Because of my many years in Environment Canada and my post as head of FEARO, I was asked by the Deputy Minister to prepare that letter on behalf of the whole of Environment Canada and FEARO. It was a demanding assignment. I began by meeting with the Minister to get a sense of his priorities and interests. Initially we spoke in French, but he moved to English because, he said, he wanted to improve his mastery of the language (and probably to avoid listening to my accent). His English was accented but erudite, reflecting his voracious appetite as a reader in both his native language and mine. His large office was lined with books reflecting his remarkably varied taste in reading material; he was a true renaissance man. I soon realized that I was dealing with a considerable intellect, a realization that was strongly reinforced in the nearly two years I worked for him.

My next step was to meet individually with the Assistant Deputy Ministers (ADMs) who headed each of Environment Canada's Services, including, of course, the Environmental Protection Service, which I used to head myself. I needed their judgement on the priority that should be given to the many activities for which they were responsible. I exercised my own judgement in pulling these sometimes competing priorities together and discussed the resulting initial draft with the Deputy Minister. After taking account of his views, I finalized my draft and laid it before the Minister. We had earlier agreed that I should prepare the initial draft in English, adjust it to take account of the Minister's comments, have it translated into French, resubmit it in that language, incorporate the Minister's changes, translate that draft back into English, and submit the final letter in both languages for signature by Bouchard and subsequent transmission to the Prime Minister.

FEARO was very fortunate to have on staff as our translator a Belgian architect, Jean Thomas, who had served in Belgium's much criticized colonial administration in the Belgian Congo before and during that unfortunate country's achievement of independence. "Graduates" of the Congo were much maligned in Belgium, which probably contributed to Jean's decision to move to Canada. His mastery of French and understanding of English were superb, and his translations must have ranked among the best in the government. All our Environmental Assessment Panels' reports were, of course, produced in both official languages, and our architect-translator not only undertook the task with great accuracy, he often uncovered inconsistencies and confusion in the original language, which resulted in better-written reports whichever language the reader chose to use.

He worked his usual magic on the draft letter in English that I had revised to reflect the Minister's changes and produced a superb French equivalent. Minister Bouchard, who was a purist in his own language, was very impressed with the result and insisted upon meeting the translator. The ostensible reason was to discuss the Minister's stylistic preferences, but, upon learning about Jean's profession and origin, the conversation quickly turned to one of the Minister's favourite subjects, European architecture. The Minister had only limited time available, and I had to push very hard to get either of them to pay attention to the draft.

Once the Minister's stylistic preferences had been incorporated in the French draft, Jean and I worked together to build these into the English version. The result in both languages was both elegant and precise. Given what happened later, it is ironic to note that one of the themes that the Minister wanted incorporated in the letter was the encouragement of national unity through the promotion of a common concern, coast-to-coast-to-coast, focused on protecting Canada's immense but vulnerable environment. Sadly, Jean passed away a few years ago. I admired him greatly, both professionally and personally.

Obviously this iterative letter-writing process was a very good way for me to develop a working relationship with my new boss. I think it is fair to say that that relationship steadily deepened as the months went by and proved especially valuable when we renewed the push to secure Cabinet approval for environmental assessment legislation. I remember well the occasion when my staff and I outlined to our new Minister the results of our public consultation on possible legislation that had been initiated under Minister McMillan. One of the most important issues we had to address was the relationship between the federal and provincial governments.

In our meetings with the provinces, two models had emerged. The first alternative would enable us, in effect, to "certify" a provincial assessment process that met the federal criteria set out in the legislation. It could then be used in place of the federal process where appropriate. The second alternative would apply both processes through such mechanisms as joint environmental assessment panels. When I explained the first alternative, Minister Bouchard's vehement response was "non, absolument non." He much preferred hands-on federal involvement. While he did not say so,

I suspect that he may also have been concerned about the political consequences of picking and choosing between provinces by certifying some but not others. In any event, it was the second model that was reflected in the draft legislation.

What we had encountered across the country from the great majority of those whom we consulted, especially industry and provincial governments, was a strong desire for certainty and predictability. There was less worry about a process being burdensome and more worry about it being erratic. While different "stakeholders" naturally emphasized different objectives and concerns, there was pretty broad support for the idea of a legislated federal process that would provide the needed predictability. FEARO staff shared these conclusions with other affected government departments in the hope that their earlier opposition to legislation would be moderated. That hope was not realized. Even the government's stated intention in the April 1987 Speech from the Throne to propose legislation to replace the EARP Guidelines Order made no difference. It took no less a body than the Federal Court of Appeal to overcome Public Service opposition.

Chapter 49

THE COURTS TURN OUR WORLD RIGHT-SIDE-UP

If this were a mystery novel instead of a memoir, the title of this chapter would clearly give away the next twist in the plot. However, what the Federal Court of Appeal did is a matter of record; what is of interest is how it happened and the effect that it had. I will do my best to answer both of those questions.

In the parts of this narrative that address environmental assessment, I have sought comments from several of my former FEARO colleagues. Elsewhere, the book is almost entirely the product of my own memories, mostly based upon first-hand experience. In contrast, what I am about to write must necessarily depend upon some second-hand information, because the key decisions that resulted in the court challenges that so transformed our prospects for legislation took place without my involvement or that of my staff. Indeed, it was not until I started writing this chapter that I came to fully understand what had apparently been going on behind closed doors. I owe that understanding primarily to an article in the *Manitoba Law Journal*, vol. 36, no. 1 (2012) by Brendan Jowett summarizing and critiquing a recent book by *Winnipeg Free Press* journalist Bill Redekop. The book is entitled *Dams of Contention: The Rafferty-Alameda Story and the Birth of Canadian Environmental Law*.

According to Redekop's account, the Rafferty-Alameda saga is many things: federal and provincial backroom political deal-making, use of public funds for political return, environmentally questionable dam construction, disregard of due process and of individual property rights, and game-changing federal court decisions that declared the federal environmental assessment guidelines order to be legally binding, not simply a guideline as previously supposed. Unfortunately for those who initiated the court action, this remarkably important result had little effect on the construction of the two dams in question.

The Rafferty dam is located in the constituency of Saskatchewan's former premier, Grant Devine, and the Alameda dam is in the nearby constituency of former deputy premier Eric Bernston. While the Rafferty dam had some local benefit, such as irrigation, the other dam's value was for seasonal flood control that only benefited downstream North Dakota, particularly the city of Minot. In Redekop's view, the real purpose of both dams was the expenditure of public funds to benefit the two political constituencies. Saskatchewan's Souris Basin Development Agency, which was responsible for building the two dams, undertook minimal public consultation despite the extensive flooding of private lands that would result and carried out a grossly inadequate environmental assessment. The assessment was needed to secure the approval of the provincial Environment Minister, who was advised by a panel that lacked expertise in the matter. Not surprisingly, the approval was readily given.

A coalition of opponents known as SCRAP sought through the courts to force Saskatchewan's Environment Minister to order a more comprehensive environmental assessment that would include a cost benefit analysis. When that effort failed, the Canadian Wildlife Federation (CWF), whose Saskatchewan affiliate was a part of SCRAP, turned its legal guns on the federal authorities.

The CWF's chief legal gun at the time was Stephen Hazell. Years later, after a stint with FEARO developing the regulations needed to bring into force the Canadian Environmental Assessment Act, he wrote an excellent book on the development of environmental assessment in Canada entitled *Canada v. the Environment*. Among many other things, it describes in a very authoritative way this game-changing legal battle. The "feds" were legitimate targets because the affected river crossed the border into the United States, thereby requiring the issuance of a permit under the International Rivers Improvement Act (IRIA). Issuing IRIA permits was the responsibility of my boss, Environment Minister Tom McMillan.

FEARO had nothing to do with issuing IRIA permits – that responsibility was held within Environment Canada – but we certainly held the view that issuance of such permits fell within the purview of the Environmental Assessment and Review Process Guidelines Order (EARPGO). In other words, no IRIA permit ought to have been issued without undertaking an initial assessment under the Guidelines Order. Moreover, given the nature of the projects involved – their size, their potential impacts, and the public controversy surrounding them – a complete initial assessment would almost certainly have concluded that holding a formal public review by an independent panel was warranted. However, under the provisions of the Order, it was the responsible authority, not FEARO, that was supposed to make that judgement. As I explained earlier, we in FEARO were constantly trying to persuade other parts of government to follow the provisions of the Order; we were therefore deeply disappointed that our own Minister would consider being less than meticulous in doing so himself. I could not, however, argue that he did not have that discretion. Moreover, because the Guidelines Order was thought to be just that – a guideline – a responsible authority could, as a matter of law, ignore it entirely.

In the event, Minister McMillan did issue the IRIA permit in 1988 without calling for a public review. Redekop contends in his book that McMillan took this action for two reasons: to secure, at the behest of the Prime Minister, provincial agreement regarding improved French-language services within Saskatchewan and to secure, in his own Department's interest, Saskatchewan's co-operation in establishing Grasslands National Park. In his much more authoritative book, Stephen Hazell, who was the key lawyer involved in the subsequent court case and for whom I have a lot of respect, makes reference to similar allegations. I have no personal knowledge about either of Redekop's contentions, but I have a great deal of respect for Elizabeth May, who resigned from the Minister's office in June of 1988 to protest eliminating the required environmental assessment to secure a political deal. She was publicly attacked for some time thereafter over her decision to leave, which merely increased my admiration for her. As a consequence, I had at the time little doubt that some kind of political deal lay behind the issuance of the permit.

We were all surprised when the federal judge hearing the court case initiated by the Canadian Wildlife Federation's Stephen Hazell concluded that the Guidelines Order was legally binding, not a guideline at all. Because the requirements of the Order had not been followed in issuing the IRIA permit, the permit was quashed. Environment Canada proceeded to undertake the required initial assessment, which determined that some of the environmental effects of the two dams were "moderately significant," a finding that should have resulted in a public review.

Despite this finding, Minister Bouchard, who by this time had replaced McMillan, reissued the IRIA permit without appointing a panel to review the project. That decision sparked another court case and a judicial decision ordering him to appoint such a panel. Specifically, the judge in that case found that "moderately significant" cannot mean "insignificant" and therefore must mean "significant," a finding that, under the Order, required a panel review. Bouchard acquiesced and successfully negotiated an agreement with Saskatchewan to stop construction on the dams, which had already begun, while the review proceeded. However, the agreement was not without cost. The Federal Government had to commit to pay $1 million a month up to a maximum of $10 million as compensation for the delay. In these bizarre circumstances, one of my most senior officers, Bob Connelly, agreed to chair the panel, which was otherwise made up of non-government experts.

While the review was underway, Minister Bouchard made his famous decision to resign from the Cabinet in order to found and head the separatist Bloc Québécois (which I will discuss later). He was replaced by Robert de Cotret, another senior minister. A subsequent meeting between de Cotret and Saskatchewan Premier Grant Devine resulted in Saskatchewan's decision to resume construction on the dams even though the public review had not been completed. Minister de Cotret denied that he had agreed to this resumption, but the bottom line is that the construction continued.

This action by Saskatchewan also caused all of the members of the environmental assessment panel, including FEARO's Bob Connelly, to resign. Bob was put under a lot of pressure to accept chairmanship of a new panel but, much to his credit, he refused. That is what Public Service integrity entails. Bob insisted that if I made reference to his decision in this book, I had to add that, as his boss, I backed him to the hilt. I recognize that this bit of mutual admiration may nauseate some readers, but I think it is important to understand what is or should be expected of professional public servants. The Guidelines Order, which governed our activities, had been declared a law of general application by the courts and it was our job to follow it, not facilitate a political deal. In the event, a new panel made up of non-government experts and chaired by a respected Saskatchewan academic was appointed by the Minister to complete the review. Construction continued, and both dams were ultimately completed.

Bob's integrity and that of his fellow panelists were clearly recognized in a strongly worded *Ottawa Citizen* editorial that also underlined the political importance of this test of the government's commitment to the environment. It is worth reproducing.

> Rafferty-Alameda Dam(s): Hold Everything Right There
>
> The Rafferty-Alameda dam project in south-western Saskatchewan, a relatively minor irrigation and power [*sic* – actually flood control] project, has suddenly taken on much larger symbolic significance. It has become a test of the Federal Government's commitment to sustainable development.
>
> It is a test not only of the new federal Environment Minister, Bob de Cotret, but of the Prime Minister himself. One of Brian Mulroney's staunchest supporters, Saskatchewan Premier Grant Devine, is defying the Federal Government and its environmental review process and proceeding with construction of the controversial dam(s). The question now is whether Mulroney will rush to the defense of his friend or of the environment.
>
> If the political and moral challenges are clear, the technical details are – as usual – complex. In December 1989, the Rafferty-Alameda Project attracted national attention when a federal court ordered the project halted pending a full environmental review. However, the Saskatchewan Government continued work on the dam over the objections of environmentalists and the federal review panel.
>
> Last week, in protest against Saskatchewan's behaviour, the five-member panel resigned. (This is a rare event in public life – someone resigning on principle – yet, apart from the chair, Robert Connelly, a federal public servant, the names of the courageous panellists are largely unknown. They are consulting engineer Hugh Mackay of Winnipeg, Robert Bell, an aquatic biologist from Le Ronge, Saskatchewan, Donald Gray, a Saskatoon University professor specializing in hydrology, and Eric Moodie, a University of Winnipeg biologist.)
>
> Whatever else the impact, the resignations made little impression on Devine. He claims de Cotret gave him tacit permission in September to resume construction on the dam; de Cotret denies any such thing.
>
> Now the Minister is threatening legal action to stop the dam project. He may also try to reclaim some $8 million the Federal Government has paid the Province to compensate for the delay.
>
> There is more at stake here than the survival of flora and fauna; there is also the Federal Government's credibility. It showed good faith in appointing a

> panel of (obviously) independent-minded professionals. We now must ensure these experts get the time and co-operation necessary to complete their task.

Sadly, the outcome for the affected landowners and adjacent wetlands was not good. That said, with the passage of time and the knowledge of what the resulting court case achieved, the outrage I once felt over the incident has inevitably diminished. Indeed, I have to admit to some relief in learning that the objectives of the political deal, on the federal side of the equation, were at least worthwhile. Prime Minister Mulroney was attempting at the time to forge a consensus across the country on a partnership between Québec and the rest of Canada (often called "ROC" by constitutional insiders) that would defuse separatist feelings among French-speaking Québécois. Responding to the needs of French-speaking minorities in other provinces was one of the means of achieving this objective. For its part, Parks Canada was attempting to include among our national parks representation from all of the many different classes of ecosystems that make up this huge country. Prairie grassland was a very important missing component, and extensive large-scale agriculture had made it difficult to find a pristine representation of that particular ecosystem. The opportunity to secure the necessary land in Saskatchewan must have seemed very attractive.

Obviously, our own Minister's decision effectively to bypass the Guidelines Order initially appeared to us as a significant setback for FEARO's efforts to persuade government departments to apply the Order's provisions. However, our frustration changed to amazement and not a little joy when the Federal Court held that the Guidelines Order was legally binding, giving it the status of a law of general application. That decision was confirmed by the Federal Court of Appeal in 1989. In 1990, the appeal court took the same position with respect to the Oldman River case in Alberta, which also involved a dam that was initiated by provincial authorities and required a federal permit. Subsequently, Alberta successfully sought leave to argue a particular aspect of that case before the Supreme Court, which ruled in 1992 that the Guidelines Order had to be applied to any project where a federal department had an "affirmative regulatory duty." In the words of the Supreme Court's decision, the Guidelines Order was "super-added" to all relevant federal legislation. Of broader and more long-lasting importance was the Supreme Court's recognition of "environment" as an area of joint federal and provincial jurisdiction. That recognition proved very important in subsequent years when FEARO's successor, the Canadian Environmental Assessment Agency (CEAA), was negotiating agreements with provinces under the newly approved Canadian Environmental Assessment Act.

Our joy over the initial decisions was soon diminished, for three reasons. The first was that FEARO was required to organize and manage two public reviews of the Saskatchewan and Alberta projects by independent panels, even though those projects were under construction and the scope for altering, much less stopping, them was so limited. While some of the two panels' recommendations did prove to have some value, it appeared as though process was being applied for process' sake. That was the antithesis of what we in FEARO believed should happen. From our perspective, the objective was not to make people jump through hoops simply because they were there. The objective always had to be to provide meaningful information that would guide decisions on whether a project should proceed and, if so, in what form. That meant that the necessary information needed to be made available well before decisions regarding a given project were made. Timely assessment was always the goal.

The second reason for our diminished joy was the imprecise wording of the Guidelines Order itself. The reader may recall that the Order was drafted in rushed circumstances in order to be brought before the last Cabinet meeting of the Trudeau government. Moreover, there had been unresolved issues respecting wording between the drafters in Justice and ourselves in FEARO. An important principle that governed our thinking was that each project should be given only the amount of assessment that it needed. The Guidelines Order did not draw a clear distinction between, for example, large and small projects, and, now that each word had been found to be legally binding, it appeared that we might have to apply potentially burdensome processes to relatively minor projects.

The third reason for our mounting concern was the realization that the Court's decisions meant that large numbers of projects that provincial governments were previously responsible to assess now had to be considered under the federal process as well. Suddenly our workload had expanded enormously. By the time I left Ottawa nearly three years later, we were dealing with projects totalling more than half of the annual capital investment in the country. I realized very quickly that, if we could not find an efficient way to deal with this new challenge, the development of our natural resource sector in particular could be affected. That could have had adverse implications for our economy and created a backlash against the concept of environmental assessment at a time when we were seeking approval for environmental assessment legislation.

Legally speaking, because the Guidelines Order was simply a Cabinet decision, it could have been rescinded or amended without reference to Parliament. However, such a move would have sent out a politically unpopular message. The only practical solution was to speed up the process of replacing the Order with legislation. Government departments that had previously opposed such legislation now saw it, properly designed, as the solution to the confusion created by the judges' decisions. The wind was now at our back, but we also had first to show that we could navigate the environmental assessment ship through the court-induced storm. In appendix IX, the interested reader will find a full account of how this challenge was successfully met.

Appendix X, meanwhile, contains an informative article that appeared in the July 18, 1989, edition of the *Financial Post* written by John Geddes providing an outsider's view of the immense pressures that were created by the Federal Court's decisions on FEARO as well as an assessment of my role in facing those pressures. A prominent environmentalist interviewed for the article is reported to have posed but not answered the question whether Robinson is "hard-assed" enough to cope. Clearly that environmentalist had not seen me vigorously pedalling on my office exercise bike. That said, the fact that I later retired to Vancouver probably provides the real answer to his question.

CHAPTER 50

LIFE ON THE HOME FRONT

I wrote earlier about transitioning in 1982 from the demanding job of heading the Environmental Protection Service to the less demanding post of chairing the Federal Environmental Assessment Review Office. I also reduced the level of my activity on behalf of the Public Service Christian Fellowship. My hope had been to spend more time at home in a less tired state in order to provide the support that my wife and children needed. Unfortunately, I was an adrenaline junkie, and the massive reduction in adrenaline production that initially accompanied my change of jobs affected me at home every bit as much as it did at work. At first, I was there in body but largely absent in spirit. In time, I came out of my adrenaline-starved funk, perhaps in part because the periodic crises created by Ardith's continuing struggles with her health had their own impact on my adrenal glands.

As the reader will have gathered from the chapter on living with schizophrenia, life at home was a lot of things, but boring was not one of them. In addition to the health-related challenges, which I will not revisit, there were the usual fun and games of raising teenagers. In her preteen years, Diana had welcomed my sitting on her bed just before she went to sleep so that she could tell me about her day. When that stopped, I knew the teenage years had begun. A few incidents stand out in my mind.

I remember one occasion leaning down to kiss Diana good night and smelling this strange sweet smell. "What is that smell?" I asked. "Oh, that's just marijuana, Dad. The smoke gets in my hair." She had been at a school dance. Happily, neither of our children got caught up in the world of drugs, but some of their friends or acquaintances certainly did.

When Diana was sixteen, she made her first visit on her own to Van-

With Ardith, James, and Diana, Ottawa, 1979: beards grow, and so do children.

couver, where Ardith's parents lived. Her seventeen-year-old cousin lived in an apartment building in Vancouver's downtown West End, and she had invited Diana to stay for a few days before moving to her grandparents' home. In my role as nervous father I telephoned to see if she was okay. "Oh, we're perfectly safe, Dad. We're in a gay building," was the cheerful response.

Of course there were incidents over the years of misbehaviour and broken bones and concussions, some sports-related, but we were spared serious illness, except for Ardith, and serious wrongdoing. James was an ice hockey goalie and, because the padding was inadequate, he often was covered with bruises. What bothered me much more when I attended his early morning games in ice-cold arenas were the ugly attitudes displayed by other parents, including those whose children were on the same team as James. They shouted abuse at him if he let a goal in. Both children were keen skiers, and James, in particular, became very proficient. Today he skies with his daughter. Diana's great love was horses.

Sometimes there were satisfying moments of parental control. After

James ready to stop the puck, Ottawa, 1978.

Ardith's father died, her mother often visited us in Ottawa and occasionally looked after the children to allow us to get away. On one such occasion, we spent two weeks at a farm belonging to old friends on Vancouver Island while they vacationed elsewhere. Our job was to look after the chickens, quite a change from my regular work. We periodically telephoned home to see how things were getting on. I grew suspicious when the children kept saying, amidst a great deal of background noise, that grandma was not able to come to the phone.

It turned out that she had been taken to hospital in an ambulance, and the children were alone at home. Our son had invited his friends for a sleepover. We knew a couple who lived a block from us, and I telephoned them at once. He was a Mountie, and she was also very authoritative. They got over to our house very quickly, sent all the partygoers home, and found out from the hospital that grandma had had a heart scare that proved to be inconsequential. She was soon home again and assured us that there was no need for us to return prematurely. There was something particularly satisfying about being able to reach across four thousand kilometres to exercise

Ardith's father and mother, James and Martha McMillan, Vancouver, late 1970s.

control over our mischievous kids: a domestic variant of the long arm of the law, complete with Mounties riding to the rescue.

Our Mountie friend and his family were a smaller version of television's *The Brady Bunch*. His wife had been left with three children when her first husband, working as a missionary in Thailand, had been killed in an accident. He also had three children and had lost his first wife to cancer at a young age. They had met at the same church which we attended, fallen in love, and moved their blended family into an attractive home a block from us. They ran a highly organized, remarkably disciplined household, and our children were in awe of them, no bad thing. Sadly, the effect of Ardith's illness on our social life prevented us from coming as close to them as we probably otherwise would have. It was nonetheless comforting to have them nearby, and they did help us out occasionally during crises. After all of their children had left the home, our friends, who were keen scuba divers, moved to the sun-drenched Bahamas, and we lost touch. I guess they were part of God's provision of which I wrote earlier.

The marriage of one's firstborn is a big event, but, in our cautious view, it came too soon. At the age of twenty, while she was studying at university for her physics degree, Diana informed us that she and her boyfriend Joe wanted to get married as soon as possible. We tried to persuade her to wait until she had earned her degree, but she was determined to proceed. Arguments about her youth carried little weight, given that she was the same age as her mother when we were married.

We were also concerned about her choice of husband. Even readers who do not share our faith might perhaps understand, given our own history, how much we believed that sharing religious views was important to making marriage work. Diana shared our faith, but her husband-to-be did not. He was a talented chef – later to be a sous chef at Ottawa's prestigious Westin Hotel – and that meant late hours and a lifestyle very different from that to which we and our daughter were accustomed. He was also a chain-smoker, and Diana's asthma, inherited from me, was affected by the constant smoke. Weeks of pleading with her achieved nothing, and Ardith and I, not wishing to create a rift between ourselves and our daughter, finally acquiesced and funded a very happy wedding. Both Ardith's mother and mine came from the West Coast for the event, and James, then eighteen, took great delight in chauffeuring them around. Sadly, Joe's family remained divided about his marriage, and neither his father nor his brother was willing to attend the ceremony. Later there was a measure of reconciliation, but Joe must have been very hurt.

Diana and Joe built their own home, doing much of the work themselves, in a small village about forty minutes from Ottawa. It was a very pretty, two-storey Cape Cod style house with blue siding and white shutters. They later sold it and built a red brick split-level. The second house was also very nice, but it did not have the oversized dollhouse charm of the first one. On our regular visits, we naturally enjoyed Joe's superb cooking, and I never failed to be amazed at how their dog Sam, a collie cross, recognized our car at least a block away and began leaping in the air. The downside of Joe's artistic cuisine was the unbelievable mess he left to be cleaned up afterwards.

Sadly, over the next few years, Joe's timetable, especially after he began working at the Westin, meant that he and Diana rarely saw one another, and his incessant smoking really affected her when they were together. To make a long, painful story short, Joe eventually stated his intention to leave her. In the event, he moved to northern Saskatchewan, and Diana came home to us. I remember her arriving on our doorstep in a state of near collapse, barely able to breathe. She was experiencing acute asthma probably

With my mother, Betty, and Diana, who is wearing Ardith's wedding dress, Ottawa, 1984.

triggered by a mix of severe stress, second-hand smoke, and seriously cold weather. She recovered physically, but I know she still carries the pain of that unfortunate series of events. Years later, she told me that one of the main reasons she wanted to get married so quickly was to get out of our highly stressed home. It is hard for me not to feel that Diana's sad marital experience was at least in part another casualty of her mother's schizophrenia.

Diana is academically gifted, and she chose physics as her primary discipline because she thought it would challenge her. Her interest in becoming a teacher developed later, partly because of the satisfaction she experienced in working as a teaching assistant at the university after receiving her degree. When Joe left, she applied to several universities to pursue studies in education and found the curriculum offered by Simon Fraser University near Vancouver to be the most appealing. By happy chance, her application was accepted a few months after we ourselves moved to Vancouver. Her career as a high school physics teacher began a few years later, and, today, twenty-three years after our return to the West Coast, she is well into her second decade of living in an attractive condominium building a block from Stanley Park and only four blocks away from us. You would almost think that someone up there was planning it all. We see her frequently, and, needless to say, we are very grateful that she is so close.

Diana's commitment to her students is truly remarkable both in terms of time and emotional energy. She really cares, and the results show. She has attracted a majority of girls in her three classes for several years running despite the fact that physics is one of the fields that continues to be male dominated. Her classes have ranked well province-wide, and one of her graduates was awarded a Rhodes scholarship to Cambridge. Another was chosen as the spokesperson for world youth at the Durban Conference on Climate Change. I saw that young woman's speech on YouTube, and I was very impressed. Diana's commitment to education goes beyond challenging those who have chosen to take physics classes. Physics students tend to be reasonably well motivated, although some may be there because of pressure from home. She insists each year on also teaching remedial math to grade 10 students, arguably the most difficult class in her school. Dealing with parents is also challenging, made more so because of the substantial differences in culture, child-rearing, and attitudes to education among so many different ethnic groups. Highly varying linguistic skills and resulting problems of communication add to the challenge.

James' life was to take a very different path. It was clear that being separated from his "mother" in New Zealand affected him, and he had more difficulty than his sister in settling into our new life in Canada. Although I regularly worked with him on his homework and tried to be supportive, it was evident that academic pursuits were not high in his priorities. Sports, especially hockey and skiing, ranked much higher. I was frankly disappointed given my own academic orientation, but I had my eyes opened to his world in an unusual way. In 1980, the four of us made our one and only car trip across our huge country. James, at thirteen, was excited at the prospect and took a lively interest in the many things we saw. Diana, at sixteen, was much too cool to display enthusiasm. She even went so far as to hang a map over her window and focus on a book lest she should by accident actually see something of Canada. Seeing animals, however, broke through the "cool." A highlight was visiting some of Ardith's relatives, who ran a lodge on a sizable island in Lake Superior. Their family pet was a very

My brother, Keith, with his first wife, Carol Ann, children Shawn and Shari, Vancouver, 1982.

large, overfed raccoon who ate his meals with his delicate little hands at the dining room table. Needless to say, Diana and James were entranced.

We took our time driving to the West Coast, nearly two weeks, in order to visit family members and enjoy sightseeing, especially in the magnificent Rockies. While on Vancouver Island, we stayed with our chicken-raising friends whose farm was not far from a roller rink. James was a keen roller skater, and I drove him to the rink and stayed to watch him do his thing. I was frankly blown away by his grace and skill. His dancing to the music was so good that he soon had a circle of admirers standing around watching him. A girl in her late teens who was employed by the rink began to dance with him, but, skilled though she was, she could barely keep up. I realized at that moment that my son was capable of doing things that I could only dream about. My respect for him soared, and I came to recognize that he was his own person and should not be expected to emulate his father. James and I drove back to Ottawa, leaving Ardith and Diana to return by plane later. We drove straight through, taking six days to cover over four thou-

My mother, Betty, her third husband Clyde Fraser, and Ardith, standing outside their home in Victoria, 1986.

sand kilometres. It proved to be a real bonding experience, and my relationship with James grew ever better in the years that followed despite many challenges and heartaches.

The only teacher who seemed to recognize James' potential was his high school accounting teacher, Mr. Scobie. He arranged for James to earn credits towards his graduation through a "co-op" program that involved working part time in one of Ottawa's best ski shops. When he left high school, James went to work there full-time. Because of his natural sales ability and enthusiasm for skiing, he soon rose to become store manager. It was not unusual for university students and even graduates to work part time at the store, and one of these told James that he was planning to enroll at Ottawa's Information Technology Institute (ITI). James realized that there was no prospect for further advancement at the ski shop (which was part of a family-owned chain), and he discussed with his mother and me the possibility of enrolling at ITI. It was expensive, but it turned out to

Ardith's brother Bruce weds Alice (seated), with me as best man, Abbotsford, 1983.

be the best investment we ever made. James found it very challenging to return to an academic environment, but he was determined to succeed.

The result was remarkable. Although he was one of only two in his class of thirty who did not have a university degree, he scored marks of over eighty percent, and he was the first to receive a job offer, mainly because of his sales experience. This was the beginning of a whole new career. Today, as the head of government relations in Ottawa of a huge multinational company based in the United States, he sells customized data management systems to both Canadian government departments and corporations as well as to some private companies and non-governmental institutions. He has been so successful in promoting innovative approaches and thereby gaining access to new customers that his company has made him a member of the prestigious President's Circle, the first Canadian to be so honoured.

A few years ago, James greatly increased the value of his own older inner city home through a beautiful renovation inside and out. That experience led him to a new venture. He and a partner started turning larger inner city properties into attractive multiple dwelling rental units. Most recently they have launched Arx Asset Management, which James describes as "a firm that assists people to grow their wealth through the acquisition of real property."

Clearly, both of our children have been successful in their chosen fields. If I sound like a proud father, it is because I am. Sadly, like his sister's, James' marriage has not been as successful as his career, but he retains a friendly relationship with Amy, his separated wife, and they share equally, in a very amicable and co-operative way, in the upbringing of their ten-year-old daughter, Portia, our only grandchild. Indeed, Amy joined James and Portia on their visit to Vancouver in 2012. Both are deeply committed parents, and it has been a source of great comfort to us to see how they have put aside their own differences for the sake of their child. I recall Portia, three years ago, when it first became clear that her parents were going to be living apart, telling me with delight that she was soon going to have two bedrooms. Parental separation can be very damaging to children, and we were naturally worried. Happily, the manner in which this separation has taken place and the way in which Portia's care is being managed offers every hope of minimizing the damage.

Chapter 51

SUCCESS AT LAST: LEGISLATION IS APPROVED

The reader will recall that the Federal Court decisions that found the Environmental Assessment Guidelines Order to be a "law of general application" created two major challenges for FEARO. I have already discussed the first, managing the huge expansion of work to avoid unreasonable delays in approving appropriately designed projects. The second was to draft and secure approval for federal environmental assessment legislation to replace the inadequately written Order. The reader will also recall that other government departments had successfully blocked the development of such legislation for more than a decade despite support for a new environmental assessment act from both major political parties. The Federal Court decisions made those departments more amenable to the principle of having legislation, but they remained just as nervous about what it might contain. My other right-hand man, John Herity, was given the daunting task of negotiating principles of legislation that would satisfy our fellow public servants' long-standing objections and still result in an effective process. He built on work earlier led by Bob Connelly.

Response across the government to John's invitation to an initial interdepartmental meeting was so overwhelming that we could not find an available government-owned conference room large enough to accommodate the attendees. We were forced to hire a huge room under the stadium where the Roughriders, Ottawa's professional Canadian football club, plied their trade. It was perhaps fitting that we should begin our efforts in a place where so many mighty battles had been fought. The dozens of public servants in the room whom John faced may not have been wearing helmets and body armour like the gladiators of the gridiron, but their head-butting attitudes were remarkably similar. I remember seeing the exhaustion in John's eyes when he dragged himself back to the office at the conclusion of each grueling session. The fact that he eventually produced a remarkable degree of acceptance, however reluctant, of a comprehensive environmental assessment act that built upon and improved the Guidelines Order is very much to his credit. John tells me that he was greatly helped in this effort by Arthur Campeau, a Montreal lawyer appointed by Prime Minister Mulroney who later became Canada's first Ambassador for the Environment. I came to know Arthur and both admired and liked him. He died very prematurely a few years later, a real loss to our country.

The next task was to secure Cabinet approval for the agreed principles of legislation before an actual bill could be drafted. That was my job. Minister Bouchard told me that I would have thirty minutes to present the principles to his fellow ministers, an extraordinarily long time for a Cabinet Committee agenda item. That generous allocation of time was a mark both of the complexity of the legislation and the degree of impact across government that it would have. John and I put together a PowerPoint presentation, and I practiced it several times. It was timed to the second and as complete as we could make it. I would like to say that, as I waited outside the Cabinet room to make my presentation, I felt calm and confident. In truth I was experiencing butterflies and the adrenaline was pumping. This moment was the culmination of more than a decade of effort by dedicated public servants. More important was what was at stake: the need for an effective, well-designed national environmental assessment process. Some departments still had objections, and, if ministers were moved to voice them, the approval process could again unravel.

Bouchard came out of the Cabinet room and told me that I would be on in about five minutes. He also said that I would only have twelve minutes to speak and answer questions. My heart sank. What was I going to do with my beautifully organized and timed PowerPoint presentation? They say that battlefield prayers are the most fervent because they are fuelled by a potent mix of excitement and fear. My prayers at that moment were similarly fuelled, and I entered the room in a somewhat stunned state. Bouchard said a few words of introduction, and I was on my feet. I decided to scrap the PowerPoint presentation and leave on the screen a flowchart showing how the process would work under the proposed law. I went through it in a minimal way and explained how it was better than the present situation governed by the Guidelines Order. There were a few questions about the burden the process might place on the affected departments, which I effectively answered by pointing out that the efficiencies made possible through the legislative scheme would make the process less burdensome than the process existing under the Guidelines Order. The chair called for a vote, and approval was unanimous. Bouchard shook my hand and congratulated me; I left with appropriate haste. Needless to say, there was great joy at the office upon my return.

Our job, however, was far from over. The next task was to work with the legislative section of the Department of Justice to turn the principles of legislation into a draft bill for submission by the Minister to the House. That job proved to be more challenging than one might have supposed, and for a very simple reason. Justice was used to writing legislation that was essentially empowering and permissive, that is to say, discretionary, rather than binding on government. I can best explain this situation by comparing the American and Canadian legislation development procedures. The differences reflect the fact that in the United States, the Legislative Branch of government is constantly attempting to control the Executive Branch, whereas in Canada a government (executive) with a majority in the House effectively controls the legislature. As a consequence, Congress typically enacts detailed legislation that requires the Executive Branch to act in a particular manner or, where the exercise of discretion is needed as a practical matter, to exercise that discretion against clearly stated criteria. If the U.S. government departments fail to follow the law, there is recourse in the judicial system with the Supreme Court as the ultimate arbiter.

In Canada, legislation is drafted by the Justice Department in consultation with the responsible department and in response to Cabinet-approved principles. The responsible Minister then introduces it to the House for consideration by the appropriate committee. The responsible departments are typically concerned with ensuring that the legislation is administratively convenient and the Justice Department, as the government's lawyers, are concerned so far as possible to avoid language that would expose the government to judicial review. The result is draft legislation that tends to be permissive and discretionary.

I can remember discussions with our U.S. counterparts during the Great Lakes water quality agreement negotiations on each other's relevant legislation. The Americans were stunned by the permissive nature of Canadian laws. "You are not required to do *anything*," they would say in astonishment. Clearly such a permissive approach would not make much sense for the wording of legislation designed to impose a requirement for government departments to follow a particular environmental assessment process. Unless the procedures are mandatory or governed by discretion that is fettered in accordance with clearly stated criteria, there is not a lot of point. To my way of thinking, unless the procedures incorporated in the legislation or in regulations issued under the authority of that legislation are vulnerable to enforcement by the courts, citizens have no guarantee that the government departments will follow these procedures. As a consequence, FEARO officials engaged in a kind of shoving match with their Justice counterparts, who were supported by affected departments, as we tried to put some teeth into the legislation. I was not personally fully satisfied with the result, but I know that our people did the very best they could in difficult circumstances.

As it happens, the bill originally submitted to the House on June 18, 1990, later benefited from a number of strengthening amendments proposed by the House Environment Committee. These followed extensive hearings during which many interested parties from across the country made presentations. Representing the provinces was Alberta Environment Minister Ralph Klein, later to become a long-serving premier, who attempted to make the case that the Federal Government should limit its involvement in the field of environmental assessment, leaving the provinces to carry the primary responsibility. His argument did not fall upon sympathetic ears, in part because he presented it very poorly. Given his later success as Alberta's Premier, I can only assume that he had either been badly briefed or had not studied his briefing material. FEARO staff and I worked with the Committee, making suggestions where appropriate and assisting in wording the amendments. From time to time I was asked to appear formally before the Committee to answer questions and comment on possible changes. In the event, the amendments were so extensive that the government decided to resubmit the bill in an improved form the following spring, coincidentally on my birthday. It was approved by the House and Senate a little over a year later, but it was not proclaimed into law until 1995, when the various regulations needed to make it effective were finally issued. Fittingly, Stephen Hazell, whose success years earlier in the landmark Rafferty-Alameda court case had placed the wind at our back in our efforts to secure legislation, joined FEARO temporarily to lead the effort to develop these regulations. The delay in their issuance was caused by a mix of their complexity and, not surprisingly, of opposition to specific provisions from public servants in various departments.

I must admit that, in my earlier periodic reporting to the House Environment Committee, I sometimes felt concern that Members of Parliament were not as effective as they should be in questioning those, such as I, who were representing government. I thought this was probably caused by a lack of staff to provide the MPs with the information they needed to challenge the answers given. However, I had not yet seen a House Committee in action when actually considering proposed legislation, rather than posing questions about current activities. I was very impressed by how assiduous MPs were in reviewing the clauses of the bill, in questioning their intent, and in pursuing options for improvement. As noted earlier, so many improvements were proposed that the government felt obliged to resubmit the bill incorporating these new proposals. This is what Committee review of proposed legislation is supposed to achieve. An even better example occurred long after my retirement when, in 2002–3, the House Environment Committee undertook a mandatory review of the Canadian Environmental Assessment Act.

My former right-hand man, Bob Connelly, represented the Canadian Environmental Assessment Agency (created under the Act to replace FEARO) at the lengthy hearings conducted by the Committee, which was very fittingly chaired by Charles Caccia. As Liberal Environment Minister under Prime Minister Trudeau, Caccia had secured Cabinet approval for the Environmental Assessment Review Process Guidelines Order (EARPGO) in 1984. In my view, the proposal for environmental assessment legislation was finally able to move forward only because of the Federal Court's finding that this Order was mandatory. When I wrote about Caccia earlier, I characterized him as a brilliant, committed environmentalist. He had not changed and clearly felt in no way limited by his government's Cabinet-approved list of improvements. Aided by fellow Liberals Clifford Lincoln (a former environment minister in the government of Québec) and Karen Kraft-Sloan and supported by the New Democratic Members on the Committee, Caccia successfully secured approval of a significant number of amendments. All were subsequently approved by the House and Senate. In Bob Connelly's judgement, taken together they constituted a strengthening of the Act. Ironically, while personally sympathizing with many of the suggested amendments, Bob had the uncomfortable job, as a good public servant, to argue against some of them because they conflicted with the Cabinet-approved proposals. Better he than I!

The ability of Members of Parliament to go beyond their own parties' positions with respect to the Canadian Environmental Assessment Act (CEAA) during both the Environment Committee's initial consideration and the review held in 2002–3 reflects the best of parliamentary tradition. It is important to note that this happened under both Progressive Conservative and Liberal majority governments. Under our system of government, the required level of independence in this situation for Members of Parliament depends in large measure on the willingness of the Prime Minister to keep from using the considerable powers in his possession to pressure the Members concerned. He can reward by promising a future Cabinet or Parliamentary Secretary appointment, or punish by refusing to sign the papers necessary to allow the Member concerned to run for the party in the next election. It is to the credit of both Progressive Conservative Prime Minister Brian Mulroney and Liberal Prime Minister Jean Chrétien that neither applied any pressure on MPs to toe the party line when reviewing CEAA.

It is a fact that our professional Public Service effectively prevented the enactment and coming into force of federal environmental assessment legislation for more than a decade and a half despite the written commitment to such legislation in the electoral platforms of the two dominant political parties of that era. Indeed, if it were not for unprecedented decisions by the courts, Parliament might never have been given the opportunity to consider, much less enact, federal environmental assessment legislation. That situation is obviously disturbing, but there is another side to this story. If I had created an op-ed page in this book for comments from those opposing the legislation, they no doubt would have pointed out that it was their job to do everything possible to prevent the imposition of requirements and procedures that could interfere with the efficient management of their legally authorized programs. They would have a point. I see merit in a system that encourages the different parts of government to fight each other on behalf of those outside government who benefit from the programs managed by the competing public servants. The problem lies in the paralysis that can be created by the effective requirement for consensus imposed by the Privy Council Office (PCO) before any matter can reach the responsible Cabinet Committee. Interested readers will find a more detailed examination of the implications for governance presented by this problem in appendix XIV. In fairness to the public servants involved in resisting environmental assessment legislation over the years, it also has to be said that if either Liberal or Progressive Conservative prime ministers had taken their respective electoral platforms' commitment to legislation seriously, each could have ordered the PCO to facilitate development of the legislation. Only after the court decisions made legislation necessary did PCO intervene in a helpful manner.

There is also the matter of the way legislation is written in this country. I can see real merit in moving the responsibility for drafting legislation out of the Department of Justice into a special unit reporting directly to Parliament. At least the bias of the drafters, when presented by government with principles of legislation, would be to produce wording that reinforces government's accountability to Parliament, through the courts if necessary, rather than minimizing it through broad use of unfettered discretion.

For some readers, it may be necessary to make very clear that environmental assessment legislation is not designed to force the government to place environmental considerations above all others. Its purpose is to ensure that decisions made about activities that could affect the environment adversely are as informed as possible. As a society, we need to understand those possible effects in order to determine what weight they should be given and how to avoid or mitigate them. If public confidence in this process is to be sustained, it is also important that such understanding be acquired and evaluated as transparently as possible. That is why the legislation required, where appropriate, public hearings, public reports, and detailed public responses to those reports from the government. For example, even if a panel review concluded that a project would result in significant adverse environmental effects, the Federal Cabinet could still decide to approve the project, but it would be expected to make its reasons public. In other words, the process remained advisory and politicians accountable to the electorate retained the responsibility for making the final decisions. That said, while panel conclusions reflecting significant unavoidable, adverse effects were rare, they, until 2012, had always resulted in a project's rejection. In that year, the Conservative government with its newly obtained majority in the House chose to approve the huge Lower Churchill

River hydroelectric project in Labrador despite the panel's finding of significant adverse environmental effects.

The last Environment Minister for whom I worked was Jean Charest, who later moved to provincial politics, changed political parties, and became Liberal Premier of Québec, serving for nine years. Not long after I moved back to Vancouver, I attended an international environment conference in that city. While walking through the conference centre, I was spotted by Minister Charest, who motioned for me to join him. He was speaking with a number of foreign visitors, and he introduced me as the man who authored the Canadian Environmental Assessment Act. That was a very generous thing for a politician to say about a career public servant, and, I have to admit, it made my day. In truth, as my account I hope makes clear, FEARO's committed personnel, like John Herity and, later, Beverly Hobby, overseen by Brian Wilson, were the real authors. They, like Bob Connelly, who continued the battle long after I left, deserve much more credit than I. And I should not forget those outside government, like Stephen Hazell, who put the wind in our sails. I am particularly grateful to our in-house lawyer, Beverly Hobby, seconded to FEARO from Justice, who put in very long hours battling skillfully and energetically on our behalf with the legal drafters from her parent department. I doubt it did her career any good, but she was on the right side of that issue.

As I was reading my manuscript yet again not long before it was to go to the printer, the news came of the death of that extraordinary global icon Nelson Mandela. Readers may recall my account of speechmaking as a young diplomat in late 1960s New Zealand. A common theme was the need to maintain international pressure on South Africa's apartheid regime. Those efforts, like the much more important decision in 1964 by External Affairs Minister Paul Martin Sr. to block a potentially huge sale of Canadian trucks to the South African police, were a reflection of Canada's long-standing policy of working, especially within the Commonwealth, to maintain that pressure. In 1986, Prime Minister Mulroney's government imposed a trade embargo on South Africa, losing hundreds of millions annually in Canadian exports. It was therefore not surprising that in June 1990, only two months after his release from twenty-seven years in jail, Mandela came to Canada to express his appreciation. He deservedly received a hero's reception wherever he went, not least when addressing Canada's House of Commons. In 2001 he was awarded honorary Canadian citizenship, the first living person to be so recognized. I admire Mandela with a passion, especially for those attitudes and policies of reconciliation that brought a remarkable measure of healing to a land that seemed hopelessly and dangerously divided. No one in the 1980s could have seriously hoped, let alone believed, that he would so quickly bring about a peaceful end to apartheid. The key was responding in a generous way to the legitimate fears of minorities, the fundamental test of a true democracy, a point I emphasize elsewhere in this book, especially chapter 56 and appendix I. It is more than fitting that Canada's current prime minister and four former prime ministers attended his funeral.

Unfortunately for me and our embattled agency, the timing of Mandela's 1990 visit to Ottawa was not the best. Gordon Harris, who did such an excellent job over the years in managing FEARO's public relations, reminded me that the South African leader's speech to Parliament coincided with the tabling in the House of our proposed environmental assessment legislation and my appearance on CBC Television to explain the content of the act. Needless to say, we did not get a lot of air time or a lot of print in the newspapers.

I am obliged to end this chapter on a sad note. The hard-won advances I have described in establishing an effective federal environmental assessment process in Canada were almost entirely reversed in 2010 and 2012 by the present Conservative government. The nature of that reversal and my reasons for criticizing both the reversal and the manner in which it was made are set out in appendix XII. I hope the reader will take time to read them. For the record, I have also set out in appendix XI a detailed description of the provisions of the Canadian Environmental Assessment Act as proclaimed into law in January 1995. Hopefully that Act will one day serve as a guide to the re-introduction of effective environmental assessment at the federal level in Canada.

CHAPTER 52

A TALE OF BETRAYAL

AUTHOR'S NOTE: I have retained this fairly technical account in the main body of my narrative rather than placing it in an appendix because I believe it important that readers understand the lengths to which the Government of Canada will go to avoid its fiduciary responsibilities to our native peoples.

"Betrayal" is a very strong word, and I leave it to the reader, after finishing this chapter, to judge whether my use of it is justified. It is my characterization of the Federal Government's attempt in 1991 to avoid its fiduciary responsibilities to the Cree and Inuit peoples of Québec as set out in the James Bay and Northern Québec Agreement.

The Province of Québec decided in 1986 to build the Great Whale River hydroelectric project as the second phase of its immense plan, first announced in 1971, to dam almost every major river running into James Bay and the much larger Hudson's Bay to the north. The first phase, commonly known as the James Bay project, was focused primarily on the La Grande River emptying into James Bay. It was constructed over a twelve-year period. The vast area to be affected by the broader plan included both traditional land of the Cree people and, to the north, of the Inuit people. Because of the fiduciary responsibility of the Federal Government to represent the interests of native peoples, a quadripartite agreement between Canada, Québec, and the two native peoples was signed in 1975 to govern the environmental and socio-economic assessment and approval procedures to be followed for the various stages of the plan. The James Bay and Northern Québec Agreement (JBNQA), as it was called, also required the appointment of "environmental administrators" representing each party. Each was given significant, largely independent decision-making responsibilities with respect to approving the adequacy and extent of the assessment procedures followed. When I was appointed Executive Chairman of FEARO, I was also appointed by Order-in-Council the Federal Environmental Administrator of the JBNQA.

If the Great Whale project had been completed, it would have been one of the world's largest hydroelectric projects, with reservoirs covering 3391 square kilometres of land environment and 1724 square kilometres of aquatic environment (lakes and rivers). The proposed three underground generating stations were planned to have installed capacity exceeding 3200 megawatts. The smaller James Bay project caused serious disturbances to the water regime and aquatic life through flooding and alteration of natural patterns of river flow and mercury pollution. There were other impacts on the lifestyle of the Cree people caused by the increased accessibility to outsiders of their traditional lands. Increased mercury levels were of particular concern because they rendered inedible so many of the fish that were an important part of the Crees' diet.

Given this history, it is scarcely surprising that the Cree people expressed strong opposition to the larger Great Whale project. Matthew Coon Come, their Grand Chief, argued that the project would alter the seasonal patterns and quantity of water flow in the affected rivers and basins, adversely affect the wildlife and marine resources of Hudson's Bay and James Bay, destroy the habitat of fur-bearing animals, disturb the migration patterns of caribou (which are very important to the Cree lifestyle), destroy the spawning grounds of fish, severely increase mercury contamination of fish, and generally harm the ecology of the region in a way that would undermine the Cree way of life and their traditional use of the land and natural resources.

The Cree initially welcomed the exchange of letters between Minister Bouchard and his provincial counterpart that reflected FEARO's success in negotiating a joint environmental assessment review process with Québec under the newly mandatory Guidelines Order. However, their welcoming attitude soon changed to concern because Hydro-Québec called for tenders for clearing and construction of the access road to the Great Whale River before any of the social or environmental assessments had even been organized, much less undertaken. Not unreasonably, the Cree expected the Federal Environmental Administrator to object to Hydro-Québec's action, and I wanted to do so. However, the Justice Department bluntly informed me that the Federal Government, meaning in this instance me, had no legal authority to prevent Hydro-Québec's action. I so informed the Cree, and they concluded that a political decision had been taken by the Mulroney Cabinet "to leave the Cree spinning in the wind."

The Cree reaction was more than simply anger. They went to the Federal Court in March of 1991 to seek an order of mandamus compelling the Federal Environmental Administrator to comply with the federal environmental and social impact assessment and review procedures of Sections 22 and 23 of the JBNQA and the James Bay and Northern Québec Native Claims Settlement Act, which was passed by the federal Parliament to give effect to the Agreement.

The Federal Government's initial response was a procedural argument that the JBNQA was merely a contract, not a law, and therefore the Federal Court had no jurisdiction. The judge dismissed this argument and was upheld on appeal.

I am ashamed to say that the first substantive federal argument was that the joint review process between Québec and Ottawa negotiated to satisfy the newly mandatory Environmental Assessment Guidelines Order was sufficient assessment, and, further, that the assessment results needed to be submitted to the Provincial Environmental Administrator only (and not to his federal counterpart) because the project was a provincial one.

The judge rejected the idea that the joint review process negotiated between Ottawa and Québec could replace the obligations under the JBNQA. He made it clear that the Great Whale Project was automatically subject to environmental and social impact assessment under the JBNQA, "especially concerning the Cree populations potentially affected." Consequently, he ruled that the Federal Environmental Administrator (me) must set up a JBNQA Evaluation Committee to determine whether the project would have any significant impact on the Cree or Inuit people or on the wildlife resources. Presumably to make sure that there could be no doubt about his views, the judge described the Ottawa/Québec joint process as "intended both to appease and circumvent the native populations" and said that it "appears to have been negotiated in an attempt to free themselves from the duties and responsibilities imposed under the Agreement." I hope I do not need to make clear that we in FEARO had no idea that the agreement for a joint environmental assessment process that we had negotiated in good faith with Québec to satisfy the requirements of the newly mandatory Guidelines Order would be used by federal lawyers to try to avoid federal obligations under the James Bay and Northern Québec Agreement (JBNQA).

Another substantive federal argument was that the JBNQA Federal Environmental Administrator had no duty to act until such time as the description of the project was submitted to him. The judge called this argument "entirely spurious." He pointed out that, in accordance with such an interpretation, the proponent of a project could decide whether or not to submit his project for review with no recourse available should he decide not to do so. He called this concept "ludicrous." He concluded, "It could not reasonably be seen to be the intention of the parties to the Agreement that the Federal Environmental Administrator would be powerless to act without the intervention of the proponent. He cannot be left to the whim of the developer."

Lest there could be any remaining doubts about his views on the matter, the judge added these further general comments:

> Sixteen years ago all parties obviously realized that there were areas exclusive to the federal domain which could be affected by any future development; that further development of Northern Québec would certainly implicate the Inuit and Cree communities. As a result, the 1975 Agreement fully recognized that at some future date two jurisdictions will be involved, as well as the aboriginal people; all parties were cognizant of the necessity of reducing to writing procedures for future co-operation. I find it incomprehensible that, on the one hand, the intervenors, the Attorney-General for Québec, and Hydro-Québec, declare themselves bound to abide by the JBNQ Agreement, but, on the other hand, other signatories to the same agreement are excluded.

Such was the poor quality of the legal advice that I was given by the Justice Department and such are the extremes to which the Federal Government was prepared to go to avoid its fiduciary duty. I find it appalling and I hope the reader does, too.

The project subsequently became bogged down in the JBNQA review process over a nearly three-year period because Hydro-Québec was unable or chose not to meet the assessment requirements laid out by the JBNQA Evaluation Committees. The Cree, the Inuit, and their environmental allies in Canada and the United States used that time to conduct effective public campaigns that resulted in cancellation of the electricity export contracts with the previously interested U.S. electrical power distribution companies. One such campaign centred on a widely reported journey down the Hudson River to New York by Cree and Inuit leaders in an unusual but highly symbolic hybrid craft. It had the prow of an Indian canoe and the stern of an Inuit kayak. The destination of the native leaders was the United Nations. In mid-November 1994, Jacques Parizeau, the premier of Québec at the time, pulled the plug, so to speak, on this ill-fated mega-project. It seems unlikely to rise again. The Cree, not a wealthy people, had to spend $8 million on their campaign to stop the damming of the Great Whale River. Ironically, as it turned out, the joint environmental review process that emerged out of the court decisions and our earlier negotiations with Québec was both unique and innovative. If carried to completion, it would have produced high-quality environmental and social information on Northern Québec based upon both science and aboriginal knowledge.

Both this sad saga and the long march I described earlier towards federal environmental assessment legislation benefited from the role of the courts. Without their intervention, the results would have been very different. The ability and willingness of an independent judiciary to review the decisions of government as needed is central to the effective functioning of our democracy. These two examples reinforce that truth.

Curiously, my involvement with the Cree did result in one very happy moment, indeed one of the best memories of my environmental career. Immediately after the Cree won their initial procedural victory in the Federal Court, I was asked for comment by a Toronto *Globe and Mail* reporter. He knew little of the subject matter because he was filling in for the regular environment reporter with whom I normally dealt. I unwisely took pity upon him and spent some time explaining the broader situation. He clearly failed to understand what I was telling him, and his report in the newspaper the next day attributed to me feelings of concern over the Cree's Court victory. He said that I characterized it as a minor victory in a long war. The implication was that I saw myself as being at war with the Cree, bearing in mind that I was the person named in the Cree's legal action.

In truth, I felt just the opposite. I was delighted that the court might strengthen the hand of the Federal Environmental Administrator (as indeed it did). Just after I read this story, I received an important West Coast visitor, the Chief of a British Columbia First Nation near Kitimat, which is on the coast well to the north of Vancouver. He had come to discuss the environmental assessment process that would apply to proposed changes in the Nechako River's Kenny power dam built by Alcan Aluminum. Alcan operated a large aluminum production facility in Kitimat. I thought my visitor might well have read the story about the Cree in the *Globe and Mail,* and I braced myself to explain what I had said. He saw the newspaper on my desk, and when I started to say something, he simply smiled and remarked, "We know your heart and we know you would not say those things." That is a moment I truly treasure.

Chapter 53

JOY IN RENOVATIONS; DELIGHT IN VISITORS

Our ties with New Zealand were periodically reinforced by visits from "down under," which always brightened our days or weeks. Presumably because of their geographic isolation, New Zealanders are inveterate travellers. They often combine their trips to Europe, especially Britain, with stops in Asia and North America because travelling to Europe one way and back the other adds little, if anything, to the cost. We have greatly benefited from this kiwi addiction to travel over the years, in both Ottawa and Vancouver. In August of 1978, Gordon and Margaret Pellow arrived in Ottawa to help us celebrate our twentieth wedding anniversary. They are the funeral director and his wife who played such a central role in our Christian conversion and the repair of our broken marriage. What could be more fitting? They gave us a beautiful piece of sculpture in china depicting two white doves with their heads touching each other. That inspiring representation of our union has sat on the coffee table in our living room for the more than thirty-five years since that anniversary. It reminds us every day how much we owe that dear couple and the God they so faithfully served.

Gordon and Margaret were very energetic, and they quickly shook us out of our customary lethargy. Their first target was our decor, which centred on the tired-looking furnishings that we had acquired before our first overseas posting in Bogota eighteen years earlier. The furnishings had also survived extensive entertaining in Wellington, a decade of use in Ottawa, and two children.

Several visits to various furniture establishments later, our living and dining rooms were utterly transformed. The centrepiece was a large, beautiful, oriental area rug, the principal colours of which were reflected in the upholstery we subsequently chose for the rooms. Gordon and Margaret's own home in Hamilton, New Zealand, was extremely elegant and beautifully situated on the high bank of a river that meanders through the centre of their city. Their very large living room was actually built around a magnificent oriental carpet, easily the biggest one I have ever seen. We had no hesitation about taking their advice on our decor. Antique occasional tables and chairs, other period furniture, contrasting modern pieces, elegant mirrors, artwork, and a beautiful chandelier for the dining room were all acquired during their extended stay with us. The transformation was both stunning and remarkably warm and welcoming. We still have all of that beautiful furniture, and it fits perfectly into our spacious Vancouver condominium apartment. One result of entertaining very little is that furniture lasts a long time.

Our ever-active guests then turned their sights on our mode of transport. A new car was the target, and the process of obtaining one proved to be quite a ride in itself. My notional budget was based on the price of a new, full-size, slightly above entry-level family car less our trade-in. We had had problems with the newer of the two cars we already owned and it was that one that we planned to replace. We visited several dealerships comparing features and prices.

At one dealership we were distracted by a beautiful sedan in the show room that was substantially more expensive than my proposed budget would permit. It was a different class of car. Adding to its appeal was the colour, inside and out, which was the same, even to the precise shade, as the dominant colour in our new oriental rug. Our friends persuaded us to make a very low offer on that beautiful sedan based on an optimistic view of the value of my trade-in while respecting my budget ceiling. The salesman, a young Jamaican newly arrived in Canada, told me that the offer would not be nearly enough, but, at our insistence, he took it to his manager. Predictably, it was turned down flat.

Encouraged by our friends, we bowed our heads briefly in prayer and told the salesman that, if God intended us to have it, it would be at that price. We talked further about our faith, and the salesman offered to find a private buyer for our trade-in, and, if he was successful, to resubmit our offer on the elegant sedan. Within two days, the young salesman called to say that he had a good offer on my car and was prepared to forward a cash deal to his manager. The manager accepted the deal, and we received delivery of this very elegant car at a price comfortably within my original budget. Our New Zealand visitors told the salesman that, in their country, a dealership would always send roses to the wife of the buyer upon selling a new car of this quality. Sure enough, roses were duly delivered to Ardith. We had that car for thirteen years, and it ran beautifully. After we moved to Vancouver, we sold it to the horse ranch where Diana used to ride. The owner of the ranch particularly liked its powerful engine.

There was, however, a very sad side to this otherwise happy tale. A few weeks later I had occasion to visit the dealership to pick something up, and I stuck my head in the show room to say hello to the young Jamaican salesman. I learned, to my horror, that he had been killed in a car accident a few days after he had helped us. I have to hope and believe that he took seriously the conversation we had about our faith in the few days he had left to live. None of us knows what tomorrow might bring.

Gordon and Margaret were never to visit us again, although we visited them several times in New Zealand. We used to joke that it was cheaper for us to make several visits down under than it would be for us to live through another visit from them. Sadly, Gordon is no longer with us, but we know we will be with him again.

Thinking of that most expensive of anniversaries reminds me that it was also the occasion of my least expensive anniversary gift to Ardith. At the same time, the gift cost me a lot. I was inspired to give it by that verse of Scripture that admonishes married couples to subject their bodies to each other. Beyond its obvious meaning, that verse to my mind also applies to keeping oneself attractive to one's spouse – in fitness, clothing, and grooming. For many years Ardith had wanted me to grow a beard, inspired perhaps by memories of the one I grew in Bogota during my long recovery from amoebic hepatitis. Once I returned to the office, the Ambassador asked me to shave it off, ostensibly because wearing a beard at that juncture in Latin America suggested identification with Fidel Castro's barbudos, his bearded revolutionary supporters. The office gossip had it that the Ambassador's wife liked it too much. I discount the latter theory, and, in any case, I was happy to get rid of it. A fan of beards I was not.

That said, I came to realize, as our twentieth anniversary approached, that I was withholding from Ardith something to which she, as my wife, had a right. I told her of my decision to stop shaving and she was delighted.

The cost to me was more than the initial discomfort – itching and the like; it was embarrassment. I had just become head of the Environmental Protection Service and few, if any, of comparable rank had beards. Later, they became more fashionable. Also, the beard was somewhat scruffy. I have since become adjusted. More importantly, the beard continues to be a symbol to each of us of our union.

From this distance in time, the years blur, and I have to use temporal landmarks to help remember the order in which events occurred. One of those landmarks was the expansion of our home in the mid-1980s. Our stone and brick bungalow had a sizable screened and roofed patio at the side of the kitchen and behind the two-car garage at one end of the house. It was an integral part of the original building, not an add-on, and I had long envisaged making it into a sunken family room with a cathedral ceiling. We had a smaller family room with a fireplace at the back of the house on the other side of the kitchen that I thought would make an attractive breakfast room. To complete the package, I envisaged two cedar decks, one shaded off the new family room and one in the sun off the planned breakfast room. Ardith wisely feared the disruption that renovations create but agreed that the concept was good. To make sure it was done well I decided to hire an architect, an expense that I never regretted. He came up with a superb design including reusing the old brick from the back of the garage on the exterior walls of the new family room to remove any sense of something being added.

The mess and the stress were not fun, and the work inevitably took much longer than promised. We had the usual disputes with the builder and his subcontractors, but these were handled very well by the architect, who had full control over the flow of payments.

What I remember most is the "plastered" plasterer whose role was vital. Our living and dining rooms had attractive cove ceilings, and maintaining the precise angle of the curve where the ceiling met the walls was important. The architect's design included French doors opening onto the new sunken family room from the dining room. To achieve maximum visual impact, the doors were set at an angle that allowed anyone entering the front door to look from that entry point through the living room and the dining room and the French doors and the sunken family room and a wall of glass to the cedar deck and the magnificent clump of silver birches that furnished the required shade. The effect was stunning and made the house seem larger than it really became and much larger than it had been.

However, placing the French doors at the correct angle meant recreating a section of the curved cove ceiling, which could be done only by a skilled hand. That hand belonged to the "plastered" plasterer. Both the architect and the builder told us that this man was a genius, truly talented, but what we saw was a very scruffy looking older man who smelt like a distillery, swayed when he walked, and swayed even more on his ladder. I expected him to fall off at any moment, but somehow, either in spite of or because of his condition, his hand moved perfectly and the final job was so good that we could not tell where the old ceiling met the new one. We were also very impressed by the floorers. Their task was to seamlessly blend our beautiful existing rosy oak hardwood floors with identical new flooring, and the result was flawless. The resulting sweep of hardwood added considerably to the visual effect created by the architect.

Renovations are not fun, and we would never do it again. That said, the result produced a lot of pleasure, especially for Ardith, which made it all worthwhile, and it undoubtedly facilitated the sale of the house. On the downside, the improvements made it that much harder to leave when Ardith's health needs made our move to Vancouver necessary.

It was not long before we were able to share our newly renovated home with much appreciated visitors, once again from far-off New Zealand. This time the visitors were Eric and Julie Sherburd. The reader may recall that Eric, a former Baptist pastor, and Julie had moved to Wellington to pursue his pastoral calling in a secular setting not long before Ardith and I became Christians. Eric, in particular, became our principal mentor during our early Christian experience, and he was especially helpful to me during Ardith's repeated health crises. The years melted away as soon as we saw them, and, even though Ardith was experiencing some emotional challenges at the time, she was able to enter into our renewed fellowship. I remember well an excursion we made to Montreal where we delighted in the "old city" quarter that is so reminiscent of Europe. I also recall how much Eric in particular enjoyed sitting in our new family room with its twelve-foot ceiling and wall of glass overlooking the cedar deck, the silver birches, and the attractively landscaped garden.

It was also our plan to accompany Eric and Julie on a very different kind of outing. I earlier mentioned the environmental exchanges we undertook with New Zealand and Australia. In all our meetings with our counterparts down under, we always included representatives of Canada's First Nations because so many of the major projects that we assessed affected native land. New Zealand did the same and, not surprisingly, relationships developed between the native peoples involved from both countries. Eric is of half-Maori descent, and he was bringing a gift from a Maori chief to the chief of the Walpole Island First Nation. It is located about fifty kilometres north-east of Detroit on six islands in the St. Clair River that forms the boundary between Michigan and Ontario. The First Nation has a registered population of about four thousand, a little over half of whom live on the islands. Corn is its principal agricultural crop. This brief extract from a descriptive website provides a quick view of that unique place.

> Walpole Island has the distinction of being "unceded territory." This fact, together with its natural and human resources, makes Walpole Island a very special place. Walpole Island is also known for its rare flora and fauna. Our local economy is highly diverse and rich. It is dependent on the bounty of the land and its fruits. Our lands and waters still support recreation and tourism. Hunting, fishing and trapping is a multi-million-dollar industry in our community. Even though we are the southernmost reserve in Canada citizens of our First Nation incredibly can still support their families through hunting and fishing, trapping and guiding activities. These traditional activities are central to our economic base and cultural integrity.

In the event, Ardith did not feel up to the journey, and Eric and Julie took off in the car that we had purchased during Gordon and Margaret's visit about eight years earlier. (We were left with the newer car carrying those meaningful licence plates that I described the end of the chapter on schizophrenia.) It is too bad that we were unable to participate in the ceremony of gift giving and acceptance that took place on Walpole Island, but we know that Eric and Julie will not forget the warm welcome they received on that special occasion. We certainly will not forget their uplifting visit to us.

We also received on two occasions brief visits to our Ottawa home from Berwyn Gibbons, our well-travelled, widowed former neighbour in New Zealand. The reader may recall that, because of her considerable contribution to New Zealand's dramatic arts, she had a hall named after her in Lower Hutt where we used to live. Her bright, inquiring mind always helped us see our surroundings in a new light, but we remember her best for the many kindnesses bestowed during our troubles while living in the house next door to hers. We visited her several times in New Zealand, and, after we moved to Vancouver, she came twice to us there as well, once with her daughter Rosemary. Diana visited Berwyn's older daughter, Denise, and her husband, Buster, in New Zealand some years ago and declared her stay on their beautiful dairy farm one of the highlights of her trip. (Visiting Eric and Julie Sherburd in Morrinsville, April Bennett in Wellington, and the Tweddell family in Tauranga were among other highlights.) Berwyn's whole family was invigorating to be around and stimulating to talk to. Our time in New Zealand was transformative in every sense, and it has been wonderful to be able to maintain these personal links with that past. They are very much part of who we are today.

We were also visited by our folk-singing friend Don Toms in his new role as a Vice President of Air New Zealand. It was great to reconnect with him, but, lacking his guitar, he was unable to serenade us. Sadly, his dear wife Jean had been lost to cancer, but he had remarried. We were to meet his new wife on our next visit to New Zealand.

PART VI

RETIREMENT AND NEW DIRECTIONS

CHAPTER 54

PREPARATIONS FOR DEPARTURE

In the chapter on living with schizophrenia, I set out the reasons behind the decision to leave my job and move back to our home province on the West Coast. As I explained, British Columbia's mental health laws played a significant part. There were reasons related to my work, as well, but they would not have been sufficient for me to leave if the need to care for Ardith had not been so pressing. Despite my relative youth at fifty-three years old, by late 1990 I was feeling tired in a deep way. Heading FEARO during the later years had been extremely demanding. Our eventual success in securing introduction into the House of an environmental assessment bill eased the pressure on that front, but the management of our court-expanded area of responsibility remained very challenging, especially under the less than ideal provisions of the suddenly mandatory Guidelines Order. We had no idea how long it would be before the much better designed legislation replaced the Order, but I think that none of us in late 1990 thought FEARO would have to function under the existing flawed regime until 1995.

One of the most exhausting human functions is nagging. I suspect that most of us can think of many occasions when we gave up pushing someone to do something and ended up doing it ourselves. In many respects, nagging was one of FEARO's primary functions: constantly pushing reluctant government departments to follow the environmental assessment procedures laid out in the Order. We also coached and educated those we nagged, and, of course, we were responsible for managing the growing number of public reviews with our panels of experts. We had long prided ourselves on being able to undertake a great deal of work with very few permanent employees, largely through the use of contracted experts such as those who served on our panels. Unfortunately, it was becoming increasingly clear that we were going to have to expand our small permanent staff significantly to handle the volume of activity both inside and outside the government. My strengths were in the analysis, visualization, and articulation of policy, and I needed the help of a strong administrator.

In recognition of our situation, I was able to obtain the temporary services of a very competent senior officer, Jean-François Martin, with precisely the skills needed. My job became much more manageable, but, after only a few months, my new, very able colleague was promoted to an Assistant Deputy Minister position in Environment Canada. I was unable to find a replacement, which was, to put it mildly, disheartening. With the pressures at home and the sense that my primary job was complete now that the legislation was before the House, it seemed to me that the time had come for a major change in my life's priorities.

Minister Bouchard had experienced his own job crisis in early 1990 with repercussions vastly greater than any change in my circumstances. The Mulroney government had for some years been trying to develop a new consensus among the provinces in support of the Meech Lake Accord. The Accord was an ultimately unsuccessful attempt to forge an agreement between Canada's elected leaders at both levels of government aimed at making changes in Canada's constitutional arrangements that would hopefully satisfy the majority of Québec nationalists, including Bouchard. Bouchard had agreed to join the Federal Government, at Prime Minister Mulroney's urging, on the understanding that Mulroney would make a serious attempt to bring about a new, closer-to-equal partnership between English and French Canada.

Both the specific content of the Accord and, of course, its acceptance, were therefore extremely important to Bouchard. It is clear in hindsight that he was increasingly worried that Mulroney was prepared to sacrifice Québec's aspirations to satisfy certain other provinces, especially the West and Newfoundland. I had travelled with him privately several times, and we had occasionally spoken of matters unrelated to our work but never about French–English relations in Canada. I cannot therefore claim any direct knowledge of the reasons behind his seemingly sudden decision, effective May 21, 1990, to resign from the Cabinet and cross the floor of the House to sit in opposition preparatory to forming and leading the separatist Bloc Québécois. I was as surprised as everyone else. The apparent trigger was an unacceptable set of proposed changes to the Accord recommended by a commission headed by Jean Charest. In two ironic twists, Charest, as I noted earlier, was himself later to become federal Environment Minister and, much later, to succeed Lucien Bouchard as Premier of Québec.

Bouchard was portrayed at the time by members of his former party, other federalists, and a significant portion of the English-language press as a "traitor," as one who had stabbed his friend Mulroney in the back. That description does not fit the man I had come to know and respect. While passionate and emotional, Bouchard was also principled and forthright. It is clear to me from my knowledge of him and from some of the things he subsequently said that he saw himself as betrayed rather than the other way around. I might add that his departure upset me very much for two reasons: I did not want to lose him as a much-respected boss, and I thought that, if there was anyone who could successfully take Québec out of Canada, it would be he. As any student of Canadian history would understand, I had good reason to be concerned. Thanks to an impressive campaign led by Bouchard, the 1995 Québec independence referendum was almost successful. The "no" side won, but only barely, with 50.6% of the vote. Bouchard's most effective federalist opponent, dubbed "Captain Canada" by the media, was Jean Charest.

Bouchard's successor as Environment Minister, Robert de Cotret, came from the administratively powerful post of President of the Treasury Board, the body that serves as the government's financial and personnel manager/comptroller. It is completely separate from the more prestigious Department of Finance, which develops annual budgets and guides fiscal policy. However, heading the Treasury Board makes it possible to facilitate expenditure approvals for ministerial colleagues and earn a lot of brownie points in the process. Having a minister who is popular with his colleagues is always helpful. As it happened, de Cotret was with us for less than a year before being replaced by the much younger, up-and-coming Jean Charest. Indeed, when Charest was first appointed to the Cabinet five years earlier at age twenty-eight, he broke the record as the youngest Canadian federal cabinet minister ever.

To return to my own story, I spoke with both Minister de Cotret and Len Good, the Deputy Minister of the Environment (who had administrative responsibility for FEARO), in late 1990 about my need to leave Ottawa to look after my wife. Both were very sympathetic, but emphasized the importance of finding a good successor before I took my leave. I began the search, and it led me to Québec city. A few years earlier, the Québec legislature had passed an environmental assessment act that, inter alia, created the Bureau d'audiences publiques sur l'environnement (BAPE), which translates as the Office of Public Hearings on the Environment. Its president was Michel Dorais. BAPE was designed to operate at arm's length from government, and the incumbent president, who was effectively my Québec counterpart, had shown that he took this independence seriously. Moreover, Michel had previously been a public servant in the Privy Council Office in Ottawa and was familiar with the workings of the federal government. He was also at least ten years younger than I and had a science background. On paper, he looked like an excellent choice, and, after securing the support of Environment Canada's Deputy Minister, I approached him. We had a very long conversation that confirmed my initial impression. I suggested that he formally apply for my position. He did so and was accepted.

News of my successor's planned departure from Québec city for Ottawa found its way to the Québec press and was quickly carried across the country. Unfortunately, the English-language press, aware of my environmental activism and my involvement in the controversy surrounding Québec's huge Great Whale project, concluded that I was being replaced by a Québec official to appease the separatist government of Québec. The Liberal Opposition had for some time been hammering the Progressive Conservative government in the House for being "soft on separatism." This news story about my departure, if true, would be grist to that mill.

I received a telephone call from Paul Martin Jr., whose mother, the reader may recall, had greeted me twenty-seven years earlier at her apartment door with the words, "Why, you're just a baby!" At the time of his call, Paul Martin Jr., who later became Finance and then Prime Minister, was the Liberal party's Environment Critic (Shadow Minister). He and I had had several courteous interactions over the years. He wanted to know whether the newspaper reports about the reasons for my departure from Ottawa were true. I explained the real reason that I was leaving my job. After expressing his sympathy, he immediately assured me that his party would not raise the matter in the House as he had no wish to add to my burdens at such a difficult time. He was as good as his word, and the news story soon disappeared. Martin, who was both gracious and competent, was yet another of those many politicians I encountered over the years who did not remotely reflect the common caricature of that much maligned profession.

Remembering Paul Martin's courtesy and kindness prompts me to say something in defence of his profession. Canadians do our country a real disservice when they seek to tar all politicians with the same ugly brush. During my career, I had direct dealings with fourteen Cabinet Ministers, both Liberals and Progressive Conservatives. While their competence and personalities varied, not one warranted the kind of dismissive generalized criticism that has become so common. Indeed, I have no hesitation in saying that, by international standards, the quality of the vast majority of individuals in government in Canada is remarkably high, whether at the elected or appointed level. I would also express the opinion that the sometimes unimpressive behaviour we see on the floor of the House of Commons is in large measure attributable to the frustrations caused by a system that fails to make use of the talents of many of those elected people.

The role of a backbench MP is constrained by strict party discipline and by the lack of resources and real influence of the House Committees through which MPs might otherwise make some impact. Positions in the career Public Service like the one I held can be much more satisfying and influential. Moreover, career public servants do not have to face the electorate or abuse from opponents or constituents. I could not begin to count the number of times I appeared before the House Environment Committee and found myself wanting to say, "Why don't you ask this or question that?" The government members were usually constrained from saying anything that might embarrass their party, and the others did not appear to have the research resources to challenge or effectively probe what was being said. Please do not misunderstand. I never lied to the members of the House Environment Committee. I merely regretted that they so often did not know what to ask me. That said, as I made clear in my account of the House Environment Committee's reviews of the Canadian Environmental Assessment Act, Members of Parliament can do a first class job when given both the information and independence needed to do so.

CHAPTER 55

SOME REMARKABLE REVELATIONS

Visitors on a very different mission from those who came to us from New Zealand were to have a long-lasting impact on myself and, subsequently, on my mother. In 1980, Michael and Jean Harper of Britain's Fountain Trust visited Ottawa from London for a conference and series of talks. Michael, as a young Anglican minister, had established the Fountain Trust in 1964 to promote the charismatic renewal in traditional churches. He had done so after having experienced the baptism of the Holy Spirit, the same phenomenon that I experienced in 1968 in our New Zealand home, six weeks after our Christian conversion.

As part of the group organizing their visit I had an opportunity to meet with them privately. I spoke of some of my spiritual and emotional struggles, and they responded by telling me of a remarkable ministry that had developed at the Anglican church in the London suburb of Hounslow where they were based. The vicar of that church had some years earlier arrived in the parish to find a tiny congregation of aging parishioners. One night in a dream he saw his parishioners as though each was horribly crippled or deformed. He came to understand that this was a representation of how they were inside, spiritually and emotionally. It became increasingly clear to him that what his parishioners needed most was the healing of this internal damage. Out of this recognition grew the ministry of the healing of memories. So successful did this ministry become that, at the time of the Harpers' visit to Ottawa, the church had grown enormously and was reaching out effectively to the community around it. In an act of remarkable kindness to a complete stranger, Michael and Jean invited me to stay in their home in London for two weeks and to meet with their vicar for healing prayer. I accepted and, a couple of months later, I found myself in the city of my birth.

Hounslow is a bedroom community of generally modest homes not far from Heathrow airport. The sound of aircraft passing overhead is almost constant. Michael and Jean lived in a tiny row house not far from the church. When I saw how small their home was, I was even more touched by their generosity in having me as a live-in guest. The sessions for healing prayer were held in the significantly larger vicarage and were conducted by the vicar himself and one of his parishioners, a woman about my own age. Each session opened with prayer for the guidance of the Holy Spirit. Initially we spent time talking about my life and, especially, my earliest memories.

When my well of relevant memories dried up, the vicar and his parishioner assistant prayed that those memories that I could not bring to mind would be revealed to them. In this way several details emerged about my birth and very early years that were totally new to me. The vicar and his assistant prayed for the healing of any hurt caused by each of the memories revealed. The effect on me as we proceeded over the two-week period was curious. It was almost as though I was regressing in age, and I sometimes felt very unsure of myself when I was on my own. To be completely honest, I cannot remember feeling particularly relieved of any pain. However, since my main objective in coming to London was to reduce my feelings of anger, the supportive, loving environment in which I found myself was scarcely the place to test the effectiveness of the process. There was nothing to trigger my anger – quite the reverse.

One of the hurts for which the vicar and his helper prayed was the effect on me of the sustained, systemic bullying that I experienced over many years at both of my boarding schools. At the heart of bullying is humiliation, which, especially when repeated over time, can leave the victim with a seriously flawed sense of self-worth. Being beaten up obviously is painful at the moment, but the resulting feeling of helplessness and hopelessness is what does greater damage in the long term. One of the worst specific instances that I experienced in Victoria was when, at the age of twelve, I was taken by some bigger boys to a forested area near the boarding school, stripped of all my clothing and left alone. I had to make my way back after dark, freezing cold and, much more importantly, profoundly humiliated. It was the humiliation, not the cold, that was lasting in its impact.

As I told the vicar, those painful experiences at school affected me in two opposite ways. On the one hand, I was left with a fierce determination to show my tormentors that I was not the loser they wanted me to believe that I was. Becoming a diplomat at so young an age and, better yet, possibly Canada's youngest ambassador, was a highly visible way of achieving that objective. On the other hand, another part of me had to fight a constant sense of inadequacy that was engendered by my youthful experiences. I often felt like a phoney, and I had an almost pathetic need for positive reinforcement, which my career, but definitely not my home life, provided.

The vicar's prayers eased much of this pain and enabled me to forgive my tormentors, but the effects on my psyche were not completely removed. Each of us is unique, and each of us has to find his or her way of coping with the kind of experiences that I have described. What I have had to keep telling myself is that my victimizers did not and do not define me. I cannot pretend that this approach always works, but I can say that it has helped. Finding faith helped even more, but I still have to choose each day to see myself in a positive light, i.e., as my Creator sees me. This means, for example, seeing myself as a loving, patient caregiver, not as a grumpy, resentful one.

There may have been little during my stay in London to trigger my habitual anger, but triggering my fear was another matter. I had a fair amount of free time, and I sometimes accompanied Michael or Jean or both as they continued their teaching work. I will never forget riding with Jean in her tiny car at breakneck speeds on very narrow winding roads in the English countryside flanked by vision-inhibiting hedgerows. The word "fear" does not really capture the mood. Stark terror comes closer. There must have been guardian angels on every fender, or wing, as they are fittingly known in Britain. At the time, surviving these outings seemed to be the greatest miracle that I experienced. Later I would come to understand how wrong I was.

The beginning of that understanding came with Ardith's reaction to me after my return to Ottawa. It was similar to her reaction the day following our 1968 Christian conversion experience in New Zealand. The reader will recall that she was so impressed by the changes in me that she cancelled her plans to fly with the children to Canada, thereby saving our marriage. This time, my general irritability was largely gone and my outbursts of anger far less frequent. Clearly, at least a measure of healing of the hurts behind that anger had taken place. Indeed, Ardith, who was experiencing a time of better health, was so enthusiastic that she wanted to go herself to London for the healing of memories. It happened that I was scheduled to attend a conference at the OECD in Paris; I made arrangements to drop Ardith in London in the care of Michael and Jean while I went on to France for a three-day stay.

When I returned to London from Paris to rejoin Ardith in Michael and Jean's home, I found her situation very different than mine had been. Ardith was never comfortable talking about herself to anyone other than, perhaps, me, especially about negative events in her past. She believed that revealing hurts reflected badly on those causing the hurts and that it was not proper to do that. I should have understood that a setting that worked well for me would not necessarily work well for her. In short, the process proved stressful for her, and the stress in turn threatened to trigger her psychotic symptoms. I had made a big mistake, and returning to Ottawa sooner than planned was clearly needed. Before leaving London, however, I took another step into my past that was to have significant consequences for me.

I decided to telephone my birth father to express my appreciation for his having paid for my private boarding school education and to let him know how well I had done with that education. (I was head of the Environmental Protection Service at that time.) Though his name was not uncommon, I had easily found him in the London phone book because of his high naval rank. My point is that there could be no doubt as to his identity. I had never met him and until my twenties had believed him dead. I asked if he remembered my mother, using her maiden name and referring to the circumstances in Ceylon (now Sri Lanka) under which they met. He responded negatively but with an upset in his voice that belied his words. I tried gently to convey why I was calling him, but he grew more and more agitated and continued to insist that I had the wrong person.

After hanging up I felt angry at myself for having upset him so. He probably had a wife and grown children and may have well have been worried about their discovering his earlier experience of fatherhood. Then a deep sense of rejection and abandonment overcame me, and I began to shake and weep. It was reinforced by memories of that terrible moment when my mother told me at age ten that my war hero dad, who had just left us, was not my real father. She was trying to comfort me over Dad's departure, but her words made my despair and anger much worse. This time Ardith tried to comfort me, much more sensitively, but to no avail. After a few moments, an inner voice proclaimed loudly an Old Testament reassurance that to this day brings tears to my eyes: "I am the God of the fatherless." My mood changed, and I began to praise God with a sense of His fatherhood that was completely new. That sense has remained with me in the many years since.

My experiences in London were also to have a life-changing impact on my mother. In the early part of this narrative I explained the circumstances surrounding my reluctant attendance at boarding school that had led to a certain coolness between my mother and me. After I became a Christian, I tried to reach out to her; however, while she and I "made nice" to each other, the warmth was simply not there. Nonetheless, I always visited her and my grandmother during my periodic visits to Canada's West Coast.

One such occasion occurred in 1979 just after my mother had been forced to place her mother, with whom she was very close, into a nursing home. "Granny," as I called her, was most upset about her change in situation, and, as soon as I saw her agitation, I felt overwhelmed with compassion. Although Mom was not so inclined, Granny read her Bible every day, and I often read it to her during my visits. I immediately did so on this occasion, and afterwards found myself comforting her by saying that she would soon be with Jesus. These words, which I had not at all intended to say, calmed her immediately, but the effect on my mother was just the opposite. As soon as we were outside my grandmother's room, Mom vigorously expressed her anger at my implying that her mother was about to die. Granny showed no signs of being near death and had been moved into the nursing home simply because my mother could no longer physically care for her. I apologized and explained that the words had simply come out. I flew back to Ottawa the next day and almost immediately received a call from my tearful mother to say that Granny had passed away peacefully in her sleep. Moreover, she had been very much at peace ever since my visit.

It was about a year later that I flew to London and afterwards called my mother to tell her about my experience with the healing of memories. I told her the details about my birth and related circumstances that had been revealed through prayer. To say that she was stunned is a complete understatement. She declared everything that I had been told to be accurate; she could not understand how anyone could have known about these very private details from so long ago. A few months later, Mom visited Ottawa. We spoke at some length about what I had said to Granny in seeming anticipation of her death and about the revelation of private information during the healing of memory sessions in London. Both had made a considerable impact on my mother, and, not surprisingly, she proved to be much more open to my belief that God is real, not a convenient invention of man, and that He wishes us to make meaningful contact with Him. I led her in the prayer that had opened the door for me to my new life, and it did the same for her. Mom died in 2004 at age ninety, so peacefully that we did not at first notice that she had stopped breathing. Two days before, she told the hospital chaplain that she was ready to go home to Jesus, almost in the words I used to comfort her mother twenty-five years earlier.

CHAPTER 56

A SOFT SPOT FOR QUÉBEC

It is impossible to write about Canada during the last half of the twentieth century and the early years of this one without addressing the perennial issue of Canadian unity. Twice, Québec separatist governments have held unsuccessful referenda on taking the province out of Canada. At the time of this writing, a minority separatist government is in office, similarly dedicated to achieving independence. To understand what lies behind these expressions of serious discontent, some historical context is needed.

The reader may recall that Ardith and I spent our 1958 summer honeymoon travelling in a leisurely manner from our home in Vancouver to Ottawa and my new career as a diplomat. We included Montreal and Québec city in our journey, and we have wonderful memories of riding in horse-drawn carriages among the beautiful old buildings in both cities. While in Montreal, we also visited wealthy Westmount, at that time a small, predominantly English-speaking city surrounded by much larger Montreal. While standing looking at the view from the crest of a hill, we were approached by a young police officer. I greeted him in my poorly accented French, and he responded in unaccented English. Wanting to practice, I continued speaking in French, but he informed me in English that he did not speak French. I was stunned to learn that a police officer on the island of Montreal could function without a working knowledge of the majority language, but I did not understand the special nature of 1950s Westmount.

I am relating this story because most Canadians today have no memory of a time when English-speaking residents of French-speaking Québec saw no need to learn the majority language and expected to be communicated with in their own language in virtually any setting. Obviously, Québec has come a very long way from that situation, but I think it is important for the

English-speaking majority in Canada to understand why Québec's French-speaking majority needed to take special steps to protect its own language. It is perhaps even more important for Canada's English-speaking majority to understand its historical debt and obligation to French Canada. That obligation has its roots in the Québec Act passed by the British Parliament in 1774, not long before the opening shots of the American Revolution.

Some additional history is needed to place that Act in context. The first French explorer, Jacques Cartier, arrived in 1534, but Québec city was not founded until 1608 and Montreal was founded shortly thereafter. The earliest British settlements to the south date from the same period. The British colonies flourished, reaching about 2.5 million people by the mid-1700s, but the French colony in Québec was much smaller, about 90,000 people. Frontier skirmishes and some battles were fought between the British and French and their respective Indian allies over the decades in North America, but it was not until 1763 that the British conquered New France in a pivotal battle on the Plains of Abraham not far from the walls of Québec city. Almost all the French aristocrats and senior government officials returned to France, leaving the Roman Catholic Church and a few large landowners to serve as leaders of the French-Canadian people. Initially, the British imposed British law, but that changed in 1774 with the passage of the Québec Act.

The passage of that Act and the initiation and progress of the American Revolution were closely linked in two very different ways. The primary British motivation behind the Act was to secure the loyalty of King George's newly acquired French-speaking subjects in the event of a war with the English-speaking colonists to the south. This objective was largely achieved through re-establishing French law in civil matters, which *inter alia* enabled the Roman Catholic Church to enforce the tithe, and changing the wording of the oath of allegiance to permit Roman Catholics to swear it in good conscience, thereby enabling them to play a role in government. The historic French seigneurial system of land management was also restored, thereby ensuring the support of French Canada's governing class. Language was not explicitly mentioned in the Québec Act, but reintroducing French law and encouraging French-Canadians to play a role in government had the effect of protecting the language and was later used in court to make arguments in support of the use of French.

From the perspective of the American colonists, the Québec Act was counted as one of the four "intolerable" pieces of British legislation enacted at about the same time that contributed so much to the instigation of the revolution. The Americans had been fighting against the French in North America for generations, and many were unhappy that their conquered enemies were now being treated in a way that would protect their French culture and Roman Catholic religion. Worse, the Colony of Québec was expanded in the Act to include the Ohio Valley and thereby block the westward expansion of the English-speaking colonies. Despite this long-standing animosity, the American Continental Congress issued an invitation in French to the people of Québec to join the newly proclaimed United States of America. No doubt in part because of that animosity, the Québécois judged that they were better off under the British and rejected the invitation. They also resisted the two invasions by the American Continental Army that followed. The tradition of French-Canadian resistance to the attractions of American liberty was maintained thirty-five years later in the War of 1812, when French-Canadian militia fought alongside British regulars and their Indian allies to turn back invading American armies.

The bottom line is pretty clear. British North America would almost certainly have disappeared if the people of Québec had accepted the American invitation to join the Revolution. The British had very few troops in Québec at the outset of the Revolutionary War. They could not have maintained control of the 90,000 French-Canadians, much less resist an American invasion, if the American colonists' popular revolt had spread to the former French colony. The United States today would presumably stretch to the North Pole, and as for Canada, well, it would not exist. As for the French language in Québec, it would probably look like that of the "Cajuns" in Louisiana. I do not think it is too simplistic to say that the French language and culture saved Canada and that Canada saved the French language and culture in North America. I cannot imagine a better basis for mutual respect and appreciation between the two founding European linguistic groups in this country. We need to understand our history and treat each other accordingly.

Canada is a country of very distinct regions, but none is as distinctive as the Province of Québec, especially the ethnically homogenous rural areas and smaller towns that are so different from multicultural Montreal. Except for the use of French as the common language of communication, it is probably fair to say that Québec's largest city has more in common with Toronto and Vancouver than it does with most of the rest of the province.

This important division between the rural and the urban lies at the heart of the minority separatist government's latest initiative that has divided the province and that has the potential to stir up divisions across the country. In August of 2013, the Québec government announced its intention to enact a Charter of Québec Values that would *inter alia* forbid the wearing in the workplace of religious symbols such as turbans, hijabs, kippas, yarmulkes, and large visible crucifixes by all public sector employees, even medical personnel, teachers, and daycare workers. The Province's Charter of Human Rights would also be amended to reflect the new values. The leader of the smaller opposition party in Québec's National Assembly has said that he is prepared to support a narrower form of the Charter, but to date the government has displayed no inclination to compromise. The proposal is portrayed as a move to protect Québec's secularism, but its practical effect would likely be to force thousands of individuals to choose between wearing the otherwise legitimate evidence of their spiritual commitment and giving up their employment. That is a huge violation of their human rights, and some would call it religious persecution. To understand the origin of this proposal some further history is needed.

The slogan that animated Francophone Quebeckers outraged by the language situation Ardith and I encountered during our honeymoon trip in 1958 is "Masters in our own House." Many, probably most, Quebeckers believed that the legitimate aspiration reflected in this slogan could be achieved without leaving Canada. The separatists, however, thought that creation of a nation state was needed. It would, like most of those in Europe, be ethnically based, that is to say, dominated by a common heritage. History has clearly demonstrated that those opposing separation were right. Francophone Quebeckers are unquestionably masters in their own house today despite remaining in Canada, and their language is far stronger than it was in the 1950s. That success was not achieved without cost. The language laws governing such matters as choice of language in education and signage were unquestionably intrusive and constituted the imposition of communal values over individual ones. I personally believe that this act of social engineering was justified in the circumstances of the time, constituting, in effect, a massive successful experiment in affirmative action. That said, personally intrusive social engineering is in direct conflict with the Canada that I have described elsewhere in this book. Generally speaking, this country is an open, tolerant society that not just accepts diversity but welcomes it. The proposed Charter of Québec Values clearly moves in a different direction.

According to the polls, the separatists initially increased popular support after first announcing their intention. Francophones outside Montreal, early polls said, overwhelmingly supported the idea, Anglophones throughout the province strongly rejected it, and other minorities also generally opposed it. Francophones in Montreal are much less supportive of the Charter, no doubt in part because almost all of Québec's recent immigrants live in that very multicultural city. Indeed, Montreal's City Council has voted unanimously to oppose application of the Charter, if enacted, within the city. It is, nonetheless, fair to ask whether the positive reaction among many Francophones to the proposed Charter means that they do not share the tolerance for diversity found elsewhere in Canada. In rural areas and small towns that is probably true, but such attitudes are not confined to the Province of Québec. Similar unease over certain kinds of immigrants can no doubt be found in some ethnically homogenous rural areas or small towns in other Canadian provinces as well. Yet proposals for comparable restrictive measures have not emerged in other parts of Canada. I believe there are two reasons for the difference: Québec's unique religious history and the current political situation in the province.

The role of religion in Québec's history has no parallel in the rest of the country. It could be said that, until the 1950s, Québec was dominated by an alliance between generally Anglophone big business and a very conservative, authoritarian provincial government led by Maurice Duplessis that had strong support from the Roman Catholic Church. The Church, in turn, had immense influence over Francophone Quebeckers, especially in rural areas. The "Quiet Revolution" of the 1960s after Duplessis' departure developed a distinct anticlerical orientation, similar in kind, though not in degree, to that experienced during and after the French Revolution. France's relatively recent decision to restrict religiously symbolic clothing was touted in that country as being in keeping with the principles of the revolution. Similar attitudes can be found in Québec. The separatist government's initiative, some have contended, is not so much an attempt to attack that which is different as it is to tap into Francophone Quebeckers' understandable desire to reaffirm this important break from what is widely perceived as a religiously oppressive past.

That said, Québec secularism is currently facing no threat from religion. Unlike France, millions of Muslim immigrants have not migrated to the province. The Roman Catholic Church is at a very low ebb in Québec, and other religions are statistically insignificant. Why tilt at windmills? Only one explanation makes sense: the separatist government was losing popularity and it needed an issue to stir up support. If the action taken also creates a rift with the rest of Canada and upsets Anglophones, so much the better. The hurt done to individuals apparently matters not at all. It is important for Canadians outside Québec to recognize what I have already underlined, that sharp division exists on this issue within the province and there are those in Anglophone Canada who would be supportive of restrictive measures aimed at forcing conformity. This is not an English vs. French issue. The separatists would like their initiative to provoke the kind of generalized uninformed anti-Québec rhetoric that would assist their cause. Hopefully, that will not happen.

Initially when considering the outcome of this proposal for a new Charter of Québec Values, but two scenarios come to mind. If, despite earlier indications to the contrary, Premier Marois had been prepared to compromise with the smaller opposition party, a narrower version of the Charter accommodating that party's views and reflecting growing criticism of the Charter's more extreme provisions could be enacted by Québec's National Assembly. However, it would subsequently be challenged in the courts as contravening Canada's Charter of Rights. That challenge would wind its way in due course to the Supreme Court of Canada, which would almost certainly sustain the challenge and strike down the Charter. (That process would presumably be faster if the Government of Canada initiated the challenge.)

What would happen next would depend on whether the separatists are still in power in Québec or have by that time been replaced by the Liberals. A separatist government would almost certainly make use of the unfortunate "notwithstanding clause" in Canada's constitution, which allows provinces to opt out of the Canadian Charter of Rights. Such action would maintain the Charter of Québec Values as valid legislation and would no doubt be characterized as Québec standing up to Canadian interference in the province's affairs. A Québec Liberal government, if it had not already removed the Charter from the books, would simply accept the decision of the Supreme Court, and the Charter of Québec Values would disappear into history.

Obviously the latter result would, from my perspective, be preferable, but the years of uncertainty and debate that would have preceded it would further divide Québec society and help marginalize those whose spiritual convictions cause them to wear religiously symbolic clothing or icons. They would be seen as not reflecting "Québec values," as not being true Quebeckers. What a pathetic, even cruel, way of seeking to gain a few points in the opinion polls! Claiming that the Charter would "unify" Quebeckers, as the separatists have done, merely adds hypocrisy to the mix.

In the second scenario, the government would offer no concessions on the wording of the Charter to the smaller opposition party but would instead press forward with its proposals intact and either call an election or bring one on by forcing a vote on the Charter in the National Assembly. Such a move would, by polarizing the electorate around the Charter, undoubtedly undermine support for the third party. It is made up of "soft" nationalists, i.e., people who share many of the separatists' nationalist feelings but who oppose leaving Canada. Many third party supporters would find the Charter attractive.

That is why the Charter is characterized as a wedge issue carefully designed by the separatists to take support away from their soft nationalist opponents. Supporters of the third party stand in the way of the separatists winning enough seats to form a majority government. A wedge issue in politics is a highly divisive initiative deliberately chosen to polarize the electorate, creating an "us against them" division that encourages people to determine their voting preference on that issue alone. Because the support in Québec for outright separation has been weakening over the years, finding another way of putting a wedge between those of French ancestry and the rest of Quebeckers has become an urgent requirement for the separatist government. The proposal for the Charter seems perfectly designed to meet that requirement.

In the event, Premier Marois decided on March 8 to call an election for April 7. It probably represents her government's best chance of securing the majority in the National Assembly needed to bring about yet another referendum on Québec separation. By focusing on the Charter, she may well be able to attract the support of many of Québec's feminists. They have demonstrated in support of the proposed Charter, apparently seeing it as a condemnation of the oppressive religious authorities who treated their grandmothers unfairly in the past. They appear unable to perceive that the Charter is not only highly discriminatory but that the majority of the victims of its most hurtful provisions and of the prejudicial attitudes and behaviour it legitimizes are likely to be women.

Many years ago, then-prime minister Pierre Trudeau contemptuously dismissed the separatist leaders as inward-looking "little men," afraid of competing in the wider Canada. I understood his point, but I thought the remark harsh and needlessly provocative. René Lévesque, the first separatist premier of Québec, was a visionary, and I can remember becoming teary-eyed as I watched his emotional "concession" speech after the defeat of the first referendum on separation. His dream had been shattered, and I felt his pain even as I rejoiced that my country remained intact and that the hurt to so many individuals that separation would cause had been avoided. It is hard, however, not to believe that Trudeau's contempt would be justified if applied to current separatist premier Pauline Marois and her colleagues.

A friend of mine has wondered whether what Premier Marois is doing could legitimately be characterized as non-violent ethnic cleansing. He argues that the effect of her policies would be to encourage those who are "different" to leave and to discourage similar people from coming into the province. I think that such a characterization is a step too far, but I do recognize that there is a "slippery slope" effect at work. Seeking to enforce outward conformity by law, especially in matters of religious observance, tends to embolden those who oppose anyone different from themselves. There have already been some unfortunate incidents in which women wearing hijabs have been verbally harassed. The separatist government has been quick to deplore them. It has also been quick to reject the suggestion that the government's own actions have contributed to a climate that legitimizes such divisive behaviour. Frankly, they cannot have it both ways. If they choose to pander to people's baser nature, they can scarcely be surprised when that baser nature increasingly shows itself.

There is one good side to this sorry situation. The proposed Charter has underlined the highly ethnocentric, possibly xenophobic, nature of the current separatist leadership. The man I worked for and admired, former separatist premier Lucien Bouchard, would never have gone to such extremes.

He has stated his preference for a much more limited assertion of secularism. Similar views have also been expressed by an earlier former separatist premier Jacques Parizeau, whose government almost won the second referendum on separation. His wife has tweeted their support for the bravery of a separatist Member of Parliament from Montreal in the federal House who has declared her opposition to the Charter. Barred from her tiny five-member caucus as punishment, she has since left the party to sit as an independent. In explaining her action, she declared that the separatists had destroyed the trust of those Quebeckers who are not of French ancestry but who had been persuaded to support the separatist cause.

Examination of Quebec's opinion polls in February 2014 makes clear why Premier Marois chose this time to roll the electoral dice in an effort to secure a majority in Quebec's National Assembly. While Quebeckers as a whole remain equally divided on support for the proposed Charter, support for Marois' government is slowly growing, with the opposition Liberals down to 34 percent, the separatists at 39 percent, and the third party at 16 percent. As for separating from Canada, only 33 percent of Québec residents are currently supportive, with those of French origin almost exactly equally divided. Polls can be notoriously unreliable and can rapidly change, but the trend to date suggests that Quebeckers may yet reject what I see as the higher road.

Separatism by its very nature is divisive, setting one neighbour against another. Adding specific legal discrimination against those whose only "crime" is a desire to display externally their inner spirituality carries the politics of division to a new low in this country. It goes against the best of what Canada, including Québec, offers to the world: total acceptance of difference, delight in diversity. If, as reflected in polls, the separatist strategy is successful in bringing about a majority government and the Charter should subsequently be enacted, I have to hope that my fellow Canadians in Québec would defiantly go into their places of public sector employment in their tens of thousands proudly wearing their turbans, hijabs, kippas, yarmulkes, and extra-large crosses, whatever their personal beliefs.

In appendix I, on the Middle East, I point out that an important test of a real democracy lies in how it treats its minorities. That truth applies in this country as well. Premier Marois needs a lesson in generosity of spirit from Nelson Mandela.

I am going to give the last word on this matter to Carol Martin, a former colleague for whom I have the greatest personal and professional respect. He is a Francophone Quebecker descended from the original colonists. I asked him for comments on my manuscript. In response he had this to say about what is going on in his own province.

> The language debates of the past could pale in comparison with what the Charter proposal is unleashing. In my youth, I witnessed "xénophobisme" (xenophobia) from the "Québecois de souche" (old-stock Quebeckers) towards everyone who was not of the same origin, including Anglophones, Jews, Italians, and others, but it was not based upon their religious beliefs and their outward expressions of them. What we are seeing now goes way beyond previous societal debates. It appeals to basic fears and ignorance fuelled by a government that seems to have neither morals nor principles of respect for diversity. Québec now runs the risk of losing much more than a few Anglos. Its government wants to create a situation that is not very different from the era of Duplessis and the predominance of the Catholic Church. That era was known as "la grande noirceur" (the great blackness or darkness). I can hardly believe what I am seeing and I am deeply concerned for my grandchildren who are growing up in that kind of society.

Chapter 57

AN UNPRECEDENTED FAREWELL

The spring of 1991 was the last that I spent heading the Federal Environmental Assessment Review Office (FEARO), a place that I had come to love and respect. Giving it a less cumbersome name – Canadian Environmental Assessment Agency – in the draft legislation before the House was the least it deserved.

One of the inevitable elements in workplace departures is the farewell party, and I was to be treated to three of these, two of which came as a surprise, one of which was unprecedented. I have already written about the joyous 1990 FEARO Christmas party, one of the happiest memories of my working career. After all that we had been through together, our little agency had become for many of us much like an extended family. The actual farewell gathering in FEARO was much less joyous. There was a lot of sadness and not a few tears, some of them mine, when I finally said goodbye.

Two very different farewell parties preceded that final goodbye. The first was hosted by Environment Canada, which I had left just over nine years earlier to take over the helm at FEARO. Coincidentally, my years serving in that department also totaled nine, the last four heading the Environmental Protection Service (EPS). I was frankly surprised that my old department would host a farewell gathering for me and even more surprised at the hundreds who turned out for the occasion. Less surprisingly, most of the attendees were from EPS, but the heads of all the other Services were there along with the Deputy Minister, Len Good, a former Deputy Minister, Blair Seaborn, as well as a smattering of senior people from other government departments. To be honest, I was blown away, and all the more so when at least a dozen present insisted upon expressing over-the-top tributes, some at unfortunate length. There was a lot of teasing humour and

This final official photo marks the close of my career: a watershed moment.

the general mood was one of celebrating my career rather than mourning my departure. It was not difficult to enter into the upbeat mood in my own speech, but it was more challenging to think of things to say in response to the many individual remarks that had been made. That said, as was evident from shouted comments, no one expected me to be brief, and they were not disappointed. Both the turnout and the tributes were very touching. Most importantly, it was a great way to recall the many challenging years I had spent working to protect the environment alongside so many committed people.

The farewell party that I characterized as unprecedented was held in no less a place than the Centre Block of the Parliament Buildings. It was hosted by Speaker of the House John Fraser, under whom I had served eleven years earlier when he was Environment Minister and I was heading EPS. He had been very active in promoting environmental causes over the decade since, and we had had periodic contact. However, I understand that the suggestion for giving me a farewell party on Parliament Hill actually came from members of national environmental organizations, especially

Sierra Club Canada Executive Director Stephen Hazell, formerly with the Canadian Wildlife Federation, with whom I had had dealings over many years. That was a very touching tribute that I prize to this day. The gathering was unprecedented in the sense that House Speakers do not normally hold farewell receptions for career public servants, with the exception of some retiring Clerks of the Privy Council (Heads of the Public Service).

While very good-humoured, the event was actually a reception rather than the party that my anticipated departure had provoked at Environment Canada. Those in attendance were also much more varied: representatives of environmental groups and of industry, politicians from three parties, media reporters who covered the environment, senior officials from several departments, senior FEARO staff, my successor-to-be Michel Dorais, and, most importantly, my children Diana and James. The event would have been too stressful for Ardith, and she remained at home.

Diana, James, and I arrived on Parliament Hill early and were met by a very pleasant young woman who was the Speaker's Special Assistant. She escorted us to the Speaker's Chambers, which are adjacent to his very comfortable apartment. (The Speaker also has available for his use an attractive country place in the Gatineau Hills on the Québec side of the Ottawa River.) The Speaker's Chambers are very impressive, in keeping with the even more impressive Parliament Buildings themselves. The Gothic architecture is striking, complete with flying buttresses, gargoyles, pointed arches, and beautifully carved stonework, especially in the interior. The interior of the stunningly beautiful circular Parliamentary Library at the back of the Centre Block overlooking the Ottawa River is mostly intricately carved wood. The carving is positively breathtaking. The Speaker's personal office where we met with him before the reception is in stone, also beautifully carved, with arched doorways and window openings and a magnificent fireplace. Hanging over the fireplace is a large portrait by renowned Ottawa photographer Karsh of wartime British Prime Minister Winston Churchill pictured standing in front of that same fireplace, one arm resting on the mantelpiece. His characteristic defiant bulldog look is very evident. I understand that the photo was taken during one of his World War II visits to Canada.

What also caught my eye was an intricately carved wooden stick at least a metre long resting near the fireplace. Speaker Fraser explained that it was a native "talking stick" carved by a noted British Columbian carver. The person holding it at a formal meeting would automatically have the right to speak. It would, of course, be handed around from person to person. Indeed, before going to another room for the farewell reception, we spent a few minutes doing just that and saying a few words each. I do not remember which of my children observed that Dad did not need a stick to talk.

Three speeches were given at the reception in addition to my own. Jim Fulton, the New Democratic party's primary spokesman on environmental issues, who was from Vancouver, spoke first. His interest in and commitment to the environment went back many years. I had had many dealings with him, especially in the context of the House Environment Committee. I remember best his observation that I was unequalled in speaking at great length while saying very little. It would be amusing to say that it went downhill from there but, in truth, the next two speakers were very kind.

The first was Charles Caccia from Toronto, a brilliant man and committed environmentalist who had served as Environment Minister during the last Liberal government under Pierre Trudeau. I much enjoyed working for him even though his efforts and mine to secure support for environmental assessment legislation had failed. Instead, we had managed to secure approval of the Guidelines Order. At the time, both of us had been greatly disappointed, but, as the reader knows, that Order, after being declared mandatory by the courts, finally opened the door to legislation.

Speaking last was our host, Speaker of the House John Fraser. Although the recently appointed Progressive Conservative Environment Minister Jean Charest also attended the reception, it was felt that Fraser should speak on behalf of the PC party, because he knew me well and Charest did not. Fraser, like Caccia, was very generous in his comments, although he made some amusing references to our initial confrontational encounter nearly twenty years earlier in Vancouver.

I was still very concerned about the implications of Lucien Bouchard's decision almost a year earlier to leave the government to lend his considerable weight to the cause of Québec separatism. For that reason, when it came time for me to speak, I wanted to say something relevant about Canadian unity in a way that meshed with the environmental assessment process that FEARO managed. The link was not immediately obvious, but I came up with the idea of telling anecdotes about the experiences of our environmental assessment panels across the country that would illustrate positive characteristics that many Canadians share. (The reader may recall that these are recorded in appendix VII.) I then went on to conclude that the generosity of spirit and tolerance that were reflected in these anecdotes would be badly damaged by the animosities that a split in our country would arouse. We would all be much the poorer as a result. Two-thirds of the speech was delivered in English and the remainder in French. I want to quote one sentence that, because of its importance, I delivered in both languages. It was composed by a young French-Canadian woman who worked for FEARO. My translation of her words reads:

> For my part, I am convinced that this is the price we must pay to preserve Canada: namely, that my "Quebecness" be affected by the Canadian experience; that the existence of the French culture affect English Canadians; and that both of us allow ourselves to be more open to the influences of native cultures and of the cultures of Canadians whose origins are neither English nor French.

In my conclusion I added the following:

> Surely that is the essence of being Canadian. That is what we give to the world – an open, tolerant, decent, orderly society where respect for the individual and for the great land we occupy must be reflected in the way we treat each other. Surely those characteristics I have described and which are found in Victoria or Québec city, in Yellowknife or Toronto, in Goose Bay or Edmonton, in Halifax or Winnipeg, in Montreal or Vancouver are worth not only protecting but fostering. I cannot but conclude that, if our country is unable to resolve its current differences, the greatest loss will be many of those characteristics, especially tolerance and mutual respect. The world desperately needs nations like ours, nations with values that enrich rather than debase human life. Canadians have an obligation to do all we can to protect those values. We in FEARO have been privileged to see Canada in a way that few have. I can tell you it is really worth saving.

Before I, metaphorically speaking, leave Ottawa, I want to emphasize that our country owes a great debt to the countless volunteers and underpaid, overworked staff members of the many remarkable environmental organizations, national, regional, and local, who have done so much to raise public awareness of the environmental challenges faced by Canada and other countries. I first became fully aware of their importance during the negotiations with the United States at the beginning of the 1970s that resulted in the Great Lakes Water Quality Agreement. Without the immense increase in the late 1960s in public concern over the environment fuelled in large measure by environmental groups, especially in the United States, the U.S. legislation upon which so much of the Agreement ultimately depended probably would not have passed. The role of the U.S. courts in ensuring that this legislation was applied meant that many of these organizations found it necessary to field impressive legal talent to achieve their objectives. The court cases and legal challenges certainly added to the environmental organizations' public profile and effectiveness, but they were also very expensive. Fortunately a happy mix of well-heeled generosity for conservation causes going back to U.S. president Teddy Roosevelt's time and more recent grassroots enthusiasm beginning in the 1960s ensured that the needed funding was forthcoming.

Under the very different system in Canada, the profile of these organizations was generally much lower, and so was their funding. In the section of my memoirs devoted to the multiyear struggle to stop acid rain, especially appendix V, I refer to the importance of the Toronto-based Acid Rain Coalition in bringing about the ultimate success of that struggle. Remembering the commitment and hard work of Adele Hurley and Michael Perley in that respect often inspired me during disheartening times. I have also spoken of Stephen Hazell's important contributions whether with the Canadian Wildlife Federation or, later, the Sierra Club. His 1999 book, *Canada v. the Environment*, provides an excellent description of the march towards Canadian federal environmental assessment legislation. The account in this narrative merely skims the surface by comparison. I think also of the impressive contributions by Don Gamble and François Bregha of the Canadian Arctic Resources Committee (CARC) over many years. CARC did a superb job of awakening southern Canadian concerns about the challenges facing our north and those who live there. We continue to benefit from that effort. The characteristic I most admire in the people I have encountered in my life is caring, and that quality abounds among those committed to protecting our environment. We should all be grateful to them.

After Speaker John Fraser's reception ended, his Special Assistant took Diana, James, and me on a tour of the principal rooms of the Centre Block of the three Parliament Buildings. (For those not familiar with Ottawa, the Centre Block is the building whose central feature is the very tall Peace Tower topped by a clock and containing a carillon, Canada's counterpart of

With the Right Honourable James, seated at the Prime Minister's desk in the House, Ottawa, 1991.

Britain's Big Ben.) The highlight of our tour was the House Chamber, the dominant colour of which is green. The somewhat more elegant Senate is red. Diana sat in the House Speaker's elaborate raised chair, and James, with his eye on the main prize, sat at the Prime Minister's centre front bench desk, clearly identified by a small Canadian flag. Photos were taken of them both, and a video was made of the speeches at the reception. It meant a great deal to me that my children were present for this event. In many ways they had paid the price for my "success," and it was only fitting that they be given a glimpse of what that success entailed. It would have been even better if dear Ardith could have been there as well, but I know she was with us in spirit.

I had begun my government career thirty-three years earlier just a few metres away in the East Block of the Parliament Buildings. At that time the East Block served as the headquarters for Canada's Foreign Ministry, then called the Department of External Affairs. As I sat at age twenty-one in my Protocol Division office overlooking Ottawa's Confederation Square in September of 1958, I could not have begun to imagine the remarkably fulfilling and varied career that lay ahead nor the wonderful conclusion to it that the Speaker's reception represented. Similarly and more importantly,

The Honourable Diana presides over the House, seated on the Speaker's throne-like chair.

I could not have begun to imagine the immense impact on our lives of the spiritual transformation that began in far-off New Zealand nor the trials and challenges that that transformation enabled us to face and even overcome. To express my appreciation in both a secular and spiritual fashion I can only say, "What a ride! Hallelujah!"

Chapter 58

A STUNNING NEW WEST COAST HOME

From a purely literary perspective, the paragraph I have just written could serve as a fitting conclusion to my narrative. There is no question that the years since have been much less interesting. However, in the hope that the reader who has persevered to this point might have some interest in what has happened to Ardith and me after our return to Vancouver, I will add a few more pages to bring our story up to date.

Some of that story has already been revealed in the passages I have written about the progress of Ardith's schizophrenia in Vancouver and the descriptions I have given of our children's lives, especially Diana's decision to move to the West Coast about a year after we did. We were particularly pleased that she chose, in due course, to purchase a condominium apartment only four blocks from us. Unfortunately, the high school where she teaches physics, psychology, and remedial math is a forty-minute drive away, which makes for very long days, especially given the time she spends after class with some of the 108 students in her care. However, we see her virtually every weekend, and knowing that she is so close is a real comfort.

Ottawa, the city we were leaving after so many years, is an attractive place, full of trees and green spaces and a remarkable amount of water for an inland city, thanks to three rivers, a canal, and some small lakes. In winter, the canal freezes and, for nearly eight kilometres, is kept clear for skaters. On the Québec side of the wide Ottawa River are the beautiful Gatineau hills covered in brilliant red foliage in autumn and, in winter, snow well-suited to skiing. Our lovely home was situated in a particularly attractive part of the city, only a ten-minute drive south from the Parliament Buildings on their hill overlooking the Ottawa River. My spacious office had a splendid view of both the River and Parliament Hill. None of this was easy to leave, but we knew that an even more beautiful place lay ahead of us.

Vancouver's temperate climate and spectacular natural setting amid sea and mountains make it one of the world's most attractively located cities. We benefited from that natural beauty immediately upon arrival. The small furnished apartment that we occupied for the first year of our stay here had a view of the water and was only a block from the sandy beaches of English Bay, so named because the early English explorers dropped anchor there. The even better beaches, which stretch for several kilometres, are found on Spanish Banks on the other side of the Bay. I leave it to the reader to figure out whose ships dropped anchor at that location.

We were also only a block away from the many attractions of huge one-thousand-acre Stanley Park (which was opened in the late 1800s by Lord Stanley, Governor General of Canada, who first presented ice hockey's most prized trophy, the Stanley Cup). While predominantly forested, the Park also contains rose and rhododendron gardens; two lakes full of waterfowl and fish; many small, furry creatures, especially squirrels, raccoons, and skunks; a few beavers; about thirty coyotes; numerous tennis courts; a nine-hole "pitch and putt"; three restaurants; an outdoor theatre; several well-equipped children's play areas, including a large outdoor pool; a very attractive day care centre; a world-class aquarium; several beaches; many secluded forest trails; and an eight-kilometre waterfront walk. Also near us were dozens of restaurants of many ethnicities and price levels as well as the other usual amenities made possible by a high-density population. We could walk to the city centre in about fifteen minutes. Living in that little apartment in such surroundings and with minimal responsibilities was like being on holiday, and we both enjoyed it enormously.

Ardith and I fell in love with our new neighbourhood, called the West End, and chose in due course to buy our permanent home there. Vancouver's West End is a mix of low- and high-rise apartment buildings together with a number of the old Victorian houses that in the late nineteenth and early twentieth century covered the area between the city's business district and Stanley Park. While most of these homes were demolished to make way for apartment buildings, a fair number remain, either as apartment conversions or single dwellings. A few have been beautifully restored, and some are open to visitors. With about fifty thousand people in a roughly ten-block square area, the West End is densely populated. Yet, at street level, largely because of the many flower gardens surrounding the houses and apartment buildings, the thousands of trees along the streets, and the numerous small parks dotted here and there, it is very people-friendly, almost like living in an extension of neighbouring giant Stanley Park.

The West End is an isthmus with walkways and marinas lining the harbour front to the north and the sandy beaches of English Bay to the south. The much wider Stanley Park, surrounded on three sides by water, forms the peninsula. The presence of so much ocean water has a significant impact on the climate, making it cooler in summer and warmer in winter. While sea-level snow is much less common in winter in Vancouver than it is in almost all other parts of Canada, it is particularly uncommon in our ocean-dominated neighbourhood. Snow on our street usually melts when it hits the ground, but, as is the case with all things weather-related, there can be exceptions, and we have photos to prove it. What attracted us most to the West End, however, was none of these things. It was the makeup of the population, so varied and eclectic. Upscale condominium apartment buildings, like our own, exist cheek by jowl with modest older rental buildings and even more modest older houses divided into apartments. As a result, every age group and socio-economic class is well represented, a characteristic that made us feel that we would grow older more slowly here.

Our move to Vancouver coincided with a serious downturn in the real estate market across the country. The downturn had hit the larger homes particularly badly, and we had been completely unable to find a buyer for our Ottawa house before our departure. Both Diana and James continued to live in the house as successive real estate agents failed to find anyone willing to make a reasonable offer. That is why we were in our small rented apartment. We were in no position to buy until we sold, especially in light of Vancouver's sky-high real estate prices. Ever since Vancouver's 1986 World Exposition, which drew Asian attention to this city, there has been an immense influx of international money into the local real estate market. The result has been to make this city Canada's most expensive for housing and one of the most expensive on the North American continent. Prices here are almost double those in Ottawa for comparable square footage, especially in what is called Vancouver West Side, where Ardith and I lived when we first met. The modest house on a very small lot where Ardith's parents lived before moving to their dream home on the side of Vancouver's North Shore Mountains happened to be for sale while we were still living in the little apartment. The asking price was sixty percent more than what we ultimately got for our very much larger Ottawa home located in an upscale neighborhood.

During our initial year in British Columbia, we naturally looked at a lot of real estate, including some places in the very affluent separate municipality of West Vancouver on the other side of the harbour (where some of the mountains are). Canada's real estate slump had hit Vancouver prices proportionately more than those in Ottawa, and that eventually worked to our advantage. We had a delightful agent, Elizabeth Wride, whose passion for the musical group the Gypsy Kings meant that we went everywhere to the sound of their rousing melodies. "Bem, bem, bem" still runs through my mind. Elizabeth and her music kept our spirits up when we encountered places we liked but then lost because our own home was still on the market.

Finally, in the summer of 1992, our Ottawa house sold, and the Taiwanese billionaire developer of the very attractive (and very empty) condominium building in the West End that had caught our eye slashed his prices by at least twenty percent. Although the unit we wanted was still priced at thirty percent more than what we sold our house for, we decided to make an offer. It was accepted, and, as soon as our furniture arrived from Ottawa, we moved in. About seven years later, Elizabeth provided the same excellent service for Diana, enabling her to purchase a very attractive one-bedroom suite in a nearly new low-rise building only four blocks from us and one block from Stanley Park. Partly because the suite was an estate sale by absent heirs, Elizabeth was able to negotiate a very favourable price. We have warm memories of visiting Elizabeth's lovely home in Vancouver's Southlands neighbourhood, where many houses have their own stables. Riding was one of her passions. She was also passionate about her dogs, three whippets (they look like small greyhounds). Watching them chase each other around Elizabeth's spacious garden at unbelievable speeds was a real treat.

We were among the first to occupy our cone-topped, architecturally striking building, but it gradually filled up. It contains thirty-six suites on twenty-one floors with a beautiful pool and hot tub area covered with a huge glass canopy opening onto a private garden enclosed with a brick wall. It is like swimming outdoors but with protection from the elements. We occupy half the tenth floor half way up the building. One benefit is a private elevator lobby, which we used as a mud room for our daughter's border collie Max. I used to clean him there during wet weather or after swimming before entering our suite. Where the building narrows slightly, the suites occupy a whole floor. The penthouse has one and a half floors and four underground parking stalls (we have two). There are three or four suites on each of the lowest three floors.

Our suite is laid out in a manner that accentuates its size. The short entrance hall leads immediately to the guest bedroom and bathroom, is wide enough for our bookcases, and opens onto a substantial circular rotunda from which are accessed, from left to right, the laundry room, where we also have more bookcases, the living and dining rooms, the den/study, the eat-in kitchen, and the master bedroom suite. The master suite has two closets (one walk-in) and a large elegant marble bathroom with a Jacuzzi tub and an extra-large separate shower stall. There is a balcony off the den. The central rotunda not only replaces narrow halls, it also gives the apartment a very open feeling, almost like a sizable house. We gave some of our furniture to our children, but the bulk of what remains fits beautifully in our new home. We are particularly pleased that the interior decor created for our twentieth wedding anniversary in our Ottawa home by our dear friends Gordon and Margaret remains intact in our new setting. There are excellent views from almost every window in the apartment. Most are floor-to-ceiling, and the curving living room window is seven metres (twenty-two feet) wide.

Our principal view to the north is stunning. It almost appears as though it had been laid out by Capability Brown, the great eighteenth-century landscape architect who designed so many of England's great country estates or parks, as they were often called. Nearest us is a line of eastern maple trees that turn scarlet in the fall. Beyond them is an expanse of green grass dotted with trees and shrubs surrounding a pond edged by stones. This pond empties through a stream under a beautiful arched and crenellated stone bridge into a small arm of the harbour that holds a marina. A forest of masts from sailing craft surround a Tudor-style building that is the Vancouver Rowing Club. It has produced Olympians in the past, and we often see the rowing sculls being used by club members. Behind the club and the marina is a wall of trees, part of Stanley Park. The taller and more distant trees are evergreens, but in front of them, along the walkway that skirts the harbour, are planted deciduous trees, many of which also turn scarlet in the fall. Behind the tall evergreens are the much taller North Shore Mountains, almost always topped with snow in winter and spring.

At night we see the moving lights of the marina reflected in the water and the decorative lights outlining the shape of the Rowing Club's peaked roof. On the lower slopes of the mountains across the harbour we can see the lights of the residential areas filtered by the trees. On the mountaintops are the much brighter lights generated by nighttime skiing, a restaurant, and the gondola housing. In daylight we can see the gondolas going up and down the mountainside. The harbour entrance, spanned by the graceful Lions Gate suspension bridge, lies between the evergreen trees and the mountains, but we cannot see it from our vantage point; the trees are too tall. We can, however, looking east, see part of the main body of the harbour, which stretches several kilometres beyond our line of sight. To the west, looking one block down our own street, we see Stanley Park's Lost Lagoon, so named because, when it was still an arm of the harbour, it would disappear at low tide. An illuminated fountain in the Lagoon forms part of our view.

Lost Lagoon is now a freshwater lake home to five thousand migratory waterfowl that visit each winter, including a dozen different species of duck. In spring and summer, there is also a migratory community of great blue herons with a hundred and fifty nesting pairs, reputedly one of the largest urban concentrations in the world. Their chicks make an appalling racket that can be heard for blocks. More spectacular to my mind is the immense bald eagle's nest, which periodically hosts nesting pairs. I once saw a family of five circling lazily above the park and harbour. Two had characteristic white heads, but the three juveniles were still brown on top. A much more common sight is the steady stream of float planes landing and taking off in the harbour, especially in the morning and evening. Many are scheduled flights to other cities, especially on Vancouver Island, but others connect Vancouver's head offices with the vast resource-rich interior of British Columbia. The province's thousands of lakes serve as landing strips.

The Greater Vancouver Regional District (GVRD), to give it its formal designation, is made up of some seventeen cities and municipalities stretching from the North Shore Mountains to the American border and inland from the ocean well up the Fraser Valley. The total population must be in excess of two million, not large by international standards, but enough to

With retirement comes more time for family, including: my first stepfather Major (ret'd) Ted Robinson, Vancouver, 1993...

make it Canada's third-largest city after Toronto (which has over five million people, including suburbs) and Montreal (which has three and a half million people in the urban area). The greatest growth is in the suburban cities, which have better funding and facilities, rather than in the city of Vancouver proper. This is why Diana teaches in a suburb.

A serious effort has been made by Vancouver's planners to make the city centre an attractive place to live through careful planning, requirements for green space and landscaping, and the maintenance of view corridors, a policy from which we have greatly benefited. The objective is to combat urban sprawl and the associated loss of valuable agricultural land. The beauty of the West End, which I have described, is one result, but the immense increase over the past twenty-five years in Vancouver's real estate prices, fuelled both by foreign investment and by the restrictions created by the local topography, has spurred the rush to the suburbs, especially for families with children. Today, less than a quarter of Greater Vancouver's population is in the city itself, and that fraction is continuing to shrink.

For those who can afford it or who are prepared to live in a very small space, Vancouver's city centre lifestyle is very attractive, except, of course, for that notorious pocket called the Downtown Eastside where several thousand drug addicts are reputed to live. It is the location of the only medically supervised injection site for narcotic users in North America. The site was established as an experiment to see whether the very high rate of hepatitis-related mortality caused by shared needles could be reversed. Apparently it has been, but the site remains controversial. That unhappy neighbourhood is presumably carefully avoided by the many foreign planners who come here regularly to gaze upon the city's achievements. Indeed, the ruler of Dubai hired Vancouver's chief planner and several of his staff some years ago. One of the major projects recently constructed in that Arab metropolis is modelled after part of Vancouver's redeveloped waterfront.

Vancouver's position as Canada's primary Pacific port underpins much of this development. The annual tonnage, though not the value, places the port among the world's greatest. Minerals, forest products, and grain brought by rail from British Columbia's interior or Canada's prairies fill the bulk carriers that wait at anchor in English Bay for their turn to enter the harbour proper. Counting them provides a remarkably accurate indicator of how the Asian economies are faring. The ubiquitous cruise ships are also very visible in season as they prepare to carry their vacationing passengers up British Columbia's mountainous coast to Alaska. Vancouver is well equipped to receive them, and there is no waiting at anchor.

I have gone into such detail describing our home and setting because the limitations on our ability to travel outside Vancouver or even to visit friends locally have, especially in recent years, made our immediate surroundings that much more important to us. Frankly, I had anticipated that our movements would one day become very restricted. Breaking the bank to buy such a beautiful place was my way of ensuring that, if we were to be caged, the cage would at least be gilded. The enjoyment that Ardith continues to experience from our stunning view and from our spacious apartment makes it very clear that we made the right choice. That said, Ardith and I were initially quite active and mobile upon our return to the West Coast, regularly making day trips to scenic spots and even climbing to the snow line on one of the North Shore Mountains.

I also continued to do some work for FEARO out of the Vancouver Regional Office over a two-year period and later accepted a five-year

... Ardith and our only grandchild, Portia, Ottawa, 2004 ...

appointment as an adjunct professor in the School of Natural Resources at Simon Fraser University (SFU), Vancouver's second-largest university. It is located in an architecturally spectacular complex on top of a mountain in suburban Burnaby. SFU has a particularly good faculty of education, and my time there coincided briefly with Diana's. She took the opportunity to audit one or two of my occasional lectures, but I usually worked as a resource person at symposia for graduate students. I found the interaction with those bright young people particularly stimulating.

In addition, I did some consulting work with First Nation bands in the Greater Vancouver area on development projects affecting them. I was very impressed by the native leaders with whom I worked for two years and much affected by the way in which their interests had been disregarded, especially in past years. It is a source of some satisfaction to me that the changes we instituted during my time at FEARO improved our capacity to understand and take account of the potential impact of various projects on native interests and values. I should also include in this list of post-Ottawa activities my role as a member of an advisory group set up by the British

... and my brother, Keith, and his second wife, Ruth, Vancouver, 2009.

Columbia government to produce draft legislation establishing a provincial environmental assessment process. I describe the successful outcome of this work in the closing sentences of appendix IX.

A vicarious highlight of our time in Vancouver has been Diana's habit of travelling to various parts of the world during the summer months. She always keeps us abreast of her adventures with descriptive e-mails and photos. The 2010 family photo in this chapter reminds me in particular of a six-month travelling sabbatical that she undertook in that year to India, North Africa, and the Middle East. She dyed her normally fair hair black to draw less attention to herself. It did not work. On her second day in Mumbai, a man on a motor scooter stared at her so hard that he ran into the back of a taxi. Fortunately only his pride was hurt. The central focus of that trip was attending a biblical history course at a university in Jerusalem, half in the classroom and half on archaeological sites. She returned home much inspired by the course but deeply saddened by the plight of women in so many of the countries she visited.

A recent acquisition has provided us with an attractive visual representation of the three segments of my life: student, public servant and retiree/caregiver. It is a one and a half-meter-long photographic/painted print

With Ardith, Diana, James, and Max, Vancouver, 2010.

on canvas depicting Vancouver's striking skyline under a glorious multi-coloured sunset sky as seen from a boat in the harbour.

In the foreground is Deadman's Island linked by a small bridge to much larger Stanley Park. The name reflects the discovery in 1862 of the bones of two hundred dead warriors in red cedar boxes lashed to the upper boughs of trees. The island was the site of an inter-tribal battle long before the Europeans arrived. Today it is occupied by HMCS Discovery, a naval training station that symbolizes some of my less-impressive student days. While at university, I was an air force officer cadet in the Reserve University Squadron. As such, I enjoyed drinking privileges at HMCS Discovery, which was the home of our naval counterparts, the University Naval Training Division (UNTD), or "untidies," as they were always called. Many a happy evening was spent in that establishment.

The symbol of my career days is a building called the Harbour Centre on the eastern side of the business district topped by a distinctive saucer-like revolving restaurant. It housed our agency's regional headquarters,

With son, James, and granddaughter, Portia, inside the aquarium in Stanley Park, 2013.

which I routinely visited and out of which I worked for two years after leaving Ottawa.

The third segment of my life is symbolized by the distinctive cone-topped apartment building where we now live. It is clearly visible at the western end of the skyline panorama, near Stanley Park.

I had to abandon most of my activities outside the home after Ardith's health worsened in 1997, forcing her into the extended period of hospitalization described in chapter 47. When she got out of the hospital, it was clear that I could leave her alone only for relatively short periods. The years that followed were steadily more constrained, especially after Alzheimer's came calling. Full-time caregiving became my way of life.

Eventually, even annual trips to Ottawa were no longer feasible, but we could still look forward to our Ottawa family visiting us. The last such occasion, to help us celebrate our fifty-fifth wedding anniversary, took place in the summer of 2013. A visit to Vancouver's aquarium, Portia's favourite place and only a short walk from our apartment, resulted in a delightful "underwater" photo.

Chapter 59

OUR BEAUTIFUL BORDER COLLIE MAX

A major compensation for having to abandon my extracurricular activities was Diana's decision in 1996 to acquire a dog, specifically a white, six-week-old border collie pup with black markings whom she named Max. Because of Diana's long hours during the week, Max became our responsibility Monday through Friday. He stayed with Diana on the weekends. Max was a part of our family for over fifteen years. I have had dogs before, both in my own childhood and when our children were young, but I never bonded with an animal like I did with Max. He was a delight in so many ways.

My first exposure to border collies had been at New Zealand's annual national sheepdog trials. At the time, there were sixty million sheep in that country and a very large number of sheepdogs, mostly border collies, to herd them. Anyone who has attended a sheepdog trial or watched one on television knows how remarkable these dogs are. Of course, we were seeing the best of the best, but it is generally recognized that the border collie breed routinely tops the canine intelligence charts. I remember reading an article in *National Geographic* describing an experiment conducted by German scientists to measure the level of canine intelligence. That experiment consisted of placing two hundred items in a room, teaching the name of each to the border collie being tested, and then instructing the animal to bring a named item to one of three persons. The border collie got it right about eighty-five percent of the time. That was impressive, but there was more. The scientists left six items unnamed and gave the border collie a name that it had not been taught. The dog brought back one of the

Max thinks delicious thoughts.

unnamed items. That achievement was a demonstration of deductive reasoning, not just of memory.

I was naturally impressed by this story but less so then I might have been had I not been exposed to Max. He was in our apartment for less than a week before he was able to tell the difference between the double ring of the enterphone and the single ring of the telephone, even though the sound was otherwise identical and came from the same instrument. The enterphone sent him rushing to the door with excitement, whereas he completely ignored the telephone ring. Not surprisingly, it was easy to teach him various words, especially commands. There was even one word that Diana used that stopped him in his tracks when he was chasing a squirrel or ball. If I wanted to exercise him and to be completely lazy myself, I merely had to point to one end of a field and then the other to have him rush back and forth.

His physical ability was also impressive, especially when catching whirling Frisbees or balls thrown high in the air. When I exercised him in Stanley Park, passersby would gather to watch. While he was still young but full-grown, I drove him for an afternoon a week over several weeks to a barn in the countryside where dogs, especially border collies, were given agility training. This involves squeezing through tubes, jumping over barriers, running through hoops, climbing ladders, walking the length of teeter-totters, and other such tasks, all as quickly as possible. He was able to perform reasonably well but would have been no good in a competition because he was too interested in the other dogs. (Also, I, his handler, could not run fast enough.) What he most enjoyed about the outing was charging around and around on the sheep paddock, chasing or being chased by other border collies.

Border collies tend to have immense energy and driven personalities, obsessed by a desire to work. Max was no exception, and he came by this characteristic very honestly. Both of his parents were working cattle dogs from British Columbia's vast cattle country, known as the Cariboo, where some of North America's largest ranches are located. That said, Diana chose him because he was homely and the runt of the litter, a veritable ugly duckling. He grew into a beautiful white and black swan, even to the point of having a soft, silky coat unlike the rough ones that so many border collies have. Unfortunately, he also shed like mad, and white hairs became the bane of our existence. Because border collies are typically so restless and because they need so much mental and physical stimulation, they do not make the best pets. One of the many dog owners I encountered during my regular outings with Max worked with Border Collie Rescue. She told me horror stories of poor dogs that became truly neurotic mainly because they were left alone too long each day. Because I had a hard time keeping up with Max's needs, I decided to make use of a dog-walking service that others in our building patronized. It was one of the best decisions I ever made.

Norman, the owner of the service, was born in Santa Marta, Colombia, of a Venezuelan mother and a Brazilian father. Coincidentally, Ardith and I had visited Santa Marta during our time in Norman's native country. A small Caribbean coastal resort town, it was popular with Colombians who wanted to spend time at the seashore without going to some of the better-known tourist destinations. It is also the place where the great liberator of northern South America, Simón Bolívar, is buried. We visited his tomb, but I remember Santa Marta best for the sandblasting effect of the strong winds along the beach. Talk about exfoliation!

Norman had a specially equipped van into which he put, each morning and afternoon, a dozen or so dogs of all sizes and shapes. (Max was part of the morning shift.) He drove them to one of Greater Vancouver's two best dog parks and beaches for a time of leash-free joy. I accompanied him on one occasion and was astounded at the control he exercised over his pack. He did screen his dogs and would not accept seriously antisocial ones. Nonetheless, I think he must have been a dog "whisperer," given the level of control he was able to maintain with what seemed like minimal effort. In the warmer weather he wore a T-shirt saying "Alpha Male," and we joked that the dogs read this and obeyed.

A former fitness trainer, Norman was himself in superb condition. He said he did what he did because he loved dogs and loved being outside no matter the weather. Max was one of the dominant dogs in the pack and was also almost always the first to catch the ball. This was not because he ran any faster, but because he started first and anticipated where the ball was going to go. He was also quite innovative. One of the dog parks was alongside a small but fast-moving river. Max figured out that, if he ran along the bank upstream for a fair distance, he could "surf" downstream on the current. Before long, Norman told me, other dogs were following suit. He also told me that he had to keep the dogs out of the water during salmon spawning season. The extra fish attracted seals, and they were capable of attacking and drowning a dog.

One of Max's worst habits was "singing" along with certain powerful female singers such as Barbra Streisand and Celine Dion. If this happened in Norman's van, all the other dogs would join in, and the resulting cacophony was horrific. When I called Norman on his cell phone I could hear the racket the "musical" animals were making through his headset. I do not know how he stood it. At home, we were simply prevented from listening to certain singers when Max was there.

It is possible that Max was protesting because the pitch of the sound was hurting his very sensitive ears. Certainly, he was bothered by the annual international fireworks competition that takes place every August on a barge anchored in English Bay about six blocks from us. (Each year it attracts hundreds of thousands of spectators, who line the beaches or occupy hundreds of small boats. We can watch it from our elevator lobby.) Max was much calmer when he got older, but I suspect that was partly because his hearing was failing.

All these things made Max entertaining, but what caused me to bond with him so tightly was his personality. Although he sometimes displayed annoying excitement when visitors came, especially when he was younger, he was actually quite reticent, not at all inclined to lick on every occasion as so many dogs do. I almost had to woo him to get a demonstration of affection. If I displayed distress, he always came to offer comfort.

That happened most commonly in our private elevator lobby as I tried to dry his long hair after we had been out walking in the pouring rain or after he had been swimming. The elevator lobby is a good size, almost like a small bedroom. When Max was feeling particularly frisky, I tried to tire him out by bouncing his ball off the walls as he jumped around trying to catch it. The room became his private "mouth-ball" court. Despite his general lack of demonstrative behaviour, Max was clearly closely attuned to my emotions. While I am better than I was years ago, I remain easily irritated and given to unreasonable feelings of anger. I struggle to suppress these feelings for Ardith's sake, and Max was a huge help in this respect. He felt my upset well before it became obvious and put his tail down and went off to hide in his bed in the laundry room. In going to comfort him, I felt my anger dissipate. Interestingly, Max was much more demonstrative in showing affection towards Ardith, even though he was more obedient to me.

When Diana made her many overseas and other trips in the summer, Max was with us full-time. At other times of the year, I was responsible for walking him each weekday afternoon, usually in Stanley Park, and at night in the streets surrounding our home. Unless it was a particularly warm day, I did not take him swimming because he had so much opportunity to do that each morning with Norman.

Whether in the Park or on the streets, wildlife avoidance was the name of the game. I used to take him running in the more distant forest trails, but, after having been shadowed by coyotes on more than one occasion, I decided to keep to the more developed areas. Coyotes occasionally came into those areas, but only singly, not in packs. I once saw one trying to interact with dogs. Perhaps it was a reject from the pack seeking some compensating socialization.

Smaller dogs could be at real risk from coyotes. I remember encountering one poor woman who was crying her eyes out, having just watched her little dog being carried off by a coyote that had come out of the bushes. We also had to watch out for raccoons. Max and I were charged by a raccoon once, but I was able to keep it at bay with my giant golf umbrella. Thank God for Vancouver's rain. We later saw young ones, and I suspect that our attacker was a mother protecting her young. One of my neighbours was clawed quite badly on his leg and had to be taken to hospital.

Our main challenge at night, however, was the ubiquitous skunk. After dark, these nocturnal creatures invaded our neighbourhood. Max's instinct was to charge them, and my arm was nearly pulled out of its socket more than once. I became very grateful for the big white stripes that made the skunks visible in the dim light of the streetlights. I guess we were fortunate that Max was sprayed only twice during what must have been thousands of outings. I did not feel so fortunate at the time, given the horrific smell that subsequently filled our apartment. Thankfully, it is no longer necessary to wash skunk-perfumed animals in tomato juice. There is a dog shampoo with a specific enzyme that targets the smell of the skunk, but I was not able on the first such occasion to purchase it until the following day. What a night! The instructions on the bottle said that I should not get the shampoo into the dog's eyes, and that meant, effectively, not washing his face. It was his face, of course, that had received the full blast of the skunk's perfume. That unwashed face smelt for weeks. Max did not get a lot of cuddling during that time. Sometime later I was telling this story to our granddaughter Portia's grade one class in Ottawa. One of the six-year-olds asked me why I did not put goggles on Max when washing him. Not a bad suggestion from a six-year-old, but finding goggles that fit and would stay on a wriggling dog does seem challenging.

At age nine, Max developed severe arthritis, to the point that this once athletic dog could barely hobble down the street. Because of her involvement with horses, Diana was aware that a product developed in Australia called Cartrophen was widely used to alleviate equine arthritis. Our inquiries revealed that there was a canine version, and we asked our vet to begin the recommended weekly injections. Within a month, there was massive improvement, and eventually Max regained almost all of his mobility. For years, an injection every six weeks proved to be an adequate maintenance dose. I was so impressed that I asked the vet for shots for me, but she said that would put her licence in jeopardy. She offered me a dog biscuit instead. Cartrophen is available for humans but only to treat a horrible-sounding ailment called "arthritic bladder." The mind boggles. Trials for broader human use are underway in Australia.

In April of 2011, our dear dog finally passed away. He had been with Norman longer than any of his other charges, and that sensitive dog whisperer was every bit as devastated as Diana, Ardith, and I were, maybe even more so. The manner of Max's going could not have been better. He and I were out after eleven o'clock at night moving slowly along the grass beside our building while he took his last opportunity to relieve himself before bedding down for the night. Max fell over, which was not unusual because his muscles had grown weak and his balance unsure over the previous six months. I went to help him up but could detect no sign of life. There had been no noise, not even a whimper, and no advance indication of difficulty. He left so peacefully, doing what he loved most, "reading" his "mail" with his sensitive nose.

A young woman passing, who kindly stopped to help, burst into tears when I told her that I thought my dog was dead. I was feeling numb, nothing at all, and I found myself comforting this perfect stranger over the loss of our pet. I told her that Max was nearly fifteen and a half years old, a good age for his breed, and that he had had a very good life. She loaned me her cell phone, and I called Diana, who came at once. Between us we got Max onto the back seat of our car and drove to the all-night emergency vet. We were pretty certain that he was dead, but it was important to be sure, and, of course, we had to dispose of his body.

The next day, as I looked at his leash, his bed, and his other paraphernalia, the sense of loss overwhelmed me, and I must have wept on and off all day. Ardith asked if I would weep as much for her, and I promised to do my best. Max has left a big hole but, with Ardith's growing need for care, the timing of his departure was as perfect as the manner of it. An old dog can be a lot of work, and my caregiving capacity was already fully occupied. Sadly, we will not have another wagging tail in our home. There would, in any case, never have been another Max.

Max's death affected me in other ways as well. I tried to maintain my regular daily pattern of walks and, indeed, I could walk much faster without the frequent stops with which all dog owners are familiar. But it was not the same. Max's delight in his surroundings, especially the smells that permeated his world, communicated itself to me. Even if I was feeling down and not wanting to go on a walk, my mood would soon lighten as I watched his bushy tail moving happily in front of me.

He also made me much less invisible. Not many people are interested in talking to an old man, but a beautiful border collie, and by association his owner, attracts a lot of interest from all ages. Walking Max could be very social. People often asked about his intelligence, and I soon developed a patter, including the story from *National Geographic* that I mentioned earlier. One of my favourite lines was that Max had become impossible to live with since he had read in a book how intelligent his breed was. There are a lot of dogs in our neighbourhood, and I soon got to know many of their owners, at least by sight. Sometimes we would congregate, but mostly we would chat individually while our respective pets interacted. There are several dog owners in our building, and sometimes I would walk with them. While Max was not normally aggressive, he was in no way submissive, and there were some dogs we had to avoid. Perhaps because of the unavoidable lack of social activity in our own home, this dog-related community became important to me, a fact that was much more obvious after Max was gone. Walks became much lonelier, especially after questions about Max's absence petered out. Invisibility returned.

As I reread this paragraph about the impact of Max's death, it comes across to me not only as sad but perhaps somewhat pathetic. That is not how Ardith and I see ourselves. Our circumstances certainly are constraining, and our inability to sustain a conversation is deeply frustrating for both of us, but our relationship is very friendly and positive, and we laugh a lot. True, Ardith no longer recognizes me as her husband and often wonders where she is, but she is warm and appreciative and always laughs at my ridiculous jokes. (Her forgetfulness is an asset in this respect.) What more could a man of my age want? The answer is help with the cooking and cleaning. A very pleasant young Filipina whom we hired to do the cleaning meets half of that need. On a more serious note, I am aware that, for many sufferers, major and even frightening personality changes can be a part of dementia. So far we have been spared this additional heavy burden, for which I am profoundly grateful. My heart goes out to those not so spared, sufferers and caregivers alike.

Chapter 60

WELCOMING THE WORLD TO VANCOUVER

I have to admit that we watched the 2010 Vancouver Winter Olympics unfold on television just like the rest of the world. Some of the big events, such as the opening and closing ceremonies, took place only about fifteen blocks from us, but they may as well have been on the other side of the country. Going to the very occasional movie with our daughter was as much exposure to crowds as Ardith could cope with at that time. Today she could not do even that.

That said, we were not unaffected by the excitement that gripped the city. The appearance of five large, illuminated, brightly coloured Olympic rings on a barge in the harbour, clearly visible from our apartment, certainly put us in the mood. There were team flags everywhere and great crowds of visitors at a time of year when tourism is normally at a low ebb. For two weeks we were treated well into the night to flashing lights and loud sounds emanating from the Vancouver Rowing Club, which is at the centre of our view. It had been taken over by the German team and renamed Club Bavaria. A large sign proclaimed "Free Party Every Night." The invitation did not go unnoticed. On a more pedestrian level, both Max and I were bemused by the disappearance of our favourite waste receptacle where I normally deposited his droppings after each walk. It had been removed temporarily to prevent its use as a hiding place for a bomb. What a world we live in!

Speaking of bombs, readers with remarkably good memories may recall mention of my musings on the Middle East in appendix I. There I indicate that Canada was obliged to spend nearly $1 billion on security for the 2010 Winter Olympics. Fifteen thousand police officers and soldiers were here to protect us from terrorists. In the event, their main focus proved to be local protestors. One morning we watched in amazement as at least two hundred police moved down our usually quiet street while police boats patrolled the harbour just in front of us and helicopters hovered overhead. It was part of a successful operation to surround and break up an anti-Olympic demonstration that had begun in the city centre twelve blocks from us and had become violent. There were many causes for the protests, but the bottom line for all the protestors was that there were better things to spend taxpayers' money on than the Olympics. There is truth in that contention, but I guess we need circuses as well as bread and housing. The TV news claimed that the violence, which extended to breaking our largest department store's Olympic-themed windows, was caused by a small group of anarchists dressed in black and wearing balaclavas. Fortunately the violence did not spread.

Many of the visiting security personnel were housed on board three cruise ships leased for the occasion. Spotting the names of the different cities on the shoulder flashes of the police officers patrolling the streets became an entertaining diversion. I talked to one from Brantford, Ontario, who expressed delight with his accommodations, with the spring-like weather, and with this very special once-in-a-lifetime assignment. I have no doubt that this feeling was widely shared.

We were spared terrorists, but Vancouver's mild climate presented problems for the organizers, who had to rely heavily on snowmaking machines in the North Shore Mountains where the snowboarding took place. Fortunately, all other skiing events were scheduled at the Whistler-Blackcomb ski resort, about ninety minutes away, where snow conditions were much better. Diana was backpacking around India at the time as part of her six-month, multiple-country travelling sabbatical. This excerpt from an e-mail I sent her about our unusually warm February weather tells the story.

> Sunday's walk with Max was amazing – bright warm sunshine with 12 degree (53° F) temperatures in the shade. I had to take my coat off. There were flowers everywhere with the cherry blossoms just starting. English Bay was full of sailboats while golfers and tennis players were hitting their respective balls and there was even a volley ball game underway on English Bay beach. Never have the palm trees looked more in place. I met some Winnipeggers who had photographed the volley ball game as they said their friends back home would

> not believe it. Some Edmontonians on their way to play golf were similarly amazed. The fourteen-day forecast contains a lot of sunshine which, despite the warmth, is much better for maintaining the snow than is rain.

While a problem for the organizers, the warm weather was great for the visitors, several of whom I met while walking Max. I chatted with a reporter from Dallas–Fort Worth who joked that she had come here get warm. They had snow in Dallas. However, while the blossoms abounded so, alas, did my allergies.

In this ice-hockey-mad country, beating the United States in very tight game for the gold medal in the men's match on the final day was seen as the crowning achievement of the Games. Nearly a hundred and fifty thousand people thronged Vancouver's downtown area to celebrate. Sixteen million Canadians, almost half our population, watched the game on TV. (Four million had watched the announcement of the team members.)

The International Olympic Committee Chairman declared that he had never seen a city embrace the Olympics to the degree that Vancouver had. He also remarked that he had the impression that hosting the Games had been a unifying experience for Canadians. I agree with that judgement, not just because of Canada's remarkable success. As I wrote to an American friend, it is not often that both our countries can be winners at the same time. The United States won the largest total number of medals in Winter Olympic history, while Canada won the largest number ever of gold medals (fourteen) at the Winter Games.

However, the unifying effect of the Olympics on Canada began well before the Games. The Olympic flame was carried further than ever before by more than a thousand runners throughout the length and breadth of this enormous country. The route was chosen to come within a two hours' drive of ninety percent of our population. Welcoming ceremonies were held everywhere from tiny villages to our largest city. No wonder the nationwide enthusiasm reached the level that it did. When the "Gold Rush" came, reminiscent of the Klondike, it merely added to an already remarkable sense of achievement. Perhaps I am being naïve, but when I saw on TV so many red-and-white Canadian flags flying in Québec, where the blue-and-white fleur-de-lis normally predominates, I thought that something special was happening. It was also exciting to see so many racial groups represented in the happy maple-leaf-decorated faces celebrating in Vancouver's streets. There was no need for hyphens. We were all just Canadians. As for the male/female relationship, three-quarters of our medals were won by women, including ice hockey gold in a hard-fought match with the United States the day before the men's encounter. Hurray for the women!

Living in the shadow of a super-patriotic giant can have strange effects. We Canadians tend to define ourselves by our differences from our far more numerous neighbours, but our unabashed glee over defeating them shows that we are not as different as we pretend. The slogan that was adopted for Canada's training program for athletes leading up to the Winter Olympics was "Own the Podium," a remarkable piece of hubris given that we had not been among the top countries in past winter Olympics. The slogan was much criticized for arousing unrealistic expectations, putting inappropriate pressure on the athletes, and being alien to the "Canadian Way." Australia's much-better-funded training program aimed primarily at summer athletics has produced results way out of proportion to the population of that country. Canada has an egalitarian streak, and our publicly funded sports training programs have historically tended not to be directed at developing elite athletes but at encouraging general participation in sport. The collective joy over the 2010 record gold medal haul has clearly resulted in a change of focus, at least with respect to the winter program. Ten gold medals and twenty-five overall at Sochi in 2014 probably mean that the Own the Podium program is here to stay.

One of the benefits of hosting the Olympic Games is the creation of infrastructure and facilities that will have real value for years after the Games are over. There is also the risk of producing rusting, underused white elephants such as those that form part of Athens' expensive Olympic legacy. Vancouver completed its own Olympic-related construction on time and within budget. Equally important, good use has been made and continues to be made of the resulting new facilities and infrastructure. The two biggest infrastructure projects were the major widening of the dramatic and very scenic Sea-to-Sky Highway that links Vancouver to the Whistler-Blackcomb Ski Resort and the underground rail-link called the Canada Line between the city centre and the airport. Both were needed, but, without the stimulus of the Games, they would no doubt still be gleams in an engineer's eye. (That engineer could well have been my younger brother, Keith, who played a major supervisory role in the construction of the rail-link.) In developing the Olympic facilities, the organizers were very concerned to meet high environmental standards. In appendix XIII, I describe three of these facilities and a transport project.

The 2010 Winter Olympics left us with some wonderful memories of great athletic achievements by so many young people from so many countries. In the process, they also underlined our common humanity, including our natural pride in our own countries and our respect for the pride and achievements of others. The mixing together of the athletes from the various teams in the closing ceremonies was designed to reflect that common humanity, the absence of distinctions between us. For the host city and country there is additional pride in knowing that we welcomed the world and were not found wanting. There is so much around the globe that is divisive. I count myself fortunate to have been up close to an event that was so unifying. The environmentally sound projects described in appendix XIII are frosting on the cake.

Chapter 61

THE JEWEL OF CHRISTIAN STEWARDSHIP

In late August of 2013, I had a jewel dropped in my lap that inspired me to write this chapter. I have earlier referred to my belief in Christian stewardship, which I define as our obligation before God to care for His creation. I treated this concept as self-evident, but in truth, not everyone who shares my faith sees that concept in the same light. With the help of my newly acquired "jewel," I will do my best to explain why I believe so strongly in what I see as both a biblically based obligation and an act of supreme common sense.

The "jewel" is a book recently published by Cascade Books called *Planted*, written by Leah Kostamo. The foreword is written by no less a person than Eugene H. Peterson, the author of the popular biblical paraphrase *The Message* and Professor Emeritus of Spiritual Theology at Regent College on the campus of Vancouver's University of British Columbia. When I first read what Professor Peterson had to say about both the quality of Leah's writing and the content of the book, I found it hard to see his superlatives as other than very gracious support for a new author. I was wrong. If I had been writing the foreword, the language would have been even stronger. I hope the little taste provided by this chapter will reinforce my point. What perhaps also reinforces my point is my decision to place this chapter near the end of my book. Otherwise, the reader would have been tempted to cast aside my prose and rush out to buy Leah's! I hope readers will at least finish what I have written before so doing. Leah would be a hard act to follow.

The bearer of the jewel was Leah's husband, Markku, an environmental scientist who is president and co-founder of the Canadian branch of the multinational Christian environmental organization with the unusual name of A Rocha. He was one of those who received copies of my manuscript while I was writing it. We were meeting face to face for the first time during one of his weekly visits to Vancouver. His headquarters lie to the south of Vancouver near the U.S. border within the watershed of a small endangered salmon river called Little Campbell. There, working out of the Brooksdale Environmental Centre, A Rocha Canada welcomes interns and volunteers from around the world to train them in actively caring for creation. Let me use some of Markku's own words to characterize A Rocha. His use of an octopus as a metaphor is particularly fitting, given that the world's largest species of that remarkable creature is found along Canada's West Coast.

> [It is] a bit like shaking hands with an octopus – which tentacle do you grasp? There's the conservation arm, the education arm, the sustainable living arm. Throw in internship programs, community outreach, our environmental centres, community gardens and suddenly you have a multi-tentacle beast! BUT, to extend the metaphor, you also have a beast with just one heart, brain and will. The variety of our work is all centred on practical action, care for creation and care for people. All of it – whether it's planting gardens with the marginalized in Winnipeg or catching frogs with day campers in Surrey, B.C. – is rooted in our mission to transform people and places into healthy communities.

Leah's book tells, in a candid, entertaining, and instructive way, the inspiring story of how she and Markku walked away from his well-paying job as a consultant to fulfill their vision of creating a God-centred, frontline, hands-on, environmentally protective "octopus" equipped for reaching out to as many people as possible while also undertaking practical, valuable, scientifically sound conservation work. Reading her words moved me, very fleetingly, to contemplate helping them weed their farm garden, no small achievement given how much I detested that task as a child. On a more serious note, Leah also sets out the theological, philosophical, and biblical base for the concept of Christian stewardship, which is the focus of this chapter.

Some might question the value of theological discussions, but, as any reader of appendix I, on the Middle East, will surely recognize, religious views and how they are interpreted can have immense consequences, both good and bad. At first glance, the hatreds and history that continue to divide that unfortunate region and make it so dangerous to the world at large seem very far removed from and much more important than conserving the environment of a small watershed in southern British Columbia. Yet, if the principles and beliefs that animate people like Markku and Leah were to be applied much more broadly among the world's nations, the transformation in the prospects for the health of the globe we all occupy could be enormous. Values have power, especially when they are rooted in religious belief and result in concrete action.

Before sharing some of Leah's words, I would make one additional observation. At least one arm of the octopus is concerned with helping people, specifically those who have difficulty helping themselves. Some environmentalists forget that mankind is a part of creation, not just the source of all the problems. Meeting the needs of "nature" should also entail meeting the legitimate needs of people. By the same token, it is also true that some of the greatest suffering that will result from, for example, climate change will be experienced by people – globally two hundred million environmental refugees are anticipated – and local pollution problems are routinely associated with human health risks. We are part of the world's ecological systems, and it is simply foolish to pretend or act otherwise.

Here, then, is some of what Leah Kostamo had to say in chapter three of *Planted*.

> "The Earth is the Lord's and everything in it," so says Psalm 24. Though seemingly benign in its simplicity the proposition that the earth actually belongs to God and not us is radical and often runs counter to popular Christian beliefs. Allow me to illustrate.
>
> I was visiting a church recently where an enthusiastic man in a plaid tie presented a power point of images taken from the Hubble telescope. His presentation – set to a soundtrack full of wavering strings and fluttering flutes – showed swirling galaxies, frosty nebulas and myriads of sparkling stars. The presenter said he was "blown away" that God had created all this – the whole universe! – just for him. Indeed, all of creation was a present, gift-wrapped in starry paper, for God's beloved: humankind. I looked around the room expecting to see mouths agape – some sign of this man's mistaken conclusion. But no, everyone wore those cheery smiles, so appropriate for modest Christian folk.
>
> I'm not sure where we got the idea that creation is the possession of people, but it sure isn't the message of the Bible. True, the creation narrative in Genesis does set humans in a unique position among the rest of creation – though, as Barbara Brown Taylor points out, we don't even get our own day, but must

share Day Six with all manner of creeping things, including cows! The specialness bestowed on our species, Genesis says, has to do with our being "created in the image of God." We reflect God's character uniquely, which, rather than giving us divine-size egos, should humble us to no end and clue us in to the fact that we might have a special role to play in the grand drama of creation.

The notion that we are image-bearers coupled with the idea that the earth belongs to God has major implications for how we live and how we respond to God's charge to Adam to "serve the garden and keep it" (Genesis 2:15). Cal DeWit, professor of environmental studies at the University of Wisconsin-Madison, helpfully sheds light on this verse when he unpacks the Hebrew words for serve ("abad") and keep ("shamar"). The first, abad, is sometimes translated till, dress, or work – all good gardening words – but it is the second word, shamar, that puts a new spin on what it means to be a good gardener for God. Shamar is sometimes translated tend, guard, take care of, and look after. DeWit contends that the word implies a "loving, caring, sustaining type of keeping." The word is the same used in the Aaronic blessing: "The Lord bless you and keep you; the Lord make his face shine upon you and give you peace." DeWit writes:

> When we invoke God's blessing to keep us, we are not asking that God keep us in a kind of preserved, inactive, uninteresting state. Instead we are calling on God to keep us in all of our vitality, with all of our energy and beauty. The keeping we expect of God when we invoke the Aaronic blessing is one that nurtures all of our life-sustaining and life-fulfilling relationships with our family members, with our neighbours and our friends, with the land, air, and water, and with our God. We ask God to love us, to care for us, and to sustain us in relationship to our natural and human environment ... The rich and full keeping that we invoke with the Aaronic blessing is the kind of rich and full keeping that we should bring to God's garden, to God's creatures, and to all of creation.

All this points to our special role in creation, which is one of care-taking or stewarding. In fact, it is our unique position as image-bearers that qualifies us to steward God's creation. "Made in the divine image, we are here to love as God loves," writes Barbara Brown Taylor. "You know how it feels under the shadow of those wings? So move over. Make room, because there is a whole creation seeking refuge, and you, you are the spitting image of the One who gives life to all."

Finally, as a kind of side bar on worship: if the Earth is the Lord's, then it's appropriate to acknowledge this once in a while. I love what Taylor has to say on this point: "For those of us who believe God is the source from which all arose, we are the first creatures to say so out loud. God may well prefer the

> sound of spring peepers, but I have to believe there was joy in heaven when the first human being looked at the sky and said, "Thank you for all of this."

By welcoming interns, volunteers, and visitors from varying backgrounds, A Rocha's activities at the Brooksdale Environmental Centre also encourage those who share our faith and those who do not to work together to promote the health of the globe we all occupy. For too long, mutual distrust has blinded both sides to the potential for that much needed common effort.

Chapter 62

A CLOSING CHALLENGE

My story has included extensive descriptions of my spiritual experiences and beliefs partly because, without them, much of the narrative would have made no sense. More importantly, shorn of those experiences, my life would certainly have taken a very different direction. In this chapter, I describe more fully the place to which these experiences have brought me. I hope the reader will find in these final words something of value that will have lasting meaning in his or her own life.

This chapter also brings my narrative to an end. That was not my original intention. My plan was to conclude with some wise observations on several of the many topics I have discussed. It would be easy to say that I abandoned this plan because I recognized that there is no automatic correlation between wisdom and my longevity. There is truth in that recognition, but I have a better reason. I began this book with the borrowed observation that the stories that make up our lives help us understand our place and determine our purpose in this world. I expressed the hope that reading my life's stories would help my children and others better understand the significance of their own stories. I want my stories to speak for themselves and for the reader to draw whatever conclusions he or she wishes from them. Wise observations from me are not needed for that to happen.

Many have observed that, in the final analysis, each of us is entirely alone. The moment of death is often cited as proof. For those of us who believe in God, that sense of being alone, even at the end of our earthly lives, is greatly diminished, indeed removed, by the certain knowledge of His presence. That said, the need for human companionship is real whatever one's beliefs. For Christians such as I who draw their guidance from biblical teachings, the New Testament, in particular, emphasizes the need for close interpersonal relationships. It goes so far as to characterize the church as a body in which each part is essential for the whole to function. I had to relearn the importance of that teaching well after my return home to Vancouver at age fifty-four.

When we first came back to the West Coast in 1991, I attended a church regularly and joined a Bible study. Very uncomfortable in group situations, Ardith remained at home. When her schizophrenic symptoms returned, it became difficult to leave her alone. Moreover, part of her paranoia included fear of my church involvement. To avoid the stress that could trigger further psychotic symptoms, I decided to confine my religious activities to Scripture reading and prayer at home, occasionally joined by a visitor or two. Even after Ardith returned from her period of enforced hospitalization and the worst of her symptoms were more or less kept under control by medication, I believed it necessary to avoid church involvement in case it triggered a return of her psychosis. That pattern continued for years and, inevitably, I became increasingly isolated.

When Alzheimer's was added to Ardith's burden in 2007, she became less and less a companion; my sense of being alone deepened further. We could not converse, and she no longer knew me as her husband. The death of our beloved border collie Max in early 2011 further underlined how isolated I had become.

It was about this time that my New Zealand mentor, Eric Sherburd, urged me by e-mail to consider attending an Alpha course. I had never heard of such a course, but his recommendation was to change my life yet again. I will describe my own experience of Alpha but I want to say something first about its origins and what it is. To ensure accuracy, I e-mailed Alpha world headquarters at Holy Trinity Brompton, a very large Anglican church in London, for their advice. The reply was very straightforward. I needed to look no further than the summary in the Internet encyclopedia known as *Wikipedia*. Clearly, the reader can do that just as readily as I can, and I will limit my description accordingly. I do, however, recommend that interested readers take the time to do so. The *Wikipedia* account is fairly detailed and remarkably balanced. It contains both praise and criticism.

Alpha is a multi-week course on Christianity that was initiated in the 1970s at Holy Trinity Brompton. It was further developed in the 1980s by Rev. John Irvine, who was succeeded in 1990 by the organization's present leader, Rev. Nicky Gumbel. Gumbel, a former London barrister, was schooled at Eton, at Cambridge, and, after a decision to join the Anglican clergy, at Oxford. Born of a Jewish father and a non-practicing Anglican mother, he experienced his own personal conversion to Christianity while studying at Cambridge.

After his ordination, he joined the staff at Holy Trinity and was soon focusing his considerable abilities on improving the Alpha course. On Easter Day, 2013, a British newspaper, *The Independent*, featured a lengthy but somewhat sceptical article that called the Alpha course "British Christianity's biggest success story." That success has not been confined to Britain. The courses have now been given in dozens of countries through churches of many different denominations from Roman Catholic to Pentecostal and have been attended by, according to the same newspaper article, about twenty million people worldwide. A couple of days later, another British newspaper, the well-respected *Guardian*, writing about the new Archbishop of Canterbury Justin Welby, emphasized his roots at Holy Trinity Brompton and his closeness to Nicky Gumbel. Interestingly, Welby's father was also Jewish. The article also reported that newly elected Pope Francis, while still a cardinal in Argentina, sent four of his bishops to London to learn about the Alpha program. More recently, an Austrian Cardinal was among a significant number of Catholic clergy at the annual Alpha Leaders' Conference in London in May of 2013. Clearly Spirit-filled, the Cardinal is also of half Jewish origin.

I have attended the Alpha course three times at two different churches a few blocks from where I live. The experience was similar each time, but I found that the depth and breadth of teaching was such that I learned new things on each occasion.

The course normally takes place one evening a week over ten weeks plus one residential weekend away from the city. On arrival, each attendee is registered and assigned to a particular small group. Only first names are taken, and there is no personal follow-up unless requested. Each group shares a buffet meal together, which provides an opportunity for participants to get to know one another. After the meal, everyone moves into the church to watch a forty-minute video presentation by Nicky Gumbel on the topic of the evening. The video is typically preceded by a few worship songs. After the video, participants divide into their assigned small groups to discuss what they have just heard.

Each group has a discussion leader and assistant normally drawn from the congregation of the host church. Leaders are strictly enjoined by the organizers not to push their own views and to be respectful of all opinions expressed, however bizarre or antagonistic. The leader's job is to throw out questions related to the presentation and to encourage everyone present to have his or her say. I played this role myself on one evening when our discussion leader was ill, and I can tell you that it is very challenging. Because of my home situation, I was not able to attend any of the residential weekends, but I could tell from what was said by those who did that the weekend experience had considerable impact on many.

While I generally enjoyed the discussions after the presentation and always appreciated cooking other than my own, the highlight for me each evening was undoubtedly the video presentation. Nicky Gumbel is a superb speaker with a real gift for explaining potentially complex concepts and an ability to relate these concepts to the challenges of everyday life. He also injects a lot of humour into his talks. Nicky does not talk down to his audience despite his obvious intellect and accomplishments. Rather, he invites those present to enter into his own struggles with faith over the years. His conclusions, to my mind, were always biblically based.

Here in Vancouver, English subtitles accompanied every presentation as an aid to many in the audience whose first language was not English. Language was sometimes a challenge in some of the small groups as well. All three of the small groups in which I participated had a majority of members from countries other than Canada. Indeed, the second of the two churches sponsoring Alpha courses which I attended includes in its congregation people from, at last count, seventy-six different countries. That sounds impressive, and it is, but, set against today's Vancouver, it is not surprising. My car insurance renewal form offers free translation for over a hundred and seventy languages.

It was not just national origin that created so much variety among participants. Personal circumstances ranged from established professionals to recently released convicts. I was stunned to learn that the middle-aged man sitting beside me one evening had just gotten out of prison after serving a long sentence for killing a fellow biker gang member. Most attendees were much younger than I, mainly in their twenties and thirties. The majority appeared to be single, but enough couples were present to warrant child care. Alpha frequently presents itself as a non-judgmental opportunity to discuss the meaning of life. That opportunity is provided in a Christian context, but the discussions include many differing views. As a reflection of British culture, Holy Trinity Brompton's small discussion groups meet in nearby pubs to discuss Nicky's talks. That would be a step too far in Vancouver, where British-style family-oriented pubs are non-existent.

There was also great variety with respect to religious experience or lack of it. I could see a few gray heads in the crowd like myself who may have been seeking to rekindle their faith or deepen their knowledge, but most people in the groups I attended were either very new to the Christian faith or simply seeking new meaning in their lives. Some were agnostics as I was at their age, but they were actively exploring alternative possibilities, something I had never done.

I found especially interesting the experiences of some of the immigrants who came from cultures so different from our own. I remember in particular a very well spoken young woman from Ethiopia who described growing up in a traditional Ethiopian Christian family. Ironically, it was not until she arrived in Vancouver that she had an encounter with Christ that transformed her much as I had been transformed decades earlier. She told us how some of her friends had been very critical of her new religious faith, arguing against its exclusivity as compared with, for example, Islam, which claims to accept Jesus Christ as a legitimate prophet but as a lesser one than Mohammed. I was reminded of her comments when I came across the text of a letter I wrote to her as a follow-up to the discussion that her comments had stimulated. Because what I wrote reflects so closely what Nicky Gumbel had to say in his video presentation that evening, I will repeat some excerpts. It will give the reader a flavour of what Alpha is about that no amount of generalities could convey.

> I was very touched by what you had to say about your faith and concerned about the arguments that your friend has been presenting to counter that faith. As it happens, the presentation which Nicky Gumbel made at the last Alpha meeting concerning the divinity of Jesus responds very directly to the points your friend has been putting forward. Let me explain by first reviewing what Nicky had to say to all of us.
>
> He began by emphasizing that the evidence for the existence of Jesus rests not only in New Testament accounts but also in the writings of both Roman and Jewish historians. Flavius Josephus, in particular, while writing about Pontius Pilate, described Jesus as a highly regarded prophet of God who gained a

large following among both Jews and Gentiles. Josephus even made reference to Jesus' capacity to perform miracles, "mighty works" he called them. Nicky went on to explain that that the Gospels and letters making up the New Testament are regarded by experts in authenticating documents as easily the best authenticated ancient manuscripts in existence. This is measured by the number of original documents that still exist and by how close in time those surviving documents are to when they were probably written.

You will remember that Nicky then focused on what Jesus said about Himself and what His followers said about Him in His presence. He quoted several Scriptures that made it clear, for example, that, when we see Jesus, we see God and that He and the Father are one. Jesus also underlined that we could come to the Father only through Him. Nicky pointed out that we can have only three reactions to Jesus' claims:

1) the claims are not true but Jesus honestly believed them;

2) the claims are not true and Jesus invented them in order to attract followers;

3) the claims are true.

The first response, Nicky argued, would have to mean that that Jesus was at least delusional and very likely insane. The second response would mean that he was a truly evil fraudster. Jesus' teachings, which provide the moral underpinnings for Western civilization, are widely regarded by Christians and many non-Christians alike as admirable and inspiring. They are also, beyond question, enduring. Are they likely to be the ravings of a madman or the creations of a fraudster?

Jesus' divinity is central to His teachings and to His willingness to become the perfect sacrifice for us all on the cross. That conflicts directly with the contention that Jesus was a legitimate prophet of God but not the greatest one. How could He be a valid prophet of God and speak blasphemy, lies, or madness? Yet His teachings are indeed blasphemous in terms of Islamic theology. To contend, therefore, that He is a prophet of God, yet reject completely His central teachings, clearly displays a poor understanding of what Jesus actually taught. Denying Jesus' divinity is a rejection of Him and the religious faith He founded. To claim recognition of Him as a prophet but deny what He taught is not an act of inclusivity; it is quite the opposite.

One of the consequences of my exposure to the Alpha courses was an invitation to join a weekly prayer group held in the home of Allan and Betty Ann Burnett. It is one of dozens of home groups associated with our church. Some of these groups are focused on particular groups of people.

One group, for example, is made up of people who work in Vancouver's very large film industry. Ours, on the other hand, is very mixed.

Allan, who is an ordained minister, regularly hosts the Alpha courses at our church in his upbeat, encouraging style, but his involvement goes well beyond that. He frequently leads teams, usually at Nicky Gumbel's request, to various parts of the world to train Christian leaders in giving Alpha courses. In the relatively short time that I have known him, these have included four countries in Africa and three in South Asia. He also travels for the same purpose to other parts of Canada. One of the stories he brought back to us from his attendance at the 2013 annual Alpha Leaders' Conference in London was the decision by the government of Ghana to send seven prison officers to the London conference because the Alpha program has so transformed Ghana's prisons.

Allan and Betty Ann's home not only provides a truly stunning setting for our worship and study each week, but is very conveniently located for me. Only a block away, their two-story apartment sits atop an attractive low-rise building at the end of our street fronting on Stanley Park's Lost Lagoon. The sizable living room enjoys superb views of water, forest, and mountains comparable to our own, but also benefits from a three-story ceiling under a dome or cupola that is the building's most distinctive exterior feature. We can see it clearly from our living room.

The group numbers about thirty in total, but an average of fifteen to twenty usually attend on any given evening. We are mixed in age with a couple of people roughly ten years younger than I, a few in their late forties or early fifties, and the majority younger. At last count there were twelve nationalities represented. Allan and Betty Ann own a wedding business and lease a chapel that is located on the ground floor of their building as well as others elsewhere in Greater Vancouver. Their own home is part of the business in that some small rooms are used for offices and their living and dining rooms are available for wedding receptions. Because a larger than usual wedding necessitated temporary removal of the living room furniture, we recently met in their good-sized kitchen. Togetherness came naturally. No encouragement was required. That said, the gathering was an especially positive and uplifting one. It gave a whole new meaning to the expression "coming together."

Allan and Betty Ann's wedding business provided me with an experience that I thought was well behind me. As I shared with my e-mail friends elsewhere in Canada and in other countries, I was once again going to be the father of the bride. I quickly explained the circumstances lest there be any misunderstanding. A young, newly arrived Chinese couple had engaged Allan and Betty Ann to arrange and conduct their wedding. They had no family or friends in Canada but wanted to have a "father of the bride" accompany his "daughter" down the aisle. I was selected for the task even though I looked more like a grandfather than a father. I have to say that the experience was a delightful change from my normal routine. I got to meet and walk with a lovely young lady, get dressed up in my best suit, participate in a moving ceremony with an uplifting message, and eat a superb meal afterwards. Not a bad day's work, and I get to add it to my résumé!

Our weekly meetings normally last about two and a half hours. The first half-hour is devoted to our hosts' superbly brewed coffee and assorted treats or veggies with dip, and socializing. We have birthday celebrations with cake and candles as appropriate. We then begin our time of worship and prayer gathered around the white grand piano in the living room with Vancouver's glorious mountains serving as a backdrop. The songs we sing can be contemporary or old, but all are full of praise. After we take our seats, Allan reads and introduces the Scripture passages for the evening. They are usually drawn from the sermon delivered by our pastor the previous Sunday. Allan encourages as many as possible to share their views, and I am often struck by the truly inspiring insights into this or that verse offered by both new and mature Christians. We conclude with Allan asking each attendee for his or her prayer requests – or expressions of thanks – before joining together in bringing those requests before God. I sometimes arrive at the meeting feeling down and overwhelmed by my role as a full-time caregiver, but I never leave feeling that way.

Christianity at its essence is not about theology and church government or rules and religious practices. It is about God's desire to bridge the gap between Himself and His most precious creation – humanity. That gap came about in large part because of His gift of free will, without which mankind could neither give nor withhold love. The bridging of the gap has to take place in each individual heart. The instrument that God uses for this purpose is grace, unmerited forgiveness paid for on the cross by Jesus' sacrifice. It is freely available to all those who seek forgiveness for their shortcomings and believe in Christ, in His resurrection, and in His promise of salvation. It is this free gift to believers that makes Christianity unique among religions. No amount of good works or religious observances can earn salvation. A simple prayer is all that is required. Christ already did the necessary heavy lifting on the cross.

I have already told the story of how my life was transformed through such a prayer of repentance forty-five years ago in New Zealand. Let me share with you the remarkable story of a similar transformation in the life of Patricia, a young mother I met near the end of an Alpha course in November of 2011. She had arrived in Vancouver two weeks earlier for a year's stay with her twelve-year-old daughter who was to be enrolled in a well-regarded Christian school on Vancouver's North Shore. She and her daughter sat beside me in the small group to which they had been assigned. I recognized her Spanish-accented English and welcomed her in my halting version of her mother tongue. I spoke fluent Spanish when I left Colombia, our first diplomatic post, but that was almost fifty years earlier, and I was, to put it mildly, out of practice. I soon learned that she lived in a very pleasant apartment in a small town on Spain's beautiful Costa Del Sol near Gibraltar. She was, however, born and raised in Colombia, very close to Bogota where we had lived for three years. Patricia soon joined the weekly prayer group under the dome near our apartment, but it was not until four months later that she told me her extraordinary story.

Patricia's Colombian family was wealthy, which made her family members targets for criminals. She was kidnapped as a child and ransomed by her parents. Partly because of this, the family later moved to the safer surroundings of the Netherlands and, subsequently, to the south of Spain. As a young woman, she spent time working in the Netherlands, where she met an English businessman who became her partner and fathered her child. Unfortunately, he proved both abusive and unfaithful, and she returned, deeply depressed, to the family home in Spain, bringing her child with her. It was not long before the family was to receive the appalling news that her older brother, who had been living in Colombia looking after the family's affairs, had been murdered by a well-known drug dealer and terrorist. Overwhelmed by her pain, Patricia tried to kill herself. Some time later, still filled with hatred and rage, she negotiated on behalf of her family with criminals in Colombia to arrange for the murder of the man who killed her brother. However, before she could finalize the contract, her life took a totally new direction.

Struck by the words of a preacher she happened to hear on her car radio, she found herself drawn to a Spanish evangelical church. As she sat off to one side listening, the preacher turned and beckoned to her to come to him. She did, and he laid hands on her head. She felt a rush of heat and energy come into her and a sense of peace and belonging that she had never known before. That encounter with Christ transformed her. She abandoned the contacts with the Colombian criminals, forgave in prayer the murderer of her brother, and sought to persuade her parents to do the same. Her brother's murderer was captured in May of 2008, four years after the murder and shortly after Patricia relinquished her hatred of him and forgave him in prayer. He was quickly extradited to the U.S. and subsequently sentenced to thirty-three years in a Florida prison.

Patricia told me that she had been a poor mother, but that had changed dramatically as well. One result was her decision to bring her daughter to the Christian school in North Vancouver that I mentioned earlier. She also forgave her daughter's father, and that act of forgiveness led him to help pay the school fees for a time. Shortly after telling me this story, Patricia sent me a moving e-mail entitled "From Broken Bits to a Beautiful Whole." In it she talked about how the "Master Craftsman" can, by putting us back together in accordance with His design, turn our brokenness into something beautiful and valuable. I cannot think of a better description of what happened to Patricia herself. She and her daughter are now back in Spain for financial reasons, but we continue to exchange e-mails. They hope to visit their friends in Vancouver when circumstances permit. Patricia tells me they miss us, and we certainly miss them.

Earlier I characterized myself as an empirical Christian. The definition I gave of Empirical Christianity, which is repeated below, was an attempt to explain the thought processes at work behind my own faith, specifically about how the miraculous experiences from which my wife and I had benefited helped me accept Jesus' divinity and His promise that He would keep with Him in eternity all those who believe that promise and accept that He is divine. I have lived long enough to have a lot of hindsight, and, as we all know, hindsight can be remarkably accurate. There is absolutely no doubt in my mind that the step in faith that I took so long ago was the most meaningful thing that I ever did. My life and that of my family benefited immensely. God the Father and His son Jesus are very real and that certainty provides me with both reassurance and hope as I look into the future without the benefit of hindsight. I do not need it. In the words of the old hymn sung by Ottawa Valley native George Beverly Shea at so many Billy Graham crusades, "I know not what the future holds, but I know who holds the future."

"EMPIRICAL CHRISTIANITY": I wrote earlier at some length about the miracles of salvation and healing that were central to our early Christian experience in New Zealand. One of the better-known passages of Scripture has to do with "doubting Thomas." In John's account, Thomas, one of John's fellow apostles, cannot believe that Jesus has risen from the dead until he actually touches His wounds. In a gentle rebuke, Jesus responds, "Because you have seen me, you have believed; blessed are those who have not seen and yet have believed." I have some sympathy with Thomas because I would almost certainly not have believed in God, much less in the claims of Christ, if I had not experienced the transformation in my own life that I described earlier. The other miracles I saw later reinforced that belief. In that sense you could say that, like Thomas, I saw (experienced) before I believed. As a consequence, I hold in awe those who believe so deeply despite not having had transforming, miraculous experiences as dramatic as mine.

I do recognize that faith, as the Bible puts it, is a gift from God so that no one can boast about having it. Yet, when my faith is tested, I am able to look back at these miracles and be encouraged. I cannot deny what I have seen and experienced. In that sense, I am an empirical Christian. Although the research scientists I later directed would have questioned the methodology, my initial prayer, however reluctant, was an experiment, and I was amazed that the results completely supported the hypothesis put forward by believers in Christ. I was not predisposed to believe, but their experiences and mine coincided, the essential element in proving a hypothesis.

Said another way, having successfully tested what I could, that Jesus is able to transform and heal in a supernatural way those who come to Him, it became reasonable to accept as valid His other claims as recorded in the Bible, such as the promise of eternal life. "Seek and you will find" is the Bible's challenge to us all, believers and skeptics alike.

I invite you, dear reader, to accept that challenge.

APPENDIX I: THOUGHTS ON THE MIDDLE EAST, THE TAIL THAT WAGS THE GLOBAL DOG

As mentioned in the main body of my narrative, the founding philosophy of the modern Israeli state came from the European Yiddish-speaking Ashkenazi Jews and is best exemplified in the communal principles that underlie the kibbutz. The Ashkenazim, given their horrific experiences in Europe, were generally inclined to look to their important allies, especially the United States, as major components of their security. The Sephardic Jews from the Middle East were much less Western-oriented. Native born Israelis, nicknamed "Sabras," were and are generally much more self-reliant in their approach to life and the defence of their country.

In the years since the 1960s, the proportion of independent-minded native-born Sabras in Israel has grown to about seventy percent of the population, despite the substantial influx of Russian Jews following the collapse of Soviet communism that clearly affected the proportion of native-born to immigrant citizens. Sabra attitudes clearly dominate the thinking of most Israelis today. The near-automatic support of the world's most powerful country and the special circumstances created by the "war on terror" undoubtedly reinforce that sense of confidence and control over their country's destiny. Perhaps spurred by that confidence, Prime Minister Yitzhak Rabin displayed flexibility and generosity in efforts to find a resolution of Israeli differences with Palestine. He had the military background, stature, and instincts that might have enabled him to lead his people in that direction. Sadly, his assassination by an extremist ultra-orthodox Jew brought his efforts to an end, and no other Israeli leader has yet emerged with comparable credentials and instincts.

To the outsider, because of its strict religious laws governing, for example, food preparation and observance of the Sabbath, Israel looks like a very religious country, almost theocratic. In point of fact, the bulk of its Jewish population is indifferent or actively irreligious. The United States, for example, is a much more religious country in terms of worship attendance. Israel's laws stem in large measure from its multi-party political structure and the fact that no one party can ever win a majority in the Knesset (parliament). The small religious parties representing the ultra-orthodox are almost always needed for a prime minister to secure the necessary majority support. They typically fill the post of minister of religious affairs and are given a near carte blanche with respect to religious laws. I remember, for example, the considerable political fight in the 1960s that occurred over the decision by Israel's international carrier El Al Airlines to allow non-kosher meals to be served on its flights.

As the centre of Jewish faith and hope, the birthplace of Christianity, and the location of Islam's third holiest site, Jerusalem is appropriately known as a holy city. Legally, under the terms of the U.N. Resolution establishing Israel in May of 1948, Jerusalem is an international city; practically, it is Israel's capital; and, historically, it is a remarkable example of endurance after having been completely destroyed by the Babylonians and again, millennia later, by the Romans.

Today it is the de facto seat of government of a nation of people who not only were exiled and scattered by the Romans throughout the Empire two thousand years ago but also experienced extraordinary persecution and near annihilation over much of the time since. Yet they were able to re-establish themselves after World War II and the horrors of the holocaust in the land to which Moses had led them thousands of years earlier after finally escaping their four-hundred–year enslavement by the Egyptian Pharaohs. There is no human saga to match it. Is it, therefore, any wonder that the minority among modern Israelis who are very religious believe that it was God Himself who made this possible? Hundreds of millions of Christians, especially evangelicals, also believe this, and, further, believe that the re-establishment of the State of Israel is central to end time theology and the return of Christ.

Ironically, Hasidic and other fervent Orthodox Jews do not recognize the present secular state of Israel as the Israel described in prophecy but rather hope for Eretz Israel, which not only would be a theocracy but would include all of Palestine, i.e., the land given by God to Moses. That is why they so fervently support the establishment of Jewish communities in Arab Palestine. Because, as I noted earlier, Israeli governments are always made up of several parties, including the small religious ones, these minority views carry much more weight than they otherwise would. Similarly, Israel's strongest supporter, the United States, is influenced by an alliance on Middle East issues between the small but influential American Jewish community and the much more numerous evangelical Christians.

On the Islamic side of the equation is a broad group of Middle Eastern Islamic countries, both Shia and Sunni, who are often at odds with each other. Despite their differences – sometimes because of them – most of these countries are committed to providing moral or material support to their dispossessed and often embittered Palestinian co-religionists. The reason for that bitterness reflects the Palestinians' long occupation of that part of the Middle East. Some claim that their ancestors were living in Palestine at the time of the Roman expulsion of the Jews two thousand years ago. Certainly they arrived in greater numbers about twelve hundred years later, after the withdrawal of the European Christian crusaders and the victory of the Muslim forces. Moreover, Islam's third holiest site, the Dome of the Rock, is in Jerusalem. That is the place from which, Muslims believe, Mohammed ascended into heaven. Clearly it is impossible to contemplate "solutions" in that part of the world without considering religion and related history.

All of us are touched by these events whatever our beliefs. For example, Canada spent nearly a billion dollars on security to protect world leaders at the Toronto G-8 and G-20 summits in 2010 precisely because of the anger and resentment fostered by this history. We had to do the same earlier in the year for the Winter Olympics in Vancouver. More broadly, the United States' interventions in Iraq and Afghanistan have at their root the animosities that both feed and flow from the ongoing confrontation between Israelis and Palestinians. The debts incurred by these multi-year interventions in addition to the huge ongoing costs of U.S. homeland security no doubt weakened America's capacity to respond to the 2008 economic crisis and the current worldwide economic slowdown. And that is to say nothing about the resulting changes for the worse in lifestyle and freedom of movement experienced in some Western countries, especially the United States. Clearly a resolution of differences in the Middle East is desperately needed, but I fear that the prospects for such are actually diminishing.

I used to think when considering the Palestinian/Israeli impasse that little has changed in that part of the world since 1967 when Israel occupied the rest of Palestine, both the West Bank and Gaza. For many years, except for the important treaty with Egypt, that remained true, but, within this century, the changes had been significant. Of particular importance were the September 11, 2001, terrorist attacks on the U.S. mainland that resulted in an even tighter alignment between Israel and the United States and the initiation of the American-led "war on terror."

President Obama's comments in 2011 about using Israel's pre-1967 borders as a basis for negotiating the borders of an independent Palestine surprised Israel, which has usually been able to take U.S. support for granted. That automatic support has undoubtedly reduced Washington's leverage in Jerusalem. However, the positive U.S. Congressional and public reaction to Israeli prime minister Netanyahu's blunt rejection of Obama's reference to the pre-1967 borders means, in my view, that Israel can continue to count on U.S. backing, especially when it matters. Adamant U.S. (and Canadian) opposition to Palestine's efforts to be recognized as a sovereign state by the U.N. reflect that reality. Texas Governor Perry, during his unsuccessful attempt to become the Republican candidate for the presidency in 2012, stated that, as a Christian, he was bound to support Israel. As he said these words, one of Prime Minister Netanyahu's top aides stood beside him. The concern for Israel is not confined to Republicans. In accepting the Democratic party's nomination for the presidency in 2012, Obama stated, "our support for Israel is unwavering." That said, Obama urged Israel during his visit to that country in March of 2013 to be more accommodating in dealing with the Palestinians' legitimate grievances and aspirations.

For those unfamiliar with the history, I should explain that, in 1967, following the defeat of its Arab neighbours in the Six Day War, Israel occupied the rest of Palestine (West Bank and Gaza) as well as Egypt's Sinai Peninsula and Syria's Golan Heights. The Sinai was returned to Egypt in 1979 as part of the Israeli–Egyptian peace treaty brokered by U.S. president Jimmy Carter. The Israeli occupation of Palestine was the most important turning point in modern Israeli history. What had been a democratic, predominantly Jewish state was, in effect, transformed into one where a huge, fast-growing minority under de facto Israeli control was non-Jewish, often hostile, and without representation in the government that effectively ruled them. That minority is only a generation away from becoming a majority. Many commentators, both Israeli and foreign, argue that such a situation is not viable in the long term and that the only real solution is Israeli withdrawal from the occupied territories, often called "trading land for peace." This is the approach – the two state solution – that is strongly argued in Carter's book on the region. Israel did withdraw from Gaza, but complete withdrawal elsewhere, especially to the 1967 borders, is not acceptable to Prime Minister Netanyahu's government.

Moreover, the Israelis believe they have reason to doubt that withdrawal from the occupied territories and recognition of an independent Palestinian state would cause the extremist Muslims to stop their attacks. Missile attacks from Gaza reinforce this point. The location of the border and other issues such as the demilitarization of the new Palestinian state, the status of Jerusalem, and the disposition of the Israeli settlements in Palestine would, the Israelis believe, almost certainly be characterized as inequitable and as justification for continued violence.

In January of 2013, Israel's voters demonstrated that they were not comfortable with Prime Minister Netanyahu's leadership. His Likud party dropped from forty-two to thirty-one seats while the newly created centrist party led by Yair Lapid secured nineteen seats. The effect was to create a virtual deadlock, with half of the seats in the Knesset belonging to Likud and its right wing allies and the other half occupied by parties favouring more moderate policies. As head of the largest party, Netanyahu remains prime minister, but the increased need to accommodate centrist opinion probably lies behind the recent resumption of peace talks with the Palestinian Authority. They have been on the back burner for four years. Lapid made the resumption of these talks a condition for his co-operation with Netanyahu. Israeli opinion polls have for years supported the notion of ceding territory if it would improve the security of Israel. The problem is that, according to the same polls, most Israelis doubt that ceding territory would result in any such improvement. The negotiations will not be easy.

Earlier I described some of the other factors that appear to constrain or inform U.S. and Israeli policy, but I am persuaded that changes within the Muslim world are equally or even more important. Specifically, I cannot help but conclude that the differences in values between the extreme fundamentalist Muslims and the democratic pluralistic West are of such a deep, enduring nature that resolution of the Israeli/Palestinian impasse would not by itself overcome them. Indeed, the fundamentalist Muslims have a vested interest in maintaining the impasse because it draws recruits to their ranks. The other side of that coin is, of course, that a solution to the differences between Israel and Palestine would help weaken the appeal of the extremists.

This broad collision of values is aggravated by what is going on within the Muslim Middle East, particularly the growing influence and obvious ambition of Shiite Muslim Iran and sometimes related spread of Sunni/Shia armed conflict. The removal of Iraq's Sunni Muslim but essentially secularist Saddam Hussein has had two important effects: the disappearance of a military counterbalance to Iran (the two countries fought a very bloody multi-year war) and the re-emergence of Iraq's Shiite majority as the dominant political force in that country. Iraq's Shiites have natural ties with, and are influenced by, Iran's Shiites, most of whose leaders are particularly fundamentalist, anti-West, and anti-Israel in their outlook. Sunni/Shia violence within Iraq is worsening despite United States pressure on Iraqi Prime Minister Al-Maliki, a Shia, to reach out to the Sunni minority rather than relying on his army to suppress them. Sunni extremists led by Al Qaeda are doing their best to prevent any possible reconciliation by bombing Shia neighbourhoods and by battling the Iraqi army in Sunni-dominated parts of the country. Iran's influence also extends to Syria, Gaza, and Lebanon, where its Shia client group Hezbollah is an extremely significant military, political, and social presence. Hezbollah displayed surprising military strength when Israel last entered Lebanon, and it is reportedly much stronger today. Iran also provides funds to the Islamic fundamentalist group

Hamas, which rules Gaza. Iran's links with Syria are more complicated and are explained below in a longer discussion of that unfortunate country.

In my view, former Iranian president Ahmadinejad's seemingly unhinged denunciations of Israel, including denials of the Nazi holocaust, and his verbal attacks on the United States were part of a strategy to occupy the extremist high ground in competition with Sunni Muslim extremists such as the Wahabists, originating in Saudi Arabia, who spawned Osama bin Laden and Al Qaeda.

Caught in the middle and under increasing pressure are the Sunni moderates best exemplified by the Saudi ruling class. They fear the Shiites and their own Wahabists, and, despite the need to maintain U.S. support, dare not appear to be soft on Israel. (Ironically, the Saudi Royals initially gained power with Wahabist support.)

For years, secularist regimes such as Mubarak's Egypt and Assad's Syria have also feared and repressed the Muslim extremists in their respective countries. Egypt has tried over time to maintain a reasonable relationship with Israel, but even Mubarak could not ignore popular concerns about Israel's treatment of Palestinians, especially Gazans, and he opened Egypt's border with Gaza despite an agreement with Israel not to do so. That was an important victory for the Gazans.

After Mubarak's forced departure in 2011 and later replacement by a Muslim Brotherhood president, the Egyptian government was under some pressure to scrap the Israeli treaty. That situation changed completely in July of 2013 when the military removed the president and revoked his Islamist constitution in response to widespread economic discontent and broad popular opposition to the president's uncompromising attempts to push secular Egypt in an Islamist direction. While new elections are promised, the decision to ban the Muslim Brotherhood bodes very badly for Egypt's future stability because of the high risk of worsening widespread violence. Relations with Israel will be the least of its concerns.

With respect to Syrian attitudes towards Israel, as long as the Israelis continue to occupy the Golan Heights, there is no prospect of any change in Syria's strong anti-Israel posture. If the ongoing civil war in Syria were to result in Assad's departure, any new Syrian government would have to maintain a similar approach.

Even Westernized, historically secular Turkey is not immune to the oratory of the extremists. In recent years, for the first time since the militantly secular Turkish Republic was founded in the 1920s, a Muslim religious party is dominating the Turkish political scene. The Israeli "murder," as the Turkish prime minister called it, of nine Turks on board a Turkish vessel on a mission of mercy to beleaguered Gaza was certainly helpful to those who want Turkey to adopt rhetoric that is more critical of Israel. Israel's refusal to apologize to Turkey added fuel to that particular fire and seemed at the time to reflect a growing sense of Israeli defiance. The Israeli government was divided with respect to this decision, which is not surprising given Israel's efforts over many years to cultivate good relations with moderate Turkey. The sharp setback experienced by Prime Minister Netanyahu in Israel's January 2013 election appears to have pushed Israeli policy in a more accommodating direction. During his March 2013 visit, U.S. president Obama persuaded Netanyahu to extend an apology to Turkey. Within Turkey, the ongoing struggle between urban liberals and the increasingly intolerant Islamist government mirror in reverse the divide in Egypt.

It is especially difficult to predict what will happen in Yemen, where Al Qaeda has been strongest. The possible collapse of the thirty-two-year-long dictatorial but pro-Western Yemeni regime worries both Yemen's Saudi neighbours and the West. What is feared is a civil war, hence the ultimately successful pressure on the leader to resign before the situation deteriorated further. Unfortunately, despite his departure, the anti-government attacks continue.

Lebanon remains divided along long-standing sectarian lines, but Iranian-backed, Shia-led Hezbollah is continuing to grow in strength, and that is not good news. Arguably, it already outclasses the Lebanese army and is now operating in Syria in support of President Assad. The risk of the Syrian civil war spilling over into Lebanon is growing. No doubt that is why Saudi Arabia has recently announced a gift of US$3 billion to the Lebanese army, the only force strong enough within Lebanon to take on Shia Hezbolloah.

Jordan has a reputation for moderation in both foreign and domestic policies. However, its large Palestinian population creates special challenges for King Abdullah's government; there is growing pressure for liberal reform.

Syria warrants more comment because of the horrific nature of what is happening in that country. Although Syria has long been one of the most efficiently brutal of Arab police states, President Bashar al-Assad's murderous repression of his domestic opponents reached new lows with the use of nerve gas. Nonetheless, it is very unlikely to provoke the kind of sustained Western intervention that was so successful in Libya. Syria has a much stronger military than Libya as well as the backing of Iran and of Russia, which has major interests there. Moreover, there is no oil in this very poor country. A major additional factor in discouraging military intervention is the sectarian division within Syria that has given Assad a firm base of support in the past.

President Assad's secular Baathist party is dominated by Alawis (sometimes called Alawites) who make up about twelve percent of Syria's predominantly Sunni Muslim population. Historically a despised, impoverished minority, their situation changed dramatically when Assad's father assumed power in a 1970 coup. The Alawis are now Syria's socio-economic elite, and they are determined to hang on to what they have acquired. In some respects there is a parallel here with Saddam's Iraq. Saddam, like Assad, was a secularist but from a Sunni Muslim background. He ruled a country that was sixty percent Shia, and he went to appalling lengths, including the use of chemical weapons, to maintain his control over the Shia and Kurdish populations.

There is another parallel with Iraq. The Christian community in Baghdad looked to Saddam as their protector, and their Syrian co-religionists, who number about ten percent of the total Syrian population, appear to do the same with respect to Assad. Many Syrian Christians hold high positions in government and business and Christians have their own courts that deal with civil cases like marriage, divorce, and inheritance based on Bible teachings. Christian civil servants in Syria are given Sunday mornings off to allow them to attend church, and schools in Christian-dominated districts have Saturday and Sunday as the weekend even though the official Syrian weekend falls on Friday and Saturday. Christians are not, however, allowed to proselytize. Some Syrian churches are reportedly fearful that these tolerant policies would be abandoned if the anti-Assad forces were to succeed in overthrowing the government. The 3.5 percent of Syrians who are Druze have also supported the Assad regime. They are heavily overrepresented among military officers.

Alawis, Christians, and Druze together make up a quarter of the Syrian population. If we add secular or nominal Sunni Muslims who have benefited from the relative stability of the Assad regime as well as moderate Sunni Muslims who fear possible extremist leadership should the rebels succeed, it could well be that Assad has had the support of around half of the population. Given the strength of his military, it is not therefore surprising that he is resisting stepping aside. Even if he were willing to seek asylum in a place where the World Court could not touch him, his supporters have too much to lose to give up control: the worse the atrocities and the longer they continue, the greater the fear of retribution. The increasing number of atrocities committed by the rebels further feeds that fear. Some observers have been surprised at how long the Assad regime has resisted the rebellion. Given what is at stake, especially for Syria's minorities, I am not at all surprised. Provided Iran and Russia continue their support, this war could last for years.

The secularist Syrian government under the Assad family has enjoyed good relations with theocratic Shia Iran for decades, initially, perhaps, because of a common dislike of Saddam-ruled Iraq. That relationship has strengthened since the outbreak of hostilities in Syria, and Tehran has sent the Assad regime both weapons and military advisers who specialize in training Alawi paramilitaries. The Alawis have their roots in Twelver Shi'ism, the form of the Shia faith practiced in Iran. Indeed, the Alawis see themselves as the furthest extension westward of Twelver Shi'ism. Based on the Alawis' practices and apparent beliefs, many Sunnis do not believe that the sect is Muslim at all. From my limited understanding of Alawi practices, which, for example, permit Western-style dress for women and do not require observance of Sharia law, I find it hard to believe that they could have the blessing of the ayatollahs of Iran. Nonetheless, the Iranians apparently see merit in a regime that represses Sunni Muslims and that claims links, however tenuous, with Shia Islam. Iran would also appreciate Syria's strong anti-Israel posture.

For its part, Sunni Muslim Saudi Arabia, long fearful of Shia Iran, is providing assistance to the anti-Assad Sunni insurgents. To some degree the Syrian civil conflict can be characterized as a proxy war between Iran and Saudi Arabia. No doubt the Saudis are also concerned at the emergence of Shia-dominated Iraq and the strength of Iran-funded, Shia-led Hezbollah in Lebanon. The fact that Hezbollah has now sent troops into Syria, helping Assad win a symbolically important victory in a border town, will deepen Saudi concern. The assassination in 2012 of Lebanon's Sunni Internal Intelligence Chief by Hezbollah underlines Lebanese vulnerability to Shia influence. Elsewhere, the Saudis have sent troops into neighbouring Bahrain to help the Sunni ruler maintain control over the restless Shia majority in that oil-rich Gulf state. Steadily growing Shia influence must appear very threatening in Riyadh, the Saudi capital.

In my view, U.S. president Obama's threat to order limited missile strikes against Syrian military installations in response to the regime's most recent use of chemical weapons against civilians was both justified and timely. Such weapons are outlawed by international treaty, and both the Russians and the Chinese had made it clear that they would nonetheless use their veto power to keep the U.N. Security Council from authorizing a concerted international response. Russia's willingness, in response to Obama's threat, to negotiate a process of removing and destroying Syria's sizable inventory of these weapons is a major contribution to the world's collective effort to prevent the use of chemical weaponry. The ensuing unanimously supported Security Council resolution setting out Syria's obligations in detail carries the force of international law, but it does not contain the threat of military force as the United States would have preferred. I do not see that as a problem. Russia has huge influence in Syria and a clear vested interest in making the U.N.-sanctioned chemical weapons removal/destruction plan work. That said, the actual removal of the weapons will be both complicated and time-consuming, especially in the middle of a civil war. The fact that the U.N. inspectors were deployed in Syria so quickly after the resolution was passed is an encouraging start. More troubling have been the recent complaints by the inspectors that the international community is not providing the technical and military support needed to undertake the task and to protect both the inspectors and the chemical weapons. More recently and even more seriously, concern has been expressed that the Syrian Government may not be revealing the location of all of the targeted weapons.

Some in the West, appalled by the death of hundreds of thousands and the displacement of millions, have supported sending weapons to the Syrian rebels, but that seems unlikely to happen. There are Al Qaeda and other Muslim extremists among the rebel forces, which raises fears that Western weapons would find their way to these groups. No one forgets that the Afghani *mujahedeen* who expelled the Russians and helped bring the Taliban to power in that country were initially armed by the CIA.

After recent events, it is hard to remember the optimism generated by the Arab Spring. For true democracy to function, there must be respect for minority rights. The manner in which the newly elected Muslim Brotherhood president of Egypt drafted that country's Islamic constitution without broad consultation and rushed it to a vote is a case in point. He has paid with his job, and possibly his freedom, for that disregard for contrary opinion. I am very pessimistic about the emergence of truly democratic regimes in the region.

Clearly, the continuing instability that comes from the collapse or serious weakening of so many authoritarian regimes creates major opportunities for Islamist extremists such as Al Qaeda. Whether by external invasion such as in Iraq or uprisings such as in Libya, Tunisia, and Egypt, police states have been removed or weakened. Syria's protracted civil war is aimed at the same objective, and other insurrections, led by Al Qaeda, continue in Yemen, Mali, and Somalia. The failure of Al Qaeda to undertake any major terrorist operations in Western Europe and North America over several years has been the basis for the contention that the United States and its allies are winning the "war on terror." That may well be true in the West, but the changes taking place in the Middle East are creating new opportunities for Al Qaeda to show that it is still a force to be reckoned with. The recent public assertion of independence by Al Qaeda leadership in violence-prone Iraq is a further reason for the Pakistani-based global leadership to display its continued relevance through concrete action, especially in the region where Al Qaeda was born.

I have concentrated on the Middle East because that is what my job in the mid-1960s entailed. However, given Canada's long frontline involvement in Afghanistan and our resulting awareness of related problems in Pakistan, Canadians know that Muslim extremism and the potential for it extend well beyond the Middle East: from the Philippines and Indonesia to northern Nigeria, Mali, other Sahel countries, Kenya's unstable neighbour Somalia, and even

Europe. Both oil-rich Nigeria, Africa's most populous country, and unstable Mali are emerging as extremist hotspots that are of growing concern to those involved in the war on terror. In Europe, the Muslim population is increasing rapidly, especially in France, where it is close to ten percent of the population. That should not automatically equate with rising extremism, but French policies such as banning religious symbols, including head scarves, play into the hands of those who promote extreme views.

In Canada, a greater tolerance of diversity fed by many years of experience with immigrants from every country on the globe has been a long-standing pattern. Far from banning head scarves, we allow our iconic Mounties to wear turbans. However, even here some would prefer a less tolerant approach. The recent proposal in Québec to ban religiously symbolic attire and icons in public sector workplaces is a case in point. That said, the dilemma faced by all Western pluralistic democracies is essentially the same. At what point should we exercise intolerance to protect tolerance? When does free speech, including religious teaching, become an unacceptable precursor to violence?

Canada has had a very limited role in the Middle East. Historically, our presence began with the promotion of and subsequent participation in the U.N.'s first peacekeeping force in response to the Suez crisis of 1956. The Canadian foreign minister at the time, Lester Pearson, was awarded the Nobel Peace Prize for his leadership in that effort. Our soldiers have also spent years wearing blue helmets along the tense border between Israel and its northern neighbours, Syria and Lebanon. Several have lost their lives in the process. As an aside, Pearson's introduction in 1965 of Canada's new maple leaf flag may have been fuelled in small part by Egypt's initial refusal to accept Canadian soldiers as peacekeepers because they served under a flag containing Britain's Union Jack and wore "British" uniforms.

Former U.S. president Carter never tires of pointing out that the Palestinians have legitimate grievances and a fundamentally just cause. Supporters of Israel would quickly respond that Israel does as well. However, as the more powerful partner in the dispute and as a "Western" democracy, Israel inevitably faces greater moral pressure to make the accommodations necessary to address those grievances. It is sadly ironic that the very success of Muslim extremism, Sunni or Shia, has understandably reduced Israel's motivation to do so. Stiffening Israeli resistance to compromise, is, of course, one of the objectives of those extremists, and so the cycle continues.

In sum, Israel and its Western supporters continue to ride an Arab and, more broadly, Islamist tiger that seems to be getting angrier rather than worn down. The rapid spread to so many parts of the Muslim world of anti-American riots sparked by an obscure anti-Islam Internet video made public a few years ago underlined the continued fragility of Western–Muslim relations even in otherwise seemingly friendly nations. The old adage "extremism begets extremism" clearly applies. Arab populism, I fear, could well feed that extremist tiger and make it even harder for the riders to get off.

Shortly before I finished reading the final version of the proof of this book, I came across an op-ed piece by Thomas Friedman, in the January 29, 2014, edition of *The New York Times*. In it Friedman stated that U.S. Secretary of State John Kerry planned to

> present a U.S. framework that will lay out what Washington considers the core concessions Israelis and Palestinians need to make for a fair, lasting deal.
>
> The "Kerry Plan," likely to be unveiled soon, is expected to call for an end to the conflict and all claims, following a phased Israeli withdrawal from the West Bank (based on the 1967 lines), with unprecedented security arrangements in the strategic Jordan Valley. The Israeli withdrawal will not include certain settlement blocs, but Israel will compensate the Palestinians for them with Israeli territory. It will call for the Palestinians to have a capital in Arab East Jerusalem and for Palestinians to recognize Israel as the nation state of the Jewish people. It will not include any right of return for Palestinian refugees into Israel proper.

Friedman further stated:

> U.S. and Israeli officials in close contact with Netanyahu describe him as torn, clearly understanding that some kind of two-state solution is necessary for Israel's integrity as a Jewish democratic state, with the healthy ties to Europe and the West that are vital for Israel's economy. But he remains deeply skeptical about Palestinian intentions — or as Netanyahu said here Tuesday: "I do not want a binational state. But we also don't want another state that will start attacking us." His political base, though, which he nurtured, does not want Netanyahu making a U-turn.
>
> Which is why — although Netanyahu has started to prepare the ground here for the U.S. plan — if he proceeds on its basis, even with reservations, his coalition will likely collapse. He will lose a major part of his own Likud Party and all his other right-wing allies. In short, for Netanyahu to move forward, he will have to build a new political base around centrist parties. To do that, Netanyahu would have to become, to some degree, a new leader — overcoming his own innate ambivalence about any deal with the Palestinians to become Israel's most vocal and enthusiastic salesman for a two-state deal, otherwise it would never pass.

I believe Friedman has accurately described the dilemma facing not just Netanyahu but Israel itself. The concessions needed for such a plan to succeed carry both risks and loss; yet the present situation also carries risks and loss and, for the long term, is probably not viable. Elsewhere in his article Friedman implies that this is a make-or-break moment in Israeli/Palestinian history. I doubt that is true. In any case, the prospects for Netanyahu successfully making such a U-turn, even if so inclined, do not appear good. Palestinian Authority President Mahmoud Abbas would also encounter internal opposition to making the commitments needed to reach a deal with Israel, especially from supporters of Hamas. The latter would not hesitate to use violence to express that opposition and to disrupt talks with Israel. Abbas does not speak for Hamas-ruled Gaza, but an agreement that excluded Gaza would still be viable.

I have said nothing up to this point about the implications of Iran's apparent attempt to develop a nuclear weapons capacity, but that attempt obviously has the potential for greatly worsening the situation that I have described. An Iranian professional whom I know has family in Tehran and makes regular visits. He believes that a carefully targeted, "surgical" attack on his former country would be warranted if it was needed to stop the development of nuclear weapons. He regards Iran's leadership as "crazy" and fully capable of launching a nuclear strike. I have not yet sought his views on the new, seemingly more moderate Iranian president Rouhani, but, in truth, the real leadership has not changed. It remains with the Supreme Religious Leader, more powerful than any medieval pontiff. There is, however, little point in discussing what Iran might do if it had deliverable nuclear weapons, because it is very clear that Israel at least and, very likely, the United States would attack Iran before such a weapon became operational. From a U.S. and Israeli perspective, both Iran's repeated threats against Israel and the special horror of a nuclear attack would warrant a pre-emptive strike.

Nonetheless, Rouhani's conciliatory tone has resulted in restarting international negotiations aimed at containing and surveilling Iran's nuclear program. The United States, the other four permanent members of the U.N. Security Council, and Germany last November reached agreement in principle to suspend by stages the economic sanctions against Iran in return for Iran limiting its uranium enrichment program to a level of five percent, i.e., well below that required to produce weapons grade material, and accepting unrestricted international inspection. That interim agreement came into effect January 20, 2014, with the start of a six-month trial period for the agreed inspection program. In response to Iran's initial disabling of centrifuges used to enrich uranium to twenty percent, the United States and the European Union announced the easing of some of the sanctions that have crippled the Iranian economy. The intent is to use the six-month trial period to negotiate a longer-term agreement limiting Iran's nuclear program. Prime Minister Harper stated that Canada's sanctions against Iran would remain. Israeli prime minister Netanyahu has expressed strong opposition to the agreement and has threatened to attack Iran even without U.S. involvement if Iran comes close to producing a nuclear weapon. Israel wants Iran to abandon its uranium enrichment program entirely. Israel's many supporters in the U.S. Congress may well try to block any easing of sanctions against Iran that does not meet Israel's concerns. Some are calling for increased sanctions.

A telephone conversation between new Iranian president Rouhani and U.S. president Obama took place not long after both men had separately addressed the U.N. General Assembly in late September of 2013. It was the first contact between U.S. and Iranian heads of state since a government-backed Iranian mob stormed the U.S. embassy in Tehran decades earlier and took hostage all but six of the Americans who worked there. The conversation followed both Rouhani's conciliatory remarks at the U.N. and on U.S. media and a reportedly constructive meeting between U.S. Secretary of State Kerry and his Iranian counterpart. However, Rouhani's welcome upon his return to Iran was, to understate it, mixed. "Long live Rouhani, man of change," shouted his supporters even as his opponents yelled in response, "Our people are awake and hate America." The opponents began to pelt the president's vehicle with various items, including shoes, a sign of contempt. Rouhani's protective detail had to move fast to shield him.

To put it mildly, Iran is not a country that normally permits attacks on its leaders, and this demonstration of displeasure may bode badly for the future of Rouhani's overtures to the West. It had been thought that Iran's real leader, Ayatollah Ali Khamenei, was supportive of Rouhani's position, but it is obvious that Iran's powerful religious hardliners take a very different view. Ken Taylor, the former Canadian Ambassador in Tehran who, along with his staff, hid at great personal risk the six American diplomats who escaped the Iranian mob in 1979, has expressed confidence in Rouhani. That is encouraging, but the real question is whether the Ayatollah himself will continue to share that confidence in the face of a hardline backlash.

As an aside, not long after his return to Ottawa from Tehran and just before assuming his new post as Canada's Consul General in New York, Ken visited my office for a briefing on Canada–U.S. environmental relations. Inevitably, our conversation turned to his experiences in Iran. I do not need to repeat the details here. There have been at least three movies made on what is known as "the Canadian Caper." I will simply say that the degree of tension and the level of danger the Canadians endured in hiding their American colleagues over many months was considerably greater than what was depicted in the films, especially the one focused on the CIA rescue plan. Canada's role in facilitating their escape was also greater than depicted.

Even if the new Iranian president's efforts to moderate Iranian policy prove unsuccessful and Iran reverts to a more bellicose posture, the credibility of his predecessor's repeated threats to attack Israel will never be known because, as already noted, Iran will not be given the opportunity to act. The more important question therefore has to be what Iran and its allies such as Hezbollah in Lebanon might do in the event that the Israelis and Americans decide that nuclear development in Iran has reached a stage that warrants a pre-emptive strike. A great deal of thought is undoubtedly being given to that very question in both Jerusalem and Washington, D.C., and there are worries in many other capitals as well. About half of the world's oil is transported by tanker and, of that half, over a third passes through the Strait of Hormuz. Iran has threatened to mine the Strait in an attempt to close it if Israel and the United States should launch an attack. A disruption in oil supply of that magnitude would significantly raise oil prices, fuel investor fears, and almost certainly bring on a major global economic downturn, especially given the current fragile state of the world's debt-ridden economy. The Middle East "tail" clearly continues to have the capacity to wag the global "dog."

APPENDIX II: LIST OF EFFECTS ON THE AUTHOR AND HIS WIFE OF HER MENTAL ILLNESS/SCHIZOPHRENIA

A) ON HIS WIFE

1. Need to transfer to private school because of "nerves" while still a young teenager.
2. Need for psychiatric consultation for anxiety while serving as a young diplomat's wife in South America.
3. Severe, prolonged postpartum depression after her first child is born in Ottawa and a deep continuing fear that she would be unable to care for her child.
4. Inability as a diplomat's wife in New Zealand to cope with social pressure, which, together with prolonged postpartum depression after her second child, led to lengthy hospitalization for "nerves."
5. Inability to care for her children, who spent most of the time being cared for by others, and resentment and fear of her husband's promotion and of the resulting increase in entertaining responsibilities.
6. Further extended hospitalization following serious psychotic episodes resulting in diagnosis of schizophrenia and repeated application of ECT without anesthetic (or husband's consent), followed by debilitating medication and substantial memory loss, most of it never recovered.
7. Periods of terror so great that resulting muscle contraction caused severe pain.
8. Return of psychosis, resulting in a third hospitalization and catatonia followed by a remarkable healing of her catatonic state in answer to prayer that made departure from New Zealand possible, two years beyond the usual assignment.
9. Return of symptoms, though less severe, followed by two hospitalizations, a dozen different medications, and a great struggle to be a wife and mother over the next twenty-one years in Ottawa.

10. Years of traumatic nightmares of being gang-raped in hospital (possibly memories of the ECT), nearly complete social isolation over decades, and frequent suicidal thoughts.
11. Resumption of serious psychotic episodes in the mid-1990s, six years after the move to Vancouver, eventually resulting in forced hospitalization and the introduction of new neuroleptic medication; this greatly moderated the incidence and severity of psychotic episodes, provided her husband was able to keep all external stress at a minimum.
12. Diagnosis of Alzheimer's in 2007, which may have arrived somewhat earlier given the presence of overlapping symptoms, such as confusion, caused by schizophrenia.
13. Inability to pursue speech therapy to compensate for the effect of Alzheimer's because the stress of the therapy triggered psychotic symptoms.
14. Decades of worry and guilt over the impact of her illness, especially threats of suicide, on her husband and on her children.
15. Near life-long shame over the nature of her illness even though there was nothing she did to bring it on or anything she could have done to avoid it.
16. Most recently, presumably as a result of Alzheimer's, almost complete loss of short-term memory, steadily expanding loss of long-term memory and inability to recognize her husband and children, remember friends, or communicate.

B) ON THE AUTHOR

1. Frustration with his wife over her inability to support his work as a diplomat.
2. Fear of the future, pain over his wife's pain, and anger over the need to abandon his dream of becoming Canada's youngest ambassador.
3. Fear of losing his wife and children when she decided to leave New Zealand with them and without him for her parents' home in Vancouver, but great relief and joy when their shared decision to accept Christ kept them together.
4. Abandonment of his diplomatic career after returning to Ottawa.
5. Strain of trying to cope over many years with ever-increasing job pressures and his wife's desperate needs at home, including further psychotic episodes and suicide threats.
6. Profound disappointment and sadness over his wife's two further hospitalizations in Ottawa.

7. Resignation from heading Canada's Environmental Protection Service to take a less demanding position.
8. Premature retirement nine years later at age fifty-four to become a full-time caregiver.
9. Decision to move to Vancouver from Ottawa because it is easier under British Columbia law to force care on a mental patient than it is in Ontario.
10. Horrendous experience of forcing his wife's hospitalization with police assistance, made bearable only because of their brave daughter's presence and support.
11. Deepening loneliness over a twenty-two-year period reflecting his social isolation as a full-time caregiver and an ever more constrained lifestyle, especially after the arrival of Alzheimer's in 2007 (or earlier) made conversation with his wife impossible.
12. Decades of worry and guilt over the effects on their children of their inadequate parenting and of their stress-filled household.

APPENDIX III: CANADA-UNITED STATES GREAT LAKES WATER QUALITY AGREEMENT, A GLOBAL ENVIRONMENTAL MILESTONE

As noted in the main narrative, my first major task in my new job managing Canada–U.S. environmental relations was to serve as co-ordinator of the Canadian inter-departmental and federal–provincial team that was responsible for negotiating an agreement to clean up the Great Lakes with the United States. The most immediate environmental problem at that time was eutrophication, the loss of dissolved oxygen in the lake waters, especially Lake Erie. Lakes Ontario and Superior reach depths of over 110 metres and 220 metres respectively. Erie was particularly vulnerable because it is much shallower, less than 20 metres on average, and because it is bordered by populous and industrialized Pennsylvania and Ohio. Ontario's industries are concentrated near Lake Ontario, not Erie. The oxygen loss in Erie resulted in the death of virtually all fish, which, in turn, led to the disappearance of many of the birds and animals that ate them. The oxygen loss was caused by the decomposition of vegetation, especially algae. The algae was fed by nutrients, primarily phosphorus, which came from detergents, insufficiently treated human and animal waste, agricultural runoff, and certain industrial activities.

The Canada–U.S. International Joint Commission (IJC) was created in 1912 under the Boundary Waters Treaty of 1909 to assist in managing boundary water issues. In 1964, both countries asked the IJC to report on the condition of the Lakes and recommend appropriate responses. Years of study followed. What gave the situation urgency and ultimately brought the two countries to the negotiating table in 1971 was the discovery by scientists at the Canada Centre for Inland Waters in Burlington, Ontario, that the eutrophication process in Lake Erie would, in a very few years, become irreversible. The anoxic (no oxygen) conditions in the bottom waters were causing a chemical reaction in the bottom sediments that was releasing ever more phosphorus into the water. Once that phosphorus production became self-sustaining, reducing human input of phosphorus into the lake water would have no benefit. The solutions were obvious: rapidly remove phosphorus from detergents and greatly improve wastewater treatment. However, the detergent manufacturers

– the "soapers," as the environmentalists called them – were vehemently opposed, crying, "Not proven." (In the 1980s, it was the coal-burning electrical utilities and other sources of sulphur saying the same thing about acid rain, and today it is the fossil fuel industry minimizing the significance of human contribution to climate change. So much for progress.) Moreover, improved sewage treatment would cost billions and that money would come from taxpayers, never a popular proposition.

Nonetheless, we gradually developed an alliance of common interest between the Canadian government, Ontario, and Québec on our side of the border, and the Great Lakes States, the newly created U.S. Environmental Protection Agency (EPA), and many U.S. congressman and senators on the American side. The opposition came from affected Canadian and U.S. industry and some U.S. congressmen and senators from more distant states. Apart from the EPA, President Nixon's Administration was not overly enthusiastic.

This reluctance was amply demonstrated when the president later had to be forced by the courts to spend money for sewage treatment facilities voted for by Congress under the Clean Water Act. It is therefore not surprising that the initial draft of the proposed agreement put forward by the U.S. State Department was very weak, offering little more than some general targets for phosphorus reduction. The Canadian delegation wanted much tighter numbers, a firm timetable, and an independent institutional mechanism to report publicly on the implementation of the goals in the Agreement. Moreover, recognizing that phosphorus inputs were only the most obvious component of more general water quality problems in the Great Lakes, we also wanted an independent institutional structure that would regularly assess the condition of the Lakes and publicly recommend new goals for the Agreement as our detection technology advanced. It was clear that the best body to play this role would be the International Joint Commission. It was very familiar with the Great Lakes and had a good track record of acting in an independent, collegial manner rather than dividing along national lines. In short, we envisaged a dynamic living agreement that would transcend the ups and downs of future environmental policies in both countries.

Many meetings in both capitals and a lot of negotiation, behind-the-scenes discussion, and lobbying followed over several months, but the effort was well worth it. The final agreement signed in Ottawa by President Nixon and Prime Minister Trudeau in April of 1972 bore considerable resemblance to Canada's first draft and contained all of the elements we wanted. For my sins, I was given the responsibility of organizing the signature ceremony, not a welcome assignment given how many things can go wrong on such occasions. A fair number of people were present from both countries and, given the egos in that room, they had to be seated with care in a strict order of precedence. You can imagine my horror when some Canadian Cabinet Ministers showed up uninvited. Under the cold gaze of the Under-Secretary, Canada's top diplomat, I frantically tried to rearrange the seating at the last moment in an effort to maintain appropriate precedence. I succeeded but sweated blood in the process. It certainly diminished the magic and triumph of the occasion for me.

The Great Lakes Water Quality Agreement was the first of its kind in the world. More importantly, it has been successful. Because eutrophication was stopped and dissolved oxygen levels restored, the fish returned to near-dead Lake Erie. However, that was just the beginning. In 1972, our ability to detect substances in the water was measured in parts per million. A few years later, we could see substances at the level of parts per trillion. That increase in detection capability enabled us to identify a wide range of chemical substances that were previously invisible or impossible to characterize. Instead of dealing only with the gross pollution we could see in the early 1970s, we were able to go after the chemical substances discharged into the Lakes that were previously hidden from us. As noted earlier, the Agreement was designed to take account of advances in both the detection and control of pollutants. Thus, the International Joint Commission was able over the years to recommend new objectives for the Agreement that resulted in significantly expanded control commitments in 1978 and 1987. In June of 2010, both governments agreed to renegotiate the Agreement's targets for the third time to address newly identified contaminants and other stresses to which the Great Lakes system is being subjected. That process is allegedly underway as these words are being written, but I admit to some concern over how long it is taking. The intent of the public reporting structures that give the Agreement its dynamic character was to put pressure on both countries, whatever the politics of the day, to tighten the pollution controls as needed and as technically feasible. It is hard not to feel satisfaction that the value of those provisions is still being demonstrated more than forty years after the first Agreement was signed.

Because I am a biased observer, I am going to give the last word on the value of the Agreement to "Great Lakes United," a non-governmental public interest group operating in both countries that is dedicated to improving the quality of Great Lakes waters. The quotation cited is an excerpt from a statement issued by the group in 2011 commenting upon the renegotiation of the Agreement.

> Many credit the 1972 Agreement for helping drive a new generation of water pollution control in both nations. For example, the U.S. Clean Water Act was signed into law that year and aggressive new controls on phosphorus pollution and a massive investment in modern sewage treatment in both countries helped revive Lake Erie and other areas choked with algae blooms and pollution. The 1978 Agree-

ment focused increased attention on toxic chemicals that were accumulating in the Great Lakes food web, and embraced the concept of managing for the health of the ecosystem. DDT had been banned in 1972, but as evidence mounted, many other "chlorinated" pesticides were banned from use in both nations. PCBs – one of the most widespread groups of contaminants in the Great Lakes – were also banned from further use.

The 1987 Protocols (additions to the 1978 Agreement) identified 43 highly contaminated harbours and other toxic hotspots, (diplomatically called "Areas of Concern") and called for their clean-up and restoration to standards that restored beneficial uses, including those such as drinking water quality and other conditions that protect human health and the environment. They also called for monitoring and controls on airborne sources of toxic pollution to the lakes, including mercury, and other measures to strengthen water quality protections.

These investments improved conditions for human health and wildlife, stimulated building booms in wastewater infrastructure, fostered a recreational fishing renaissance in Lake Erie, and built scientific capacity in freshwater ecology and related fields that has solved problems around the world.

NOTE: Shallow Lake Erie is again under threat of eutrophication. Extensive growth of algae fed by agricultural run-off rich in phosphorous and other nutrients used in fertilizer threatens to re-create the lake-water conditions of the 1960s. This so-called non-point source form of pollution is very difficult to control. Significant changes in fertilizer composition and use may be necessary to protect oxygen levels – and fish life – in Erie's waters. Securing these changes will not be easy.

APPENDIX IV: ENVIRONMENTAL PROTECTION SERVICE: REFORMS AND TRADE-OFFS

In my day, the Environmental Protection Service (EPS) was divided into three headquarter directorates and five regional districts with several more sub-regional offices from the Atlantic to the Pacific to the Arctic. The responsibilities of the three directorates were divided between water pollution; air pollution; and environmental contaminants, hazardous waste, and polluted site cleanup. While most of my time was necessarily spent in Ottawa, I visited all the regions regularly and most of the sub-regional offices at least once.

A major focus of the third directorate was the classification of the large and growing number of chemicals in industrial use. Part of that effort included developing appropriate protocols governing the testing of new chemicals. Every industrial country and many less developed ones faced the same challenge, and our concern was to promote international standardization of such testing, initially among member nations of the Organization for Economic Cooperation and Development (OECD) headquartered in Paris. Simply put, if we could rely upon each other's testing it would greatly reduce duplication, cost, and time. I made a number of overseas visits to promote this concept and also attended conferences on the subject in Paris.

One of the holdouts was Australia, whose Liberal-Country party coalition government did not rank environmental protection among its priorities. Like Canada, Australia is a federation, and the two parties in coalition forming the Commonwealth (Federal) government at that time were disposed to leave environmental matters to the states. The Labour party held the opposite view, and the Commonwealth government would typically adopt more interventionist environmental policies when Labour was in power. As a result, after making my obligatory courtesy calls in the national capital, Canberra, I made my round of most of the state capitals preaching the gospel of standardized testing protocols. New South Wales, Victoria, and South Australia were receptive, and Australia in due course supported the OECD's effort to develop these protocols.

Early in my tenure as head of EPS, I attended an international conference that was wrestling with whether the developed world should apply its environmental standards to less developed countries or even to poor areas within an otherwise developed country, if the result were to deprive poor people of chances to better themselves economically. Stated more succinctly, does poverty trump pollution? That is, should potentially hazardous waste dumps or industrial activities be placed in poor areas because the people, desperate for economic opportunities, want them? Is it an imposition of Western middle class values to deny these poor people what they want, or are we by so doing legitimately trying to avoid exploiting the poor?

Many southern Canadians oppose some kinds of economic development in Canada's sparsely populated north because of their potential for harming relatively pristine areas already affected by rapid polar warming. Some of the natives who live there are facing worsening economic conditions as that warming disrupts hunting and other traditional activities. Not surprisingly, they are increasingly open to development initiatives that offer community benefits, jobs, and even equity positions in the development companies. Should the conditions of development be left to the local authorities to determine, or should they mirror the standards expected in southern parts of the country? Should standards more stringent than those down south be imposed because of the special character of the Arctic regions?

Another example is the process for developing environmental regulations. Regulation development processes can be highly incestuous. As was underlined so clearly during the world's 2008 credit crisis, the distance between government regulators and financial institutions in many developed countries, including the United States, was far from arm's length. I discovered the potential for a similar problem with respect to environmental regulation when I was first appointed to head EPS.

Our regulations were developed by task forces made up of federal and provincial officials and their industrial counterparts. The environmental groups claimed that they were all in bed together. That was an exaggeration, but I did find that EPS' engineers and scientists and the companies' counterparts had gone to the same schools, had often worked with the same industrial processes, and were in many respects interchangeable. Consciously or not, they often applied similar value judgements to the problems that faced them.

My response was to invite environmental and community representatives to join in the deliberations, although only the government officials signed off on the recommendations. To balance concern with the environment, there was also a legal obligation to produce a socio-economic impact assessment with formal public input before any regulation could be proclaimed. More difficult to address was the day-to-day enforcement of regulations, especially since we had a practice of trying to negotiate a solution to a pollution problem and using the possible laying of an information, as it was called, as leverage. Company executives were often more concerned with their public image than the generally inadequate fines imposed by the courts. My staff and I were more interested in results than in putting notches on our legal guns, but spills always resulted in immediate charges. The potential for undue accommodation certainly existed, and the environmental groups often decried our seeming slowness to act. Getting the right balance was always a challenge.

Another illustration of a more specific nature is the way we dealt with Giant Yellowknife, at the time one of our largest gold mines, located near Yellowknife, capital of the Northwest Territories. Because the ore in that mine is low grade, it has to be extracted through what is called a gold-roasting process. This process produces emissions containing arsenic trioxide. As these are released into the atmosphere, they contaminate the precipitation (in that latitude mostly snow). This contamination was particularly worrisome for native communities because, during the long dark winter, melted snow is their primary, if not only, source of water. Not surprisingly, blood levels of arsenic, which in low concentrations is considered a potential carcinogen, were elevated among the First Nations peoples dependent upon that supply of water. One solution – closing down the mine – would have devastated the local economy. Technology existed to curb the release of arsenic into the environment in the form of "bag houses" – huge filters through which emissions from the gold-roasting process would be moved – but the number of bag houses needed to achieve near zero release of arsenic would render the mine inoperable at gold prices in the early 1980s. To make things more complicated, science at that time (or even today) could not produce data that would tell us at exactly what level arsenic trioxide in the atmosphere, drinking water and, ultimately, blood became unsafe.

I therefore decided to obtain expert advice from various sources on anticipated increases in the price of gold. The predictions, as it turned out, were very conservative, but they were high enough to justify installing several bag houses and keeping the mine open. More importantly, blood levels of arsenic among the affected people dropped significantly. Did they drop enough? I cannot say with absolute certainty, but I have to believe that the impact of closing down the region's largest employer and principal income generator (other than the federally subsidized territorial government) would have caused public health problems flowing from poverty and stress that would have been significantly greater than those caused by the very small amounts of arsenic still being released. Was that a reasonable judgement to make? I leave it to the reader to decide.

As illustrated by this example, decisions related to pollution control are often very difficult, and not just because a choice frequently has to be made between sharply competing objectives that cannot be compared in simple economic terms. Much of the time we are also managing ignorance, because even today science often cannot tell us with certainty what concentration of this or that potential contaminant will cause cancer or birth defects or inhibit neural development. In my view, managing ignorance requires applying value judgements or bias and the bias of an agency such as I headed must be towards what we called "prudence." For us, that meant mandating, where possible and reasonable, control technology or changes in industrial processes to minimize or prevent the release of industrial chemicals or their potentially harmful by-products into the environment. "Prudence" for industry usually meant the exact opposite: not making expenditures unless the benefits could be precisely determined and evaluated.

Fortunately, over time, it has been increasingly recognized that, in many sectors, industrial processes that minimize releases of substances tend also to be more efficient. Similarly, processes that minimize energy consumption have both environmental and economic benefits. That said, mandating the environmental view of prudence remains necessary in certain areas, and it is that philosophy that underpins, for example, the policy reflected in the most recent version of the Canada–United States Great Lakes Water Quality Agreement. It requires zero discharge of certain industrial chemicals into those waters (around which live almost fifty million people).

It is the nature of man not to be far-sighted. Unfortunately, it is precisely that quality which is often needed to protect ourselves and our environment from the side effects of our economic and other activities. I have, however, noticed one encouraging trend with respect to global warming or climate change, about which I received my first briefing over thirty years ago. While many politicians in many countries seem unable to see beyond the next election, there is a growing number of exceptions, and some prominent business leaders are being much more far-sighted than their political counterparts. That first briefing was remarkably accurate, but completely underestimated the speed at which temperatures would likely rise, especially in polar regions. Particularly accurate was the prediction of much stronger and more frequent extreme weather events, including droughts and floods, as weather patterns changed and warmer oceans fuelled more intensive storms.

However, in uncertain economic times, environmental issues tend to take a back seat, and I see no change in that reality. I also remain pessimistic about environmental policies in the world's emerging economies, especially China and India, where a combination of an understandable sense of entitlement ("our time has come") and resentment at the industrial West for creating the problem in the first place is colouring their response. We reap what we sow, and we have sowed all too well.

It is also the nature of man to want simple solutions to complex problems. The ubiquitous "sound bite" so loved by TV news editors responds both to the need of that medium and the taste of the public. I used to use a humorous illustration in my speeches to bring home to audiences how difficult it can sometimes be to determine clear cause and effect relationships in the environmental field. I cited statistics demonstrating that between the 1950s and the 1970s sperm counts among college age males in the United States had dropped significantly. At the same time there was an equally significant increase in the concentration of certain persistent contaminants in the seminal fluids. Clearly one was causing the other. Or – was it tight pants?

APPENDIX V: CANADA'S MULTI-YEAR CAMPAIGN TO PERSUADE THE UNITED STATES TO CONTROL TRANS-BOUNDARY ACID RAIN

As I noted in the narrative, the single issue that most dominated my years heading the Environmental Protection Service (EPS) was acid rain. During the 1970s, Fisheries Department monitoring and testing programs in selected lakes in Ontario's Canadian Shield were yielding ever more alarming results. The acidity of these lakes was steadily rising, and some had reached the point at which fish life could no longer be sustained. I was, of course, aware of these results before I became Assistant Deputy Minister, but we needed to fully understand what was causing the problem before we could move to correct it. The acid was arriving in the form of precipitation or airborne dry deposition, a fact most dramatically demonstrated by the phenomenon known as pH shock. (The pH scale is how acidity and alkalinity are measured.) This is caused by the spring-time melting of snow that has experienced months of acid deposition. The sudden rush of highly acidic water into the lakes commonly results in a fish kill. The Canadian Shield is largely bare granite because so much soil was removed during the last ice age. There is therefore very little alkaline material to provide a buffering effect to combat the incoming acid. Clearly, our first challenge was to establish the source of the airborne acid.

We turned for help to Environment Canada's Atmospheric Environment Service, as Canada's weather service is properly known. AES not only has the largest computer in the country, it also has the best atmospheric chemists and physicists. As it happened, the Assistant Deputy Minister in charge of AES at the time was my old friend and colleague Jim Bruce, with whom I had worked so closely during the negotiations that led to the Great Lakes Water Quality Agreement. Once again we were to work together in a major enterprise to secure U.S. co-operation in addressing a serious trans-boundary environmental problem. We would, however, have been greatly dismayed if we had known how long it would take to achieve success.

Analysis of the acid showed that it was primarily sulphurous in origin. Jim's atmospheric chemists explained that sulphur dioxide emissions from industrial activities such as coal-fired electric power plants and nickel refineries were being transformed through photochemical reactions driven by the sun into sulphuric acid that came down to earth in the form of acid precipitation or dry deposition. Similarly, nitrogen dioxide emitted from such sources as vehicles was being transformed into nitric acid. Jim's atmospheric physicists and their computers worked their magic and soon created mathematical models showing where the principal sources of the sulphur emissions were located. All but a few of the power plants were located in the United States, especially the Ohio Valley. The nickel refineries were in Ontario, but their contribution to the problem was significantly smaller than that of the power plants. Armed with this information, I got in touch with David Hawkins, the U.S. Environmental Protection Agency's (EPA) Assistant Administrator for Air Quality, and invited him to a presentation on the subject in Ottawa.

I need to explain that I was dealing at the time with President Carter's EPA. Those he had appointed to the top positions in that Agency included many environmental activists. David was one of these, a brilliant young environmental lawyer who shared our commitment to protecting North America's environment. However, for him acid rain was a pretty small problem and therefore low in priority. He was faced with much bigger issues, notably the widespread "non-attainment" of air quality objectives mandated under the U.S. Clean Air Act in dozens of American cities. David sat through our presentation and asked the appropriate questions, but was noncommittal in response to my efforts to promote a co-operative approach to addressing trans-boundary acid rain.

That evening I took him out to dinner at an excellent restaurant on the Québec side of the Ottawa River. While the meal was superb and the atmosphere convivial, it was very much a working session, and we spent hours going over the issues that had been addressed earlier in the day. By the end of the evening, David agreed to look at the issue more seriously upon his return to Washington. Before long, the United States agreed to a Memorandum of Intent governing Trans-boundary Air Pollution that would commit the two nations to "commence formal negotiations no later than June 1, 1981 of a Cooperative Agreement on Trans-boundary Air Pollution." The Memorandum also created four joint Canada–U.S. task forces to examine what should be in that agreement.

The task forces were up and running not long after the Memorandum was signed on August 5, 1980. They focused on four areas: (A) atmospheric movements and chemistry, (B) the impacts of sulphur emissions on the receiving environment, (C) appropriate pollution control technology, and (D) the legal and institutional mechanisms needed for effective enforcement and monitoring. The task forces reported to a Canada–U.S. Steering Committee chaired by

David and myself. Task force (B) had the widest-ranging set of responsibilities in that it was to examine not just impacts upon the lakes but on other receptors as well. For example, acid rain was damaging buildings and statuary, especially those made of limestone, including Canada's historic Parliament Buildings. Of potentially greater concern was the impact on human health, especially respiratory problems, when the sulphur dioxide emissions were concentrated in the form of fine particulate matter. In addition, subsequent research determined that soil biology and chemistry could be seriously damaged by acid rain both by killing important microbes and leaching out minerals needed for the growth of both trees in forests and agricultural plants. Determining "loadings" that could be tolerated by the receiving environment was clearly essential but by no means easy.

A common sense of purpose quickly developed, and we made good progress in producing a set of agreed-upon task force reports that would provide the basis for negotiating a comprehensive control agreement similar in many ways to the Great Lakes Water Quality Agreement. When President Ronald Reagan replaced Jimmy Carter in January of 1981, we wondered what the effect might be on EPA and on our task forces. Initially the indications were reassuring. The new president's first foreign visit was to Ottawa in March of 1981, where he specifically affirmed his administration's intent to meet the commitments in the Memorandum of Intent on Trans-boundary Air Pollution signed by the previous administration. Unfortunately, that affirmation was not reflected in the policies and practices adopted by the new management at EPA.

Before describing the problems that arose, I want to say something about President Reagan. As a former diplomat, I greatly respect President Reagan's formidable communications skills and the role that he played in international affairs, especially with respect to the Cold War with the Soviet Union. Given my own experiences with what he called the "evil empire," I have long recognized that the exercise of superior strength, short of war, was the only way to deal with such an oppressive regime. However, on environmental issues, the first Reagan Administration was clearly out of step with both actual environmental needs and, as it eventually proved, U.S. public opinion. The second Reagan Administration clearly recognized that fact; both the policies pursued and the new appointees leading EPA responded more closely to needs identified by their scientists.

President Reagan's first administration was committed to rolling back many of the Carter administration's policies and regulations affecting the environment. Those appointed to EPA's top positions reflected that commitment. David's Republican replacement was very candid in making that clear to me, and he was as good as his word. The papers written by the task forces had reflected a consensus of participating experts from both countries. To our amazement, they were completely rewritten by U.S. officials in a fashion that made any concerted action impossible. Meetings became increasingly pointless and, on more than one occasion, U.S. experts who disagreed with their new political masters were removed from the room. Several resigned. On one occasion that I will never forget, I led a Canadian team to Washington for a meeting, but no U.S. officials appeared. The U.S. State Department claimed that it was a simple error in scheduling. My colleagues in Foreign Affairs and I decided that there was no point in continuing this charade, and we began to devise a completely new strategy.

Despite the attitude of the Reagan Administration, we were not without American allies on the acid rain issue. Many senators and congressmen, especially from New York, Pennsylvania, and the north-east where damage from acid rain had been documented, were sympathetic to our cause. The immensely popular Muskoka "cottage country" north of Toronto with its thousands of lakes boasted tens of thousands of summertime American residents, many of whom owned properties in the region. Some of these visitors were very influential and not reluctant to express concern about the impact of acid rain on their favourite vacation destination. Then there were the U.S. fishermen and duck hunters worried about the impact of acid rain upon their favourite occupations. As had been the case in the cleanup of the Great Lakes, the governments of adversely affected states were also potential allies. Finally, there was the substantial and growing environmental movement in the United States. Our challenge was to inform and work with all these potential allies in an effort to move American public opinion towards support for acid rain control.

The first and most important target had to be Congress, which in the late 60s and early 70s had played the leading role in promoting environmental protection. Historically, the Canadian Embassy in Washington, D.C., had tended to focus its attention on the Administration, primarily the State Department and the White House, rather than on Senators and Congressmen. Perhaps because of this history, there did not appear at the outset to be much of an appetite on the part of Canada's diplomats for a major lobbying effort with Congress, and we initially aimed our efforts elsewhere.

That was to change in 1981 with the appointment of Allan Gottlieb, a brilliant career diplomat who became the most activist and, arguably, the most effective Canadian Ambassador in Washington since diplomatic relations were established. He correctly recognized that the United States has, in effect, two governments, one centred in the White House and one on Capitol Hill. For foreign governments, the United States can be very difficult to negotiate with. Whatever is agreed after many trade-offs and much compromise at the negotiating table must then pass the test of obtaining congressional support for funding and legislative changes and sometimes even receiving formal "advice and consent" by the Senate for treaties. Other countries have recognized the importance of wooing Congress, but none is as successful at it as Israel. In fairness, there are special reasons for Israel's success, and these, the reader will recall, are set out in appendix I. Canada had little experience of operating in that fashion.

Accordingly, before Ambassador Gottlieb's new approach opened the door to Capitol Hill, we took a number of steps to reach people and organizations outside Congress. An initiative that ultimately proved to be very valuable was hiring a respected American freelance writer to submit articles on the impact of acid rain to American magazines that catered to fishermen, duck hunters, and other outdoor enthusiasts. He met periodically with my staff and me for briefings on the latest scientific findings and then incorporated these in articles designed to stimulate concern on the part of his readers. This activity continued for years, eventually resulting in clear-cut support for acid rain control from one of America's most powerful lobby groups, the National Rifle Association (NRA). Apparently the NRA has a lot of duck hunters among its membership.

I used to look forward to the freelance journalist's visits to my office. He always provided a very colourful picture of what was going on among those he was seeking to influence. He had a habit of referring to me as the "Great White Chief of the Ottawas." ("Ottawa" is the name of the tribe that originally occupied the area of Canada's capital.) I remember him asking about the beautiful Maori carving that sat on the coffee table in front of my office sofa. I explained that it was a feather box in which a Maori chief would keep the special feather he wore to mark his rank on ceremonial occasions. He asked what was in it, and I replied, "Nothing." On his next visit, he presented me with two eagle feathers, both of which are still in that box. It now sits in our living room. I have yet to find an appropriate ceremony at which to wear the feathers.

We also provided funds to help support the presence in Washington of Adele Hurley, a young woman who had proved to be a very effective voice for acid rain control while working alongside the equally talented and committed Toronto-based Michael Perley. They led the Canadian Coalition Against Acid Rain. Adele's job in Washington was to motivate, inform, and energize the major U.S. environmental groups to make acid rain control a matter of priority in their own lobbying efforts. She ran into the same problem I had when I first met with David Hawkins of EPA. There were so many other environmental challenges that seemed more important to American environmentalists. I always tried to lunch with Adele on my visits to Washington as a form of encouragement and to learn what was going on. There were many people over the years who became deeply involved in the struggle to stop acid rain. No one was more dedicated or worked harder than Michael and Adele. Canada and the affected U.S. states owe them a lot.

As explained earlier, Ambassador Gottlieb's arrival in Washington opened the door to direct lobbying of Congress. The first step in that process was a presentation to the appropriate committee of the House of Representatives by Jim Bruce, the head of the Atmospheric Environment Service, and myself as head of EPS. Jim focused his part of the presentation on the atmospheric dynamics and the impacts so far identified on the receiving environment, especially the lakes, in both countries. He emphasized that there were literally tens of thousands of lakes at risk. I discussed the pollution sources both in Canada and the United States and the sort of controls that would be needed to address the problem. I also emphasized the long history of co-operation between our two countries in dealing with trans-boundary pollution, citing the success of the Great Lakes Water Quality Agreement and praising the U.S. Congress for its past leadership in environmental matters. As it happens, our presentation was the first time that Canadian officials, speaking on behalf of the Government of Canada, had testified before a U.S. Congressional committee. Our officials had appeared before such committees on previous occasions, but only to provide information on a matter of interest to the committee, never to plead a case on behalf of Canada.

Was it worth it? Did it have any real impact? I cannot answer those questions definitively, but I suspect that it was not particularly effective. That said, it was perhaps a necessary prelude to the behind-the-scenes work of lobbying the senior "staffers" serving key Senate and House committees and those in the offices of key Senators and Congressmen. That activity had real value, and we developed some very useful contacts and relationships over time. I encountered some extremely impressive people during that process who helped me better understand the great importance and power of the U.S. Congress under the American "separation of powers" between the executive, legislative, and judicial branches of government. I remember in particular a very senior Senate committee staffer who hailed from Texas. He spoke with an elaborate drawl, which I suspect he used to mask the remarkable intellect behind it. He was willing to spend some time explaining how the U.S. Senate and, more broadly, the Congress works. Coming from a much simpler system of governance, I was initially inclined to be critical of the seemingly cumbersome U.S. governmental structure. I changed my views during my periodic visits to Washington and came to see many benefits in the U.S. system.

Ambassador Gottlieb was to stay in Washington for about eight years, and during that time he cultivated substantial relationships with that city's power brokers, including many senators and congressmen. My successor as the head of EPS, Bob Slater, ably continued the campaign in the United States that we had started, as did his successor, Peter Higgins. Finally, in 1991, Canada and the United States signed an acid rain control agreement. Several factors besides the campaign we had begun brought about this long-awaited success. These included the more benign environmental policies followed by the Reagan Administration after his re-election in November 1984; similar policies followed by his successor, President Bush; the excellent personal relationship between Canada's Prime Minister Mulroney and President Reagan, which continued with President Bush; and the success of Ambassador Gottlieb's carefully-targeted activism.

The content of the Agreement was such that we could probably have negotiated something similar as early as 1982 on the basis of the work of our task forces, if there had been any political will on the U.S. side to do so. Instead, we enjoyed nine unnecessary years of unabated acid rain. As the reader might well imagine, I look back upon this period of my life with mixed feelings. We fought the good fight, and it was an extraordinary learning experience. However, it took the work of many others over many years to harvest the crop that we had worked so hard to sow.

APPENDIX VI: AUTHOR'S SPEECH TO THE NATIONAL ACADEMY OF SCIENCES IN WASHINGTON, D.C., "THE RULE OF LAW BETWEEN NATIONS – AN ACID TEST," OCT. 4, 1982

"The Government of Canada and the Government of the United States of America ... share a common determination to combat trans-boundary air pollution in keeping with their existing international rights, obligations, commitments and cooperative practices, including those set forth in the 1909 Boundary Waters Treaty, the 1972 Stockholm Declaration on the Human Environment, the 1978 Great Lakes Water Quality Agreement and the 1979 ECE Convention on Long Range Trans-boundary Air Pollution."

That is a quotation from the Memorandum of Intent between Canada and the United States concerning trans-boundary air pollution signed in Washington on August 5, 1980, more than two years ago. Its meaning is clear. The efforts of both countries to deal with trans-boundary air pollution, specifically the activities outlined elsewhere in the Memorandum, should be undertaken in a way that reflects "existing international rights, obligations, commitments and cooperative practices." To understand the Memorandum and to appreciate what it means in the context of Canada–United States environmental relations, we need to examine what these rights, obligations, commitments, and practices are. I propose in what is really a brief presentation for such a large topic to look at the history of our environmental relationship, to draw some conclusions about it, and to consider what effect the present activities under the Memorandum of Intent are having on the principles underlying that relationship. I should add that the paper I am about to present to you is also drawn from extensive personal experience reflecting nearly eleven years of my own continuous involvement in Canada–United States environmental relations over the period from early 1971 to the end of last year.

That involvement began for me, when I was still a diplomat, in a venture that symbolizes in many ways the aspirations which those responsible for environmental policy in both countries at that time strongly shared. That venture was the first Great Lakes Water Quality Agreement, signed by President Nixon and Prime Minister Trudeau in 1972. Those of us who served on the Canadian and American negotiating teams were very conscious in 1971 that we were breaking new ground, that we were trying to create a set of concepts and an institutional framework that would stand the tests of both time and political change. The word we used was "dynamic," denoting both strength and flexibility. Indeed many of us were persuaded that we were at last bringing into being a system of managing trans-boundary environmental problems – we called them challenges – which could rise above the traditional short-sighted we/they attitudes which often accompany international disputes.

Lest I appear to be falling into the error of contending that the true light in these matters was discovered by our little band in 1971, I must put aside nostalgia for a few minutes and focus on what went before – on the considerable heritage which set the stage for the Great Lakes water quality negotiations. To do this properly, I must go back to the beginnings of this century and pay tribute to some intelligent and far-sighted men in Washington and Ottawa who perceived that the sharing of a continent would be more orderly and peaceful if some rules governing certain kinds of trans-boundary behaviour were established. This perception led to the Boundary Waters Treaty of 1909, a landmark instrument which has served ever since as the principal basis for responsible Canada–United States dealings with respect to boundary waters and, by extension, to other trans-boundary environmental issues.

In my paper today, I shall focus on three elements in the Treaty: (1) the principle underlying a number of its articles to the effect that one nation may not take certain actions unilaterally within its borders which would injure the other nation; (2) the absolute prohibition in article IV against injurious trans-boundary water pollution and (3) the creation of the International Joint Commission and the uses to which the Commission has been put.

The Treaty was designed to create a framework of principles and an institutional mechanism to bring about rational management of the waters flowing across and along the international boundary. The underlying concept was the acceptance by both countries that each ought not to disregard the interests of the other country when deciding upon some action which could affect that other country. The Treaty therefore limited each country's right to do as it wished with an important segment of the continent's waterways. Specifically, in article IV, the Treaty required the agreement of the other country or the approval of the newly created International Joint Commission before taking actions which would raise water levels on the other side of the boundary. In addition, in article II, while the Treaty reaffirmed the traditional right of upstream users effectively to reduce the flow of water to downstream users, the downstream users were accorded the same legal remedies as if the injury took place in the same country as the causative action. In short, our ancestors saw the unwisdom of one country acting without regard to effects on the other country and moved to limit or influence such actions.

While the Treaty is primarily focused on water flow, it also contains a brief but very strong reference to water quality. Article IV reads in part "it is further agreed that the waters herein defined as boundary waters and waters flowing across the boundary shall not be polluted on either side to the injury of health or property on the other." The principle underlying this article is clear – we should not damage our neighbour by lowering to an injurious level the quality of the water we release to him. The practical application of this prohibition is much less clear since it depends in each instance on a definition of injury. No general definition of injury appears in the Treaty and some have viewed this as a serious shortcoming. Yet, as I reflect upon it, I would have to say that this shortcoming is more theoretical than real. An abstract definition of injury would in any case have to be applied in an ad hoc manner in each instance. A specific judgement would still have to be made. Accordingly, what becomes more important than a general definition is the means by which we make such a judgement in each situation.

That brings me to the third element in our discussion of the Boundary Waters Treaty – the creation of the International Joint Commission made up of six appointees, three from each nation. Because of its importance, I am going to spend some time talking about the way in which the Commission functions. I will begin with a basic truism. The Commission would have little unique to offer to the better management of Canada–United States relations if, within it, business were to be conducted along national lines. Let me elaborate. If all matters brought before the Commission were to result in a division between Canadian and American Commissioners, the effect would be to create yet another forum for negotiation between the two countries. Canada and the United States have no need for such a forum – they can argue with each other very readily elsewhere. What they need is a place that encourages the solution of a given problem based on the facts of the case in an atmosphere one or two steps removed from competing national political or diplomatic interests. By and large, successive Commissioners over the years have recognized this point and have opted to operate as a collegial whole. The success of their efforts can be seen in the fact that on only two or three occasions since it began to function in 1912 has the Commission divided along national lines The need to preserve this heritage of collegial objectivity has never been greater than it is today. Obviously, to sustain this objectivity, the individual Commissioners must be independent of national government direction. It is most important that both our national governments recognize this truth in making appointments to the

Commission and in conducting business with it. This same concept of independent objectivity has historically applied to the Commission's technical advisers as well and I will say more on that point later.

The Treaty envisages the Commission playing essentially three roles: (1) to approve applications for raising the level of waters flowing across the boundary; (2) at the request of one or both governments, to inquire into and report upon any matter arising between them (Note: this is not confined to boundary waters.); and (3) to arbitrate between the parties at the request of both parties.

We can dismiss the third role – arbitration – very quickly as the parties have never used the Commission in that fashion. The first role – approving applications for raising water levels – requires the Commission to operate in a quasi-judicial fashion. When an entity in one country wishes, for example, to build a dam and, *inter alia,* flood a portion of the other country, the agreement of the second country must be sought or an application must be submitted to the Commission. In practice the latter route – application – is almost always followed.

Upon receipt of an application, the Commission normally appoints a technical advisory board usually made up of well-qualified expert officials drawn equally from each federal government. Sometimes state or provincial government officials are also appointed. The technical board becomes in effect a technical mini-commission with co-chairmen and an equal number of Americans and Canadians. The board members are expected to operate on a collegial basis and to give their best professional advice to the Commission, not simply relay their respective employers' views. In due course, the board submits its recommendations to the Commission, which may accept, reject or amend them. Often the Commission holds public hearings related to an application. In due course the Commission issues or not the required Order-of-Approval sanctioning the project described in the application and setting out conditions as appropriate. The St. Lawrence Seaway, for example, is covered by several Orders-of-Approval issued by the Commission. In conjunction with the Order-of-Approval, the Commission normally appoints a control board with a composition similar to that of a technical advisory board to monitor the sanctioned activity and to advise the Commission on progress and any changes needed in the Order-of-Approval's conditions. Again, the control board is expected to operate on the basis of technical expertise and collegial objectivity.

The second role is the one where the Commission has probably made its greatest mark. Requests by governments for the Commission to inquire into and report on various matters are normally called Article IX references after the relevant Treaty article. While references can be submitted by either government singly, they are almost invariably submitted jointly. Needless to say, careful Canada–US negotiation of the precise wording of a reference normally precedes its submission to the Commission. As I said earlier, in theory virtually any matter arising between the two countries could be the subject of a reference to the Commission. In practice almost all references have dealt with trans-boundary environmental issues, some of which, however, have involved air rather than water quality. The Commission's method for dealing with references is essentially the same as that for applications except that the final product is a report to the two governments of a purely advisory nature, rather than an order carrying legal force.

There have been many references over the years but, before providing some examples to demonstrate the utility of this process, I would like to cite another event which has contributed some important principles to the Canada–United States environmental relationship. In the 1920s a dispute arose over damage caused by sulphur dioxide fumes to crops in the State of Washington from a zinc smelter in Trail, British Columbia. Initially the Commission was asked to examine the cause and extent of the damage, recommend what damages should be paid and identify what should be done to prevent further damage. Subsequently the United States and Canadian governments decided to move to binding arbitration using an ad hoc arbitration tribunal established for that purpose rather than relying upon the Commission. The reasons for this change are not relevant to this paper. What are relevant are the tribunal's conclusions delivered a decade later. As well as assigning specific damages and laying down a stringent emission control regime that is still in force today, the tribunal stated "under the principles of international law, as well as the law of the United States, no state has the right to use or permit the use of its territory in such a manner as to cause injury by fumes, in or to the territory of another, or the properties or persons therein, when the cases are of serious consequence, and the injury is established by clear and convincing evidence." While different from the water pollution prohibition in article IV of the Boundary Waters Treaty and, of course, not carrying the same force as a treaty provision, this principle was certainly compatible with the behaviour pattern encouraged by the Treaty. Moreover, it served to encourage those involved in the management of Canada–United States trans-boundary environmental issues to apply to air quality the concepts already in place for water quality.

I will single out two references to illustrate the value of the article IX referral mechanism. In 1964, the governments of Canada and the United States asked the Commission to report on Great Lakes water quality. Six years and a great deal of work later, the Commission submitted a report which laid the basis for the negotiation of the first Great Lakes Water Quality Agreement. (The Agreement was renegotiated and updated in 1978.) That report was based on one prepared for the Commission by a technical advisory board made up equally of Canadians and Americans which functioned in a completely collegial fashion. The Commission's report provided the two governments with an agreed scientific base and set of recommendations upon which a legally binding agreement could be based. In its work over this six-year period, the technical advisory board, partly because of its broad membership, drew upon a sizable number of federal, state, provincial and private sources of knowledge on both sides of the border. A pattern of cooperative study and analysis emerged and we are still benefiting today from that pooling of knowledge and talent. The experts were able to interact with one another without specific governmental direction and the resulting report represented a wide cross-section of expert opinion on both sides of the Great Lakes Basin. It was this cross-fertilization of ideas and research, stimulated by the Commission and its collegial processes, that eventually produced the agreed conclusion, among many others, that Lake Erie was on its way to a total loss of dissolved oxygen through eutrophication; it was further concluded that rapid action was needed to reduce phosphorus inputs if irreversible damage was to be avoided. The detergent manufacturers and some others argued "not proven" but the preponderance of evidence and scientific judgement indicated otherwise. We know today that we were right to have moved when we did. There is an obvious lesson here for our present acid rain controversy.

In 1975, the Commission was asked to report on the trans-boundary effects of the planned Garrison Diversion irrigation project in North Dakota. As originally proposed, the bulk of the return flows from about 250,000 irrigated acres would have entered into the Souris and Red Rivers, both of which flow into Canada. These flows would have contained high concentrations of leached materials from the soils which, particularly in the case of the smaller Souris River, would have greatly hardened the river water making it, without treatment, unusable for a wide variety of purposes. In addition, the link established by the project between the Missouri system and the Red River system flowing into Lake Winnipeg would have introduced new kinds of fish harmful to existing species. The Commission had to conduct its investigation in a highly sensitive political climate with great emotion generated in both countries on both sides of the issue. The official Canadian view, I might add, was that the project as originally conceived would have violated the pollution prohibition provision in article IV of the Treaty. Notwithstanding this sensitivity, in January 1977, the Commission, aided by a technical advisory board operating in a collegial manner, was able to agree on a report essentially calling for major changes in the project. The Commission's report was, of course, only advisory but both governments were then able to make their judgements, which may differ, on an essentially common database and set of conclusions. In a de facto though not a legal sense, the Commission was effectively defining what in this particular instance constituted injurious pollution under article IV of the Boundary Waters Treaty.

These examples deal with water quality but we have also used the Commission extensively for air quality issues in addition to the Trail smelter case already cited. Currently there are two air pollution boards reporting to the Commission, one of which has a standing instruction to report on air pollution problems from coast-to-coast. The other regularly reports on the progress of pollution abatement programs to improve air quality in the Detroit/St. Clair Rivers area on the Michigan/Ontario border.

I spoke at the outset of my remarks of the brave new world we were creating with the signing of the 1972 Great Lakes Water Quality Agreement. As you can see from the heritage that we brought to the Great Lakes negotiations, we may or may not have been "brave," but we certainly were not particularly "new." We were building not just on the Commission's specific recommendations for the Great Lakes, but on six decades of evolving co-operative mechanisms and ever clearer principles of conduct. Both negotiating teams were very conscious of this history and the preambular paragraphs of the Agreement ring with the sound of past cooperative accomplishments. In short, we sought to apply through the specific mechanisms of the Agreement the general concepts that have served both countries so well for so long. Let me illustrate.

The Agreement – and its more comprehensive successor signed in 1978 – specifically recognizes the general obligation of both parties in article IV of the Boundary Waters Treaty not to pollute one another. The relevant preambular paragraph reads, "Reaffirming in a spirit of friendship and cooperation the rights and obligations of both countries under the Boundary Waters Treaty, signed on January 11, 1909, and in particular their obligation not to pollute boundary Waters..." In effect the Agreement goes on to define that obligation by establishing specific water quality objectives. However this de facto definition is not static, it is dynamic. The objectives are meant to be reviewed as further scientific data are produced. Indeed the 1978 version of the Agreement made some significant changes in and additions to the 1972 objectives. The new version even added a provision addressing depositions of pollutants from the air, a mark of our growing understanding of air as a medium of transport for pollutants whose primary impact is experienced on the ground or water. Perhaps it is more accurate to view the objectives as a practical guide leading to the achievement in the Great Lakes of the intent of the article IV prohibition against injurious pollution rather than as a de facto definition of the prohibition. Either way, the Great Lakes Agreement sought to reflect the article IV basic obligation in a form that was measurable and achievable.

Another concept reflected in the Agreement is respect for the differences in each other's governmental procedures. Both sides are agreed on the goals but, with some exceptions, each recognizes that the other may choose to work towards a given goal in a different way. Thus, to use phosphorous input as an example, the Canadian side moved to restrict phosphorus in detergents at the outset of the Agreement while the US initially chose to go a different route. The point is that each country has a right to expect a certain result or impact from the other's efforts but should not demand that identical methods be followed on both sides of the border

The third concept in the Agreement that I wish to emphasize is the use of the International Joint Commission to monitor and regularly report publicly, if it chooses, on the progress of the Agreement. Indeed the Commission is expected not merely to state whether the objectives are being met but also to assess the adequacy of the objectives themselves using emerging data on the state of the Lakes. The Commission thus becomes the central mechanism for promoting the dynamism built into the Agreement.

To help the Commission, two advisory boards were established. One, called the Great Lakes Water Quality Board, was as usual made up equally of Canadians and Americans. However, unusually, the Agreement required that the Board members be representatives of the two federal governments and of each state or province involved in the Agreement. The Board has eighteen members to accommodate the eight Great Lakes states and each is a senior representative of a federal or provincial/state agency carrying out programs covered by the Agreement. Never before has the Commission been served by a board which is so large, so senior in its membership and, most importantly, so representative of the agencies whose programs the Commission is charged to evaluate. Some critics have pointed out that because the Commission is generally dependent for technical advice on the Board, it is therefore dependent on the very agencies whose performance the Commission is supposed to judge. Moreover, how, the critics ask, can a board with such a membership act in the objective collegial manner expected of Commission boards. As one of the authors of this structure, I have to concede that in theory these criticisms have validity and indeed caused the negotiators of the Agreement some concern. Unfortunately we could not come up with a better way of including all the Great Lakes states in the management mechanisms of the Agreement. Fortunately, in practice there are compensating factors. Most importantly, the very "representativeness" of the Board members makes it difficult for individual members to be unduly defensive about their programs because of the pressure from their peers. The conclusions drawn by the Board are similarly affected by the balance in the membership. Each of the different governments represented is able to keep a suspicious eye on the others. I guess you could call it an international monument to the effectiveness of federalism. The Commission also has its own small staff to advise it, including a modest regional office in Windsor, Ontario, across the river from Detroit, and is not therefore dependent solely on the Board for technical advice.

The other board, the Great Lakes Science Advisory Board, is appointed along more traditional lines although a considerable effort is made to include senior personnel from the principal research organizations around the Great Lakes. The creation of such a board with its focus on improving and coordinating research reflects the importance of ever better research in resolving the many challenges presented by the efforts to protect and improve the quality of this vital water source and waterway. Inadequate attention to research results in fighting the war against pollution with one hand tied behind one's back.

Valuable as these cooperative mechanisms are, they will fail to do the job required if governments do not provide them with the resources needed. That is why the Great Lakes Agreement expressly states in article XI "The parties commit themselves to seek (A) the appropriation of the funds required to implement this Agreement ..." Recent budgetary proposals in the United States run the risk of failing to meet this obligation, as is reflected clearly in the Commission's biennial report on the Agreement issued this past July. Indeed the forthrightness of the Commissioners' expressions of concern underlines once again the Commission's independence and the need for it. (As you may know, a recent report by the General Accounting Office of the US Congress expressed similar concerns.)

In concluding my remarks about the Great Lakes Water Quality Agreements of 1972 and 1978, I would say this – these agreements, building on decades of experience and guided by well-tested principles and practices, have created a very effective mechanism whereby our two countries can address in an efficient way the environmental problems facing the important Great Lakes basin that is home for so many of our people. The plumbing has been put in place, so to speak, and the design is tested and true. But if the resources required to maintain it are not adequate; it will soon spring leaks. The damage will not be confined to the Great Lakes – it will affect the whole Canada–United States relationship. What is at issue is commitment – commitment to the written word and to decades of cooperative practices. That commitment can be undermined through resource starvation just as readily as through overt rejection of co-operation.

While the situation in the Great Lakes is cause enough for great concern, I would be less than honest if I did not say that the acid rain negotiations bring out even more starkly the existing threat to the principles and practices about which I have been speaking. Before I develop that theme, let me emphasize the seriousness of the Great Lakes and acid rain problems. My paper today is deliberately focused on principles and practices because of their importance but I do not wish by implication to downplay the substantive concerns which we have about the issues those principles and practices are designed to address. Acid rain, unchecked, will transform for a very long period, perhaps forever, the ecology of a huge portion of North America and the effects will be very damaging in economic and other terms to both of our countries. Quantifiable costs will almost certainly reach several billions of dollars a year and much of the damage is not readily quantifiable. There are very real economic costs involved in inadequate water quality in the Great Lakes as well, but there the focus of attention is primarily on threats to public health. Public and professional concern about these is mounting on both sides of the border and effective responses are very much needed. In a word, I am not discussing principles and practices in a vacuum. I am talking about tools that are absolutely essential if we, the United States and Canada, are to deal effectively with serious environmental problems along our common border.

I have placed a great deal of emphasis on the International Joint Commission in this paper because the Commission both symbolizes and facilitates our long-standing cooperative practices. One might therefore legitimately wonder why we have not used the Commission to deal with acid rain. Before describing the current situation, I will answer that question.

Historically we have submitted joint references to the Commission in situations where it appeared that the insertion of an objective third party could help the two countries resolve a difference. Where good progress was being made in bilateral discussions between governments on the issue, we would not normally need such third-party contribution.

The Memorandum of Intent which Canada and the United States signed on August 5, 1980, indicates clearly that there was at that time no basic disagreement between the United States and Canada on the acid rain issue. Experts in both our countries agreed that acid rain is a menace to us both. We recognized that the problem is real. I quote from the preamble to the document.

> The Government of Canada and the Government of the United States of America share a concern about actual and potential damage resulting from trans-boundary air pollution, including the already serious problem of acid rain.

The Memorandum says that both countries, and I quote again, "recognize this is an important and urgent bilateral problem, as it involves the flow of air pollutants in both directions across the international boundary, especially the long-range transport of air pollutants."

When President Reagan visited Ottawa in March 1981, one of the first items discussed in the bilateral talks was acid rain. The President specifically affirmed his Administration's intent to meet the commitments in the Memorandum of Intent signed by the previous Administration.

In these circumstances the initial involvement of the Commission was not perceived as necessary. However, that involvement may yet occur. Consideration will no doubt be given to using that unique institution to monitor the implementation of a possible air quality agreement just as it is now used to monitor the Great Lakes Water Quality Agreement.

I would like to comment further on the commitments under the Memorandum of Intent and in particular on the cooperative practices and structures established through it. Please bear in mind as we do this that the Memorandum does not introduce totally new concepts; rather it sets out an administrative framework for fulfilling the existing principles and practices that I have already been discussing. It also starts from the premise that we have a serious urgent problem to address and that we had better move quickly to deal with it. Listen, for example, to three of the preambular paragraphs.

> Canada and the United States ...
>
> note scientific findings which indicate that continued pollutant loadings will result in extensive acidification in geologically sensitive areas during the coming years, and that increased pollutant loadings will accelerate this process;
>
> are concerned that environmental stress could be increased if action is not taken to reduce trans-boundary air pollution;
>
> are convinced that the best means to protect the environment from the effects of trans-boundary air pollution is through the achievement of necessary reductions in pollutant loadings.

As one who was deeply involved in negotiating the wording of this Memorandum, I can assure you that this language was not inserted lightly. These words reflected the consensus of experts in both countries. Not surprisingly, the first operative paragraph of the Memorandum was similarly imbued with urgency. The two governments agreed:

> (A) to establish a Canada/United States coordinating committee which will undertake preparatory discussions immediately and commence formal negotiations no later than June 1, 1981, of a cooperative agreement on trans-boundary air pollution; and
>
> (B) to provide the necessary resources for the committee to carry out its work,

> including the working group structure as set forth in the annex. Members will be appointed to the work groups by each government as soon as possible.

The central instrument for action created by the Memorandum was the joint work group structure. It was modeled after the Commission's practice of appointing technical advisory boards. The difference was that the work groups would report directly to the parties rather than to an independent Commission. This was deemed appropriate since the parties, as stated in the Memorandum, were broadly agreed on the nature of the problem. What was needed was detailed advice from experts in various fields in order to devise a reasonable response.

There were five work groups, each with Canadian and United States co-chairmen. Work group I concentrated on the effects of acidic precipitation on a variety of receptors – lakes, fish, forests, wildlife, crops, buildings and human beings. A prime objective of this group was to come up with a target loading, with the help of both European and North American data, for the principal pollutant of concern – sulphur.

Work group II concentrated on atmospheric modeling, attempting to trace or predict the movement and transformation of pollutants through the air. A prime objective of this effort was to estimate through the application of atmospheric mathematical models the effects of emissions of acidifying pollutants (especially sulphur dioxide) from a given location on depositions in other parts of eastern North America. The group eventually worked with eight mathematical models which had been developed independently by Canadian and US agencies. The results were displayed in the form of so-called transfer matrices and carefully compared with network observations, sometimes characterized as "ground-truthing."

Work group III was divided into two – III A and III B. III A was responsible for developing alternative pollution control scenarios for both countries based on the information provided by the other work groups. The concept of a jointly developed series of control scenarios reflected our appreciation that neither country could develop a reasonably sophisticated control program, especially if linked to loadings, without understanding the general levels of reduction which could be achieved by the other country's program. Work group III B had the task of identifying, assessing and costing control technologies and of quantifying pollutant emissions. Work group IV focused on legal principles and the design of possible institutional mechanisms.

I will try to place this description in a reasonable conceptual framework by tracing the relationship between the groups. Group I would produce loading reduction targets based primarily on lake sensitivity about which there is a considerable amount of data. The Group would make use of observed and model estimates of loadings generated by Group II. Group II, using the emissions information from Group III B, depositions information and atmospheric models, would seek to link levels of deposition reduction in the receiving areas identified by Group I with reductions of emissions in the principal source areas. Group III B would provide estimates of cost and of emission reduction effectiveness for various control methods. Group III A would bring all this information together to produce a number of possible control scenarios that would serve as a basis for negotiating an air quality agreement between the two countries. The object was to negotiate around a common database and a set of mutually acceptable alternative control scenarios.

As with the International Joint Commission's various boards, the key to success lay in an open, cooperative, collegial approach in each of these work groups. Thus, instead of arguing over every scientific conclusion or assumption, the negotiators, working from a common set of scientific and technical conclusions, would focus on timing and cost of control. While differences would undoubtedly remain, they would at least be of a type which would permit informed political judgements to be made. It was not long after the change in the US Administration in January, 1981 that we realized that the rules of the game were also being changed even as the game was underway.

Perhaps to establish the mood, the incoming Reagan Administration quickly decided that Group III A would not develop control scenarios as set out in the wording of the Memorandum of Intent. Instead such work would be done separately by both sides as and when they chose to do so. Group III A would simply oversee the work plans of the other groups and coordinate activities as needed. Not long thereafter and despite substantial agreement among the scientists in the various groups on the wording of draft reports, we were also treated to the sight of non-experts re-writing scientific conclusions and of unhappy US scientists being quietly reassigned. Some US scientists actually quit. As a result, we have had major turnovers in US membership of one group and three US co-chairmen in succession in another. You can imagine the effect these changes have had on a reasonable work program.

This pattern of external interference or inadequate support of the work groups has continued over the past year and a half. Our scientific experts have attended scheduled meetings and had virtually no one turn up on the United States side or were greeted by people whom they had never before seen. (The meetings are usually held in the United States because of the lack of travel money for the U.S. participants.) Despite the frustration of operating under such conditions, our people have occasionally succeeded in laboriously putting together a draft only to have it greatly changed by United States officials who were not involved in the discussions which produced it.

A major casualty of this manipulation of expertise has been an earlier agreement among Work Group I scientists on an environmental loading objective. There was general acceptance during the work group process that a loading of twenty kg of wet sulphate per hectare per year would offer a reasonable level of protection for most aquatic systems. Now, at the eleventh hour, the United States side of the work group completely refuses to accept this figure as a loading target. What makes this situation particularly disturbing, even absurd, is that at a twenty-three nation conference in Stockholm on acid rain last summer, the United States representative endorsed a total sulphur loading target approved by the conference that is nearly twice as demanding as the one produced in the Canada–US work group. The Stockholm target is expressed in terms of total sulphur deposition, which complicates the comparison, but if you calculate the emission reductions required to achieve that target, it is almost twice as stringent as the target earlier accepted within the work group.

Another example of the climate in which the new Administration has obliged us to work is the US approach to "peer review" of the work group reports. We have no objection to peer review. On the contrary we welcome it as an aid to accuracy and objectivity. Indeed informal peer review – broad consultation with informed experts in the field – has been a standard practice in workgroup circles. Even experts within industry have been consulted. Accordingly, in response to US concerns, we suggested a joint approach, using as reviewers our hosts today, the National Academy of Sciences in the United States, and its Canadian counterpart, the Royal Society. However, the United States Administration insisted on separate "peer" reviews with the American one overseen by the President's Science Adviser. Given our experience to date and the context I have described to you, what are we to think of such an attitude? What confidence are we to have in the results?

The Canadian Government made its unhappiness with this whole situation very clear last summer both privately and publicly. We wondered out loud if our national interest was being served by continuing to participate in the work group structure, particularly since some in Congress who were opposed to control action were arguing that the United States should take no action while the matter was being examined by the Canada–United States work groups. Since then Work Group III B has finally been able to agree on a report but it is focused primarily on what control technology is available, a less controversial area than environmental effects or atmospheric transport. At the time I prepared this text, the Work Group on atmospheric transport showed some signs of achieving agreement. However, in the crucial area of loading targets we are still faced with a reluctance to accept figures that were clearly acceptable earlier and which are much less demanding, as I explained a moment ago, than those accepted by the United States in a multi-national forum.

Some in Canada, with the advantage of hindsight, feel that we should have referred the whole matter to the International Joint Commission rather than rely on bilateral work groups. Others, even more disillusioned, feel the same interference would have occurred in Commission advisory boards. One can only speculate about that possibility but it is very clear that the Memorandum of Intent – supposedly defining agreed intent – is currently masking two very different intents – one to resolve the problem – the other to dissolve it – to make it disappear in a torrent of alleged scientific doubts. Indeed a new term has been coined to describe this torrent – informational haze. The central tenet of this haze or propaganda barrage is that we do not know enough about acid rain to take action to control it. Before continuing my remarks let me face this critical haze head-on. To do so I am going to cite a source who may seem a bit surprising. He is Dr. Stuart Warner, vice president for environmental affairs of INCO, operator of Sudbury's large nickel smelter, which is Canada's principal emitter of sulphur dioxide.

I will be quoting from a letter written last February from Dr. Warner to the US Congress' General Accounting Office in response to an inquiry from that Office. Responding to the controversy surrounding the science of acid rain, he admits frankly that the real issues are economic and social – even emotional – and must be faced now rather than wait, perhaps indefinitely, for a conclusive scientific answer. As some others have put it, we are not likely to find a smoking gun. If we, nonetheless, should obtain absolutely conclusive evidence linking specific smokestacks to distant environmental acidification, Dr. Warner writes and I quote "I have seen no scientific argument advocating increased emissions of sulphur and nitrogen oxides. I have seen many arguments that even present levels of emissions are too high. The minimum response I expect from someone who places great weight on science would be to ensure that no increase in emissions be tolerated. This is not what we are seeing in the United States." Needless to say, it is the view of our work group experts and, as best we can judge, most independent US experts that what is needed now is a major reduction of emissions. Reflecting this view, Dr. Warner outlines elsewhere in his letter INCO's plans for further substantial reductions in sulphur emissions from the Sudbury smelter.

For nearly four years I headed Canada's counterpart to the US Environmental Protection Agency. I saw, as a non-scientist, that most questions facing government could not be resolved by science alone. Dr. Warner is right on this point. That said, I also saw that scientists, if allowed to proceed to the limit of their knowledge and to draw their conclusions in an independent fashion, could often significantly narrow the areas where non-scientific judgements had to be applied. This is what we want the work groups to do. The alternative – to seek to influence scientific judgements to produce politically or administratively convenient conclusions – is extremely dangerous. With such an approach it would not be long before it would be impossible to distinguish between fact and fancy. I fear that in parts of Washington that has already happened with respect to acid rain. No doubt an audience of scientists like this one could produce additional examples drawn from other fields involving the administratively convenient "adjustment" of scientific conclusions.

That there are doubts about specific aspects of the acid rain problem is beyond question, but none is significant enough to undercut the conclusion reached by an independent scientific committee established by our hosts today – the National Academy of Sciences. The committee's conclusion was that acidic precipitation is a real and worsening problem calling for urgent control action. This was the same conclusion as reached by the twenty-three nation meeting in Stockholm on acid rain that I mentioned earlier and which secured the support of all national delegations, including that from the United States. Specifically, the relevant paragraph, number eleven, of the agreed ministerial statement issued at the conclusion of the meeting reads "the acidification problem is serious and, even if deposition remains stable, deterioration of soil and water will continue and may increase unless additional control measures are implemented and existing control policies are strengthened." I repeat, the United States delegation endorsed the statement and yet the obvious effort in this country to delay or relax emission controls continues. Let me also read an excerpt from the same paragraph eleven that specifically addresses the North American situation.

> The governments of Canada and the United States are developing a bilateral agreement that will reflect and further the development of effective domestic control programs and other measures to combat trans-boundary air pollution and are taking interim actions available under current authority.

That is certainly a statement of what ought to be but from what I have said today you can see that it does not describe what in fact is happening despite the Memorandum of Intent and President Reagan's reaffirmation of it in Ottawa during his first foreign visit. Indeed, the "interim actions" so far taken in the United States (in contrast to those taken in Canada) have generally had the effect of relaxing controls and adding to the problem.

For our part in Canada, we are willing now to bring about a fifty percent reduction in our own sulphur dioxide emissions during this decade as our contribution to achieving the twenty kg wet sulphate loading mentioned earlier, provided the United States also does what is needed to meet this objective. As I said before, this will not be enough for our most sensitive lakes – there is certainly no risk of imposing unnecessary controls – but it will buy us some time to bring further precision to our research and to refine and extend our control actions as needed. We have sought compatible – not necessarily identical – action in the United States, but the response from the Administration, unlike some parts of Congress, has so far been completely negative. Given what I have said about our beleaguered work group structure we can perhaps be forgiven for wondering if our experts will ever be allowed to produce what is needed to change this response.

This situation would be a bitter enough pill to swallow if it affected only the serious menace of acid rain. Unfortunately it affects much more. The denial of needed resources to implement the Great Lakes Water Quality Agreement and the blatant efforts to manipulate the acid rain work groups despite the explicit commitments in the Memorandum of Intent cut across – indeed risk destroying – more than seventy years of trans-boundary respect and practical cooperation between Canada and the United States.

The concept that one nation or person should seek to avoid damaging another is basic to the societies which exist in both our countries. The opposite is unthinkable. It is really the rule of force – might is right. That is why I entitled this paper "The Rule of Law Between Nations – An Acid Test." Unless there is a major change in policy, we are going to lose that test and we shall all be much the poorer for it.

APPENDIX VII: INSTRUCTIVE ANECDOTES DRAWN FROM PUBLIC REVIEWS OF PROJECTS ACROSS CANADA CONDUCTED BY FEARO'S INDEPENDENT ENVIRONMENTAL ASSESSMENT PANELS

In every public review that FEARO managed we saw our fellow citizens working hard to influence decisions that could affect them, almost always in circumstances that were controversial and sometimes deeply stressful. Everywhere we found a deep concern for the natural environment, a sense that, collectively, we are and must be faithful stewards of this great land. The settings have been dramatically different: a tiny Inuit church on Baffin Island in the Arctic, an elegant ballroom in downtown Vancouver, a community hall in rural Prince Edward Island, a native meeting house near Shefferville, Québec, a local resident's home in Etobicoke near Toronto's Pearson airport, a farmer's field next to Moose Mountain Creek in Saskatchewan, and an open-air First Nations' potlatch on the Pacific coast. The variety is infinite, but there are some common characteristics Canadians display in these different settings that warrant comment.

Let me speak first of courage and civility. I think of a community hall in Borden, Prince Edward Island, which, despite blowing snow, was packed, mainly with ferry workers and their families worried that a proposed bridge to New Brunswick would put them out of work. One after another, they rose to tell the panel about their fears and their anger. After some time, a diminutive businessman came to the microphone and, with voice shaking, declared that the bridge's time had come. He unwisely went on to observe that he had heard no one saying it was a bad thing. The room erupted in shouts of "it's a bad thing!" Undaunted, the businessman completed his statement and received a warm round of applause for his courage.

Similarly, in a log building packed with First Nations people in Fort Smith, Northwest Territories, on the banks of the Slave River, a lone non-native voice was raised supporting the proposed replacement of the diseased bison herd in Wood Buffalo National Park. Native representative after native representative had strongly attacked the concept, yet they heard the dissident view with courtesy and calmness. So impressed was the speaker by the respectful reception he received that he declared (in an undoubted exaggeration), "I don't think there's too many places in the world where people resolve their differences through a process quite as well developed and civilized as this sort of process."

Another characteristic is humour, sometimes with a sense of drama. A lot of funny things happen at hearings, but most are involuntary or accidental, such as using a meeting room in a suburban Victoria hotel next to a striptease bar. Witnesses had to compete with highly distracting sounds coming through the wall, but proceedings ground to a stop altogether when the performers left or arrived, passing by the back of the meeting room. Distraction notwithstanding, that particular panel review resulted in a ban on exploratory offshore hydrocarbon drilling on the West Coast that still stands.

Some years later, a panel reviewing proposed highway expansion through the fabled Rogers Pass in the Rockies was similarly forced to compete with a neighbouring striptease bar in Golden, British Columbia. Somewhat embarrassingly, that happened just as Blair Seaborn, the Deputy Minister of the Environment, was making a rare visit to see a panel in action. Later, after his retirement, he was to chair some of our panels, notably one reviewing the proposed underground disposal of nuclear waste, but he was mercifully spared "musical" competition. I guess "concentration" would be another characteristic that could be associated with these distractions. That would also be true of the unfortunate panel that held a hearing immediately above a bowling alley. The challenge for those giving testimony was to try to time their most dramatic points just before a strike and the accompanying cheers, no mean feat.

The panel that survived the bowling alley went on to achieve a considerable strike of its own. It was assessing a proposed uranium refinery project to be located in Port Granby, Ontario. It not only recommended against proceeding with the proposal but included in its report sharp criticism of the related regulatory body, the Atomic Energy Control Board. Given that the panel was chaired and supported by public servants, this was a rare if not unprecedented event at that time (the late 1970s). The government accepted the recommendation, and the refinery was never built. I am told that some of those working in FEARO at the time wondered if the environmental assessment process would survive the backlash from the energy community and the economic departments of government.

Creativity is another characteristic sometimes on display at panel hearings. Our panel reviewing low-level NATO military flying activities in Labrador and the adjacent parts of Québec was treated to a creative event at a hearing in Montreal. A mini play was presented to show the impact of these activities on people and animals, but the electronic soundtrack, filled with the sounds of low-flying jet fighters, effectively drowned out the dialogue. No doubt that was the intent.

Two other characteristics worth mentioning are dignity and hospitality. While such characteristics are not confined to our indigenous peoples, they are particularly evident in indigenous culture, and I will use an example reflecting that culture. When the panel reviewing the possibility of undertaking exploratory drilling for hydrocarbons off the Pacific Coast visited Skidegate, the principal centre of the Haida Nation on Haida Gwaii (formerly known as the Queen Charlotte Islands), they were received in a most impressive fashion by magnificently costumed chiefs and with a ceremonial banquet, extensive oratory, and traditional dances. The intent was to do honour to their visitors in a manner in keeping with the dignity of the Haida Nation. That meant to receive the visitors as foreign ambassadors.

Dignity is a characteristic that sometimes requires flexibility to protect. That same panel also visited the Nisga'a village of Kincolith on the northern coast of the British Columbian mainland. The school gymnasium where the meeting was to be held was arranged in the usual manner with the table for the panel located at the head of the room, tables for witnesses and proponents along opposite sides, and chairs for the audience facing the panel. The chief and his council arrived, concluded that the arrangements were not in keeping with their own status in that community, and took their seats at the panel's table. The panel sat in the audience and received a thorough airing of the issues as seen by that community.

Another characteristic panels saw in abundance was common sense: popular wisdom. A good example occurred in a tiny Inuit hamlet at Frobisher Bay on the southern tip of Baffin Island. Picture a small wooden church overflowing with local residents and visitors in a magnificent scenic setting in the most barren part of Canada – not a tree or bush in sight. The panel reviewing possible hydrocarbon exploration in South Davis Strait was listening to an expert on ocean currents explain how it would be virtually impossible for an oil spill to come ashore; the oil would go out to sea. An elderly Inuit, speaking Inuktitut, calmly inquired, "If what you say is true, how is it that we often find driftwood on our shores?" The expert was unable to give a satisfactory answer.

The last of the characteristics I want to illustrate with an anecdote are those of trust and mutual respect. These do not come easily. They have to be earned, although the basic decency and tolerance of Canadians makes that easier. I think of a difficult session with a group of citizens in neighbouring Etobicoke who, feeling betrayed by the government's expressed intention to expand Toronto's Pearson airport, were in no mood to trust a panel to undertake a balanced review of those expansion plans. Yet, through reasoned discussion and examination of how the process works, these Etobicoke residents came to the conclusion that, as one of their leaders said later during the hearings, "I do believe that now, finally, somebody is listening to what is happening at Pearson International Airport." I think of a heated discussion among supporters and opponents of the Rafferty-Alameda dam project gathered, along with the panel reviewing the project, in a farmer's field scheduled for expropriation next to Moose Mountain Creek, Saskatchewan. At the conclusion of the discussion, the owner of the field, a strong opponent of the project, said to the panel chairman with great emotion, "You have made my day," a reference to his confidence in the process.

Perhaps I can best conclude these examples of trust by quoting both a supporter and an opponent of a proposed uranium refinery at Wanup near Sudbury, Ontario. First, the supporter from the Sudbury Citizens' Committee, who said:

> The very open democratic process that I think these hearings have demonstrated helps explain why so many of us really do enjoy living in the Canadian climate in contrast to some of the other places that we might be.

He certainly was not talking about the weather. The opponent, representing the Wanup Citizens' Group, had this to say:

> Ordinary people where I come from, faced with a situation like this in Wanup, would simply have said "they" will do what "they" want to do, for "they" must know what "they" are doing. In my first encounter with authority, "they" have faced me. "They" have had faces, "they" have had names, "they" have listened, and "they" have shown that "they," like me, were very human. In spite of the fact that these hearings were overbearing and frightening to me at first – I must tell you that my knees used to shake under this table – you allowed us to speak, you did listen, you did not overpower us with your expertise, you all tried to be as fair as possible.

I cannot resist making an editorial comment. The words I just quoted, which are typical of the reactions that the informal user-friendly EARP hearing process engendered, constitute an eloquent testimony to the value of that process in bringing our governmental institutions closer to the people. There is a widening gulf between the governors and the governed that needs to be bridged. Open, responsive, accessible decision-making, if applied more widely and consistently, could be a key component in bridging that gulf.

My penultimate anecdote is taken from hearings that I chaired myself dealing with a proposed additional runway at Vancouver International Airport. In some ways it sums up all of the other anecdotes. Our twelve days of sitting, often as late as one o'clock in the morning, contained moments of humour, drama, anger, brilliance, dignity, frustration, and determination. There were many smiles in the room when the head of the nudists' society rose to complain about the small aircraft, including helicopters, which she called "flying chainsaws," that routinely buzzed Wreck Beach, a "clothing optional" location at the foot of a cliff below the University of British Columbia's campus. I expressed sympathy but had to explain that that issue was beyond the mandate of the panel.

One highlight stands out in my mind. It is a deeply moving statement made by the elected chief of the Musqueam Band whose reserve borders the airport. She put aside the impressive technical submission that the Band had prepared and poured out her heart about the repeated indignities experienced by her people. They had watched helplessly while lands that had been theirs, including the airport itself, were increasingly put to uses incompatible with their hunting and gathering culture. In short, the Musqueam people had been marginalized. The next speaker was the Mayor of Richmond, the suburban city where the airport is located. Capturing the mood of the room, he opened his presentation with the words, "I feel very small." There were sharp exchanges and tense moments over the twelve days and it was tiring for all. But, when it was over, I found myself very proud of my fellow citizens, of their civility, of their competence and professionalism, of their intelligence, of their compassion, and above all of their tolerance and respect for one another.

I was not alone in noting these things. One of the most impressive witnesses was a top-ranked expert on airport noise from California. His superb performance reflected not only his competence but his experience all over the United States in giving testimony on similar occasions. He sat through the twelve days of hearings and, at their conclusion, sought me out to say how enormously impressed he had been by the proceedings, far superior to anything in his previous experience. He spoke of our civility; our respect for one another; and our focus on issues, not personalities or posturing, as well as of the quality of our dialogue. He doubted that such could be duplicated in his own country.

His last observation may be overstated, but surely we owe all the citizens of our country the opportunity to contribute their thoughts, insights, and talents towards taking care of this enormous piece of the world's environment. Open, consultative decision making allows and encourages that to happen. As for the substance of that review, the airport panel recommended approval of the proposed additional runway but also recommended, among other things, an innovative condition: the creation of a multi-stakeholder advisory committee to monitor the project. That recommendation was accepted.

The other two panels I chaired personally had to do, respectively, with the Yukon section of a proposed natural gas pipeline from Alaska to the lower forty-eight states and the deep rock disposal in Ontario of nuclear waste from power-generating reactors. (Because of my expanding workload, I found it necessary to turn over chairmanship of the latter panel to my old boss, Blair Seaborn, who was by that time retired.) These experiences helped me understand how challenging it can be to chair such panels. Managing sometimes boisterous public meetings while extracting useful information and keeping the peace is a true art form. Chairing private meetings of the panels themselves can be equally challenging. Panel membership is regarded as an honour, and we were able to attract first-class people who would normally command much more than we could afford to pay them. They came from different disciplines and had different values. Disagreements were inevitable, but the chairperson had to try to produce a consensus and a unanimous report. My favourite technique for defusing tense situations was humour, and we used to enjoy much laughter in the panel meetings that I chaired. I learned a lot from fellow panelists.

The Alaska gas pipeline project in the Yukon was my first opportunity, very early in my FEARO career, to chair a panel. I will draw my last anecdote from that eye-opening experience. It was unusual in that the most vigorous exchanges did not take place between proponents and opponents but between technical experts working for the company proposing the project and those engaged to advise the panel. The burning issue was the effect of "secondary frost heave" on construction standards. I will spare the reader a detailed explanation of this phenomenon (assuming after so many years I was capable of providing one) and describe instead the effect that the debate had. A real meeting of minds eventually occurred, and the company agreed that it was appropriate to re-examine their engineering design.

During the course of the debate, one of the experts had mentioned flying over a major pipeline corridor in the Soviet Union and seeing the pipelines meandering like rivers. They had presumably been affected by primary frost heave (alternate thaw and freezing) and a lack of appropriate compensating engineering standards. I could not help but make the observation that we were fortunate to be living in an open society like Canada where the government had in place processes such as National Energy Board hearings or FEARO's panel reviews which, because of full open debate, ensure that the Soviet experience was not repeated here. To his credit, the primary spokesman for the proponent company quickly agreed. Curtailing that kind of unrestricted public exchange carries real risks both to the environment and to the quality of governance.

APPENDIX VIII: CONTRIBUTIONS BY CANADIANS WITHIN OR OUTSIDE THE FEDERAL GOVERNMENT TO THE ADVANCEMENT OF ENVIRONMENTAL ASSESSMENT METHODOLOGIES AND PROCEDURES DOMESTICALLY AND INTERNATIONALLY

I wish to pay tribute to individual FEARO "graduates" who have continued to make their contributions, sometimes internationally, to the advancement of environmental assessment and to other Canadians with whom we worked closely over the years. My purpose is to underline how rich the Canadian experience has been in this respect.

My former right-hand man, Bob Connelly, continued to play a central role in transforming FEARO into the larger and increasingly authoritative Canadian Environmental Assessment Agency, which replaced it. During those years and after his retirement, he was also active in the work of the International Association for Impact Assessment (IAIA). While still at FEARO, Bob chaired the U.N. working group that developed the only international convention on environmental assessment, The United Nations Convention on Environmental Impact Assessment in a Trans-boundary Context, completed in 1991. In recognition of his work, the Norwegian Environment Minister presented him with a lovely old map of the world at the first meeting of the parties to the convention in 1994. Sadly, the United States chose not to ratify the convention, essentially rendering it irrelevant to Canada. However, it is actively applied in Europe and is integrated into the European Union Directive on Environmental Assessment. Now "retired," Bob continues to chair panel reviews of projects and provide advice to the Government in resolving environmental disputes under the North American Free Trade Agreement.

Not long after I left Ottawa for Vancouver, my other right hand, John Herity, became Environment Canada's Director of Biological Diversity. He played an important role in shaping Canada's contribution to the goals of the 190-member Convention on Biological Diversity signed in Rio in 1992. Canada was the first industrialized country to sign that convention.

Former Vancouver regional director Dave Marshall worked with me both at EPS and FEARO. He managed the extensive and challenging Beaufort Sea Hydrocarbon Development Environmental Assessment Review from 1980 to 1984 and has directed the Fraser Basin Council since its inception in 1997. The Council is a unique, collaborative governance structure made up of representatives from the federal, provincial, local, and First Nations governments; the private sector; and civil society. It works within British Columbia and beyond to promote environmental sustainability through inter-jurisdictional co-operation. Its focus is the Fraser River Basin, which is the size of California and discharges into the Pacific Ocean south-west of Vancouver. Dave's work has also included collaborative watershed management in Indonesia and the Philippines, and he helped to restore the Marshlands in southern Iraq after they had been devastated by the previous Saddam regime in the late 1980s.

Others, like Carol Martin, have become successful consultants. Fluent in Spanish, he was particularly active in Latin America even before he left FEARO. For example, Pat Duffy and he taught a course on environmental assessment focusing on an industrial development project in a Mexican municipality. It even included a mock public hearing. In Costa Rica, as part of a Dutch-led project, Carol conducted a condensed environmental assessment of a small gold mine owned by Canadians and produced a report recommending environmental assessment regulations for the Costa Rican government. Subsequently, Costa Rica adopted a review process similar to that used in Canada. Farther south, Carol led conferences on the Canadian approach to environmental assessment before a variety of governmental, public, and university audiences throughout Argentina. After leaving FEARO, Carol focused his attention on El Salvador for two years, helping its Government Environment Secretariat to develop environmental assessment legislation containing a number of features reflecting Canadian practice. He also worked with the Canadian International Development Agency on a six-year project on the modernization of the electrical energy sector in all of the Central American countries. His role was to provide advice on what environmental assessment processes and practices should be applied.

International recognition of Canada's contribution to the understanding and practice of environmental assessment has been truly remarkable. For each of the past twenty-eight years, the International Association for Impact Assessment (IAIA) has granted its prestigious Rose-Hulman award to "a past or present member of IAIA for a major contribution to the field of impact assessment over a sustained period." In ten of those years, the recipients have been Canadian. I have been privileged to know all but three of them, and I hope the reader will bear with me as I name each in turn.

In 1987, the award was given to trail-blazing Thomas Berger, whose Mackenzie Valley pipeline inquiry many years earlier established the standard for such reviews. The award of 1988 went to Dr. Gordon Beanlands, whose work with the Canadian Environmental Assessment Research Council (CEARC) was central to its success. In 1991, CEARC itself was the award winner. In 1993, it went to Robert Goodland, who played a central role in developing the Environmental Assessment process at the World Bank. Barry Sadler was the winner in 1996. An academic and consultant based in my hometown of Victoria, he worked closely with CEARC and spent a sabbatical with FEARO. The 1998 winner was Dr. Husain Sadar, one of FEARO's most valued employees. In his post-FEARO career as Professor of Environmental Sciences at Ottawa's Carlton University, he has published dozens of articles and several books. Dr. Shirley Conover of Halifax received the award in 2002. An academic, a consultant, and the chair of one of our Environmental Assessment Panels, she made a major contribution as a member of CEARC. Bob Connelly, who needs no introduction, was the 2006 winner. Bill Ross was the co-winner in 2009. A Calgary academic and consultant, he was a member of CEARC, spent a sabbatical with FEARO, and has served on or chaired several Environmental Assessment Panels. Most recently he chaired a panel examining a major mining project. In 2012, the award again went to a Canadian, Peter Croal, who works for the Canadian International Development Agency and has been over many years a tireless advocate for the application of environmental assessment procedures to foreign aid projects.

One active IAIA member not on that list but who epitomizes a lifetime commitment to promoting the application of well-conceived environmental assessment is Dr. Pat Duffy. When, on the occasion of his eightieth birthday, I asked how he was enjoying his retirement, he replied that he was still open for business. Lest the reader suppose that his response reflected octogenarian bravado, I should report that he completed a mission to Cambodia earlier that year and also gave lectures and participated in symposia in this country. Pat was a member of the small group in Environment Canada who developed the first Cabinet Directive on environmental assessment in 1973. As one of FEARO's regional directors, he played a central role in many public reviews.

Later, as a consultant, he made contributions in many countries over the years, but I want to single out one in particular. I have a recent letter from a senior official at the headquarters of the U.N.'s Food and Agricultural Organization (FAO) in Rome attesting to Pat's central role in encouraging and enabling FAO to develop environmental guidelines for impact assessments of FAO projects. It took many years to get these approved, but, as my correspondent makes clear, Pat's persistence and professional contribution respecting content were central to bringing the guidelines into being. In recognition of his lifetime contribution to excellence in impact assessment, the IAIA Board of Directors designated Pat as the recipient of the Outstanding Service to IAIA award in 2013.

One of our regional directors, Phil Paradine, who was later ordained in the U.S. Episcopalian (Anglican) Church, worked with the Canadian International Development Agency (CIDA) in Indonesia and later at the World Bank headquarters in Washington, D.C., where he was highly regarded. Phil tells me that he studied at Virginia Theological Seminary while at the World Bank. Although ordained as a deacon in Ottawa, he returned to the United States to become a priest and initially undertook outreach work among foreign refugees in Virginia. He is now doing mission work in the Appalachians. His socio-economic interests developed while working with FEARO's environmental assessment panels and later with former Soviet Bloc countries on behalf of the World Bank. I should also mention Paul Wolf's work introducing environmental assessment into CIDA and his later related activities in Zambia.

I also wish to pay tribute to another long-term FEARO employee, Dr. William Couch, who, after retirement, spent many years teaching environmental assessment at the University of Warsaw's Centre for Environmental Studies. After Poland joined the European Union, it was obliged to enforce the Union's Directive on Environmental Assessment as well as other environmental policies. Protecting the environment was never a priority behind the Iron Curtain, and Poland, like other Eastern European countries, had a lot of catching up to do. Poland's commitment in this respect has been impressive, and the Centre where Bill taught was in the forefront of that effort. He also spent years compiling a detailed history of the development of environmental assessment in Canada. One of our leading universities has recently accepted his manuscript for publication. It contains many useful lessons and will be an important addition to the professional literature. Bill recently returned to Ottawa to live near his children and grandchildren, which means that I can no longer talk about having e-mail friends from Warsaw to Wellington. It had a nice ring to it.

The bottom line is obvious: graduates and associates of Canada's Federal Environmental Assessment Review Office and its successor, the Canadian Environmental Assessment Agency, have contributed remarkably to bettering our world. I am proud of every one of them.

APPENDIX IX: BRINGING ORDER TO ENVIRONMENTAL ASSESSMENT IN CANADA OUT OF COURT-INDUCED CHAOS

In my narrative, I used the somewhat overblown metaphor of steering the environmental assessment ship through a court-induced storm. The reader may recall my contention that the best way of addressing the resulting massive expansion in federal responsibility for environmental assessment was to develop a co-operative federal–provincial system of assessment across the country. The idea was to share the increased workload and avoid unreasonable delays in approval for well-designed projects. Achieving such co-operation was made more difficult by a mix of long-standing resentment of "federal intrusion" and anger at the result of the court cases on the part of some provinces. The provinces that have been most sensitive about the role of the Federal Government are Alberta and Québec. I will begin by focusing on what happened in Alberta.

The first Alberta project that warranted a public review under the newly mandatory Environmental Assessment Guidelines Order was a proposed pulp and paper mill on the Athabasca River in northern Alberta called the Alpac project. At that time, Alberta did not have a structured environmental assessment process except for that provided by the Alberta Energy Resources Conservation Board, which reviewed projects only in the energy sector. Bob Connelly, my right-hand man, went to Edmonton, accompanied by a Justice Department lawyer, to explain the legal requirement for a review and our desire that it be a joint one with the province. Bob told me that he walked into one of the most hostile meetings he had ever attended. There were over a dozen senior provincial participants in the room who argued vigorously that the federal process should not apply and that the federal officials might as well pack their bags and go home. We arranged for a conference call between Minister Bouchard and his Alberta counterpart. Sensitive to what had happened in the Rafferty-Alameda situation, Bouchard did not give an inch, and it was agreed that a joint review would take place.

Neither Bob nor I remember whether the issue of appointing review panel members came up in that ministerial discussion, but the appointment story is worth recounting. We learned that one of the Alberta appointees under consideration was the owner of a car dealership in the town nearest the project who had taken out newspaper ads welcoming the industry to the area. Bob pointed out to Alberta officials that, under the federal Guidelines Order, such a person might be viewed as less than impartial and this could lead to a legitimate legal challenge. Despite this warning, Alberta made the appointment, and a major public outcry resulted. Perhaps not surprisingly, this unfortunate appointee resigned before the review began, much to the relief of others involved.

The federal panel appointees were Bill Ross of the University of Calgary, who was a member of the Canadian Environmental Assessment Research Council and a veteran of several reviews, and David Schindler, a highly regarded fisheries biologist at the University of Alberta in Edmonton, who, in an earlier career, had played a pioneering role in documenting the impact of acid rain on the lakes of Ontario. The surviving Alberta appointee was Gerry DeSorcy, chair of the Alberta Energy Resources Conservation Board, a man of considerable competence and integrity who later sat on the panel that examined a natural gas development project at the Suffield military base in Alberta.

The Alpac panel recommended that the project not proceed, largely because of concerns about the chlorine bleaching process and its effects on the river and the fish. The recommendations were accepted and the company returned with new, cutting-edge technology that eliminated residual chlorine in the bleaching process effluent. The project was approved. Later, Alberta enacted environmental assessment legislation, which created the Alberta Natural Resources Conservation Board to review non-energy projects. Joint federal–provincial reviews with that board and the Alberta Energy Resources Conservation Board have subsequently been held on several projects in the province. In sum, the federal–provincial Alpac review resulted in the introduction of new, environmentally sound paper bleaching technology, the creation of a legislated provincial environmental assessment process, and an effective, mutually acceptable mechanism for co-operation between the two orders of government. Not a bad result!

The corresponding project in Québec that warranted the first joint review under the now mandatory Guidelines Order was a huge hydroelectric project on the Great Whale River flowing into southern Hudson's Bay. As explained in chapter 52 of the narrative, because the assessment and approval of that project was also covered by a unique agreement between the federal government, provincial government, and the Cree and Inuit peoples for which I had a significant personal responsibility, I kept at arm's length from the federal–provincial negotiations that were needed to develop the specifics of that joint review. FEARO was represented by Carol Martin, our Regional Director for Québec, ably supported and guided by my temporary second-in-command Jean-François Martin. They were assured of strong support from Minister Bouchard. Some will, no doubt, see irony in the Minister's support for asserting the federal role in Québec given his later decision to resign from the Federal Cabinet and the Progressive Conservative party to found and lead the separatist Bloc Québécois regional party in the federal House. In point of fact, his first question to FEARO staff was, "What is best for the environment?" It was also clear that he wanted to be even-handed in dealing with Alberta and his own province.

Along with Carol Martin, I had earlier been exposed to the depth of Québec's resentment against what was seen as Ottawa's intrusion into the management of the province's resource sector at a meeting in Québec city held to discuss the general implications of the Federal Court decisions respecting the Guidelines Order. The senior Québec officials present made it very clear that they regarded this federal intrusion as an attack upon their sovereignty, specifically their freedom to develop their resources as they saw fit. I remember in particular a passionate comment to the effect that hydroelectricity is to Québec what oil is to Alberta.

In the event, given that the Federal Court decisions applied equally in Québec as elsewhere in Canada, Carol and Jean-François were able to develop a joint review process for the Great Whale project that we thought meshed well with the procedures set out in the Agreement governing that project. I have discussed that Agreement at some length in chapter 52. It produced one of the most stressful experiences of my career.

Co-operative arrangements with other provinces were developed over time across the country. In some instances, provinces such as British Columbia that had previously been without structured environmental assessment processes decided to establish them. Indeed, after my move to Vancouver from Ottawa, I was invited to become a member of an advisory group that was developing environmental assessment legislation for the British Columbian legislature. My involvement was aimed at ensuring that the legislation would mesh well with the federal process. Many years later, I encountered a senior provincial official with whom I had worked at that time. He told me how pleased they had been over the effectiveness of those components in the legislation that governed joint reviews with the "feds." His compliment created a very satisfying moment for an aging, full-time caregiver.

APPENDIX X: *FINANCIAL POST* ARTICLE "THE BARK BEHIND THE BITE OF ENVIRONMENTAL OFFICE," JULY 18, 1989, BY JOHN GEDDES

OTTAWA – Until recently most politicians and bureaucrats in Ottawa knew next to nothing about the Federal Environmental Assessment Review Office and its Executive Chairman, Ray Robinson.

They're learning fast.

Robinson and FEARO are at the centre of the Conservative government's efforts to weld environmental protection to economic policy.

Legislation to strengthen FEARO is expected to be ready for Cabinet approval this summer. A recent court decision has indicated that the environmental review process is more powerful than anyone realized.

Some provinces, industry groups and even federal departments are alarmed by FEARO's growing power.

Meanwhile, Robinson is plowing ahead with reviews of contentious projects, ranging from the proposed Prince Edward Island bridge link to New Brunswick to Atomic Energy of Canada Ltd's plans to dispose of radioactive waste.

The key to reforming FEARO, Robinson said, is to get the agency in on the ground floor of decision-making. "The whole tradition of environmental concerns being an add-on at the end of every process is the bane of our existence."

Robinson, 52, took over FEARO in 1982. He had earlier spent 9 years in senior positions at Environment Canada, including a stint lecturing Americans on the dangers of acid rain as the Department's director of Canada-US relations.

An elaborately carved Maori feather-box displayed prominently in Robinson's office testifies to an earlier career. He held foreign service postings from New Zealand to Colombia for 15 years.

Diplomacy may once again be in order as FEARO shoulders its way to a new position of power. "There are many bureaucrats in Ottawa who are appalled that FEARO has turned out to be as powerful as it is," said Don Gamble, a critic of FEARO and Executive Director of environmental group Rawson Academy of Aquatic Sciences.

FEARO's profile has steadily grown since a landmark Federal Court decision in April. The court found Ottawa negligent for failing to conduct a full review of Saskatchewan's Rafferty-Alameda dam project.

The decision surprised the government by concluding that the 1984 Order in Council that laid out the environmental assessment review process has the force of law.

While FEARO's power is rising, legislation being prepared will not reverse present policy, which gives federal departments responsibility for considering the environmental impact of their own projects.

"If you are a serious about integrating economic and environmental objectives, then the place to do it is where the economic decisions are being made," Robinson said.

But he added that the legislation will probably give FEARO power to take over the assessment role in the early stages, if it decides a department is not giving environmental concerns adequate attention.

"The initial assessment process has been sloppy," he says. "I would anticipate a considerable smartening up of the system across government."

But Gamble is not sure Robinson is tough enough to play the strong hand he has been dealt at FEARO.

"No-one has better instincts on what constitutes a full and fair environmental review [than Robinson]. On sincerity and integrity, he's hard to match. The question is does he have the kind of hard-assed bureaucratic profile you need in Ottawa to carry the day," he said.

"When you start questioning whether the Finance Department is behaving in an environmentally responsible way, you have to ask what kind of guy can go up against [Finance Minister Michael] Wilson and his senior bureaucrats."

Robinson will also face resistance from the provinces. Already FEARO is locked in difficult negotiations with Alberta over an environmental review of new pulp and paper mills and with Québec over the second stage of the giant James Bay power development.

Previously, environmental assessments of resource projects were generally left in the hands of the provinces. But the Rafferty-Alameda decision means that Ottawa can no longer defer to the provincial reviews, Robinson said.

Instead, a system of co-operative assessment must be worked out, even for projects where federal involvement is limited to a small financial contribution, he says. Up to now, FEARO conducted full environmental assessment reviews only on large projects in areas of clear federal control, such as developments on federal lands.

"The concern is that the provincial economic agenda will become secondary to the federal environmental agenda," says Doug Bruchet, environmental director of the Canadian Petroleum Association.

And Bruchet worries that when FEARO's role is entrenched in legislation, more Canadian environmental issues will end up in the courts.

Already a trend towards litigation is emerging. Court challenges, prompted largely by the Rafferty-Alameda ruling, have been launched over both the Oldman River dam in Alberta and Québec's James Bay development.

Robinson says he is dedicated to keeping the review process from turning into a cumbersome impediment to economic growth. "The key is to give a project the degree of assessment it warrants."

He supports the basic structure of the current system, in which federal departments first screen projects for environmental impact, then proceed as necessary to an environmental overview called an Initial Environmental Evaluation.

Only a minority of projects – about 30 in FEARO's history – are subject to the much more thorough, independent assessment.

APPENDIX XI: AUTHOR'S 1995 PAPER "THE FEDERAL ENVIRONMENTAL ASSESSMENT PROCESS – FROM GUIDELINES ORDER TO THE CANADIAN ENVIRONMENTAL ASSESSMENT ACT"

Note: this presentation was made to the Canadian Institute's Conference on the Changing Face of Environmental Law and Regulation in Western Canada held in Vancouver, British Columbia, on May 29, 1995.

INTRODUCTION

This paper will briefly examine the federal Environmental Assessment and Review Process (EARP) and, in greater detail, the new Canadian Environmental Assessment Act which replaced the EARP last January. The paper will also touch on efforts to harmonize the federal and provincial environmental assessment procedures with particular reference to Alberta and British Columbia.

THE FEDERAL ENVIRONMENTAL ASSESSMENT AND REVIEW PROCESS (EARP)

The EARP was first introduced through a Cabinet decision in 1973. It was altered with a second Cabinet decision in 1977. In 1984, the EARP was strengthened and updated with the issuance of the Environmental Assessment and Review Process Guidelines Order. The Guidelines Order ceased to apply, except for certain transitional arrangements, last January when the new Canadian Environmental Assessment At was proclaimed.

The EARP was primarily a planning process, not a regulatory one. Its basic objective was to ensure that proposed projects that require some level of federal decision-making were assessed for their potential environmental and directly related socio-economic effects early in the government decision-making process in concert with initial economic and engineering studies. When used properly, the process was an effective tool in marrying or integrating the concepts of sound economic development with those of environmental sustainability, thereby promoting the principles of "sustainable development."

Central to the EARP was the principle of self-assessment. Federal departments and agencies responsible for project decisions were also responsible for determining the appropriate level and scope of the environmental assessment to be carried out. They were required to ensure that appropriate environmental assessment studies were completed and that those assessments were fully considered in making project decisions. There is much to commend this principle. In particular, it may instill in project managers and decision-makers a sense of environmental responsibility and stewardship that probably would not be there if the environmental assessment requirements were determined and directed by an outside agency. This principle, however, has been criticized, and with reason. Indeed, it has been likened to putting the fox in charge of the hen house. While some elements of self-assessment remain, this criticism is addressed in the new Canadian Environmental Assessment Act by, in effect, giving the Environment Minister control over the comprehensiveness – and by extension, quality – of the assessments undertaken.

Under the 1984 EARP Guidelines Order, the process applied to any project that was to be undertaken by a federal Department that may have had an environmental effect on an area of federal responsibility or that involved federal funding or that was located on federal lands. In large measure, the new Act is similar, but with certain defined limits and with much greater specificity.

The EARP was designed to ensure that the appropriate level of effort was applied to each project requiring assessment. Accordingly, projects with the potential to cause major environmental effects or generate significant public concern were subjected to a detailed and thorough assessment with opportunities for public input. Projects with less significant effects or which generated less public concern were subjected to less rigorous review and assessment. The rules governing these distinctions were, however, somewhat vague. They are much clearer under the new Act.

After the initial general decisions under the EARP are made, a number of more specific decisions could follow:

1. the project may have had effects that were not significant or could be readily mitigated – in that event the project could proceed or proceed with appropriate mitigation;
2. the project was likely to cause significant adverse effects that were not mitigable – in that event the project had to be modified or abandoned;
3. the project required further study before a decision on its environmental significance could be reached – in that event a more detailed assessment had to be carried out and
4. if, in the opinion of the responsible minister, the project could have had potentially significant environmental effects or have caused

> public concern such that a public review would be desirable, that minister was required to refer the project for formal public review by an independent environmental assessment panel appointed by the Minister of the Environment.

Under the new Act the conditions described in paragraphs (1) and (2) above remain substantially the same. However, the projects to which paragraph (3) refers are now listed by category in a regulation which also sets out the nature of the comprehensive assessments required. As for paragraph (4), the Environment Minister now has authority to decide on the need for a formal public review by an independent panel regardless of the opinion of the Minister responsible for the project. The responsible Minister may, however, request that such a review be held.

Much of the attention given to the EARP has been focused on those projects that require a full public review by an environmental assessment panel. Although this is understandable given the high public profile of these reviews, the vast majority of projects subject to the EARP were never elevated to the level of a panel review. One could compare the EARP to an iceberg. The tip of the iceberg, the panel review stage, was highly visible. However, the bulk of the process was much less visible, but equally important. The cumulative environmental effects of the many non-panel EARP reviews, if not properly mitigated, could well have been greater than the impacts associated with the relatively few projects subjected to panel reviews. That was one of the reasons for the creation of a "comprehensive study" regulation under the new Act. Projects covered by it can now be assured of an assessment even though, say, ninety percent or more of them would not warrant review by an independent panel.

The independent panel review process established under the EARP is changing very little under the new Act mainly because it has worked so well over the years. At the height of the confusion created by the series of court decisions in the late 1980s and early 1990s, which effectively broadened and strengthened the EARP, more than twenty reviews covering projects valued at tens of billions of dollars were underway at one time. That was an aberration. The current number of active panel reviews – eight – is more typical.

Panels are independent advisory bodies appointed by the Environment Minister, usually comprised of three to five members, all of whom, except for the chairperson, were for many years drawn from outside government. Historically, the Executive Chairman of FEARO or his designate chaired such panels but, more recently, panel chairpersons have almost always been drawn from outside of government and that pattern is expected to continue under the new Act. Strict rules governing conflict of interest applied to the selection of panel members and every effort was made to ensure that panels contained a range of relevant expertise and perspectives. For example, it was common to have at least one native member on panels reviewing projects with significant impacts on native interests. Where proposals entailed decision-making at both levels of government, joint federal/provincial panels have frequently been established in a variety of configurations. These range from panels all of whose members are jointly appointed by both governments to panels containing, say, two members appointed by each government with either a jointly appointed chairperson or co-chairpersons appointed separately. A new pattern is, however, emerging whereby federally appointed members are sometimes added to an existing provincial review body, provided that body, in terms of its configuration and procedures, meets the test of openness and independence reflected in the new Act (and the old EARP).

Although each panel review has been unique and the review steps and procedures followed by individual panels have varied, the following elements have been common to most such reviews:

1. Panel appointment and the issuance of specific Terms of Reference by the Minister of the Environment;
2. Increasingly frequently, allocation of funding by an advisory committee separate from the Panel to help participants prepare their presentations;
3. Identification by the Panel in consultation with the public (often using a workshop) of specific issues and concerns to be addressed during the review;
4. Development by the Panel, in consultation with the public (often using a workshop) of guidelines for an environmental impact statement (EIS);
5. Completion of environmental studies by the proponent and submission of an EIS to the Panel;
6. Public review of the EIS culminating in a determination by the Panel on the adequacy of the EIS for purposes of proceeding to the hearing stage;
7. Informal but structured public hearings held by the Panel to allow all interested parties to express and discuss their views on the project;
8. Preparation by the Panel of its report to government containing its findings, conclusions and recommendations – it is important to underline that panels make recommendations, not decisions;
9. Public release of the panel report by the Minister of the Environment and the Minister of the decision-making Department; and

10. Detailed public response (decision) by government on the Panel's recommendations.

Under the new Act, there are three changes to the panel process – the panels now have subpoena powers, a formal Cabinet decision is required to respond to panel recommendations, and participant funding is mandated for all panel reviews.

An important final step in the EARP, whether it be for projects subjected to panel reviews or for non-panel reviews, was a follow-up program. Procedures are needed to ensure that panel recommendations accepted by government or mitigation measures identified through non-panel reviews were implemented if the project was to proceed. A longer term post-assessment monitoring and surveillance program was also established for a few projects. Under the new Act, such a program is now mandatory.

COURT DECISIONS AFFECTING THE EARP

There is no point in this paper in revisiting the various court decisions that changed the EARP so fundamentally during the final years of its life. It is sufficient to say that those changes both emphasized the need for reform and facilitated its achievement.

REFORMS TO THE FEDERAL ENVIRONMENTAL ASSESSMENT PROCESS

Since it was first introduced in 1973, and with increasing vigour in the late 1980s, environmental assessment practitioners and other interested parties have suggested a number of changes to the EARP. Public interest groups, native organizations, industrial and commercial associations and government agencies have, over the years, become increasingly aware of the EARP and the important role that it plays in federal government decision-making. This increasing awareness and understanding of the process and its significance for government decisions as well as the court decisions mentioned above brought to light a number of flaws and weaknesses and resulted in calls for change.

Following a process of public consultation, the Government formally stated its intention to introduce environmental assessment legislation to replace the EARP in the Speech from the Throne of April, 1987.

The Government's initial package of proposed environmental assessment reforms was announced in June, 1990. It consisted of three main elements:

1. passage of a Canadian Environmental Assessment Act – which addressed the environmental assessment projects;

2. introduction of a requirement for the environmental assessment of all proposals submitted to the federal Cabinet – which addressed the environmental effects of government policies and programs; and
3. initiation of a participant funding program to help affected public participants in all panel reviews of major projects.

CANADIAN ENVIRONMENTAL ASSESSMENT ACT – DETAILED PROVISIONS

The Canadian Environmental Assessment Act, which was enacted by Parliament and given Royal Assent in June, 1992, was proclaimed into law in January, 1995. It is the cornerstone of the reform package. The Act sets out a clear environmental assessment process aimed at helping ensure that the concepts of "sustainable development" are fully reflected in the factors to be considered when making decisions on projects covered by the Act.

As under the EARP, the Act requires each federal authority – including federal Ministers, departments and agencies – to be responsible for the conduct of environmental "self-assessment" on projects falling within its decision-making authority. However, the conduct of the more significant assessments is now subject to regulation and, as noted before, the Minister of the Environment now determines the need for the public review of a given project by an independent environmental assessment panel.

Projects covered by the process include all physical works and specified physical activities where a federal authority:

- is the proponent;
- provides several funding;
- administers several lands; or,
- in prescribed circumstances, regulates some aspect of the project.

This last category warrants further explanation. As earlier noted, there has been confusion over what federal regulatory actions trigger the current EARP especially in the wake of various court decisions. Under the new legislation regulatory authorities covered by the Act are specifically listed – statute by statute, indeed clause by clause – in a regulation known as the "Law List."

Like the EARP, the new Act is designed to ensure that assessments are completed as early as possible in the planning stages of projects. Unlike the EARP, the Act specifically prohibits the making of any federal decision to proceed with a project covered by the Act until the requirements of the Act have been met.

Another change from the EARP is the new, more open process for initial assessment. Public access to assessment information and opportunities for the public to be consulted at this stage are strengthened.

The Act divides projects into one of four categories:

- excluded projects;
- class assessment projects;
- listed major projects; and
- all other projects.

Projects which are known not to pose any risk to or harm the environment or for which the environmental effects are negligible are excluded. This exclusion is effected through regulation in two different ways. "Physical Works" to be excluded are listed by categories. "Physical Activities" not related to a "Physical Work," on the other hand, will be excluded unless specifically included. Examples of "Physical Works" which are excluded are minor construction projects, routine maintenance activities and simple renovations. Examples of "Physical Activities" that are included are low-level flight training activities conducted by the Department of National Defence and the testing or operation of a mobile PCB treatment system. There is also provision in the Act for the exclusion of projects which are carried out in response to an emergency situation or, as defined in regulation, where there is minimal federal involvement.

For projects which are routine and repetitive in nature and are known not to cause significant or unmitigable effects, "class" assessments can be utilized. The determination of what constitutes a class assessment will be made by the new Canadian Environmental Assessment Agency, which replaced the Federal Environmental Assessment Review Office (FEARO) when the Act was proclaimed last January. Class assessments may be used for such activities as dredging, highway maintenance, and the rebuilding of facilities on the same site. Information generated through post-project monitoring will provide valuable input and guidance for future projects in the same class. All class assessments will be tailored to take into consideration local circumstances.

Projects for which the environmental impacts are known to be significant require a comprehensive study. Categories of projects requiring comprehensive study are prescribed by regulation. These projects tend to be of a large scale and often generate public concern. Examples include:

1. oil and gas developments beyond a specified size or located offshore;
2. uranium mining facilities and nuclear reactors;
3. water management projects beyond a specified size;
4. industrial plants such as pulp and paper mills; and

5. marine terminals designed to handle vessels beyond a certain size.

There is a common misunderstanding that because a project falls into a category identified on the comprehensive study list, it automatically requires an assessment under the federal process. This is not so. For there to be a federal comprehensive study, a project must not only be on the comprehensive study list but must require a federal decision of a type which would trigger the federal process.

For projects requiring comprehensive study, the responsible department or agency must prepare a report that considers:

- the project's environmental effects and their significance;
- mitigation measures;
- comments from the public;
- the purpose of the project;
- alternative means of carrying out the project;
- the need for and the requirements of any follow-up programs;
- cumulative impacts associated with the project;
- the conservation and sustainable development of any renewable resources that are likely to be significantly affected by the project, and
- any other matter the decision-making department or its Minister may require.

Following completion of a comprehensive study report, it is submitted to the Canadian Environmental Assessment Agency. The Agency in turn publishes a notice advising of the report's availability and provides an opportunity for public review and comment. Once comments have been received, recommendations are submitted by the Agency to the Minister of the Environment and it is at that point up to that Minister – not, as under the EARP, the Minister of the decision-making Department – to decide whether further review by a panel or a mediator is needed. The latter Minister may, however, as noted earlier, request a panel review.

Projects that do not fall into one of the above categories, i.e. excluded projects, class assessment projects, or listed projects requiring comprehensive assessment, undergo initial assessment or environmental screening in order to determine the existence and extent of possible environmental effects. Upon completion of the environmental screening, projects which, in the opinion of either the Minister of the decision-making Department or the Minister of the Environment, are likely to result in potentially significant environmental effects or arouse major public concern, will be subjected to further review by a mediator or an environmental assessment panel. For projects that do not require this further level of review, a decision will be made at this point on whether the project should be allowed to proceed and, if so, what mitigating measures are appropriate.

The basic objectives of the varying levels and types of assessment are:

1. to determine the effects of a project on the natural environment and the impact of the changes on human health and socio-economic circumstance;
2. to ensure that federal decisions relating to these projects take full account of that determination; and
3. to do so in a cost-effective way by ensuring that the amount of effort put into the assessment is in proportion to the likely risk presented by the project to the environment.

The option of appointing a mediator under special circumstances instead of a panel is designed to make the process more flexible and potentially more cost-effective.

Projects suitable for mediation include those where all stakeholders are willing to participate and consensus on the outstanding environmental issues is considered likely. Other factors to be considered in choosing a mediation process are the number, ideally small, of readily identifiable stakeholders and the scope and number of the environmental matters at issue. In short, the process must be manageable and the prospects promising.

Environmental mediation is a form of environmental assessment which can avoid the cost of a full public view by a panel. However all environmental factors would still normally be considered. It is also recognized that, if mediation fails, a panel may still be required. Mediation can in addition be used as an adjunct to a panel review, i.e. some issues amenable to mediation may be referred to mediation while other more problematic matters may remain as part of the panel's mandate.

Panels under the Act continue to be advisory and not decision-making bodies but for the first time, as noted earlier, they now have subpoena powers. They will otherwise function much as they did under the EARP. For example, panels and mediators under the new Act must submit their findings and recommendations to the Minister of the Environment. The report of a mediator or of a new review panel must also be made public. However, unlike the EARP, as noted earlier, a formal Cabinet decision, made by a public explanation, is required to respond to a panel's recommendations.

One of the most important new aspects of the process outlined in the Act is the follow-up program. Several feedback mechanisms are to be implemented to ensure the new process is effective. For example, comprehensive study reports for major projects are to include follow-up monitoring plans designed to verify the accuracy of the predictions contained in the environmental assessment and to determine the effectiveness of any required mitigating measures. There is also a requirement for a follow-up plan to be prepared following approval of the project for those projects that are not subject comprehensive study. These follow-up plans and the final reports are to be made available to the public. The effective result should be that approval of any project is conditional, *inter alia*, on the establishment of an effective follow-up process.

The Act is also designed to minimize duplication of services between jurisdictions without abdicating any federal decision-making powers. This is achieved primarily through enabling the Minister of the Environment to appoint a review panel jointly with another party, such as a provincial government, a foreign state or a body set up under a comprehensive native land claim agreement. Joint panels must, however, meet the same key requirements, such as openness and independence, as federal panels. In addition, the Act allows for close cooperation with provincial governments during the initial assessment or screen phase. The specifics of this cooperation between jurisdictions are expected to be codified in a series of federal/provincial agreements based on a framework agreement approved in November 1992 by the Canadian Council of Ministers of the Environment, about which more is said later.

In cases where a federally constituted body equipped to hold public hearings on environmental issues already exists, such as the National Energy Board, the Minister of the Environment may accept such a body as an adequate substitute for a panel review. It is anticipated that in such circumstances, which are expected to be rare, the Minister might also name an additional person or persons to the substitute body. Ministerial discretion also exists, if certain criteria are met, to recognize a First Nations environmental assessment process and related claims agreement arrangements as a substitute for the procedures under the Act.

The Act also provides the Environment Minister with power to order a panel review of a project not otherwise under federal jurisdiction which is anticipated to have significant adverse environmental impacts across an international, inter-provincial or provincial/territorial boundary as well as across boundaries between First Nation and other lands and around federal parks. This provision includes the authority to seek, if necessary, an injunction from a court to prevent such a project from proceeding before the review is complete. The procedures contained in this section of the Act are designed to ensure that every effort is made to promote the co-operative assessment by the parties involved before any federal decision to intervene is taken.

In addition to encouraging direct public participation in the review of major projects, the Act provides opportunities for public participation by all stakeholder groups in virtually every other aspect of the environmental assessment process from regulation development (setting the rules for assessments) to follow-up and evaluation programs and from initial screening, where appropriate, to panel reviews. Public participation is highlighted as one of the main purposes of the Act.

The Act also outlines an improved public notification system and ensures that information on projects under assessment is more accessible to the public by requiring the establishment of public registries (libraries containing all relevant documentation) located near such projects. Efforts are well advanced in establishing an electronic data base including key information about all projects subject to the new Act that will be widely accessible across the country.

For the process established under the new Act to become effective, four regulations had to be issued. Proclamation of the Act necessarily awaited their completion. A Regulatory Advisory Committee with representatives from industrial associations, environmental organizations, native groups, provincial governments and federal departments was established under FEARO's chairmanship to assist in drafting the regulations. The four key regulations now in force are:

1. a list of major projects requiring a comprehensive study;
2. a list, normally called the Law List, of federal statutes and regulations that will trigger the environmental assessment process;
3. a list of physical works to be excluded; and
4. a list of physical activities to be included.

Other regulations that are still under development at this time include those providing:

1. language defining what constitutes minimal federal involvement in a project and, therefore, does not require the application of the Act;
2. procedures for carrying out environmental assessments where First Nations are the primary decision-makers;
3. special procedures associated with projects and activities related to the provision of foreign aid; and

4. special procedures for commercially competitive Crown Corporations and the Harbour commissions. (These will not be covered by the Act until the appropriate regulation is in place.)

As noted earlier, the Act provides for the creation of the Canadian Environmental Assessment Agency to replace FEARO. The Agency, which came into being when the Act was proclaimed last January, is charged with promoting uniformity in the application of the process across the country, conducting training, supporting mediation and review panels and promoting research into more effective and efficient ways of assessing environmental impacts. Of particular importance is its role in advising the Minister of the Environment on the need for reviews by panels or mediators of given projects. That responsibility gives the Agency the influence it needs to ensure that assessments conducted by government departments are of good quality. It will also report annually to Parliament through the Minister on the administration and implementation of the process across the federal government.

It is also expected that the Agency will play an increasingly important role in working with the provinces on the harmonization of environmental assessment processes and procedures for projects where both levels of government have jurisdiction.

PARTICIPANT FUNDING

As noted earlier, the second component of the environmental assessment reform package is a participant funding program.

Often public participation provides essential information which not only facilitates the integration of economic development and environmental protection, but also increases sensitivity towards the people and circumstances of a particular region that is not readily obtained through other means.

Prior to the announcement of the environmental assessment package in 1990, there was no regular program for the provision of funds to assist participants in EARP public reviews. Participant funding was available for reviews on an ad hoc basis. The reform package introduced for the first time a regular program for participant funding to assist stakeholders taking part in panel reviews. That program has now been reinforced with specific language contained in the Act. While the principal objective of the program is to improve the effectiveness of public reviews by increasing the quality of the information provided to the panel, it also helps ensure that all participants have an equal opportunity to prepare and present informed views.

The program works as follows. A certain amount of funding is established for each panel review. Local groups, organizations or individuals may apply for small grants from these funds to carry out a specific project or analysis or investigation as part of their review of the project. A small committee, with non-governmental representation separate from the panel, reviews each proposal and recommends to the Agency who should receive assistance and how much. The committee must assess the relevance and value of the work describing each application against criteria reflecting a panel's terms of reference.

In addition, successful applicants must meet other broader criteria. For example, participants must be affected by the proposed project or represent those who will be affected. In particular, participants who need the most help in preparing and presenting their views will be given priority. Participants representing all sides of the issue will be equally considered for funding, but not the proponent. The amounts of money involved are generally modest and typically represent only a portion of the costs incurred by participants.

POLICY REVIEW

The third component of the environmental assessment reform package is a process for assessing the environmental implications of all submissions to the federal Cabinet.

Given the broad scope of policy assessments and the need for a greater degree of confidentiality than is the case for project reviews, the policy assessment procedures are, of necessity, different from those used for project assessments. The Cabinet decided, therefore, to exclude policy assessment from the new Canadian Environmental Assessment Act, depending instead on a Cabinet directive.

Under the policy assessment process, the Minister of the Environment provides advice to other departments on procedures for assessing the potential impacts of their policies and programs on the environment. The actual assessments are carried out internally by the Department or department responsible for the policy, with no requirement for public involvement. However, a department may choose to consult the public if it so wishes. This internalization of the process is in keeping with the confidential nature of Cabinet deliberations. However, at the time the government policy or program is announced, the responsible Minister is required to publish a statement summarizing the results of the environmental assessment of the policy or program.

Only policies and programs with implications that are environmentally relevant will require substantive assessment. The great bulk of Cabinet decisions deal with matters that have no environmental implications.

The federal government has, as yet, limited experience with methodologies for policy assessment but work is underway in this area. Necessarily, there will be a period of adjustment and learning during which new procedures will be developed, tested and adopted.

Although the policy assessment process is not as open as the project assessment process outlined in the new Act, it represents an important, and to some, radical change in the way government conducts its business. For the first time, government planners and decision-makers will be obliged to build environmental factors in the development of government policies and programs. Clearly, so doing is essential to pursuing the principles of sustainable development.

WORKING TOWARDS HARMONIZED FEDERAL/PROVINCIAL ENVIRONMENTAL ASSESSMENTS

The expansion of the EARP as a result of court decisions mentioned earlier resulted in some duplication and overlap between the federal and provincial environmental assessment processes. As a result, the federal government and the provincial governments have been working to ensure that the two levels of process requirements are harmonized and duplication is minimized. And while the Canadian Environmental Assessment Act does not provide for delegation of federal environmental assessment decisions to the provinces, it does, as noted earlier, contain a number of provisions encouraging joint assessments and other co-operative arrangements.

Under the direction of the Canadian Council of Ministers of the Environment (CCME), steps are being taken to facilitate cooperation between the federal and provincial governments in the future conduct of environmental assessments. A CCME framework agreement between the federal and other governments setting out how each would cooperate with the other in matching the various provincial environmental assessment processes with those set out in the Canadian Environmental Assessment Act was approved by the CCME in November 1992. The intent is to use the framework as a basis for negotiating individual bilateral agreements that would reflect the specifics of individual provincial systems.

The first province to take up the challenge of translating the principles of the CCME framework into a specific bilateral agreement was Alberta. Canada and Alberta signed the Canada-Alberta Agreement on Environmental Assessment Cooperation in August 1993. Building on the principles set out in the CCME framework, the Alberta Agreement reflects:

1. recognition by both parties that the procedures and requirements of each government's environmental assessment process are consistent in principle and intent and that environmental assessments must be

undertaken in a manner which avoids unnecessary duplication, delays and confusion;

2. agreement that both governments will establish a designated office to act as the main point of contact on matters relating to their respective environmental assessment processes and the application of these processes to the review and assessment of specific projects; accordingly, the federal agency has now established a small office in Edmonton; the Province's designated office is managed by Alberta Environmental Protection; and
3. agreement that for projects where both governments conclude that there is a need for a full public view, a joint review panel will be established to conduct the review; for most projects in Alberta, the federal requirements for a public review will be met through special arrangements e.g. adding temporary federal nominees to provincial bodies with either of Alberta's two environmental hearing bodies – the Energy Resources Conservation Board or the Natural Resources Conservation Board. The first joint federal/provincial panel under this arrangement was established with the Natural Resources Conservation Board; the recently completed review, now awaiting governmental response, was of the Pine Coulee Water Management Project.

In British Columbia, negotiations on a similar agreement have been initiated; it will reflect procedures under both the new BC Environmental Assessment Act, now awaiting proclamation, and its federal counterpart.

Another major challenge for the harmonization of environmental assessment procedures, especially in BC but also elsewhere, is related to the settlement of First Nation land claims. The BC Treaty Commission received statements of intent to negotiate land claims agreements from nearly forty First Nations and there may be more still to come. Each of these agreements as it is negotiated is expected to include provisions for environmental assessment procedures.

Both the federal and BC governments agree that the various environmental assessment procedures that are expected to be included in these separate settlement agreements should not result in a proliferation of distinct and potentially incompatible environmental assessment processes across the province. Avoidance of duplication and overlap will be a major objective of the negotiations.

CONCLUSION

The process and practice of environmental assessment in Canada, especially at the federal level and here in BC, is in transition. The EARP, since its introduction in 1973, has become an increasingly important and critical component of federal government decision-making. During its early years, the EARP went largely unnoticed or unheeded. Its application was spotty and its main claim to fame was focused on a few high-profile panel reviews.

The Federal Court decisions declaring the EARP Guidelines Order to be mandatory, the subsequent passage of the new Canadian Environmental Assessment Act and the other reforms described in this paper have served to raise the profile of environmental assessment at the national level. They have also brought much-needed attention to an activity that will be a crucial tool in helping this country face the environmental and developmental challenges that will dominate the balance of this century and that show no sign of disappearing beyond the year 2000.

Nonetheless, processes alone, however well-designed and -implemented, will not meet the need. The real requirement is broad recognition that all sectors of society and all levels of government need to cooperate in designing our collective future. Without that cooperation, environmental sustainability will remain a dream.

APPENDIX XII: CRITICISM OF BOTH THE EVISCERATION IN 2010–12 OF THE CANADIAN ENVIRONMENTAL ASSESSMENT ACT AND THE RELATED ABUSE OF PARLIAMENTARY PROCESS

I said in the main narrative how much I admired the commitment and professionalism of the people with whom I worked. I was also very lucky to be in a field of work that encourages such commitment. What we did mattered, and it still does. Unfortunately, the present Conservative government of Canada does not appear to share that view. As I understand it, Prime Minister Harper believes that it is necessary to minimize those federal procedures and regulatory authorities that are designed to protect the environment in order to facilitate rapid development of our natural resources, most obviously oil from Alberta's tar sands. As a result, my story about the decades-long struggle to create environmental assessment legislation in Canada has a very unhappy ending, at least for the time being.

The beginning of that unhappy ending was the mandatory review of the Canadian Environmental Assessment Act (CEAA) conducted by the Conservative-chaired House Environment Committee in 2010. There was no consultation outside Ottawa, and a limited list of witnesses was called. The recommended amendments were contained in what the minority Conservative government called an omnibus budget bill that could be defeated by the combined opposition only by bringing on a general election, which the opposition parties at that time were not prepared to do.

After the Conservatives secured their majority in the House in 2011, the process of change became even more draconian. In 2012, the Conservative government, using its majorities in the House and Senate, secured rapid enactment of two "omnibus" bills that amended a large number of acts with virtually no House Committee examination of these amendments. Only the House Finance Committee undertook quick, cursory reviews. Among the changes were those that effectively removed most of the triggers, such as all nuclear and nearly all other energy projects, for CEAA and virtually all the inland water pollution control provisions under the Fisheries Act. Another change restricted public participation in the hearings held under CEAA. (CEAA was actually replaced, not just amended, in one of the 2012 omnibus bills.)

The effect is to greatly reduce the federal role in environmental assessment and water pollution control and reduce public influence on federal decision-making, thereby undoing decades of work. Moreover, very loose criteria permitting the use of provincial processes in place of the federal one make it likely that the independent federal panel public review process, including joint reviews with provinces that had proven so successful, has effectively come to an end. An agreement with British Columbia signed in March of 2013 has had that effect, and other provinces are expected to follow suit. British Columbia First Nations leaders have expressed their outrage and have threatened to take the Federal Government to court. Native leaders elsewhere in Canada have already done so. The Supreme Court of Canada's decision on the Oldman River Dam in 1992, which recognized the environment as a joint responsibility of the federal and provincial levels of government, has clearly been ignored. The second omnibus bill in 2012 limited the application of the Navigable Waters Protection Act (NWPA) to about one hundred lakes and rivers across the country, greatly limiting the capacity of the Federal Government to protect inland waters in this country. It was the need for a federal permit under the NWPA that led to a federal environmental assessment of Alberta's provincially sponsored Oldman River Dam and the subsequent game-changing Supreme Court decision. Prime Minister Harper has ensured that that situation will not be repeated.

The parliamentary procedures followed – bypassing relevant House Committees – further marginalize the Members of Parliament. Review of legislation by Committees constitutes the most important means by which ordinary Members of Parliament influence the governing of our country. Despite its Conservative majority, the Senate Committee reviewing the 2010 omnibus bill actually criticized the House for its inadequate scrutiny of the legislation. The Senate as a whole, however, went on to approve it. How sad it is that a committee of the anachronistic appointed upper house found it necessary to criticize the elected lower house for failing to do its democratic duty.

With a few exceptions, I have managed to avoid strong language in telling the stories that make up my life, and I have also tried to be impartial politically. However, I cannot avoid expressing my distress in the strongest terms over this abandonment of basic federal constitutional responsibilities and the accompanying violation of parliamentary process. These omnibus bills have done real harm both to the Federal Government's ability to protect the environment and the right and obligation of Members of Parliament, on behalf of those who elected them, to examine as thoroughly as possible all proposed legislation, especially legislation of such significance. In matters of environmental protection and management, we Canadians must not forget that our country is the second-largest, territorially, in the world. Surely we have an obligation to all mankind to be responsible stewards of this immense piece of the world's landmass.

With respect to our democracy, I suspect that most Canadians who bother to think about such things have for a long time considered minority governments as undesirable because they are inherently unstable. I certainly held that view. After witnessing this abuse of power by our present Prime Minister, I am starting to rethink that issue. If Parliament is to exercise the authority that it theoretically holds under our Constitution, it may be that minority governments are the only way to ensure that it can continue to do so. In the final analysis, democracy should be defined by such words as accountability and responsiveness, not by words like efficiency and stability.

There is an impact from this decision by the Prime Minister that may not be obvious to some. The decision sends out a signal to corporations that, at least at the federal level, environmental protection is a much less important issue than it used to be. FEARO engaged a consultant during my time there to do an assessment of the impact of our environmental assessment process on corporate behaviour. What we found was very heartening. Company after company had established environment departments staffed by appropriate professionals to advise them on the effects of their activities and to contribute to the design of those activities. In many companies, these environment departments reported directly to the CEO or were headed by a vice president who sat at the management table. The practical result of these changes was that the projects proposed were generally much better designed from an environmental perspective.

It is reasonable to suppose that corporate boardrooms will now give less weight to advice from their environment departments and probably downsize them. Such action could have an impact that would last beyond any future restoration of appropriate environmental procedures and regulations. I am thinking specifically of an exodus of environmental professionals from this country to greener fields south of the border. It could take a long time to replace that professional infrastructure, thereby weakening Canada's competitive capacity in a global industry of growing importance: the science and technology of environmental management and protection. Short-sighted policies can be so harmful at so many levels.

The environmental challenges faced by Canada and other nations are growing, not diminishing. A policy of deliberately closing our eyes to these challenges does not make them go away. Nor is it part of Canada's long-standing tradition of support for the international community to turn our back on multilateral efforts to overcome those challenges that no nation can address alone. At a deeper level I also have to question the morality of deliberately choosing not to know the possible harmful consequences of our actions in case such knowledge might interfere with our policy objectives. The reader will therefore surely understand why I wonder what has happened to our traditional values, our collective national conscience. Where is the Canada of which I was so proud as I stood in the freezing cold on Parliament Hill, shouting my heart out as I watched our new Maple Leaf flag unfurl for the first time?

APPENDIX XIII: EXAMPLES OF THE HIGH ENVIRONMENTAL STANDARDS GOVERNING THE CONSTRUCTION OF VANCOUVER'S OLYMPIC FACILITIES

I have chosen three examples of these facilities, although the first, a stunning, environmentally sustainable harbour-front convention centre, was not directly related to the Games. However, the decision to build it was based in large part upon the anticipated increase in world attention that Vancouver would attract as a result of receiving the Olympic nod. The centre's environmental elements include a living, carbon-absorbing, oxygen-producing roof with six acres of grassland, sea water heating and cooling, on-site water treatment, and fish habitat built into the foundation (which extends into the harbour). The other two facilities – the Olympic Village and the Richmond Olympic Speed Skating Oval – were directly related to the games and have become Olympic gifts that go on giving. Like the conference centre, they were designed with the environment in mind. The Olympic Village was envisaged as the starting point for a new, environmentally friendly central neighbourhood housing up to fifteen thousand people.

According to the architects, the Olympic Village is even greener than the Conference Centre because of its "exceptional levels of sustainability." The initial one thousand residential dwellings were built to what are called minimum LEED Gold equivalence levels. LEED is an acronym for Leadership in Energy and Environmental Design, a green building rating system developed by the U.S. Green Building Council. The community centre meets LEED Platinum standards, while the building containing seniors' housing is designed to meet the "Net-Zero" standard, which represents annual energy, water, and carbon neutrality. All of the buildings feature green roofs, passive solar design, above-code installation and glazing, and low or no VOC (volatile organic carbons) paint and carpets. Rainwater is retained in cisterns to be used for irrigation of the green roofs and landscaping. All buildings are heated and cooled using an in-slab hydraulic system connected to a hybrid heating and cooling system powered by high-efficiency natural gas boilers, which use both ground-source heat pipes and an innovative heat exchange system tied into the sewer pipes to recover their latent heat. I apologize to readers if, like me, they find this description hard to follow, but the bottom line is simple enough: this is state-of-the-art green construction.

The Richmond Olympic Oval is located south of Vancouver near the airport on an island in the Fraser River delta. From the air, the roof takes on the stylized shape of a Great Blue Heron's wing, a tribute to the Salish First Nation and to that large wading and fishing bird that inhabited the riverbank at first European contact two hundred and thirty years ago. The Oval's principal environmental feature is the material of which it is built: mountain pine beetle kill wood.

The engineers responsible for the building won a prestigious award acknowledging outstanding achievement in structural design from the Institution of Structural Engineers. Runners-up included the 2008 Olympic Games' Beijing National Stadium (a.k.a. the Bird's Nest), London's Wimbledon Centre Court roof, and the new Elephant House in Copenhagen. The award citation focused on the "fully integrated and multi-faceted sustainable design ... that opens up new possibilities for the use of mountain pine-beetle kill wood which has proven to be a unique, durable and aesthetically pleasing material." This is a reference to the millions of British Columbia trees that were killed a few years ago in a massive mountain pine beetle infestation. That infestation resulted in large part from climate change, specifically because winter temperatures were not low enough to kill the pine beetle larvae. The infestation stopped only after British Columbia ran out of the mountain pine trees that fed the voracious beetle. All those dead trees constitute, of course, a major fire hazard, and, while logging them as quickly as possible is obviously desirable, the sheer quantity involved means that there is little hope of significantly reducing the fire risk.

A distinctive feature of the Oval's design is its unique "wood wave" roof. This roof, which is one of the longest clear spans in North America, is made of one million feet of mountain pine beetle kill wood linked together in undulating sections to create a beautiful rippled effect. Also of note are the structurally innovative design for the flat ice surface and the architectural piers used to support the roof structure. The lead project architect was involved in the design of both the Calgary and Salt Lake City Olympic speed skating tracks.

After the Olympics, the Oval was converted to a multi-use sport facility that includes two Olympic-sized ice rinks, up to eight hardwood ball sport courts, a gymnasium, a two hundred metre track, and a rubberized turf area. The speed skating oval is covered with removable flooring and could still be used for competition.

Although it is neither a contribution to our infrastructure nor a facility as such, I want to mention one other environmentally significant project that was stimulated by the Olympics: the creation of the world's largest fleet of hydrogen fuel cell buses. The twenty buses are part of the BC Transit bus fleet in Whistler, home of nearly all the Olympic ski events. These buses, operating on hybridized hydrogen fuel cells, provide a sixty-two percent reduction in greenhouse gas emissions relative to their diesel equivalents and have a range of five hundred kilometres before refuelling. BC Transit's new depot in Whistler also serves as a hydrogen refuelling station. The fuel cells were designed and made by Vancouver-based Ballard Power Systems, which is the exclusive provider of fuel cells to Mercedes-Benz (Daimler). The plan is to evaluate life cycle costs for the fuel cell buses through to 2014 to assess how they compare with current internal combustion engine technology.

APPENDIX XIV: AUTHOR'S 2006 PAPER "LESSONS FOR GOOD GOVERNANCE DRAWN FROM THE HISTORY OF THE ENVIRONMENTAL ASSESSMENT AND REVIEW PROCESS (EARP)"

SUMMARY

Recent events have given rise to calls for the Public Service of Canada to display greater transparency and public accountability in the management of government business. The application of environmental assessment processes within government, with their constant emphasis on openness, public consultation and responsiveness, has created a level of transparency and accountability within those programs where it is applied that more than responds to these calls. However, there has been a long history of resistance to these processes within the Public Service and a study of that resistance is instructive in understanding those elements of current practices that require change if greater openness and responsiveness are to be achieved across government. In conclusion, several suggestions are made aimed at improving transparency, public accountability and professional expertise, especially at the top levels of the Public Service.

POSITIVE EFFECTS OF EARP

Environmental assessment experts studying the history of Canada's Environmental Assessment and Review Process (EARP) and its agency, FEARO (which became the Canadian Environmental Assessment Agency in 1995), would no doubt focus on the significant advances that have occurred in methodology and instrumentation designed to produce ever better predictions of environmental and social impacts. However, the influence the Process has had on stimulating broader improvements in governance is equally important.

Federal environmental assessment processes typically require public consultation early in decision making. Analyses that at one time would have remained confidential are routinely made public and comments are invited. Indeed, there is usually a need to respond to such comments including, where appropriate, justifying conclusions and recommendations formulated by public servants. For major projects, panels of independent experts may hold hearings and submit analytical reports, including recommendations, directly to the responsible Minister. Funds are often made available to help intervenors improve the quality of their presentations at these hearings. The panel reports are always made public as are the required governmental responses. Consultation with the Environment Minister customarily informs those responses. Some or all recommendations from a panel may be rejected by Ministers but a public explanation would be expected. The environmental assessment process has had a major impact on those areas of governmental decision making where it is routinely applied. Specifically, it has opened up to public scrutiny and, therefore, to more effective accountability, a formerly closed decision-making system that arguably placed too much power in the hands of senior public servants. In short, the affected decision-making processes have become almost completely transparent as well as highly responsive.

REQUIREMENT FOR CONSENSUS

The Privy Council Office (PCO) is responsible for preparing the agendas of the various Cabinet committees. Typically, a proposal affecting more than one department would be expected to reflect interdepartmental consensus or near-consensus before being placed on the relevant agenda primarily to reduce the demands on Ministers' time. As a result, senior officials in the affected departments are in these circumstances given the primary responsibility for making the value judgements and tradeoffs that are a normal part of significant decisions. This is of concern because the public might reasonably expect such trade-offs to be made by publicly accountable elected politicians. Continued failure to reach a consensus among affected departments can doom a proposal even though a Minister or two may support it. (A strong Minister can usually get his proposal onto the relevant Cabinet committee's agenda without such consensus but often at the cost of having all or most of his colleagues briefed to oppose him. A common result is a decision to send the proposal back to officials to seek consensus once again.)

OPPOSITION TO ENVIRONMENTAL ASSESSMENT LEGISLATION

The long struggle to produce environmental assessment legislation is a perfect example of the worst effects of this system. The United States enacted its comprehensive environmental assessment legislation in 1969 but Canada chose instead to rely on a very brief 1973 Cabinet decision calling for the application of environmental assessment to projects funded or approved by the Federal Government. Procedures evolved gradually over the next ten years but they were often ignored in whole or in part because they were perceived by many managers as optional and unduly burdensome. Both the victorious Liberals in 1980 and the victorious Progressive Conservatives in 1984 called specifically in their respective election platforms for the enactment of such legislation. However, it took until 1990 to secure Cabinet approval for the introduction into the House of Commons of the Canadian Environmental Assessment Act (CEAA). Moreover, although it was enacted within two years, it took until 1995 to have it proclaimed. (The CEAA required regulations to become operational and opposition within the Public Service was such that it took years to secure their approval.) Senior officials opposed to the CEAA correctly saw the proposed Act as a threat to their control over the flow of information and advice to Ministers. That control is normally tightly held and, as a result, adamant opposition to any form of environmental assessment legislation came from all across the Government, even from those departments which were philosophically sympathetic to the objectives of environmental assessment processes. It was only because of a series of remarkable court decisions in the late 1980s that it finally proved possible to bring the CEAA before the Cabinet.

INTERVENTION BY THE COURTS

A word of background is needed. In 1984, the last Trudeau Cabinet meeting had approved the Environmental Assessment Review Process (EARP) Guidelines Order, which codified in some detail the environmental assessment processes as they had evolved to that point. At the time, the Order was perceived merely as a guideline and constituted a sop to the Environment Minister. His proposal to introduce legislation as promised in the party platform had not been allowed to get anywhere near the Cabinet table because of widespread opposition across departments. Ironically, what the courts did in a series of decisions on different construction projects beginning in 1989 was to characterize the Guidelines Order as a law of general application, meaning that the procedures set out in it potentially applied to every federal action and law. The effect was massively to expand the scope and power of the EARP. The Government was also bound to apply every word of the Order, which had been less than perfectly written because of the last minute urgency of its preparation and because it was regarded as a mere guideline. Some provinces, alarmed by the resulting Federal intrusion into areas of their competence, appealed the decisions to the Supreme Court but without success. For a time FEARO was overseeing the assessment of projects worth more than half the annual capital investment in Canada. More seriously, the Order's inflexible wording made it difficult to tailor the level of assessment to the environmental significance of each project. Because the Government was not prepared politically to rescind the Order, the obvious solution was to replace it with a carefully drafted, well thought through piece of legislation. There were still many battles over details but, because the existing situation was seen as more intrusive and burdensome than the proposed CEAA, it proved possible to achieve the level of consensus needed to meet the requirements of the PCO gate keepers. It is worth noting that FEARO had, with Cabinet's blessing and before the court decisions were handed down, conducted a thorough coast to coast public consultation on the need for legislation and had found broad support from industry, provinces, first nations and environmental groups for a legally based, clearly defined, predictable process. This support had in no way mitigated opposition from career public servants.

EFFECTIVE PUBLIC SERVICE VETO AND THE DOCTRINE OF MINISTERIAL RESPONSIBILITY

In theory, public servants are accountable through their own hierarchies to their Ministers who are in turn accountable to Parliament. In practice, most Ministers are greatly dependent on public servants, especially (as amply demonstrated by the CEAA experience) with respect to initiatives needing the support of other departments. The bottom line is that unelected officials were able over many years to prevent action on a political commitment made by successive governments of both major parties. It took a decision by the judiciary to overcome what was in effect a Public Service veto. The doctrine of ministerial responsibility, which holds that government employees should be accountable to the public solely through Ministers, not only fails to address this problem but may in fact perpetuate it by shielding public servants from the public they are supposed to serve. This doctrine is, of course, intended to protect democracy by ensuring the supremacy of those who are elected over those who are not. That is a legitimate intent despite some practical negative consequences and measures to overcome these negative consequences must therefore be crafted with care to avoid undermining the role of Ministers. However, it does not help to pretend that there are no problems and that only Ministers exercise power.

POSSIBLE IMPROVEMENTS

Measures to enhance accountability and address the invisible exercise of too much power by unelected officials might include a greater role and more resources for parliamentary committees in reviewing discretionary decisions such as draft regulations (as in Britain) and otherwise dealing directly with senior officials, more public consultation with real dialogue on major issues of public policy, greater use of white papers in seeking public input on policy proposals before recommendations are finalized, expanded program review by the Auditor General or Environment Commissioner, a policy of actively disseminating governmental information in the public interest rather than simply responding to requests, more powers for the Information Commissioner, appointment of a well staffed ombudsman to assist the public in dealing with Government and an educational program for selected public servants to equip and motivate them to function in a transparent manner. Changing the way federal legislation is drafted would also be helpful. For example, future legislation should no longer be designed for the convenience of administrators, i.e. with maximum discretionary authority and minimal obligation upon Government to act in a prescribed manner. Rather, such legislation should detail the Government's obligations in mandatory language and contain prescriptive language governing the exercise of discretion, thereby facilitating judicial review if the requirements of the legislation are not followed. Such an approach would assure the public and parliamentarians that the wishes of Parliament, as expressed in legislation, will, not just may, be carried out.

THE IMMENSE VALUE TO GOOD GOVERNANCE OF COMMITTED KNOWLEDGEABLE SENIOR PUBLIC SERVANTS

There is also need for a cultural change in the Public Service, especially in the senior ranks, to reinforce that sense of obligation or service to those outside Government for whose benefit the various programs are operated. Prior to the late 1960s, most senior officials, including deputy ministers, had come up through the ranks of individual departments. They therefore typically possessed extensive knowledge of their departments, strong commitment to their objectives and programs, loyalty to their staff and a sense of responsibility for the welfare of those segments of the public whom the programs were designed to help. (In his 1989 book, *Keeping Deputy Ministers Accountable*, former Clerk of the Privy Council and Head of the Public Service Gordon Osbaldeston recounts that these characteristics were highly prized by virtually all of the 21 private sector CEOs he interviewed for his book.) In the interdepartmental battles that often accompany the development of public policy, these senior officials would normally fight hard on behalf of their departmental interests and the broader interests in society which their departments exist to protect or promote. A glance through a federal telephone directory quickly reveals how broad these interests are – Agriculture, Energy, Labour, Health, Welfare, Industry, Fisheries, Environment, Transport, Consumers, Native Affairs, Immigration, Trade, Aid, Foreign Affairs, Defence, Veterans, Northern Affairs etc. Each department has its "clients" and those "clients" reasonably expect that their interests will be vigorously advanced by "their" department in interdepartmental policy discussions. Constructive interaction of this kind contributes in an important way to good governance. Concentration of too much power in one place has the opposite effect.

THE PERILS OF OVER-CENTRALIZATION

The trend towards appointing Deputy Ministers (DM's) to head departments where they had no background began in the 1960s primarily because of a perception that broad management skills were more important than specific knowledge and experience. In the early 1970s, Michael Pitfield, Trudeau's Clerk of the Privy Council, carried this appointment pattern much further. Pitfield rightly recognized that senior officials' departmental loyalties made his task more difficult in that policies enunciated by the "centre" (PCO, Finance, Treasury Board etc.) would be resisted by these officials if judged inimical to an individual department's interest. Moreover, attempts to save money by finding "fat" in the system would run into walls of non-cooperation. As a result, the Government was often forced into blanket reductions rather than selective cuts. Efficient departments would be cut the same as less efficient ones thereby punishing efficiency since those departments could absorb the cuts less easily than could their fatter cousins. Pitfield's solution, implemented gradually and still not universal even today, was to change the way top level officials were selected. A pattern emerged in which most DMs and an increasing number of ADMs were appointed to departments where they had no history or commitment and often moved before they could develop that depth of understanding needed to serve Ministers as they should. (Mr. Osbaldeston's book cited earlier emphasizes this policy's substantial costs in general effectiveness and in the provision of well informed advice to Ministers.) Potential high-flyers quickly recognized that their futures lay with pleasing the centre — to be team players, not boat-rockers. (In his book, Mr. Osbaldeston also reported that private sector high flyers were prized for their knowledge of their specific business in sharp contrast with the over-emphasis on central agency experience within government.)

Over time the culture of the Government-wide team player has increasingly dominated the Public Service. At its best, this results in the application of a broad perspective and experience to the management of a given program. At its worst, the legitimate interests of a particular program may be sacrificed on the altar of inexperience or even personal ambition. For example, in his zeal to please the centre by offering up cuts in a given program, the responsible DM or ADM may inadvertently undermine his department's capacity to meet the legally mandated objectives of that program. The risk increases if his knowledge of the field and, perhaps, of the relevant legislation is limited. Indeed, it can be fairly argued that the working climate created by this pattern of appointment encourages senior officials to lose sight of the fact that their primary obligation must always be the full implementation of the programs legally entrusted to them. It is easy to understand why some would conclude that a culture in which most decision-making processes are far from transparent and in which some, perhaps many, senior officials are overly prepared to proclaim "ready, aye, ready" to wishes from the centre helped foster the failure to control the abuses of public trust documented by Judge Gomery and the Auditor General.

The changes carried out by Michael Pitfield and further encouraged by his successors also had a negative effect on the potentially constructive interaction described earlier between departments with legitimately competing perspectives. Instead of pursuing the tough exchanges that the various departmental "clients" have a right to expect and which can contribute so much to good governance, officials involved may be more concerned to achieve a consensus pleasing to the centre as quickly as possible, i.e. to avoid rocking any boats. That scenario will almost invariably minimize responsiveness to legitimate interests outside government.

While greater public accountability will help in addressing the problems outlined in the three preceding paragraphs, further measures, such as longer appointment periods and greater emphasis on relevant knowledge and expertise in the selection of both DMs and ADMs, are clearly needed.

CONCLUSION

Those outside government with legitimate interest in policies or decisions that affect them and, indeed, the public at large need to have confidence in the Government's policy development and decision-making systems. Programs where environmental assessment processes are routinely followed have already achieved a level of openness that meets this need. Elsewhere in government, similar attitudes need to be cultivated and effective public consultation mechanisms as well as other measures such as those suggested earlier put in place. In addition, the criteria used in appointing and moving senior officials and the relationship between those officials and the PCO need to be rethought with the intent both of increasing the transparency of Public Service decision-making and policy development processes and also of ensuring that recommendations submitted to Ministers by public servants are both balanced and responsive to legitimate public concerns.

AUTHOR'S NOTE:

This paper was written before the publication of Judge Gomery's second report. The similarity between the conclusions of that report and those of this paper is not, however, coincidental.

ADDED NOTE:

Readers unfamiliar with Judge Gomery's inquiry need to know that he was appointed by the subsequently defeated Liberal government to inquire into a scandal involving the misuse of public funds paid to public relations firms and to recommend measures to prevent its re-occurrence. According to the opinion polls, the incoming Conservatives' electoral victory was greatly aided by this Liberal scandal. Assurances of more transparent accountable government were central to the Conservatives' campaign. Indeed, the central theme of transparent decision-making at the conference for public servants for which this paper was prepared was chosen in response to Prime Minister Harper's promises in this respect. Judge Gomery recommended various measures to strengthen the independence of career public servants and to increase the transparency of governmental decision-making to inhibit inappropriate political interference in certain kinds of decision-making, especially in the management of public funds. The incoming Conservative government not only failed to act upon these recommendations; it reduced both Public Service independence and general governmental transparency. Instead, Parliament enacted legislation adding complexity to the process of awarding government contracts, an action deemed unnecessary by Gomery, who thought existing procedures adequate. (They had been bypassed.) The net effect has been to make the contracting out process needlessly more difficult and expensive, potentially making government more inefficient by inhibiting outsourcing.

INDEX

Note: A page number in italics indicates a photograph. The initials RR in the subheadings refer to Raymond M. Robinson.

CPSIA information can be obtained at www.ICGtesting.com
Printed in the USA
LVOW05s1920150414

381843LV00004B/11/P